HOMER ON THE GODS AND HUMAN VIRTUE

Creating the Foundations of Classical Civilization

This book seeks to restore Homer to his rightful place among the principal figures in the history of political and moral philosophy. Through this fresh and provocative analysis of the *Iliad* and the *Odyssey*, Peter J. Ahrensdorf examines Homer's understanding of the best life, the nature of the divine, and the nature of human excellence. According to Ahrensdorf, Homer teaches that human greatness eclipses that of the gods; that the contemplative and compassionate singer ultimately surpasses the heroic warrior in grandeur; and that it is the courageously questioning Achilles, not the loyal Hector or even the wily Odysseus, who comes closest to the humane wisdom of Homer himself. Thanks to Homer, two of the distinctive features of Greek civilization are its extraordinary celebration of human excellence, as can be seen in Greek athletics, sculpture, and nudity, and its singular questioning of the divine, as can be seen in Greek philosophy.

PETER J. AHRENSDORF is the James Sprunt Professor of Political Science and an affiliated professor of classics at Davidson College. He is the author of *Greek Tragedy and Political Philosophy: Rationalism and Religion in Sophocles' Theban Plays* and *The Death of Socrates and the Life of Philosophy: An Interpretation of Plato's Phaedo*; the coauthor of *Justice Among Nations: On the Moral Basis of Power and Peace*; and the cotranslator of *Sophocles' Theban Plays*. He is also the author of many articles and essays on Plato, Thucydides, Hobbes, Sophocles, Sarmiento, and Homer. Ahrensdorf has received a Fulbright scholarship to study and teach in Argentina, two National Endowment for the Humanities fellowships, five Earhart Foundation fellowship research grants, a Boswell Faculty fellowship, and the Hunter-Hamilton Love of Teaching Award from Davidson College.

HOMER
ON THE GODS AND HUMAN VIRTUE

Creating the Foundations of Classical Civilization

PETER J. AHRENSDORF
Davidson College

CAMBRIDGE
UNIVERSITY PRESS

32 Avenue of the Americas, New York, NY 10013-2473, USA

Cambridge University Press is part of the University of Cambridge.

It furthers the University's mission by disseminating knowledge in the pursuit of education, learning, and research at the highest international levels of excellence.

www.cambridge.org
Information on this title: www.cambridge.org/9780521193887

First published 2014

Printed in the United States of America

A catalog record for this publication is available from the British Library.

ISBN 978-0-521-19388-7 Hardback

To Thomas L. Pangle

Contents

Acknowledgments

Over the many years that I have worked on this project, I have incurred many debts and it is a pleasure to acknowledge them. An earlier and somewhat different version of portions of this book appeared as "Homer and the Foundation of Classical Civilization," in *Recovering Reason*, edited by Timothy Burns (Lanham, MD: Lexington Books, 2010), pp. 3–16. I thank Lexington Books for kindly granting me permission to use this material.

For their generous financial support, I thank the Boswell Fellowship Program and its founders, Thomas and Cheryl Boswell; Davidson College; the Earhart Foundation; and the National Endowment for the Humanities. My thanks go as well to Beatrice Rehl, my editor at Cambridge University Press, for her enthusiastic and timely support for this project, her patience, and her always valuable advice. I also wish to express my gratitude to her assistant, Isabella Vitti, for all her help, and to the anonymous reviewers for the Press for their suggestions and comments.

I am grateful as well to those who invited me to lecture on Homer at Emory University, the University of Texas at Austin, Smith College, Rhodes College, Michigan State University, and Boston College. I benefited greatly from the excellent questions, comments, and criticisms of the students and professors at these institutions.

It was my great good fortune to study Homer with such remarkable teachers and distinguished scholars as James Winn and Kevin Crotty at Yale University and David Grene at the University of Chicago. I also thank the lively and enlivening students at Davidson College who took courses with me on Homer and taught me much about his poems. I am grateful as well to Timothy Burns, Steven J. Kautz, Carmen Nakassis, Dimitri Nakassis, Judd Owen, Lorraine Pangle, John Paulas, Richard S. Ruderman, Brian J. Shaw, and Nathan Tarcov for their friendly advice and assistance. I also wish to express my gratitude to my daughter, Lucia, and my son, Matias, for supporting me in so very many ways and, in particular, for helping me in the preparation of this manuscript for publication. Finally, I thank my wife, Alejandra Arce Ahrensdorf, who, as always, provided me with the wisest counsel, the most timely encouragement, and the most indispensable support of all.

Introduction

Homer has always been celebrated as one of the greatest poets – "the best and most divine of the poets," according to Socrates (*Ion* 530b9–10)[1] – but it is forgotten today that such philosophers as Plato, Montaigne, and Nietzsche considered him to be a foundational political, moral, and philosophic *thinker* as well. In Plato's *Republic*, Socrates identifies Homer not only as "the first teacher and leader" of all the tragic poets (595b9–c2) but also as a man widely believed to know "all the human things that have to do with virtue and vice and also the divine things" (598d7–e5) and to teach about "the governance of cities and the education of a human being" (599c6–d2).[2] In his *Essays*, Montaigne goes so far as to claim that Homer "laid the foundations equally for all schools of philosophy" (1976, 377; see also 371, 455).[3] According to the eighteenth-century political philosopher Giambattista Vico, all philosophers from Plato up to his own time regarded Homer as a philosophic thinker

[1] Consider also, for example, Rousseau 1979, 453; Nietzsche 1967, 63–64. Even Vico, who denies Homer's existence as a single individual (1999, 363, 381), nonetheless declares him to be "the most sublime of all the sublime heroic poets" (364; see also 149, 318, 370, 372). On this point, see Porter 2004, 329–330. See also Wolf 1985, 47, 210.

[2] Consider also, for example, Horace *Epistles* 1.2, where Horace compares Homer favorably with the philosophers Chrysippus and Cantor. In Griffin's words: "Homer, says Horace, is the best of all moral philosophers at teaching the bad consequences of the passions" (1995, 28).

[3] It is also noteworthy that in the concluding chapter of his *Two Treatises of Government*, Locke presents Homer's Odysseus as the model of a man who righteously but prudently resists oppression (1998, 416–417).

who founded Greek civilization and as "the source of all Greek philosophies [*il fonte di tutte le greche filosofie*]."[4] And in *The Genealogy of Morals*, Nietzsche contends that Homer constitutes *the* fundamental theoretical alternative to the entire tradition of Platonic philosophy: "Plato versus Homer: that is the complete, the genuine antagonism" (1969a, 154).[5] It is the goal of this book to restore Homer to his rightful place among the principal figures in the history of political and moral philosophy and to do so by elucidating, in particular, his education of the Greeks.

According to Plato, Herodotus, Thucydides, and Xenophon, as well as Machiavelli, Montaigne, and Nietzsche, Homer was the educator of the Greeks, the theoretical founder of classical civilization.[6] Herodotus judges that it was Homer, together with Hesiod, who created the gods in the form in which the Greeks worshipped them (2.53), a judgment reiterated by Nietzsche, who declares that Homer is the man who "gave the Greeks their gods – no, who invented his own gods for himself!" (1974, 242).[7] Socrates proclaims that Homer taught the Greeks about such great and

[4] Vico 1999, 355–387, especially 355–356, 386. For the passages in Italian, see Vico 1977, 543–584, especially 583.

[5] Consider also the identification of Homer with the origin of Enlightenment made by Horkheimer and Adorno (1972, xvi, 13–20, 32–36, 43–80; see also Ruderman 1999, 145–150). See as well Lukàcs's treatment of Homer as a theoretical figure of capital importance: "if no one has equalled Homer, nor even approached him . . . it is because he found the answer [to the question: how can life become essence?] before the progress of the human mind through history had allowed the question to be asked" (1977, 30; see also 47). On the identification of the *Odyssey* in particular with philosophy, see Hall 2008, 147–159. Hall contends, "The *Odyssey* and philosophy have been inseparable since antiquity" (147).

[6] Plato *Republic* 606e1–607a5; see also 376e2–377e4. See also Herodotus 2.53; Thucydides 1.2–11; Xenophon *Symposium* 3.5; Machiavelli 1998, 58–60, 68–71; Montaigne 1976, 569–571, 442–443; Nietzsche 1974, 242–243; 1968, 205; 1969a, 154; 1984, 161.

[7] Consider as well Nietzsche 1984, 88; Montaigne 1976, 701. Herodotus also claims that the Greeks received many of their religious beliefs from the Egyptians (2.41–51). On the significance of Homer as a religious teacher of the Greeks, consider as well Hegel 1956, 237; Voeglin 1957, 72; and Manent 2010, 42–48. Manent goes so far as to say, "It is, in the first place, inasmuch as he was a 'theologian,' or a poet who authored 'theologies,' that Homer was the educator of the Greeks" (2010, 42–43 – my translation). Burkert notes, "Only an authority could create order amid such a confusion of [religious] tradition. The authority to whom the Greeks appealed was the poetry of Hesiod and, above all, of Homer" (1985, 120). See also Bowra 1977, 215; Finley 1978, 135–136.

noble matters as generalship, statesmanship, and human virtue (*Republic* 599c6–d2), a claim echoed by Alexander the Great, who – possibly because of the influence of Aristotle – deemed the *Iliad* a portable treasure of "military virtue" (Plutarch *Alexander* 15.4–5).[8] In his essay celebrating Homer as one of the three "most outstanding men" who ever lived, Montaigne declares: "It was against the order of nature that he created the most excellent production that can be. For things at birth are ordinarily imperfect; they gain in size and strength as they grow. He made the infancy of poetry and *of several other sciences* mature, perfect, and accomplished" (1976, 570 – emphasis added). As all these thinkers testify, it was Homer who provided the Greeks with a common moral understanding by providing them with vivid and compelling models of human excellence. It was Homer who revealed to the Greeks the nature of the gods and illuminated their relations to humans. It was Homer who guided the Greeks in their reflections about human nature and in their imaginings of human and divine greatness.[9]

These thinkers also stress that Homer presented his teaching in a distinctively poetic, artful, and oblique manner. As Socrates suggests, in both Plato (*Republic* 378d3–e1) and Xenophon (*Symposium* 3.6, *Memorabilia* 1.2.58–59), Homer's teaching is not always immediately accessible, for it is "composed among hidden thoughts [ἐν ὑπονοίαις πεποιημένας]" (*Republic* 378d6). Similarly, in Plato's *Protagoras*, Protagoras identifies Homer as a sophist, that is, as one of those who both possessed and taught wisdom, but who also sought "to make a disguise for themselves and to cover themselves with it [πρόσχημα ποιεῖσθαι καὶ προκαλύπτεσθαι]" out of fear of hostility (316d3–9). In *The Prince*, Machiavelli points to Homer as a wise teacher of

[8] According to Richardson, "There was a strong ancient tradition that Aristotle gave his pupil Alexander the Great a special text of the *Iliad*." Richardson surmises, "Alexander's own passion for Homer must derive in part from Aristotle's influence." At any rate, Aristotle himself "quotes Homer some 114 times, with a strong bias towards the *Iliad*" and evinces "a close and sensitive psychological reading of the text" (1992, 36; see also 37–40).

[9] In the words of Burkert, "To be a Greek was to be educated, and the foundation of all education was Homer" (1985, 120). According to Scott, "Homer was the greatest single force in making of the Greeks a kindred people and in giving them a mutually understandable language and common ideals" (1963, 98). See also Hunter 2004, 246. For the didactic role played by Homer in the later classical world, consider Farrell 2004; Long 1992; Browning 1992.

princes who taught subtly and "covertly [*copertamente*]" such heterodox but vital lessons as the need for rulers to imitate the harsher qualities of beasts as well as the finer qualities of men.[10] In the preface to his translation of Homer's poems, Hobbes praises Homer especially for his "discretion" (1894, iii–x). In *The New Science*, Vico claims that all philosophers until his day characterized Homer's wisdom as an "esoteric wisdom" – or "hidden wisdom [*sapienza riposta*]" – one that can only be uncovered after considerable intellectual exertion by his students.[11] As these thinkers emphasize, Homer conveys his theoretical teaching about, for example, the nature of the divine or the character of human excellence with circumspection, indirection, and even misdirection. Although Homer is not as reticent as such thinkers as Plato – who never speaks in his own name in his dialogues except for the titles[12] – Homer does primarily address us indirectly, through the speeches of his characters rather than in his own name.[13] Moreover, Homer's narrative is far from straightforward, for its structure is exceedingly complex and its roughly 450 similes[14] – almost none of which are repeated[15] – can be as perplexing and thought provoking as they are arresting and moving.[16]

[10] Machiavelli 1998, 60, 68–70, 77–79. For the Italian text cited, see Machiavelli 1966, 107.

[11] Vico 1999, 355–356; 1977, 543–545.

[12] Strauss 1964, 50–62.

[13] As Griffin notes, "More than half of the Homeric epics consists of speech by characters, not narrative by the narrator . . . some 55 per cent of the total of the two epics" (2004, 156). In the *Iliad*, almost 45 percent of the lines (7,018 of 15, 690) are in direct speech; in the *Odyssey*, almost 70 percent of the lines (8,225 of 12,103) are in direct speech. Consider also Richardson 1990, 70–82.

[14] Moulton 1977, 18. On the challenge of counting Homeric similes, see Buxton 2004, 146–147; Edwards 1991, 24; 1987, 102–103. See also Scott 1974, 190–212; 2009, 189–205.

[15] See Edwards 1991, 24; 1987, 102–103; Buxton 2004, 146; Redfield 1975, 188.

[16] As Buxton observes, "the Homeric narrator himself intervenes in order to point out likenesses through the medium of similes" (2004, 148; see also Clay 2010, 21–22). Similarly, as Edwards points out when speaking of the *Iliad*, "The Homeric long simile is a masterpiece of poetic art, and brings us as close as we can hope to get to the perceptions and sensitivities of the genius who constructed the monumental poem" (1991, 41; see also 34, 39 on the didactic function of the similes, as well as Edwards 1987, 104–105). Consider especially such extremely surprising, so-called reversal similes as in *Iliad* 22.93–97, 24.477–484, and *Odyssey* 8.523–531, 16.16–21, 23.233–240. See Moulton 1977, 114–116, 128–132, 134; Felson and Slatkin 2004, 105; Silk 2004, 38–39. See also Buxton 2004, 153–154; Stanley 1993, 216–217; Schein 1984, 107.

Just as Homer's Odysseus is a crafty, artful figure, a man of many ways, so is Homer himself an artful teacher, whose poems possess many layers of meaning, whose plots and characters undergo many changes, and who leads us through many stages of reflection before we may arrive at the heart of his teaching.[17] By prompting us to identify and to strip away the many layers of his presentation of, for example, the gods and the heroes, Homer prompts us to consider and reconsider our initial beliefs about the nature of the divine and the character of human excellence. In this way, Homer invites us to embark on an intellectual odyssey of our own.

The greatness of Homer as a thinker is, however, overlooked in our times. Prominent scholars of Homer identify illuminating insights concerning such themes as the nature of the divine or the character of human excellence in the epic poems, but they tend to treat those insights as inherited cultural beliefs or as flashes of naive, poetic inspiration rather than as the cohesive political, moral, and theological teachings of a theoretical mind. Beginning with the publication of *Prologomena to Homer* (1795) by Friedrich August Wolf and culminating with the work of Milman Parry and Gregory Nagy, the so-called Analyst/Oralist thesis that the *Iliad* and the *Odyssey* were a collection of stories, composed by multiple generations of "illiterate," "simple," "primitive"[18] bards and later written down in various forms by various hands, has tended to prevail. Wolf's key contention is that, since the *Iliad* and *Odyssey* emerged in illiterate, primitive times – at "the slender beginnings" of Greece – they must themselves be intellectually and artistically primitive works simply offered for the entertainment and applause of the immediate audience and continuously altered by different bards for different audiences (consider, e.g., Wolf 1985, 75, 104, 209). As Wolf puts it, "whether I contemplate the progress of the Greeks themselves or that of other races, I find it

[17] As Griffin notes, Homer's characters "express strong and clear moral judgments, which the narration does not... We are meant to judge, but not to be bullied into judgment by the poet" (2004, 162).

[18] Fowler 2004, 220. See also Moulton 1977, 16. Parry uses the term "primitive" only with some reservation (1971, 377), whereas Nagy emphatically avoids it, possibly in favor of the adjective "young" (1996, 149–150). Nagy does acknowledge, however, that modern Homeric scholarship tends to view Homer as "primitive": "In terms of such ideas, Homer was not really classical or preclassical: he was primordial. Such a primordial Homer, whether or not his name was Homer, was some kind of primitive; if he was a genius, he was a primitive genius" (2009, 3).

impossible to accept the belief to which we have become accustomed: that these two works of a single genius burst forth suddenly from the darkness in all their brilliance" (1985, 148). This "historicist approach" – based on the historicist thesis that the human mind is fundamentally shaped by its historical circumstances and is consequently incapable of rising above and even shaping those circumstances – "swept the field" of classical scholarship.[19] As James Porter observes,

> Instantly, the timeless Homer of popular and literary imagination became an object of scientific historical analysis and damning critique, albeit on a somewhat irrational basis[20] . . . Henceforth, the Homeric texts themselves began to appear as something like an archaeological site, with layers of history built into them in a palpable stratiagraphy: the disparate effects of multiple compositional layers (some, including, Jebb would actually call them "strata") and the intrusive hands of editors could all be felt in the poems. (2004, 336)

So powerful is the influence of Wolf today that even though, to cite one example, Robert Fowler acknowledges that Wolf's fundamental "premise that Homer lived in an illiterate age" is one "we now know to be false,"[21] Fowler nonetheless insists that the poems "had to be the creation of tradition, not of any one bard" and hence "it is retrograde to argue that we can go on reading him [Homer] like Virgil or Shakespeare" (2004, 220–222).[22]

The natural, though possibly unintended, effect of the Analyst/Oralist triumph has been to discourage students from seeking in Homer's poems the

[19] Porter 2004, 336; see also Grafton 1985, 26–28; Whitman 1958, 1–9; Clay 1983, 4–5. For an account of the overall impact of Wolf and also of the criticisms of Wolf made by Goethe and Schiller, see Reinhardt 1997b, 217–220. See also Myres 1958, 75–76, 83–93.

[20] Porter explains the "somewhat irrational basis" of Wolf's Homeric scholarship as follows: "Wolf was at bottom an intuitionist whose touchstone was his philological *sensus* ('feeling'), while his science was an *ars nesciendi*, or 'art of ignorance'" (2004, 336).

[21] See Wolf 1985, 75–102. For Nagy's convincing argument "that Homeric poetry does indeed refer to the technology of writing" at *Iliad* 6.168, 6.176, 6.178, and most emphatically at 7.89–90, see 1996 14, 36.

[22] But consider Griffin: "Romantic scholars used to believe that the [Homeric] epics were created by the whole people (Volkspiele); now institutions and rituals get the credit. It is as if we argued that the plays of Shakespeare were the product of the circumstances of his time: of course the artist is influenced by his period and himself influences it, but we are left with the question why (if we have ruled out individual genius) the plays of Shakespeare are so much better than those of his contemporaries" (1995, 8).

wisdom attributed to him by thinkers from Plato to Nietzsche.[23] As Wolf declares, "The Homer that we hold in our hands now is not the one who flourished in the mouths of the Greeks of his own day, but one variously altered, interpolated, corrected, and emended from the times of Solon down to those of the Alexandrians" (1985, 209). Ulrich von Wilamowitz-Moellendorff – perhaps "the most important analyst" and "Wolfian" (Reinhardt 1997b, 219) – went so far as to judge the *Iliad* as it stands "a wretched patchwork" (Whitman 1958, 2; consider also Reinhardt 1997a, 173, 177–183). Parry's monumental effort to prove, on the basis of his analysis of the *Iliad* and the *Odyssey* and his studies of Yugoslav oral poets, that Homer's poems were composed in the manner of "the illiterate bards of Yugoslavia" had the understandable effect of seeming, at least, "to bring Homeric art down to the level of the quasi-mechanical" (Whitman 1958, 5–6). For even though Parry himself evidently felt great affection for the Homeric poems – he declares with evident enthusiasm, "When one hears the Southern Slavs sing their tales he has the overwhelming feeling that, in some way, he is hearing Homer" – he nonetheless suggests that those poems are not fundamentally different from the tales of Yugoslav singers, since their artistry and even their very ideas are "the same" (Parry 1971, 378; consider also, e.g., 375). As Adam Parry says of his father's scholarship on the *Iliad* and the *Odyssey*, "What holds Parry's attention in all his writing is the tradition, never the poems in themselves" and again, "The poet, then, is essentially subordinate to the tradition; and it never occurs to him to depart from it, or even to fashion it so as to produce any personal vision of the world" (1971, liii, lii). In Milman Parry's own words regarding Homer, "The poet is thinking in terms of formulas. Unlike the poets who wrote, he can put into verse only those ideas which are to be found in the phrases which are on his tongue, or at the most he will express ideas so like those of the traditional formulas that he

[23] Wolf, with apparent inconsistency, on occasion seemingly praises Homer's individual "genius" (1985, 47; see also 210). Grafton, Most, and Zetzel argue that Wolf's ambiguity was "deliberate," for it "allowed him to bring off two crucial tours de force. In the first place, he was able to sit on both sides of the fence – that is, to continue to maintain the beauty, the artistry, the coherence of the poems he was chopping to bits. . . In the second place, Wolf's deliberate ambiguity had a preservative effect on the bulk of what he wrote . . . he invited the reader time and again to join his revolution; but he did not spell out its exact nature" (1985, 34). For his part, Nagy lauds the "rich, complex, and, yes, subtle . . . Homeric tradition" (1996, 144–146).

himself would not know them apart" (1971, 324). It is therefore not surprising that Henry Theodore Wade-Gery went so far as to claim that Parry may be called "the Darwin of Homeric Studies," for just as "Darwin seemed to many to have removed the finger of God from the creation of the world and of man, so Milman Parry has seemed to some to remove the creative poet from the *Iliad* and *Odyssey*" (Wade-Gery 1952, 38–39).

More recently, Nagy has followed in the footsteps of Parry, of Parry's student Albert Bates Lord, and ultimately of Wolf himself,[24] first by contending that with regard to the question of the intent of the creator of the Homeric poems, "this intent must be assigned not simply to one poet but also to *countless* generations of previous poets steeped in the same tradition" (Nagy 1979, 3 – my emphasis), and later by going "as far as urging scholars to avoid expressions in which 'Homer' is used as the name of an individual" lest they "start thinking of 'Homer' in overly personalized terms" (Graziosi 2002, 16; Nagy 1996, 21; see also 25–26).[25] For, as Nagy maintains – repeating a claim made by Wolf himself[26] – just as the Greeks commonly attributed "any major achievement, even if this achievement may have been realized only through a lengthy period of social evolution, to the episodic and personal accomplishment of a culture hero who is pictured as having made his monumental contribution in an earlier era of the given society," so the Greeks "retrojected" Homer "as the original genius of epic" (Nagy 1996, 21).[27] In words that echo Wolf (1985, 209), Nagy sums up his approach to Homer as follows: "The textual tradition as we have it, in all its variations of form and content, defies a unified explanation in terms of one single person's great achievements of observation, in terms of one 'big bang'" from "a single creative mind of a single person called Homer or whatever his name might be" (2010, 312–313; see also 1996, 92–93). Accordingly, the study of the theoretically rich and profound

[24] As Nagy observes admiringly: "For Wolf, there was no Homer to recover. He argued that the Homeric text had emerged out of oral traditions, which could not be traced all the way back to some 'original' single author" (2004, 41–42).

[25] For Nagy's debt to Parry and Lord (especially Lord 1960, 1991), see, for example, Nagy 1979, 1–3; 1996, 10–11.

[26] "The Greek race always had the reprehensible desire to trace each of its most notable institutions back to the earliest times, and to attribute virtually every useful component of later culture to the discoveries of its own heroes" (Wolf 1985, 78).

[27] Fowler suggests that Nagy "stakes out an extreme oralist position" (2004, 230). See also Graziosi's very qualified reservations (2002, 16–17).

philosophic poet Homer has given way to the study of a primitive, nameless tradition that produced the poems.

In opposition to the Analysts and Oralists, the so-called Unitarians have arisen to defend the grandeur of Homer as an individual artist.[28] Jasper Griffin, for instance, insists that "the *Iliad* did not arise spontaneously from the mere existence of an epic tradition" but "must have been the creation, essentially, of a singer of great powers, . . . whom the people of later antiquity, who knew nothing about him, called Homer" (1995, 7). But, notwithstanding their extremely valuable and helpful insights into Homer's poems, even the Unitarians have tended to concede that Homer was not a great thinker, that he did not fundamentally shape and enlighten ancient Greece, but rather that, in an admittedly imaginative and creative fashion, he simply reflected and transmitted the cultural beliefs of his time. For example, even though Cedric Whitman considers the *Iliad* and the *Odyssey* to be "wonders of the poetic world," he also judges Homer's mind to be "the archaic mind, prephilosophic, primarily synthetic rather than analytical, whose content is myths, symbols, and paradigms" (1958, 13–14). Ruth Scodel elucidates the moving character and "exceptional sophistication" of Homer's narrative, but she ultimately deems him a "tradition-bearer," albeit an "exceptionally strong" one, rather than a foundational thinker and poet (2004, 45–46). Charles Segal points out that, "Whether or not the *Iliad* was composed with the aid of writing, it is certainly not the naive or primitive voice of Volk, nature, or the pure warrior spirit, in the way that eighteenth and nineteenth century critics from Vico and F. A. Wolf to Ruskin and even Gilbert Murray would claim" (1992, 14). Yet, while he celebrates Homer's "narrative self-consciousness" and "control of the narrative," Segal goes on to conclude that far from being an enlightened teacher of the Greeks, the "Homeric bard . . . is the voice and the vehicle of an ancient wisdom" and "remains, above all . . . a purveyor of pleasure . . . and a preserver of traditions" (1992, 27–28; see also 23).[29]

To discover the fundamental arguments against the traditional view that Homer was a philosophic poet and therewith the principal cause of the

[28] Consider, for example, Bowra (1977: originally published 1930); Whitman (1958); and Griffin (1980, 1995, 2004), whom Nagy calls a "neo-unitarian" (1996, 134).

[29] Griffin does, however, claim that the *Iliad*, at least, embodies "a clear and *unique* vision of the world, of heroism, and of life and death" (1980, xvi – my emphasis).

dramatic decline in Homer's reputation as a thinker, we must look beyond the philologist Wolf to the political philosopher Giambattista Vico (1668–1744): the author of *The Principles of a New Science of the Common Nature of Nations*, "the true father of historicism" – in the judgment of Isaiah Berlin and possibly R. G. Collingwood and Leo Strauss as well[30] – and the thinker who may justly be considered the founding figure of modern Homeric scholarship.[31] George Grote identifies Vico as "that eminently original thinker" and the "profound" "precursor of F. A. Wolf in regard to the Homeric poems" (1861, 351–353; see also Michelet 1971, 340–341). Berlin points out that, "Three-quarters of a century before Wolf and his school, Vico saw in Homer not an individual who wrote the *Iliad* and the *Odyssey*, but the national genius of the Greek people itself, as it articulates its vision of its own experience over centuries" (2000, 76).[32] According to Benedetto Croce (1964, 270), Collingwood (1956, 259–260), and Max Fisch and Thomas Bergin (1963, 69), Vico exerted a direct and indirect influence on Wolf and through him all subsequent Homeric scholarship. Indeed, although Wolf himself never explicitly refers to Vico in his *Prologemena to Homer*, Wolf later published an article entitled, "G. B. Vico on Homer," "grudgingly acknowledging Vico's priority" (Fisch and Bergin 1963, 69). Even Nagy himself remarks, "If we adopt a teleological view of the *Iliad* and *Odyssey* as the culmination of a long tradition, then the intuitions of Giambattista Vico on Homer will prove to be more fruitful than the labors of early analysts like l'abbé d'Aubignac or even F. A. Wolf" (1974, 11; see also Grafton 1999, xxi). As Porter observes, "it was Giambattista Vico who first articulated the view . . . that Homer was not a person but an idea . . . created

[30] Berlin 2002, 66; Collingwood 1956, 63–71; Strauss 1971, vii. Consider as well Berlin's remark with regard to Vico's thought: "This is the whole doctrine of historicism in embryo" (2000, 58). See also Berlin 2002, 7–8, 53–67; Ambler 2009, 167–168, 170–172.

[31] For Vico's broad theoretical influence, see especially Croce 1964, 236–244, 268–278; Fisch and Bergin 1963, 61–107; Berlin 2000, 8–12, 112–121; Lilla 1993, 1–6; Grafton 1999, xii–xiii.

[32] Consider as well Jullien's remark, in her fascinating essay on Jorge Luis Borges's two stories about Homer – "El hacedor" (Borges 1971) and "El inmortal" (Borges 1974) – the latter of which refers as well to Vico (1974, 24–26): "Giambattista Vico, who preceded F. A. Wolf in seeing the Iliad as an amalgamation of composite fragments, appears as a character in the story . . . Vico's theory . . . de-individualizes Homer, making him a 'symbolic character' of the Greek people" (Jullien 1995, 143).

by the Greeks (though believed in by them)" (2004, 329).[33] It is Vico, then, who is responsible for the thesis that has gone on to dominate Homeric scholarship, namely, that Homer was either a primitive poet or simply a fictitious name for a tradition of primitive bards.

One might go further back in time and attribute the decline in Homer's reputation as a thinker to Francis Bacon, the philosopher whom Vico himself singled out in his *Autobiography* as "a man of incomparable wisdom both common and esoteric, at one and the same time a universal man in theory and in practice, a rare philosopher and a great English minister of state" (1963, 139; see also 146, 155).[34] As Gerrard Passannante suggests, Francis Bacon, "appears unexpectedly as a crucial but forgotten figure in the long history of Homeric readers – a forbear even to the great critical legacies of Giambattista Vico, F. A. Wolf, and Milman Parry" (2009, 1015–1016).[35] In the first place, Bacon specifically denied that there was any esoteric wisdom or "inwardness" in Homer's "fables" (1974, 99). Furthermore, and more importantly, through his work, the *Advancement of Learning* (1605), Bacon launched a broad intellectual revolution, one that sought to replace an unreasonable prejudice in favor of classical antiquity with a reasonable prejudice against it:

> Antiquity deserveth that reverence, that men should make a stand thereupon and discover what is the best way; but when the discovery is well taken, then to make progression. And to speak truly, "Antiquitas saeculi juventus mundi [The age of antiquity is the youth of the world]." These times are the ancient times, when the world is ancient, and not those which we account ancient *ordine retrogrado*, by a computation backward from ourselves. (1974, 38)

In the wake of Bacon's contention that the writers of antiquity were primitive by virtue of being ancient, the French author d'Aubignac called into

[33] Porter wittily characterizes Vico's extremely influential thesis as follows: "Vico here is playing out the logic of disavowal that would typify Homer's reception for centuries to come, and which runs: 'Homer was the best poet ever, but he never existed (and here are the proofs for both claims – his poems)'" (Porter 2004, 329–330).

[34] For Bacon's influence on Vico, see Fisch and Bergin 1963, 20–26, 42–43, 59–60, 80–81; Verene 1981, 128–134; Collingwood 1956, 63–64; Berlin 2000, 26, 144–145; Ambler 2009, 173, 177; Grafton 1999, xxiii, xxvi–xxvii. For an account that stresses Vico's critique of Bacon, see Lilla 1993, 14, 47–52, 108, 125–126.

[35] See Passannante 2009 as a whole, for an intriguing argument that Bacon sought to "atomize" the text of Homer and therewith, it seems, the authority of Homer.

question the very existence of Homer in particular (1670)[36] and Charles Perrault, with the support of Bernard Le Bovier de Fontenelle, initiated the momentous "Quarrel of the Ancients and the Moderns" with his *Parallel of the Ancients and Moderns in all that Regards Arts and Sciences* (1687) by broadly assailing the "pre-eminence of the ancient writers" and insisting that "Homer described a primitive, not a noble world."[37] Around the time that Vico wrote on Homer, Richard Bentley – the man celebrated by Wolf as a "great" man (1985, 118; see also Haugen 2011, 232–233) and excoriated by Jonathan Swift as "the most deformed of all the Moderns" (1975, 159–160) – dismissed the belief that Homer "designed his Poem for Eternity, to please and instruct Mankind" (1713, 18). In his *Remarks upon a late Discourse of free-thinking: in a letter to F.H. D. D. by Phileleutherus Lipsiensis* (1st ed. 1713, 8th ed. 1745), Bentley declared,

> Take my word for it, poor Homer in those Circumstances and early times had never such aspiring thoughts. He wrote a sequel of Songs and Rhapsodies, to be sung by himself for small earnings and good cheer, at Festivals and other days of Merriment; the Ilias for the Men, the Odysseis for the other Sex. These loose Songs were not collected together in the form of an Epic Poem, till Pisistratus's time about 500 years after. (1713, 18)[38]

Nevertheless, as Anthony Grafton argues with reference to Perrault and Bentley in particular, "Vico's reading of Homer was far more sustained, and the consequences he drew from it more radical, than these men's remarks" (1999, xxiv).[39]

It was Vico, in his work, *The Principles of a New Science of the Common Nature of Nations* (1st ed. 1725; 2nd 1730; final 1744), who first fully and

[36] Porter 2004, 329; Parry 1971, xii. See d'Aubignac 1925 as a whole.

[37] Macaulay 1903, 319; Grafton 1999, xxiv. Barchilon and Flinders remark that Perrrault's "favorite device is to find some passage of Homer which does not conform to the mores or good manners of the seventeenth century, and then suggest that he was a barbarian" (1981, 49–50). In his work, *A Full and True Account of the Battel Fought Last Friday Between the Antient and the Modern Books in St. James's Library*, Jonathan Swift recounts that Homer, who "appeared at the Head of the Cavalry, mounted on a furious Horse . . . took Perrault by mighty Force out of his Saddle, then hurl'd him at Fontenelle, with the same Blow dashing out both of their Brains" (1975, 156–157).

[38] For Bentley's influence on classical scholarship, see as a whole Haugen 2011, especially 230–245.

[39] Consider also Adam Parry's judgment that Vico's understanding of Homer was "more deeply historical" than that of d'Aubignac (1971, xiii).

self-consciously asserted and argued for much of what went on to become the dominant scholarly view of Homer[40]: namely, that Homer's poems were "unworthy of a wise man" (1999, 356); that "Homer knew nothing of philosophy" but "was simply a commoner" (363); that "the Homer of the *Odyssey* is different from the author of the *Iliad*" (359; see also 383); indeed, that Homer "never existed as an individual" but rather as "an idea or heroic archetype of the Greeks who recounted their history in song" (381); that "the Homeric epics were composed and revised by several hands in several ages" (363); that the division and arrangement of Homer's books into the *Iliad* and the *Odyssey* were made or commissioned by "Pisistratus and his sons, the tyrants of Athens" and that "Before this, Homer's poems were evidently a confused aggregation of material" (375); and, consequently, "In the future, then, we should highly esteem the Homeric epics" – not for their humane wisdom – but "as two great repositories of the customs of early Greece," at a time when "the barbarous Greeks" possessed "the crude, boorish, fierce, cruel, volatile, unreasonable and unreasonably headstrong, capricious, and foolish morals of early peoples" (387, 355, 358).

How persuasive is Vico's account of Homer? Vico acknowledges that all philosophers up to his time, from Plato on, believed Homer to be a philosophic thinker – indeed the philosophic founder of classical Greece (1999, 355, 386). But Vico sets out on "the search for the true Homer" in order to prove quite specifically that Homer was not a philosopher (355–387). Vico addresses the question, as he puts it, of "whether Homer was in fact a philosopher" in two ways, one general and one textual (355). Throughout his discussion of Homer, Vico makes two general arguments in support of the thesis that Homer was not a philosophic thinker. First, he argues that, since "Homer shared the popular feelings and customs of the barbarous Greeks of his times," and, since, as the *Iliad* and the *Odyssey* show, the morals of Homer's time were "crude, boorish, fierce, cruel, volatile, unreasonable and unreasonably headstrong, capricious, and foolish" and "such behavior can only be found in people who have the mental weakness of children, the vigorous imagination of women, and the seething passions of violent youths, we must deny that Homer possessed any esoteric wisdom" (355, 358, 300–301; see also 372).

[40] See Porter 2004, 329–330, 336.

It is important to note that this general argument is based on Vico's textual interpretation of the Homeric poems, for it is on the basis of that textual interpretation that he claims that the morals of Homer's time were savage. Vico does acknowledge the possible counterargument that even though Homer's times may have been savage, he himself may have been morally and intellectually superior to his times. "Poets," he declares, "are the teachers of the masses, and the aim of poetry is to tame their savagery [*la ferocia del volgo*]." But Vico goes on to argue, again evidently on the basis of his textual interpretation of Homer's poems, that because Homer celebrates savage behavior, especially through his "greatest characters," his own activity as a poet "was unworthy of a wise man [*Non era d'uom saggio*]" (1999, 356–357; 1977, 545). Vico's second general argument is that, since "it is impossible for anyone to be both a sublime poet and a sublime metaphysician," because "metaphysics draws the mind away from the senses, while the poetic faculty sinks the whole mind into them," Homer, as "an incomparable poet,. . .could in no way have been a philosopher [*non fu punto filosofo*]" (1999, 369, 386; 1977, 583). Vico, however, does not clearly support with evidence or argument his assertion that it is simply impossible for one individual – for example, a Plato or a Dante (Ambler 2009, 184) or a Machiavelli – to combine a poetic imagination with a philosophic mind.[41] The clearest basis for Vico's argument that Homer is not a philosophic thinker, then, would seem to be his textual interpretation of the poems.

Vico focuses his interpretation of Homer's poems on Achilles. It was "the hero Achilles, whom Homer sang to the peoples of Greece as a paragon of heroic virtue" (1999, 19; see also 318). According to Vico, in the course of describing the man Homer celebrates as "the greatest of the Greek heroes, Homer records three qualities which run contrary [*tutto contrarie*] to the philosophers' three ideas" (1999, 300; 1977, 476). First, Achilles contradicts the philosophers' rational understanding of justice when he "savagely [*feroce*]" denies that he shares a common humanity with the Trojan Hector (1999, 300; 1977, 476). Second, Achilles contradicts the philosophers' "notion of glory

[41] In the *New Science*, Vico always refers to Plato simply as a philosopher (1999, esp. 56, 78, 100, 124, 204, 213–214, 218, 355, 456–457, 490); to Dante simply as a poet – "the Tuscan Homer" (359), who possessed a "barbarous nature ... incapable of reflection" (367) – without any reference to such works of political philosophy as *De Monarchia* (197, 244, 359, 367–368, 405); and to Machiavelli simply as a political philosopher without any reference to such plays as *Mandragola* (439, 490).

conceived as fame won by beneficial service to humankind" and "devotion to his homeland" when he withdraws from the war against the Trojans and "shamelessly rejoices with Patroclus at Hector's slaughter of his fellow Greeks"; and "when he finally aids the Greeks it is only to assuage his personal grief because Hector has killed his friend Patroclus!" (1999, 300–301, 358; see also 356–357). Third, Achilles contradicts the philosophers' "desire for immortality" by proclaiming to Odysseus in Hades that he would rather be "the ignoblest slave among the living" than a king in Hades (300–301). Vico also indignantly decries Achilles at the end of the *Iliad* when, "unmindful of Priam's good faith in coming alone and placing trust in Achilles, unmoved by the many great misfortunes of such a king, by pity of such a father, or by the veneration due such an old man, and disregarding their common lot, which is the strongest motive for compassion – Achilles flies into a bestial rage [*montato in una collera bestiale*] and thunders that he will cut off Priam's head!" (1999, 358; 1977, 547). Since Homer celebrates such "knaveries [*villanie*]" of his heroes, as well as of his gods, Vico concludes that "Homer's capricious [*leggieri*] gods and heroes could scarcely have been created by a mind in which the study of the philosophers' wisdom has instilled consistency" (1999, 356–357; 1977, 545–546). And it is largely on the basis of his thesis that Homer and his poems celebrate villainous heroes and gods that Vico reasons that the poems must have been put together in barbarous times by a number of simple, primitive bards (consider, e.g., 1999, 355–359, 363, 375, 381, 387).

Vico's reading of Homer's poems is not, however, as clearly supported by the text as one might expect. In the first place, even though Vico claims that Homer celebrates Achilles for his cruelty to both the Trojans and the Achaians (1999, 19, 350–351, 356–358), Homer himself explicitly criticizes Achilles in the opening lines of the *Iliad* by stating that the "destructive" anger of Achilles led to the death of "countless" numbers of his fellow Achaians (1.1–7) and later by stating, in his own name, that the prayer of Achilles' mother for the suffering of Agamemnon and the Achaians, inspired by Achilles' anger at them, is "beyond measure [ἐξαίσιον]" in its harshness (15.598–599; see 1.407–412, 16.233–238).[42] Furthermore, Achilles is sharply criticized for his anger and his lack of compassion in the course of the poem,

[42] Translations are my own, though I have found especially helpful Richmond Lattimore's wonderful translations of both the *Iliad* (1992) and the *Odyssey* (1999). The text of the poems that I use throughout is the Oxford edition of Thomas W. Allen.

not only by Agamemnon (e.g., 1.174–177) – as Vico notes (1999, 356) – but also – as Vico fails to note – by the god Apollo – "Thus Achilles has destroyed pity" – and by those whom Achilles himself claims are by him the "most beloved of Achaians" and "the most beloved men" – Odysseus, Phoinix, and Ajax – by his companion Nestor, and, most remarkably, by his most beloved and honored companion, Patroclus.[43] Moreover, Homer goes out of his way to provoke his audience's compassion for the Trojan victims of Achilles, for example, by presenting in such detail, and so vividly and unforgettably, the heartrending sorrows and moving laments of Priam, Hecubae, and Andromache (22.25–92, 22.405–515, 24.159–168, 24.477–804). What is more, even though Vico claims that Achilles acts heartlessly toward Priam at the end of the *Iliad* (1999, 358), Homer shows Achilles both expressing compassion as well as admiration for Priam and giving content to that compassion, not only by returning to Priam the corpse of his beloved son, but also by freely granting Priam and the Trojans a twelve-day truce during which they may bury Hector in peace, even though the gods did not demand such a truce and Priam had not even requested it (24.512–551, 24.596–670). Notwithstanding Vico's claims to the contrary, Homer never presents Achilles flying into "a bestial rage" at Priam or threatening to cut off his head (1999, 358).[44] It would seem, then, that rather than praise Achilles for his anger and cruelty, Homer criticizes Achilles for his anger and cruelty and praises him for eventually, in some measure, rising above them. And insofar as Achilles does indeed raise profound and far-reaching questions regarding the value of glory, loyalty, and the desire for immortality, as Vico suggests (1999, 300–301; see *Iliad* 9.314–327, 9.400–416; *Odyssey* 11.473–491), Vico does not clearly explain why such questioning would be *un*philosophic rather than philosophic.

There are other reasons to question the care with which Vico read Homer's poems. Even though Vico claims that Homer simply celebrates Achilles as the greatest hero (1999, 19), Homer focuses one of his two epic poems on the alternative heroism of Odysseus, in the *Odyssey*, a poem Vico

[43] 24.39–54, 9.198, 9.204, 9.300–302, 9.434–438, 9.483–523, 9.624–642, 11.655–667, 11.761–763, 18.79–82, 11.647–653, 16.29–35.

[44] Achilles does warn Priam against provoking his wrath, but Achilles does so precisely because he wishes to restrain his wrath and show compassion to Priam, as he proceeds to do (24.559–672).

tends to ignore (Alvis 1995, x). Vico claims that a single individual, Homer, must not have composed both the *Iliad* and the *Odyssey*, because the *Iliad* appeals to "pride, anger, and thirst for revenge" and celebrates Achilles, "the hero of violence," whereas the *Odyssey* celebrates Ulysses, "the hero of wisdom" (1999, 383). Yet it is the *Iliad* that concludes with Achilles exhibiting not violence, but compassion toward the father of the warrior he has slain, and it is the *Odyssey* that concludes with Odysseus exhibiting violent anger against the relatives of the suitors he has slain (*Iliad* 24.476–804; *Odyssey* 24.494–544).[45] Vico claims that "In the *Odyssey*, Homer himself describes two blind poets who sing at the banquets of the great: Demodocus at Alcinous's banquet for Ulysses, and Phemius at the suitors' banquet" (1999, 380). Homer, however, never describes Phemius as blind (see *Odyssey* 1.153–155, 1.325–327, 22.330–356, 24.439). Vico, in the course of denouncing the wrath of Homer's Achilles, remarks with indignation, "The beautiful princess Polyxena, who is the daughter of the once rich and powerful Priam, and is now a miserable slave despite her royal birth, must be sacrificed on Achilles' tomb, so that his ashes, thirsty for vengeance, may soak up the last drop of her blood!" (1999, 358). But Homer never even mentions Polyxena in either of his poems. Finally, Vico's idiosyncratic and often extremely harsh judgments of Homer as a poet – that, since "nearly all of Homer's similes are based on wild animals and other savage things . . . it is clear that no mind civilized and refined by philosophy could have succeeded in inventing such similes" (357; see also 363, 371, 384–385); that "no mind rendered humane and compassionate by philosophy could have created the truculent and ferocious style which Homer uses in describing the great variety of bloody battles, and the great variety of extravagantly cruel kinds of slaughter, which constitute the particular sublimity of the Iliad" (357, 385); that "Homer's heroes exhibit the capriciousness of children, the vigorous imagination of women, and the seething passion of violent youths" (371; see also 358); and that "Homer's clumsy and indecorous passages reflect the awkwardness under which the Greeks laboured to express themselves while their language was still taking shape and was extremely poor" (371;

[45] Consider also Schein's observation that "the *Odyssey* is no more different from the *Iliad* artistically, intellectually, or spiritually than, say, the *Tempest* is from *King Lear*" (1984, 37; see also 1996, 6–7).

see also 384) – may also lead one to wonder how persuasive Vico's interpretation of Homer is.[46]

One may reasonably question, then, the reading of Homer on which Vico bases his argument against the traditional view that Homer was a philosophic thinker. Nagy himself characterizes Vico's study of Homer as one consisting of "intuitions" rather than careful analysis of the text (1974, 11). John Alvis describes Vico's reading of the *Iliad* as "less than fully satisfactory in its impatience of careful treatment of detail" (1995, x). Indeed, according to Grafton, Vico "knew Homer only at second hand, through Latin translations" and "knew the Greek world more distantly still, through scholarly compilations" (1999, xxi–xxii). In his *Autobiography*, Vico himself states that he "decided to abandon Greek" at a certain point in his studies and later admits at least one error in his account of Homer (1963, 134, 196). Croce observes that even though Vico's "new departure in Homeric criticism brought with it implicitly a complete revolution in the history of ancient literature," Vico himself "was no specialist" on Homer and his account of Homer was not "strictly logical" but rather "exaggerated and one-sided" (1964, 190–192). One may reasonably doubt, then, that this founding figure in modern Homeric scholarship possessed an authoritative mastery of Homer's text or a compelling interpretation of his poems.

A number of scholars have even wondered whether Vico's primary intention in arguing that the ancient and venerable Homer, if he existed at all, was a primitive poet, was not rhetorical and political rather than scholarly and theoretical: namely, to challenge, in an oblique and politic manner, the ancient and venerable authority of the Bible and the Catholic Church, at a time when the Inquisition in Italy, for example, was still powerful.[47] For even though Vico speaks in pious tones in the *New Science* – Berlin accordingly maintains that "Vico was a pious Roman

[46] Grafton suggests that Vico's reading of Homer was heavily influenced by a sixteenth-century commentary written by Julius Caesar Scaliger, "who saw Homer's literary crimes as clearly as Vico" (1999, xxiv). According to Grafton, Scaliger, in addition to "subjecting Homer to a literary mugging," deemed "Homer's heroes far too plebeian" (1992, 161, 163). Consider Vico's apparent praise of Scaliger (357) but also his criticisms of him (149, 188, 363–364).

[47] Fisch and Bergin observe, "Vico says nothing of the Inquisition in his autobiography, but his writings are not fully intelligible to one who does not bear in mind that it was active in Naples throughout his lifetime" (1963, 34; see 34–36 as a whole). See also Ambler 2009, 185.

Catholic, and he believed that the Church alone could provide the answers" (2002, 8; see also 60–63; 2000, 29, 70, 87, 91–93, 98–102) – the Dominican G. F. Finetti, who wrote a work entitled *Defense of the Authority of Sacred Scripture against Giambattista Vico* in 1768, "claimed that Vico's invocations of divine providence and the Bible were merely exoteric covers for a scandalous teaching regarding man's feral beginnings" (Lilla 1993, 244). According to Fisch and Bergin (1963, 63), Finetti

> saw more clearly than others that the *New Science*, however innocent in intent, was by no means innocuous in effect. To admit the feral state as the starting-point for the rise of humanity, and to make the development of society a matter of internal dialectic, was to put the entire structure of Catholic thought in jeopardy. He saw too that Vico's theory of the origin of religion was Lucretian, not Christian; and that the disintegration of the personality of Homer and of other heroic characters would open the way to the ultimate disintegration of Moses, the patriarchs and the prophets.[48]

Insofar as Vico's reading of Homer is, taken at face value, unpersuasive and insofar as he may have even used Homer as a stalking horse for the religious authorities of his time, it is not at all clear that Vico's momentous and influential account of Homer constitutes a genuine refutation of the traditional, pre-Vichian understanding of Homer as a philosophic educator of the Greeks.

If Homer was the educator of the Greeks, what was the purpose and content of that education? What form of human excellence, for example, did Homer seek to foster among the Greeks: military and political or philosophic and contemplative? What understanding of the divine did he seek to convey? Vico identifies the two principal obstacles that any serious student of Homer, always and everywhere, must wrestle with: his bewildering portrayal of the gods as "capricious" and of the apparently greatest hero, Achilles, as "savage" (1999, 357, 300–301). If Homer genuinely possessed wisdom concerning the divine and sought to enlighten the

[48] For a fuller account of this "interpretation of Vico as esoteric atheist" made by a variety of scholars, see Lilla 1993, 243–245. Consider also Collingwood 1956, 76–79. According to Ambler, "Strauss wonders also whether Vico's extended discussion of Homer is an implicit comment on the Bible" (2009, 178; see also 174, 177–180, 182–183, 185). On the other hand, Lilla's whole book on Vico is largely devoted to arguing against the "unconvincing interpretation" of Vico as "an atheistic Epicurean writing against the Catholic church" (1993, 243).

Greeks concerning the nature of the divine (Plato *Republic* 598d7–e5; see also 595b9–c2, 599c6–d2, 378d3–e1), why did he portray the gods in such a seemingly frivolous and comic manner? And if Homer genuinely possessed knowledge of human virtue and vice (Plato *Republic* 598d7–e5; Plutarch *Alexander* 15.4–5; Machiavelli 1998, 68–70), why did Homer present the seemingly selfish and wrathful Achilles, rather than the dutiful Hector or the prudent Odysseus, as the greatest hero of his poems? Such are the questions this book aims to address.

The emergence of the postmodern critique of rationalism and the influence of that critique on contemporary intellectual life render a study of Homer's education especially urgent. For much of modern times, there was little theoretical interest in the question of Homer's teachings because of the widespread view that, thanks to historical progress, not only in technology and power, but also in wisdom and virtue, we modern human beings have little to learn from the classical Greeks. Schiller and Hegel – in some measure following Rousseau and ultimately, as we have seen, Vico and Bacon – viewed Homer, for example, as a great but naive poet, who went on to found a civilization that represented the infancy or adolescence of the human spirit.[49] But Nietzsche persuasively challenged this confident view of human progress – most dramatically, as Max Weber points out, through his "devastating criticism of those 'last men' who 'invented happiness'" (Weber 1958, 143; see also Nietzsche 1954a, 129–130) – and the condescending view of Homer such belief in progress fostered[50]:

[49] For Schiller's identification of naiveté with childhood, see 1981, 21–28, and for his discussion of the Greeks as a whole and of Homer in particular as naive, see 1981, 32–38, 65–66. For Hegel's identification of the Greeks with adolescence, see 1956, 106–107. For examples of Hegel's view of the Greeks as beautiful and impressive but primitive, consider also 1956, 233–250. In this context, Hegel also remarks: "the poets were . . . the teachers of the Greeks – especially Homer" (1956, 236). Consider also Rousseau's description of Homer as "a poet born in times which, in comparison with the times that followed, still preserved something of the childhood of the human spirit" (1986, 277).

[50] Nietzsche argues against the account by Rousseau and Schiller of Homer as a "naive" poet whose genius arises naturally, "reared at the bosom of nature," that Homer's so-called naiveté can be understood only as a willful, artistic veiling of "the terror and horror of existence" and hence as a product of "the wisdom of suffering" (1967, 42–44).

> Before . . . the innermost dependence of every art on the Greeks, from Homer to Socrates, was demonstrated conclusively, we had to feel about these Greeks as the Athenians felt about Socrates. . . And so one feels ashamed and afraid in the presence of the Greeks, unless one prizes truth above all things and dares acknowledge this truth: that the Greeks, as charioteers, hold in their hands the reins of our own and every other culture, but that almost always chariot and horses are of inferior quality and not up to the glory of their leaders, who consider it sport to run such a team into an abyss which they themselves clear with the leap of Achilles. (Nietzsche 1967, 93–94)[51]

In the light of Nietzsche's critique of modernity and the powerful doubts it has raised – doubts that have in so many ways shaped our postmodern world (Rorty 1989, 27–30, 39–43, 61–66, 96–121; 1991, 32–33) – it seems reasonable to consider the possibility that we postmodern human beings have much to learn from classical civilization and the philosophic poet who founded it.

But what is the teaching of Homer? What kind of civilization did he seek to establish? Nietzsche's postmodern attack on the Western tradition of liberal, democratic rationalism was launched in the name of the tragic heroism of Homer. Nietzsche argued that Homer and the tragic poets founded a noble civilization – the noblest human beings have ever created – based on a pessimistic, tragic view of life; on a celebration of the life of the heroic warrior; and on a rejection of rationalism.[52] But that civilization was destroyed by Socrates: "Who is it that may dare single-handed to negate the Greek genius that, as Homer, Pindar, and Aeschylus, as Phidias, as Pericles, as Pythia and Dionysus, as the deepest abyss and the highest height, is sure of our astonished veneration?" (Nietzsche 1967, 88).[53] Socrates destroyed the Homeric, tragic culture and replaced it with a rationalistic, optimistic, anti-tragic one that proclaims that reason can lead human beings to happiness, and hence that the life based on reason is the wisest, happiest, and best way of life for a human being (1967, 95; see also 1954b, 473–479). But this anti-tragic Platonism paved the way for a sub-tragic, sub-heroic, sub-spiritual democratic enlightenment that has culminated with the "*the over-all degeneration of man*" and the

[51] Consider as well Lukàcs's contention that Homer enables us to understand "the secret of the Greek world: its perfection, which is unthinkable for us, and the unbridgeable gulf that separates us from it" (1977, 30–31).

[52] Nietzsche 1967, 17–18, 87–97, 106; 1968, 448–453; 1969b, 270–274; see also 1989, 201–202, 204–206; 1954b, 562–563.

[53] See also Lukàcs 1977, 36.

"animalization of man into the dwarf animal of equal rights and claims" (1989, 2–3, 118, emphasis in original). Thanks to Socrates and Plato, the "master morality" taught by Homer has been eclipsed by the "slave morality" of Christianity – "Platonism for 'the people'" – and ultimately by the "herd animal morality" of the modern democratic world (1989, 2–3, 115–116, 204–208; 1984, 46–47). To avoid the final victory of the democratic, peaceful, sub-tragic, and sub-heroic "last man," Nietzsche calls for a rebirth of tragic heroism. This new tragic culture must replace the model of the serene rationalist Socrates with the model of the angry and suffering warrior Achilles, "the greatest hero" (1967, 43) and with the model of Homer himself: "With this Homeric happiness in one's soul one is also more capable of suffering than any other creature under the sun" (1974, 302; see also 1984, 108–109). As we have noted, Nietzsche crystallizes his understanding of Homer as a thoroughgoing opponent of rationalism with the formulation: "Plato versus Homer: that is the complete, the genuine antagonism" (1969a, 154).

Nietzsche offers a brilliantly provocative account of Homer, one that has the virtue of taking Homer seriously as a thinker.[54] But is it a convincing account of the substance of Homer's thought? Was Homer, the educator of the Greeks, truly an enemy of the rationalism that proved to be a hallmark of Greek civilization? When examined in the light of Homer's texts, Nietzsche's interpretation proves to be deeply questionable. For example, Nietzsche simply takes it for granted that Achilles is the greatest of Homer's heroes (1967, 43). Yet, Homer devoted one of his two epic poems to exploring the rival heroism of Odysseus, a hero who comes to sight as an embodiment of rationalism, insofar as he, in contrast to Achilles, defeats his enemies by his wits and cunning. Furthermore, even though Achilles is famous for his greatness as a warrior, Homer focuses the *Iliad* on Achilles' *questioning* of the passionate, spirited, warlike life that Nietzsche celebrates and on Achilles' consideration of the possibility that the life characterized by peace, friendship, and reflection might be superior (see, e.g., 1.149–171, 9.308–429, 18.98–110, 24.476–670; see also 9.185–191). Moreover, Nietzsche assumes that Homer simply admires the heroes he presents (see, e.g., 1969a, 39–43). Yet, as we noted earlier, Homer explicitly criticizes Achilles, for example, in the opening lines of the *Iliad*, and he

[54] For an argument that Nietzsche "was not in fact a strict unitarian" in his reading of Homer's texts, see Silk and Stern 1981, 152, and 150–154 as a whole. See also 189.

repeatedly focuses the reader's attention and sympathy on the sufferings of Achilles' Achaian and Trojan victims. Finally, while Nietzsche's sharp opposition between the rationalist Socrates and the anti-rationalist Homer seems to draw support from Socrates's sharp critique of Homer's heroes in the *Republic*, it ignores the distinction Socrates himself draws between his critique of Homer's heroes and his admiration for Homer himself.[55]

My own study of Homer suggests that in his two epic poems, Homer offers a systematic critique of both the tragic warrior heroism represented, for example, by Achilles and Hector, and the seemingly rational heroism represented by Odysseus. In the *Iliad*, Homer shows that the core of the heroic life is a desire to render oneself worthy of honor by devoting oneself nobly and selflessly to one's community, as Achilles and Hector devote themselves to their communities. But Homer calls the wisdom of such devotion into question, both through the suffering of Hector, his family, and his people, but most of all through the agony and fate of Achilles. In the *Odyssey*, Homer turns to examine the case for a seemingly more sophisticated and enlightened brand of heroism, embodied by the wily and self-interested hero Odysseus. Yet, Homer demonstrates that Odysseus's self-interestedness leads him to act with considerable inhumanity, not only toward his companions, but also toward his family. Moreover, Homer shows that the seemingly enlightened heroism of Odysseus is ultimately less rational than it seems and that indeed it is ultimately less rational than the seemingly more passionate heroism of Achilles. For, while Achilles is generally more dominated by the passions, especially by the moral passion *par excellence* of anger, than Odysseus is, Achilles ultimately rises above his anger in the last book of the *Iliad*. In sharp contrast, Odysseus reveals throughout the final books of the *Odyssey* that, for all his apparent thoughtfulness, he remains entirely in the grip of the passions and especially in the grip of anger. Furthermore, it is Achilles, not Odysseus, who raises the most far-reaching questions concerning justice, happiness, and the gods. Homer indicates that Achilles is ultimately the best of the Achaians because he is the most thoughtful of the Achaians and hence because he is the one who comes

[55] See Plato *Republic* 595b9–c3, 606e1–608b2; *Apology of Socrates* 40e4–41a8; *Ion* 530b9–10; consider also Bolotin 1995.

closest to Homer himself.[56] My investigation of Homer suggests that the alternative between the sub-heroic rationalist and the noble irrationalist presented by Nietzsche is false. For Homer shows, through such examples as that of the thoughtful and compassionate Achilles of Book XXIV of the *Iliad*, that genuine rationalism is both noble and humane. Indeed, Homer bears witness to the possibility of a noble and humane rationalism above all through his own example. For the more one reads his epic poems, and studies and ponders his splendid characters – human and divine – the more one comes to admire the wisdom, the heart, and the humanity of Homer himself.

[56] For accounts of Homer's rationalism that stress the superiority of Odysseus to Achilles, see Benardete 2005, 1997; Clay 1983. Consider as well Deneen 2000 and Zuckert 1988, 19–20. For accounts of Homer's rationalism that are more critical of Odysseus, see Bolotin 1989; Ruderman 1995, 1999. Consider as well Alvis 1995. For accounts of Homer's rationalism that highlight the thoughtfulness of Achilles, see Burns 1996, as well as, again, Bolotin 1989. Consider as well Saxonhouse 1988; Lutz 2006. For an argument that Homer ultimately teaches the importance of recognizing the "limits of reason," see Dobbs 1987, 493.

CHAPTER 1

The Theology of Homer

THE UNGODLIKE GODS OF THE ILIAD?

The modern reader of Homer is most immediately surprised and bewildered by his portrayal of the gods. In contrast with what we expect of divine beings, in contrast with the Bible in particular, Homer's gods seem undignified, even frivolous.[1] Some scholars attempt to explain the frivolity of the Homeric gods by suggesting that they are not distinctively divine beings but simply human beings writ large. Richmond Lattimore, for example, contends that "The gods of Homer are mainly immortal men and women, incomparably more powerful than mortals, but like mortals susceptible to all human emotions and appetites."[2] Similarly, Cecil Bowra claims, "The gods are a delightful gay invention [who] were only like human beings and

[1] Vico describes Homer's gods as "capricious [*leggieri*]" (1999, 357; 1977, 546). Reinhardt coined the phrase "a lofty lack of seriousness" or "sublime frivolity [*ein erhabener Unernst*]" to describe the gods of the *Iliad* (1960, 25). See also Redfield 1975, 76. Even Griffin, after stressing the instances in which the gods appear dignified, acknowledges that, "every reader of Homer is aware that the gods are often seen very differently, as frivolous, cynical, and all too human" (1980, 172). Consider also his admission that the gods in Homer "do not seem to fulfil all the demands which mortals make of their gods, either in awesomeness or in concern for justice" (1995, 11).

[2] Lattimore, 1992, 54; see also Finley 1978, 135–136, 141; Edwards 1987, 138; Lateiner 2004, 21. According to Lukàcs, Homer "made purely human beings out of" the gods (1977, 102).

therefore often laughable."[3] Yet Homer often presents the gods as appearing much more ridiculous than human beings. For example, Book XIV of the *Iliad* presents Zeus, the greatest of the gods, as forgetting completely about the climactic and tragic life and death battle between the Achaians and the Trojans because he suddenly gets the hots for his wife, the goddess Hera. Moreover, Zeus is not only ridiculously out of control in his sexual passion but also amazingly inept and unwise. When the human Paris is overcome by erotic desire for his wife, Helen, he suavely and gallantly declares: "But come, let us go to bed and turn to love-making. For never before has love thus enfolded my mind, not when I first sailed from lovely Lacedaimon in sea-faring ships, having seized you, and in the island Kranae I mingled with you in love-making, in bed, not even then, as now I love you and sweet longing has taken hold of me" (3.441–446). On the other hand, when Zeus is overcome by erotic desire for his wife, the god clumsily and foolishly proceeds to proclaim his love for her by referring to love affairs he has had with seven other goddesses and mortal women! Zeus declares to his wife:

> But now let us go to bed and turn to love-making. For never before has love for any goddess or woman so melted about the heart inside me, broken it to submission, as now: not that time when I loved the wife of Ixion who bore me Peirithoos, equal to the gods in counsel, nor when I loved Akrisios's daughter, sweet-stepping Danae, who bore Perseus to me, pre-eminent among all men, nor when I loved the daughter of far-renowned Phoinix, Europa, who bore Minos to me, and Rhadamanthys the godlike; not when I loved Semele, or Alkmene in Thebe, when Alkmene bore me a son, Herakles the strong-hearted, while Semele's son was Dionysos, the pleasure of mortals; not when I loved the queen Demeter of the lovely tresses, not when it was glorious Leto, nor you yourself, so much as now I love you, and sweet longing has taken hold of me." (*Iliad* 14.313–328)[4]

[3] Bowra 1977, 222. Bowra goes so far as to claim, "this complete anthropomorphic system has of course nothing to do with real religion" (1977, 222). Redfield maintains that Homer's *Iliad* tells "not of gods conceived as actual, but of literary gods" (1975, 76). See also Murray 1924, 265: "The gods are patronised, conventionalised, and treated as material for ornament"; and Kirk 1962, 345: "The gods provide other forms of diversion ... These divine scenes successfully avert the threat of monotony." Kirk suggests that "certain divine actions ... may be little more than *façons de parler*" (1974, 292). See also Whitman 1958, 222.

[4] Bowra comments that this "long list of erotic triumphs is ... well compared to Leoporello's Catalogue in *Don Giovanni*" (1977, 223). In Mozart's opera, however, it is not Don Giovanni himself who pronounces this list.

What can it mean to worship such a comical figure as the greatest of gods? How can we take seriously a poet who presents the greatest of gods in this way?

Homer's poems occupied a place among the Greeks comparable to that occupied by the Hebrew scriptures among the Hebrews. We may go so far as to say without too much exaggeration that Homer's poems, and especially his *Iliad*, were the Bible of the ancient Greeks.[5] Yet if we compare the *Iliad* with the Bible, we cannot help but be struck by at least one clear and startling contrast between the two works. While the Bible clearly and emphatically focuses our attention on God and His doings, the *Iliad* emphatically directs our attention and our admiration toward the speeches and the deeds of its *human* heroes.[6]

To be sure, the Hebrew Bible presents a galaxy of great and unforgettable human heroes and heroines, above all, Abraham, Moses, and David.[7] But what is characteristic of the Biblical heroes is that they attribute their heroic deeds to God and hence focus our attention on God. David, who of all Biblical heroes most resembles Achilles, who, like Achilles, is a great warrior, a great friend, and a lover of music and poetry, declares to Goliath just before he kills him:

> You have come against me with sword and spear and dagger, but I come against you in the name of the Lord of Hosts, the God of the ranks of Israel which you have defied. The Lord will put you into my power this day; ... the whole world will know that there is a God in Israel. All those who are gathered here will see that the Lord saves without sword or spear; the battle is the Lord's, and He will put you all into our power. (I Samuel 17:45–47)

[5] As Long remarks, "Throughout classical antiquity and well into the Roman Empire, Homer held a position in Mediterranean culture that can only be compared to the position the Bible would later occupy... Like the Bible for the Jews, Homer offered the Greeks the foundation of their cultural identity" (1992, 44). See also Bacon 1974, 99: Homer "was made a kind of scripture by the later schools of the Grecians." Consider as well Schein 1984, 38; Hunter 2004, 246; Farrell 2004, 268; Griffin 1995, 1. For comparisons of various passages in or aspects of the Homeric poems and the Bible, see Bowra 1977, 228–229; Griffin 1980, 150–158, 171–172.

[6] As Kearns puts it, "these are not poems about Gods, but about human beings" (2004, 71).

[7] The ensuing discussion of the Bible owes a great deal to Fradkin 1995, 55–66. For an extremely helpful discussion of Abraham's distinctive, unclassical heroism, see Pangle 2003, 127–171.

As this example of David indicates, human heroism in the Bible tends to be dwarfed by the greatness of a God who not only creates the heaven and the earth but also founds a people, rules them, leads them into war, and vanquishes their enemies. God engages in and dominates those political and military activities that are usually associated with heroism. God always comes to sight as the true hero – the only true hero – of the Bible.[8] Consequently, the Bible teaches that the greatest human excellence is humility: the bowing down in awe before God, the awareness of human smallness in the face of God, the full recognition of God's towering greatness and perfection.

Now, the gods of the *Iliad* also play an absolutely crucial role in the events of the poem. As the opening words of the poem show, it is a goddess who ostensibly narrates much of the story of the poem. Moreover, it is Zeus who ostensibly plans much of the action of the *Iliad*. And it is the gods as a whole who determine in large measure who wins and who loses in battle, who shall live and who shall die, who shall attain great glory and who shall suffer terrible sorrow. As Achilles says to Priam near the end of the poem (24.527–531):

> For two urns lie on the door-sill of Zeus that give evil gifts, but the other one, good things. Should Zeus who delights in thunder mingle these and give them to someone, he sometimes encounters something evil, sometimes something noble. But when Zeus gives from the urn of sorrows, he makes one the victim of outrageous deeds, and the evil hunger drives him over the divine earth, and he wanders, honored neither by gods nor by mortals.

Nevertheless, it is the human heroes of the poem, not the gods, who excite our interest and admiration. It is, for example, the human conflicts between Achilles and Agamemnon and between the Achaians and the Trojans, and not the divine conflict between Zeus and Hera, that move and engross us. Indeed, in the light of the human conflicts of the poem, the divine conflicts – such as the bickering between Zeus and Hera – seem petty and silly. While the gods of the *Iliad* are beings of great splendor and considerable charm, they never seem to achieve the nobility and the dignity of such characters as Andromache, Priam, Hector, Patroclus, or Achilles. The gods' feelings seem

[8] Consider also St. Augustine's remark regarding the Christian martyrs: "If it were not contrary to the usage of the Church, we might call those martyrs our 'heroes'" (*City of God* 10.21, St. Augustine 1984, 401).

shallower, their souls thinner, and their characters smaller than those of the greatest heroes and heroines of the poem.[9]

Now, this strange portrayal of the gods may tempt us to dismiss Homer as a primitive thinker whose understanding of the divine was itself shallow and whose belief in such gods was crude and even bizarre. Yet Homer's seemingly frivolous portrayal of the gods in fact reflects a coherent and even a profound understanding of what divine beings must be like. One may even say that Homer's understanding of the divine is, in its own way, as profound as the understanding presented in the Bible. But to arrive at the heart of Homer's teaching about the divine, we must set aside our own expectations about what divine beings must be like and consider what expectations and beliefs the human characters in Homer's poems cherish about the gods.[10] Homer's teaching concerning the gods unfolds in stages, and in order to grasp that teaching, we must begin by trying to see, naively and simply, how the gods come to sight to the humans in the first and more fundamental poem, the *Iliad*.[11] Our natural inlet into Homer's understanding of the gods is, to begin with, the views of the gods expressed by the human characters in the poem. For, as Homer indicates, for example, by addressing human characters in the poem on eighteen occasions, as well as us, his audience, the singer Homer wants and expects his audience to identify with his human characters – especially with Menelaus, whom he addresses seven times in five separate books – and to take their beliefs seriously, even though he ultimately leads us beyond those beliefs.[12]

[9] Even Griffin concedes that the gods' "concern cannot rival in intensity that felt by such human watchers as Priam or Achilles" (1980, 201). See also Alvis 1995, 8.

[10] Dodds aptly warns against simply judging the piety to be found in Homer by "the kind of thing that enlightened Europeans or Americans of today recognize as being religion" (1973, 2).

[11] See Griffin 1995, 1; Clay 1983, 26. I discuss the portrayal of the gods in the *Odyssey* in Chapter 4.

[12] Menelaus, whom Homer addresses seven times throughout the poem, prays to "Father Zeus" twice (4.127, 4.146–47, 7.104–107, 13.602–603, 17.679–681, 17.702–704, 23.600; 3.349–354, 17.18–28; see also 3.365, 13.631–639). Homer also addresses Patroclus nine times, all in book XVI (20, 584–585, 692–693, 744, 754, 787, 788–789, 812–813, 843), the Trojan warrior Melanippus once (15.582–583), and Achilles once (20.1–3). Homer of course implicitly addresses the audience throughout the poem, but there are occasions in which he seems to address us in particular, as individuals, by using the second person singular. See 4.223–225, 4.429–431, 5.85–86, 15.697–698, 17.366–367. Homer also

PIOUS BELIEF IN THE ILIAD

How do the human beings of the *Iliad* view the gods? Even though the gods as Homer portrays them may appear frivolous to us, these gods are prayed to, honored, and revered by his human heroes and heroines.[13] Indeed, the human characters in the poem believe that the gods, led by Zeus, are providential gods, wise and just beings, who care for human beings, protect the innocent, and punish the wicked. In the first place, the human characters describe the gods, especially Zeus, as beings who rule over human beings. Hector declares that Zeus "rules all mortals and immortals" (12.241–242). Menelaus, Ajax, and Achilles all refer to Zeus as "Ruler" or "Lord" (ἄναξ).[14] Calchas, Achilles, Odysseus, Pandarus, and Glaucus refer to Apollo, the son of Zeus, as "Lord" as well.[15] Homer too refers to Zeus as one "who rules over gods and human beings"[16] and refers to Apollo,[17] Poseidon,[18] Hades,[19] Hephaestus,[20] and Hermes[21] as "Rulers" or "Lords" as well. Hera herself affirms, twice to Zeus: "you rule over all immortals."[22]

But the clearest sign of the widespread belief in divine providence in the *Iliad* is that the Achaians and Trojans alike refer to Zeus – twenty-seven times – as "Father Zeus."[23] The gods themselves – including his siblings

addresses the goddess (presumably an individual Muse) twice (1.1–7, 2.761–762); the divine Muses as a whole, who dwell in Olympus, four times (2.484–487, 11.218–220, 14.508–510, 16.112); and Apollo twice (15.365–366, 20.151–152). See also Clay 2010, 19–26; Richardson 1990, 170–182.

[13] See Griffin 1980, 148–150.

[14] 3.351 (Menelaus), 7.194 (Ajax), 16.233 (Achilles), 18.118 (Achilles).

[15] 1.75 (Calchas), 1.390 (Achilles), 1.444 (Odysseus), 5.105 (Pandarus), 16.514 (Glaucus), 16.523 (Glaucus).

[16] 2.669. See also 1.502, 1.529, 7.200.

[17] 1.36, 7.23, 7.37, 16.804, 23.863.

[18] 13.28, 13.38, 15.8, 15.57, 20.67. See also Zeus's reference to Apollo as "ruler" (15.158).

[19] 20.61. Poseidon too refers to Hades as one who "rules" (15.188).

[20] 18.47, 18.42. Poseidon (15.214) and Thetis (18.137) also refer to Hephaestus as "ruler."

[21] 2.104.

[22] 4.61, 18.366. But Hera also tells the god Sleep, "the brother of Death," that he is "ruler of all gods and of all human beings" (14.233).

[23] 2.371 (Agamemnon), 3.276 (Agamemnon), 3.320 (the Achaians and Trojans), 3.365 (Menelaus), 4.235 (Agamemnon), 4.288 (Agamemnon), 6.259 (Hecubae), 7.132 (Nestor), 7.179 (Achaians), 7.202 (the Achaians), 8.236 (Agamemnon), 12.164 (Asios), 13.631 (Menealus), 13.818 (Ajax), 15.372 (Nestor), 16.97 (Achilles), 17.19 (Menelaus), 17.630 (Ajax),

Hera and Poseidon – also refer to Zeus as "Father" nineteen times.[24] Homer himself echoes his characters by referring to Zeus twenty-nine times as "Father"[25] and thirteen times as "the Father of Gods and Men."[26] From start to finish, the *Iliad* identifies Zeus as a fatherly being, and therefore, it would seem, a loving, caring, and just being, looked to for assistance by one and all. In the first prayer in the poem addressed to Zeus, Thetis, speaking on behalf of her son Achilles, calls him "Father Zeus" (1.503). In the last prayer in the poem addressed to Zeus, Priam calls him "Father Zeus" (24.308). Zeus, then, is not only a ruler over all gods and human beings but is also a fatherly and hence, presumptively, a benevolent and beneficent ruler.[27]

To be sure, like many a father, Zeus often inspires anger, blame, and bewilderment among his children. Menelaus declares, in a moment of fury: "Father Zeus, no one else of the gods is more destructive than you" (3.365; see also 13.631–639, 12.164–165). Agamemnon, denying all blame for his disastrous dispute with Achilles, insists that it was Zeus who "took away his mind" and thereby inexplicably caused him to quarrel with Achilles: "But what could I do? A god accomplishes all things" (19.137, 19.90; see 19.83–144, 2.371–378; and also 9.17–28, 19.268–275). Similarly, Priam, gallantly denying that Helen is at all to blame for the nine-year Achaian war against his people, blames the gods instead for inflicting war upon him (3.162–165). Nevertheless, time and again, twenty-five times in all, Menelaus, Agamemnon, and Priam, along with Achilles (directly and through his divine mother), Hector, Ajax, Nestor, Automedon, Asios, and all the Achaians and Trojans pray to Zeus as they

17.645 (Ajax), 19.121(Alcmene, as reported by Agamemnon), 19.270 (Achilles), 20.192 (Achilles), 21.83 (Achilles), 21.273 (Achilles), 22.60 (Priam), 24.287 (Hecubae), 24.308 (Priam).

[24] 1.503 (Thetis), 1.578 (Hephaestus), 1.579 (Hephaestus), 5.33 (Athena), 5.362 (Aphrodite), 5.421 (Athena), 5.457 (Apollo), 5.757 (Hera), 5.762 (Hera), 5.872 (Ares), 7.446 (Poseidon), 8.31 (Athena), 8.360 (Athena), 8.420 (Iris), 11.201 (Iris), 21.512 (Artemis), 22.178 (Athena), 22.221 (Athena), 24.461 (Hermes).

[25] 1.533–534, 2.146, 4.23, 5.662, 8.69, 8.245, 8.397, 8.438, 8.460, 10.154, 11.66, 11.544, 13.796, 14.352, 14.414, 15.236, 15.637, 16.227, 16.250, 16.253, 16.676, 17.46, 17.498, 17.648, 21.506, 21.508, 21.520, 22.209, 24.100. See also 21.469.

[26] 1.544, 4.68, 5.426, 5.764, 8.49, 8.132, 11.182, 15.12, 15.47, 16.458, 20.56, 22.167, 24.103.

[27] I therefore think Fustel de Coulanges goes too far in claiming that the term "father" "was synonymous with the words rex, αναξ, βασιλευς" (1900, 97–98). The term "father" connotes a more (though not entirely) reliably benign ruler or king.

would to a father, for protection, wisdom, and justice.[28] According to Menelaus, humans believe that Zeus "surpasses all others in his mind, both men and gods" (13.631–632; see also 13.354–355; consider too 8.141–144). Agamemnon reports that humans deem Zeus "the best of men and gods" (19.95–96). And Achilles calls him simply "the highest and best of gods" (23.43). Moreover, Achilles, Agamemnon, Odysseus, Diomedes, Chryses, Glaucus, Pandarus, Theano, the Trojan women, Achaian youths, and the Achaians as a whole also pray for assistance to two children of Father Zeus – Apollo and Athena – and to all the gods, sixteen times in all.[29] Notwithstanding, then, their occasional frustration with the gods, Homer's human characters believe in divine providence and repeatedly look to the gods, led by Zeus, "the Father of Gods and Men," for effective and righteous rule.

The story of the *Iliad* virtually opens with a plea to Apollo, "the son of Leto and Zeus," for justice (1.9). The Achaians have stormed and plundered the city of Thebe and have given to their mighty king, Agamemnon, the captured daughter of Chryses, a priest of Apollo (1.366–69). In the very first words spoken by a character in the poem, the old priest begs the king for the return of his "beloved ... child" (1.20–21). The distraught father offers the king and the assembled Achaians "boundless ransom" (1.13). He also offers a public prayer that the gods grant the Achaians success in conquering Troy and returning home safely. The priest beseeches Agamemnon to free his

[28] 1.500–516 (Thetis, on behalf of Achilles – see 1.393–412, 15.72–77, 18.74–77), 2.371–374 (Agamemnon), 2.411–418 (Agamemnon), 3.275–291 (Agamemnon), 3.297–301 (the Achaians and Trojans), 3.319–323 (the Achaians and Trojans), 3.349–354 (Menelaus), 4.288–291 (Agamemnon), 6.475–481 (Hector), 7.177–180 (the Achaians), 7.200–205 (the Achaians), 8.236–244 (Agamemnon), 8.526–528 (Hector), 9.171–178 (Nestor and the Achaian elders), 11.735–736 (Nestor), 12.162–172 (Asios), 15.370–378 (Nestor), 16.97–100 (Achilles), 16.231–249 (Achilles), 17.19 (Menelaus), 17.498–506 (Automedon), 17.645–647 (Ajax), 19.257–266 (Agamemnon), 21.272–283 (Achilles), 24.306–316 (Priam). See also 7.132–135 (Nestor).

[29] For prayers to Apollo, see 1.35–45 (Chryses), 1.450–457 (Chryses), 1.472–474 (Achaian youths), 4.118–121 (Pandarus), 4.288–291 (Agamemnon), 16.97–100 (Achilles), 16.513–529 (Glaucus). For prayers to Athena, see 4.288–291 (Agamemnon), 5.114–122 (Diomedes), 6.286–296 (Theano and Trojan women), 10.277–282 (Odysseus), 10.283–295 (Diomedes), 10.460–464 (Odysseus), 11.735–736 (Nestor), 16.97–100 (Achilles), 23.768–772 (Odysseus). For prayers to all the gods by the Achaians, see 8.343–347, 15.367–369. Consider as well 3.275–291 (Agamemnon), 6.475–481 (Hector), 7.132–135 (Nestor), 8.526–528 (Hector).

daughter and thereby show reverence for Apollo. So morally compelling is this demand from the wronged father and priest that "all" of the Achaians beg the king to yield the girl (1.23). But the king responds by dismissing the old man, says Homer, "in an evil way" (1.24–25). King Agamemnon threatens the priest, twice, and cruelly boasts that he will keep the girl as his slave until she grows old, doing his work and sharing his bed. And the Achaians acquiesce in this decision. Terrified, impotent, and desperate, the old father leaves and "he went silently along the shore of the much-roaring sea" (1.34). Overwhelmed by the wickedness of the powerful king, the moral cowardice of the Achaians, and his own helplessness, the old man prays to "the lord Apollo" for justice: "Hear me, Silver-bowed One .... Let the Danaans pay for my tears with your shafts" (1.37–42).

Similarly, in Book II, as the Achaians and the Trojans are about to swear oaths to respect the terms of a truce and the result of a duel between Menelaus and Paris to decide the outcome of the war, Agamemnon prays to Zeus and other deities to enforce the truce and punish those who violate it: "Father Zeus, Thoughtful One, from Ida, Most Glorious, Greatest, and Helios, You Who watch over all things and listen to all things, and rivers and earth and You Who under the earth punish weary human beings, whoever has sworn a false oath, You be witnesses, guard the oaths of trust" (3. 276–280). Both the Achaians and Trojans then proceed to pray: "Zeus, Most Glorious, Greatest, and the Other Immortal Gods, let those, on either side, who attack in violation of the oaths sworn before, let their brains flow on the ground as this wine does, both theirs and their children's, and let their wives be broken by other men" (3.298–301). And as the duel is about to proceed, the Achaians and the Trojans again pray: "Father Zeus, Thoughtful One, from Ida, Most Glorious, Greatest, whichever man has made these deeds to take place among both sides, grant that he die and go down to the house of Hades, and that for us there come to be sworn oaths of friendship and trust" (3.320–323). Then, as he begins the duel, Menelaus prays for justice to "Father Zeus": "Zeus, Lord, grant me to punish him who first did evil things to me, divine Alexandros, and break him beneath my hands, so that someone of humans born hereafter will shudder at doing evil things to one who received him as a guest, who has offered him friendship" (3.350–354; see also 2.588–590).

Later, when the sworn terms of the duel and truce are broken, and his brother Menelaus is treacherously wounded, an outraged Agamemnon affirms,

> Thus the Trojans struck you and trampled on their sworn oaths. But in no way will the oath and the blood of the lambs be in vain, nor the unmixed libations and the right hands we trusted in. For, if at once the Olympian has not accomplished it, he will accomplish it hereafter, and they will pay a great penalty, with their own heads and wives and children. For I myself well know this in my mind and my spirit. A day will come when sacred Ilium will perish and Priam and the people of Priam of the ash spear, and Zeus, the son of Cronus, high-throned, dwelling in the upper air, will shake the black aegis over all, seething in anger at this deception. These things will not go unfulfilled. (4.157–168)

Agamemnon goes on to rally the Achaians against the Trojans by assuring them that "Father Zeus" will inflict terrible sorrows on the Trojan "liars" (4.234–239). We see, then, through all these examples, that the characters of the poem, on both sides of the conflict, are wholly convinced that the gods are enforcers of justice, that they especially enforce oaths solemnly sworn to by human beings by punishing without mercy those who violate them, and that, in general, they favor those who are truthful and dutiful and hospitable and visit destruction on the treacherous and deceitful.[30]

The most prominent example in the poem of one who expresses this belief in providential gods is the central hero of the poem, Achilles. In Book I, Achilles suffers what he believes to be an outrageous injustice. As the plague sent by Apollo in response to Chryses' prayer threatens to destroy the Achaian army, Achilles intervenes to save the army from disaster. He calls an assembly, asks the seer Calchas to speak, and guarantees his safety (1.53–92). Achilles then succeeds in inducing Agamemnon to return his mistress to her father and thereby brings the deadly plague to an end. Agamemnon, however, rewards Achilles' good deed by dishonoring him. He denounces Achilles and then humiliates him by robbing him of his *own* mistress (1.101–187). And even though Achilles has just saved the army from disaster,

[30] I therefore believe that Dodds overstates his case when he says that there is "*no* indication in the narrative of the *Iliad* that Zeus is concerned with justice as such" (1973, 32 – emphasis added; see also 52). Even Adkins, after arguing that the Homeric gods "are far from just," admits that, in portions of the Homeric poems, the gods are believed, at least, "to guarantee some moral relationships" (1960, 62, 65). I agree with Lloyd-Jones that "the protection of justice must have been one of Zeus' attributes," at least insofar as he is speaking only of how Zeus appears in the eyes of Homer's characters (1971, 8; see also 5). Kearns, after noting that "ethical considerations . . . are not a major concern of its [the *Iliad*'s] Gods," observes that, "In the *Iliad*, there is some human expectation that Zeus, at least, will punish wrong-doing" (2004, 67–68).

not a single man in the army speaks up on Achilles' behalf or intervenes in his defense. Forsaken by all, overcome by anger and frustration, Achilles looks to the gods for justice. As he declares to Athena: "If a man obeys the gods, they heed him greatly as well" (1.218). Consequently, Achilles urges his divine mother to ask Zeus to punish Agamemnon and all the Achaians for their injustice:

> Remind him of these things, sit beside him, and take his knees, if in some way he might be willing to help the Trojans, to pin the Achaians against their sterns and the sea, being killed, so that they may all have profit of their king, and that the son of Atreus, wide ruling Agamemnon, may also recognize his folly, that he did not honor the best of the Achaians. (1.407–412; see also 1.231, 1.421–422)

Achilles' prayer to Zeus for justice and his faithful expectation that Zeus will answer that prayer reflect his conviction that Zeus, together with the other gods, enforces justice, a conviction he shares with Chryses, Agamemnon, Menelaus, and indeed all the Achaians and Trojans.

The simple, pious belief that the gods, led by Zeus, are wise, just, and providential, then, is widely expressed by the human characters of the poem. Homer evidently presumes that his audience comes to the poem with this belief. Furthermore, Homer appears, on the surface of the poem, to support and champion the belief that the gods, led by Father Zeus, provide for human beings. Homer, as we have noted, himself refers to Zeus as "Father" twenty-nine times and also calls him "the Father of Gods and Men" thirteen times. He also nourishes the belief in divine providence through his opening and repeated appeals to goddesses, the omniscient Muses, "the daughters of aegis-bearing Zeus," to inform ignorant mortals regarding the providential "plan" of their father and other details of the story: "Tell me now, Muses, Who have homes in Olympus – for You are Goddesses, are there, and know all things, but we hear only the fame and we do not know at all – which were the rulers and leaders of the Danaans?" (2.484–492; see also 1.1–7, 2.760–762, 11.218–220, 14.508–510, 16.112–113). Throughout the poem, Homer recounts instances in which the gods care for human beings, pity them, and hearken to their prayers. Hera "cared" for the Achaians, "pitied" them, heeds their prayers, and intervenes on a number of occasions to help alleviate their suffering.[31] Apollo "heeded" the prayers of

[31] 1.55–56, 1.194–196, 5.711–909, 8.343–353, 18.165–168, 18.239–242.

Chryses and Glaucus.[32] Athena "heeded" the prayers of Odysseus and Diomedes and saves the life of Menelaus.[33] Poseidon "pitied" the Achaians and helps them and feels "grief" for Aeneas and rescues him.[34] Aphrodite saves Paris and her "beloved son" Aeneas (3.373–382, 5.311–318). Above all, Zeus, in Homer's account, repeatedly is said to feel pity and sorrow: for Agamemnon and the Achaians, for Hector, for Sarpedon, for Ajax, for Achilles and the principal Achaian warriors, for Priam, and even for Achilles' horses.[35] Zeus goes so far as to weep great tears of blood when his son Sarpedon is slain (16.458–461). And Zeus declares, on the eve of Hector's death: "My heart sorrows for Hector" (22.169–170). Homer recounts, on a number of occasions, that Zeus also "heeded" the prayers of human beings.[36] In all these ways, Homer lends support and encouragement to the pious hopes and longings of his audience.

Homer supports the belief in divine providence most visibly by opening and closing the story of the poem with the lesson that Zeus and his children answer the prayers of human beings for justice.[37] In Book I, the heartrending prayer to Apollo for justice by the wronged father and priest Chryses is answered swiftly and effectively. Apollo responds with righteous wrath, sending a terrible and deadly plague that ultimately compels the cruel king Agamemnon to return the girl Chryseis to her "beloved father" (1.441). It is hard to imagine an example that would inspire in the audience greater sympathy for the helpless victim of injustice or greater moral satisfaction at the outcome.[38] The story of the *Iliad*, then, opens with a terrible wrong righted by the rough justice of "the son of Leto and Zeus," Apollo (1.9). In this way, the poem begins by affirming the justice of the gods and the effectiveness of their providence (see also 1.442–445).

Similarly, at the end of the poem, we see the gods, led by Zeus, intervene to assist another old father victimized by another cruel tormentor. After Achilles slays the leading Trojan defender Hector, and the other Achaians repeatedly stab his corpse, Achilles proceeds to drag the corpse around the

32 1.35–45, 1.450–457, 16.513–527.
33 5.114–122, 10.277–295, 10.460–513, 23.768–772, 4.127–129.
34 13.10–38, 15.41–44, 20.288–340.
35 8.245–246,15.12, 16.431, 17.648, 19.340, 24.332. See also 17.441–442.
36 8.245–246, 15.377–378, 17.648–650, 21.273–298, 24.314–316.
37 See Scodel 2004, 53, 49; Crotty 1994, 24; Griffin 2004, 162.
38 See Gagarin 1987, 297.

walls of Troy, before the eyes of Hector's parents and people (22.369–375, 22.395–411). King Priam, Hector's father, overcome with grief, is powerless to stop the now triumphant Achaians from outraging the corpse of his beloved son, day after day. We see the hitherto splendid and prosperous king reduced by his impotent sorrow to a pathetic, sobbing old man who rolls around in excrement and smears himself with it (22.412–429, 24.160–165). Zeus, however, commands Achilles to return the corpse of Hector to Priam and sends his own beloved son Hermes to escort Priam to and from the Achaian camp. The uncertain Priam prays to "Father Zeus" for success on this dangerous mission and Zeus apparently grants it (24.308–309). Thanks to the gods' intervention, the powerless old Priam recovers the corpse of his beloved son and leads his family and city to mourn and bury their champion.

The first and last prayers in the *Iliad* are made by victims of injustice who turn to the gods for help and whose prayers are effectively answered.[39] Homer begins and closes the story of the poem by assuring the audience that the gods as a whole, led by Zeus, effectively protect the just and pious, no matter how weak, against the cruelty of the wicked, no matter how strong. Homer appears, then, on the very surface of the poem, to be a champion of piety, a poet who justifies the ways of the gods to men, and who therefore encourages in us the hope that Zeus, the Thoughtful, Compassionate, and Righteous Father of Gods and Men, loves us, cares for us, and ensures that justice is done. Therefore, piety, a simple, conventional trust in the governance of wise and caring gods, is our natural beginning point in approaching the poem, the threshold across which we may enter the Homeric universe. However, Homer proceeds to challenge this conventional piety most powerfully in the course of the poem. To understand this challenge, let us consider more carefully how the poem unfolds.

THE QUESTIONABLE PROVIDENCE OF THE GODS

Homer begins the *Iliad* by raising a question concerning the justice of the gods. The poem opens: "Sing, Goddess, of the wrath of Peleus's son, Achilles, which was destructive, which put countless woes upon the Achaians, hurled forth many mighty souls of heroes into Hades, and

[39] I therefore think that Adkins goes too far in stating, "The relations between such gods and mankind are *clearly* not founded on justice" (1960, 62 – emphasis added).

prepared them as food for dogs and all birds" (1.1–5). Up to this point in the opening sentence, the singer appears to condemn the anger of Achilles.[40] It was "destructive" to Achilles' own people, to his fellow soldiers, and it led, not only to their deaths, but also to the desecration of their corpses. Moreover, by focusing on the consequences of Achilles' anger rather than on the cause of that anger, the singer seems to belittle the cause and therefore seems to imply that the anger was not justified. But then, there is a twist. We learn that "the plan of Zeus was accomplished from the time when the two first stood apart, striving, the son of Atreus, lord of men, and divine Achilles" (1.5–7). Apparently, Zeus somehow approved of Achilles' anger and aided it with his plan, even though it was destructive of Achilles' fellow Achaians. But how could Zeus, the Father of Gods and Men, support injustice?[41] It would seem, contrary to the first impression given by the opening, that Achilles' anger must have been just. But how could it be just to cause such tremendous harm to one's own people? The singer seems to turn to the goddess to address his perplexity concerning the relation between justice and the gods, on the one hand, and justice and loyalty to one's own people, on the other.

Now, as we have seen, there is indeed reason to believe that Achilles' anger at Agamemnon and the Achaians is just. Agamemnon selfishly and recklessly endangers the survival of the Achaian army, which has been fighting at Troy for nine years to recover *his* sister-in-law, because he wishes to keep as his slave and concubine the daughter of Chryses, a priest of Apollo. When Achilles single-handedly saves the army from Agamemnon's outrageous behavior, Agamemnon humiliates him by taking away his mistress, and none of the Achaians speak up on his behalf, just as none of the Achaians intervened on behalf of Chryses against Agamemnon.[42] So perhaps the anger of Achilles, though destructive of the Achaians, is just, and perhaps then Zeus's plan to avenge Achilles is just.

Yet, even if we stipulate that Achilles is right and Agamemnon is wrong, the poem raises a further question concerning the justice of the gods early in Book I. For when Achilles considers responding to Agamemnon by killing him, Athena suddenly appears and informs Achilles that Hera wants him to refrain from attacking Agamemnon because she loves and cares for both men

[40] See Clay 1983, 38.

[41] See Lutz 2006, 112.

[42] Consider Redfield 1975, 12–14; Bolotin 1989, 47; Clarke 2004, 25–26.

"in the same way" (1.208–9; see also 1.195–6). But if Agamemnon is unjust, and Achilles is just, and Hera loves and cares for them both in the same way, must Hera, at least, not be indifferent to justice?[43]

We might answer that, even if Hera is indifferent to justice, Zeus himself, the greatest of the gods, the Father of Gods and Men, must care for justice and must try to benefit humans by seeing that justice is done among them. Yet, it is not immediately clear how deeply Zeus cares about justice. When Achilles urges his mother to ask Zeus to punish Agamemnon and the Achaians, Thetis informs him that she will have to wait because Zeus "went yesterday among the blameless Ethiopians in search of a feast, all the other gods followed him," and he will not return for twelve days (1.423–424)! This account stands in troubling contrast with that given in the opening lines of the poem. There, the singer portrays Zeus as a god who plans and directs human action. Here, Zeus goes off to party and leaves all humans, other than the Ethiopians, to their own devices for twelve days. Father Zeus seems a distant, even an absentee father here. How truly, then, does even Zeus care about justice or about humans as a whole?

When Zeus and the other gods return to Olympus, Thetis goes there and explains to "Father Zeus" that Agamemnon dishonored Achilles (1.503). She then beseeches Zeus: "Now exact payment for him You Yourself, Olympian, Thoughtful Zeus. Put strength into the Trojans so that the Achaians may repay my son and enlarge him with honor" (1.508–510). Now, this demand would seem to deserve considerable reflection and deliberation from Thoughtful Father Zeus, since it requires him to inflict on the Achaians, as Homer notes in the proemium, "countless woes" (1.2). Does the injustice Achilles has suffered warrant such a punishment of the entire Achaian army (consider 15.598–599)? Might Zeus not take another course of action, for example, by commanding Agamemnon and the Achaians to atone for their injustice by honoring Achilles, as he later commands Achilles to relent in his cruelty against Priam by returning the corpse of his son? Zeus, however,

[43] As we will see, Achilles' belief in the justice of the gods appears to be shaken by this incident.

I therefore disagree with Kirk's claim that Athena's intervention here is little more than a figure of speech (1974, 292), as well as Redfield's claim that Homer's audience would take this scene "as having little to do with the relation between man and god as they would normally understand that relation" (1975, 78). Consider Griffin's critique of Kirk and Redfield on this point (1980, 147–148, 158–160).

simply grants Thetis's prayer, albeit with one complaint: "This is a disastrous matter when you send me into hostilities with Hera, and she provokes me with words of reproach. Since even as things are, forever among the immortal gods, she quarrels with me and speaks of how I help the Trojans in battle" (1. 518–521). The only concern Zeus expresses here is for the nagging and the reproach that he must suffer at the hands of his wife, an annoyance that he apparently handles quite easily, with a simple threat to Hera, a great feast among the gods – marked by "unquenchable laughter" – and a night together in bed (1.560–569, 1.595–611). Zeus agrees to Thetis's demand, without even considering any alternative response and without expressing any concern whatsoever for the terrible sorrows the Achaians will suffer – sorrows that Homer devotes the rest of the poem to describing – nor for the injustice Achilles is suffering. How truly thoughtful, then, is Thoughtful Zeus and how truly provident is Father Zeus?

THE DOUBTFUL TRUSTWORTHINESS AND WISDOM OF THE GODS

The central example of divine providence in the *Iliad* is Zeus's "plan," in accordance with the prayers of Achilles and Thetis, to kill "many" Achaians beside their ships and thereby drive them to honor Achilles (2.1–6; see 1.1–7, 1.407–412, 1.508–510). During the four days after he agrees to grant the prayer of Achilles and Thetis – recounted in Books II–XVIII – we see Zeus's plan apparently succeed completely. By the end of the first day, the Achaians have been so badly beaten by the Trojans that they are driven to build a wall to protect their ships (7.336–344). The Achaians, who for nine years have been besieging the Trojans, are now besieged by them. At the end of the third day, Agamemnon begs Achilles to return to the war and offers him boundless gifts and honors of all kinds, which Achilles refuses. On the fourth day, the Trojans smash the Achaian forces, break through their wall, and start to set their ships on fire. This impending catastrophe prompts Achilles to send his companion Patroclus and his soldiers to save the Achaians. When Patroclus is killed, Achilles accepts the honors offered by Agamemnon and the Achaians and returns to the war. Insofar as the Achaians acted unjustly against Achilles by dishonoring him, then, Zeus effectively punishes them for their injustice and induces them to shower him with honors. As Thetis remarks to her son, "These things have been accomplished through Zeus, as before you prayed, raising your hands, that all the sons of the Achaians be pinned against the sterns of their ships, feeling their need for you, and that they suffer grievous deeds" (18.74–77; see also 16.236–238). In this way, the *Iliad* appears to vindicate the wise, just, and caring providence of Zeus, the Father of Gods and Men.

Yet, as Homer stresses, Zeus's plan almost fails utterly, twice, right from the start: first, when the Achaians attempt to leave Troy and, second, when the Achaians and Trojans agree to a truce and a duel between Paris and Menelaus to end the war and Menelaus wins (2.155–156, 3.369–375).[44] Through his account of these near failures and the manner in which they are averted, Homer raises the most far-reaching questions concerning the trustworthiness, the wisdom, the justice, and the benevolence of Zeus, and concerning the nature of the gods as a whole.

Once he has promised to answer the prayer of Achilles and Thetis to punish the Achaians, Zeus, after pondering "in his mind," resolves that he shall "destroy many men beside the ships of the Achaians" so that they may "honor Achilles" (2.3–4). The "plan" that appears "best" to him is to send a "destructive dream" to Agamemnon to tell him to lead the Achaians on a rash, self-destructive, frontal assault against Troy. The dream, appearing to Agamemnon in the guise of Nestor, tells him: "But now, hear me quickly. For I am a messenger from Zeus, who, from far away, cares greatly for you and takes pity on you. He bids you to arm the flowing haired Achaians for battle with all haste. For now you would take the wide-wayed city of the Trojans" (2.26–30). The dream, following Zeus's instructions, goes on to assure Agamemnon that all the gods now support him and therefore he will succeed in conquering Troy on this very day.

Now, this dream sent by Zeus to Agamemnon represents the first direct intervention by Zeus into human affairs in the *Iliad*. And this dream is wholly deceptive. While Zeus assures Agamemnon that the Achaians will conquer Troy on this day, in truth he intends to use the Trojans to destroy many

[44] One might argue that Zeus's plan also comes close to failing when Hera beguiles Zeus with Eros and Sleep in Book XIV and consequently Ajax knocks Hector out of the fighting. However, Homer refrains from suggesting here, as he suggests in the other two cases, that, for example, if Zeus had not woken up and intervened, the Achaians would have conquered or destroyed Troy or even that Hector would have been killed (cf. 15.4–11 with 2.155–156, 3.373–382; consider also, for example, 16.698–701).

Achaians. This incident invites us to wonder, more broadly, whether Zeus merely pretends to care for and pity the Achaians, whether he genuinely "cares greatly" for them or for the Trojans, whom he is simply manipulating here, or indeed for any human beings (apart from Achilles). Indeed, it is noteworthy that the first time in the poem that the claim is made that Zeus "cares for" and "pities" human beings is in an unambiguously deceptive and destructive dream sent by Zeus. Accordingly, Homer calls Agamemnon a "fool" for putting his trust in Zeus – the first time in the poem that Homer calls any one a fool: "So he [the dream] spoke and went away, and left there one [Agamemnon] who believed things in his spirit that were not to be accomplished. For he thought that he would take Priam's city on that day – fool! – who did not know what deeds Zeus was devising. For he was to put woes and groaning on both the Trojans and the Achaians through mighty conflicts" (2.35–40). Homer emphasizes here that it is foolish to trust in the truthfulness of even the greatest of gods. He thereby invites us to wonder whether it may not be foolish as well to believe that even the Father of Gods and Men cares for human beings at all.

Later in Book II, Homer again sharply juxtaposes Agamemnon's trust in the truthfulness of Zeus with Zeus's apparent unworthiness of that trust. When Agamemnon makes a sacrifice to Zeus and prays that Zeus will fulfill his promise and ensure that, on this day, the Achaians will conquer Troy (2.412–418), Homer observes to his audience: "So he spoke, and the son of Cronus did not accomplish any of it, but he accepted the sacrifices and increased the unwished for toil" (2.419–420).

But furthermore, through his account of the aftermath of the dream, Homer suggests that one should not only distrust the truthfulness of the gods, but also their wisdom. For even though the deceptive dream Zeus sends to Agamemnon does convince him to attack Troy on this day, Agamemnon, on his own, decides first to "test" the Achaians' eagerness to attack Troy by telling them a lie of his own. He tells them, falsely, that great Zeus commands that all the Achaians leave Troy and go home and that he, Agamemnon, agrees that they should all flee "with our ships to the beloved land of our fathers" (2.73–74, 2.110–141). Agamemnon evidently believes that the Achaians are so eager to keep fighting the Trojans that his deception will provoke them to reaffirm and renew their determination to conquer Troy rather than retreat in shame, though he does take the precaution of urging the commanders of the army "to restrain with words" any soldier who might choose to flee (2.75). But Agamemnon wholly misjudges the spirit of his soldiers after nine years of war. For his words stir in "all" of them the desire to run to their ships and sail away from Troy (2.142–154). Indeed, according to Homer, they would have gone home if Hera had not intervened (2.155–156).

Now, this whole episode highlights, of course, the folly of Agamemnon, who is evidently himself so eager to conquer Troy, so unfamiliar with the hardships of warfare, and so unenthusiastic about returning to his own wife and home that he grossly underestimates the fatigue and homesickness of his soldiers (see 1.163–168, 1.225–231, 1.109–115; consider also 2.225–238, 3.284–291). Agamemnon is also evidently so blinded by his hatred for Achilles that he fails to see the demoralizing effect the withdrawal of Achilles apparently has on the Achaian soldiers (see especially 2.239–242). But this episode also highlights the folly of Zeus. For, as we have seen, Zeus evidently sent the dream to Agamemnon in the expectation that the Achaians would rashly attack Troy, that they would then be driven back in headlong flight to their ships by the Trojans, and that so many Achaians would be killed that they would turn to Achilles, in desperation, and honor him (2.3–5). But the dream backfires, for it almost leads all of the Achaians to return home, safe and sound, without honoring Achilles at all. Zeus does not foresee the folly of Agamemnon. He does not understand either the gulf that separates Agamemnon, who is eager for conquest, from his men, who are sick of war and eager to return home, or the failure of Agamemnon to understand that gulf. But furthermore, Zeus, like Agamemnon, evidently takes it for granted that the Achaians are eager to continue fighting because, even more than Agamemnon, he himself is altogether unfamiliar with the hardships of war (and the possible appeal of monogamous marital life) and hence grossly underestimates the fatigue and homesickness of the human soldiers. The episode is, then, a comedy of errors about these two rulers, divine and human, each of whom tries to manipulate his subjects through deception. For each ruler's scheme backfires because each fails fundamentally to understand his subjects.[45] Yet this comedy, insofar as it touches Zeus, is most unsettling. For if the Father of Gods and Men is so

[45] Homer stresses here that both Zeus and Agamemnon are rulers, that Agamemnon is a king nourished by Zeus, and that he wields the scepter that Zeus himself wielded, just before he presents Agamemnon's foolishly deceptive speech to his men (2.95–109).

unwise and inept, how can we human beings reasonably look to him for protection and justice?[46]

Now, one might defend the wisdom and providence of the gods here by arguing that, even though Zeus admittedly acts unwisely by sending the dream, his wife, the goddess Hera, does, as Homer suggests, effectively prevent the Achaians from going home. In this way, one might argue, the goddess wisely corrects the perhaps temporary lapse in judgment of her husband and supports and maintains his providential plan. Yet, through his depiction of the aftermath of Hera's intervention, Homer shows that it is not Hera, or Athena, but a human being, Odysseus, who stops the Achaian retreat and thereby saves the Achaian expedition against Troy, and also the plan of Zeus, from failure. In this way, Homer suggests, for the first time in the poem, that a human being may, in a certain sense, be a wiser and more effective ruler of human beings than a god.

Hera instructs Athena to go through the fleeing Achaian army and "restrain each mortal with your gentle words" (2.168–169). Athena, however, does not simply obey Hera but rather finds one mortal, Odysseus, and instructs him to go throughout the army and "restrain each mortal with your gentle words" (2.180). Now, both goddesses evidently believe that all the soldiers can be easily persuaded, by gentle words alone, to postpone their homecoming and return to the war against Troy. They evidently assume, as Zeus evidently assumes, that it is reasonable and congenial for men to fight in wars, far from home, and hence that it is only necessary to remind the Achaians, gently, of their desire to continue the war to induce them to stay and fight. And Odysseus does go on to effectively restrain all of the Achaians from sailing home (2.207–211).

Odysseus, however, departs from the goddesses' instructions in three crucial ways. First, before even attempting to dissuade any of the Achaians from leaving Troy, he runs to Agamemnon and obtains from him "the scepter of his fathers, always imperishable," handed down from Zeus, the symbol of his royal and divine authority (2.185–186, 2.100–108; see also 1.277–279). It is only once he has this scepter in his hands that he attempts to restrain any of the Achaians from fleeing. Unlike Hera and Athena, Odysseus, then, understands that "gentle words" alone cannot induce men from fleeing the battlefield and returning home but that a symbol of royal and divine authority is also

[46] As Clay puts it, "A gulf appears to exist between men's beliefs about the gods and their reality" (1983, 149).

necessary. Second, Odysseus only uses "gentle words" at all with the leading men in the Achaian army, the kings and outstanding warriors (2.188). When Odysseus encounters a man of the demos or multitude, he strikes him with the scepter, berates him, affirms the authority of King Agamemnon, and reminds him that Zeus stands behind the king: "Let us not have in any way all Achaians rule as king here. It is not good to have the rule of many. Let one be ruler, one king, to whom the child of crooked-counseling Cronus gave his scepter and righteous laws, so that he might deliberate for them" (2.203–206). In contrast with the goddesses, Odysseus understands that gentle words can only persuade a few human beings to keep fighting, that force and the threat of force, human and also divine, are needed to persuade most human beings to keep fighting because most human beings do not find fighting in a war so clearly reasonable and congenial.[47]

Indeed, it is not clear that gentle words suffice to persuade even most of the leading commanders and warriors to continue fighting. For even though Homer does state that "whenever he overtook some king or outstanding man," Odysseus "was restraining him with gentle words," the words he reports Odysseus as speaking are far from being simply gentle:

> Daemonic one, it is not seemly for you to be afraid like an evil man, but you yourself sit down and sit the other people down. For you do not yet know with certainty the mind of the son of Atreus. Now he was testing, but soon he will smite the sons of the Achaians. For did we not all hear what sort of thing he said in the council? May he not become enraged and do something evil to the sons of the Achaians? For great is the spirit of kings reared by Zeus, and their honor is from Zeus, and Thoughtful Zeus loves them. (2.188–197)

Although Odysseus does not strike these men, he clearly appeals to their fear of the angry king and of the mighty god who loves him. And while Odysseus does go on to attempt to persuade the Achaians to stay at Troy and continue to fight by speaking gentle words – by, for example, appealing to their sense of shame, their self-interest, and especially their pious hopes – he does also harshly rebuke and beat the leading proponent of leaving Troy and thereby implicitly threatens others as well (2.284–332, 2.244–269; see 2.333–335).[48]

[47] See Benardete 1997, 123.

[48] Indeed, none of the leaders of the Achaians who speak here, neither Nestor nor Agamemnon, simply use gentle words to persuade them to remain at Troy. Nestor harshly appeals to the men's desire for vengeance: "Therefore let no one be eager to go home until he has lain in bed with a wife of the Trojans to avenge the struggles and groans of

We see, then, that it is Odysseus who prevents Thoughtful Zeus's plan from backfiring, that it is Odysseus who prevents the Achaian army from disbanding, and that he does so by departing from the commands of the gods rather than simply following them. Unlike the gods, Odysseus understands that human beings cannot be easily persuaded – with gentle words – to risk life and limb, far from their loved ones. And Odysseus understands this because, unlike the immortal gods, he is a mortal being who knows from experience, as a divine being cannot, the fear of death, the homesickness, and the suffering that are essential to war. As Odysseus remarks,

> And indeed, anyone who remains one month away from his wife is impatient with his many-oared ship, which wintry gusts of wind and the surging sea keep back. For us now this is the ninth year that is coming around to us as we remain here. Therefore I am not indignant with the Achaians for their impatience beside their curved ships. (2.292–297)[49]

By presenting the deceptive and maladroit interventions of Zeus, Hera, and Athena in the episode of the dream and its aftermath, Homer calls into question not only the gods' truthfulness but also their capacity to understand human beings. And through the case of Odysseus in particular, he invites his audience to wonder whether human beings are not capable of a wisdom and a providence that is, in some respects, at least, superior to that of the gods. By highlighting not only the deception but also the ineptitude of the gods, and specifically their lack of understanding of how to rule human beings, Homer challenges the conventional, trusting, pious belief in the wise providence of the gods.

THE DOUBTFUL JUSTICE AND BENEVOLENCE OF THE GODS

After Odysseus prevents the Achaians from going home and Agamemnon leads them to attack Troy, Zeus's plan to use the Trojans to punish the Achaians and thereby induce them to honor

Helen" (2.354–356). And both Nestor and Agamemnon threaten those who leave with death (2.357–359, 2.391–393).

[49] It is noteworthy that, even though Odysseus has just single-handedly prevented the Achaian army from leaving Troy, the divine Muse, daughter of Zeus, praises Ajax – who plays no role whatsoever in preventing the Achaians from disbanding – as the best of the Achaians, after Achilles (see 2.761–762, 2.768–770; see also 2.484–492).

Achilles is again almost thwarted, this time by the combined efforts of the Achaians and the Trojans. Just as they are about to start fighting, the Trojans and the Achaians suddenly call a truce and decide together to end the war by having Paris and Menelaus duel for Helen. Had they succeeded, Zeus's plan would have failed entirely. Now, this whole episode (at the beginning of Book III), like the episode (at the beginning of Book II) of the dream sent by Zeus to Agamemnon to incite him and the Achaians to attack Troy, calls into question the wisdom of Zeus. For Zeus evidently takes it for granted that both the Trojans and the Achaians are eager to fight each other to the death, overlooks entirely the longing for peace on both sides of this conflict, and therefore fails to foresee the possibility that they will try on their own to settle the war peacefully, once and for all.

But unlike the previous episode, this one also calls into question the justice and benevolence of Zeus. For the decision of the Trojans and Achaians to end the war by having Paris and Menelaus duel for Helen seems eminently just and seems to reflect a genuine attachment to justice, as well as a longing for peace, on both sides. Indeed, this is an absolutely crucial moment in the story of the *Iliad*. After nine long years of war, the Trojans and the Achaians agree to a settlement that, had it succeeded, would have spared the lives of many Achaians and Trojans – including Sarpedon, Patroclus, and Hector – would have avoided the deaths by violence of Achilles and Priam, and would have saved Troy from its final destruction (see 18.95–96, 22.56–76). Insofar as Zeus has a fatherly concern for the Achaians and Trojans, one would think that he would welcome such a settlement. Yet Homer reveals to us that Zeus deliberately wrecks that settlement, in a singularly treacherous manner, and plunges the Trojans and the Achaians back into the "miserable war" (3.112).

When the Trojans march out to fight the advancing Achaians, Hector, the leading Trojan warrior, sees his brother Paris flee in terror from fighting with Menelaus, whose wife he stole and thereby provoked the Achaian war against Troy. Hector, in his first words in the poem, angrily denounces the cowardice and injustice of his brother:

> Evil Paris, best in looks, crazy for women, deceiver, would that you had not been born and that you had died unmarried! I would indeed wish it. It would have been more profitable than thus to be an object of outrage and contempt from others. The flowing haired Achaians, I suppose, laugh out loud, saying that you are our best champion, because of your noble looks, but there is no violence or strength in your

> mind. Were you like this when you sailed across the sea in sea-faring ships, having gathered faithful companions, and you mingled with foreigners and led away a good-looking woman from a far off land, the sister-in law of courageous spearmen, a great sorrow to your father and city and people, a joy to our enemies, and a disgrace to yourself? And you would not stand fast before Menelaus, beloved of Ares? Thus would you know what sort of mortal he is, whose blossoming wife you possess. The lyre and the gifts of Aphrodite would not help you, nor your hair or looks, when you have mingled in the dust. But the Trojans are frightened. Otherwise, you would wear a tunic of stone, on account of the evils which you have done. (3.39–57)

Hector, the military leader of the Trojans, here affirms that the Trojan cause is unjust, confirms that Paris began this nine-year-old war by an act of deception and adultery, and laments that the cowardly Trojans have not stoned him to death for his evil deeds (see also 6.281–285).

Apparently impressed by Hector's powerful rebuke, Paris proposes not only to face Menelaus in battle but also to decide the outcome of the war, once and for all, by dueling Menelaus for the reward of Helen and all her possessions:

> But now, if you wish me to wage war and do battle, make the rest of the Trojans sit down and all of the Achaians, and in the middle bring together Menelaus, beloved of Ares, and me, to do battle for Helen and all her possessions. Let whoever of us wins and proves himself stronger take the possessions fairly and the woman and lead her home. As for the rest, having sworn oaths of friendship and trust, may you dwell in fertile Troy and may they go to horse-nourishing Argos and Achaia, the land of beautiful women. (3.67–75)

Hector, delighted, orders the Trojans to sit down on the battlefield, publicly explains Paris's proposal to the Achaians, and publicly blames Paris for the war (3.86–87). Menelaus readily agrees to this proposal, as long as Priam swears an oath to respect the outcome of the duel: "For this sorrow above all comes to my spirit, and I am minded that the Argives and Trojans at last may be separated from one another, since you have suffered many evils because of my quarrel and because Alexandros began it" (3.97–100). Menelaus explains here that he embraces the proposal above all because it seems just to him that the quarrel should be settled by the two principals, without causing any more suffering to either the Achaians or the Trojans. Like Hector, Menelaus agrees not only that Paris is to blame for the war but also that it is wrong for both sides to continue to suffer for his wrongdoing. Homer then reports: "So he spoke and both the Achaians and the Trojans rejoiced, hoping to put a stop to the miserable war" (3.111–112). We then learn that even before hearing about the proposed duel, leading Trojans have been urging that Helen be returned to Menelaus (3.159–160). Even King Priam himself, on learning of the proposed duel, immediately agrees to it, though he does fear "his beloved son" Paris will lose (3.259–260, 3.304–309). So evidently reasonable and just is Paris's proposal that, with the qualified exception of Agamemnon, who prays to Zeus that, if Menelaus wins, the Trojans should offer some additional, fitting honor to the Achaians, the Achaians and Trojans all unreservedly swear oaths to honor the terms and outcome of the duel (3.284–287).

Furthermore, the subsequent victory of Menelaus over Paris in that duel seems just, since all evidently agree that, at the very least, Paris wronged the hospitable Menelaus by stealing away with his wife. Homer stresses that, consequently, the Trojans themselves hated Paris so much that none of them was willing to help him in any way: "But no one of the Trojans or their glorious allies was able then to show Alexandros to Menelaus, beloved of Ares. They would not indeed have hidden him for love, if any had seen him. For he was as hated by them all, as black death is hated" (3.451–454). Indeed, it would seem that, precisely because he is aware of his own wrongdoing, Paris does not dare to pray to the gods for help before facing Menelaus in combat. Menelaus, on the other hand, confident as he is that Paris is in the wrong and he is in the right, does pray to Zeus for justice: "Zeus, Lord, grant me to punish him who first did evil things to me, divine Alexandros, and break him beneath my hands, so that anyone of human beings born hereafter will shudder at doing evil things to one who receives him as a guest, who has offered him friendship" (3.351–354; see also 2.588–590, 3.27–28, 3.366).

The victory of Menelaus would seem, then, to be a victory for justice. Yet Zeus thwarts that victory. In the first place, his daughter Aphrodite rescues Paris from certain death at the hands of Menelaus. Menelaus, who has been temporarily disarmed, grabs Paris by the helmet and pulls him toward the ranks of the Achaians. In Homer's words: "And now he would have dragged him away and won for himself boundless glory if the daughter of Zeus, Aphrodite, had not then keenly observed him, and broken the chin strap, made with strength from a slaughtered ox" (3.373–375). She then miraculously transports Paris to the safety and sensual comfort of his bedchamber in Troy. Now, it is true that Homer does not say that Zeus sent Aphrodite to foil the attempt of the Trojans and the Achaians to end the war. She appears to act on her own initiative, out of fondness for Paris, as Helen suggests (3.406–409). But on the other hand, Zeus never expresses disapproval here for what his daughter does. Indeed, he goes on to follow up on her action by restarting the war in the most shocking manner imaginable.

After Paris mysteriously vanishes, Agamemnon proclaims, in the midst of the confusion, that, since Menelaus clearly won, the Trojans should now return Helen, her possessions, and some additional honor, so that the Achaians may sail home and the Trojans may live in peace. The Achaians immediately agree, but the Trojans, even though they all hate Paris, apparently hesitate (see 3.449–461). At this moment, Zeus sends Athena to destroy the truce and resume the war by inducing the Trojans to violate the sworn agreement: "Very swiftly, go to the host of the Trojans and the Achaians and try to make it so that the Trojans, by overstepping them, violate their oaths to the surpassingly glorious Achaians" (4.70–72; see 4.86–147, 4.220–222). What makes this action by Zeus so singularly shocking is that, in the eyes of the human beings of the poem, he is the *enforcer* of oaths. Indeed, the clearest feature of Zeus's justice toward men and also gods is his respect for oaths and the enforcement of oaths.[50] When Menelaus originally agrees to the duel with Paris, he insists that the agreement be sealed with oaths to Zeus: "Bring two sheep, one white, the other black, for Earth and the Sun. For Zeus we will bring another. And bring the strength of Priam, so that he himself may swear an oath, since his children are overbearing and untrustworthy, lest someone, through transgression, violate the oaths of Zeus" (3.103–107). Menelaus does not trust in the promises of "untrustworthy" men but trusts that Zeus will punish those who "violate" their sworn oaths. But we now see that it is Zeus who is untrustworthy, since he induces the Trojans to violate this very oath (cf. 3.107 with 4.72). As we have already seen, when the Trojan Pandarus violates his oath and almost kills Menelaus, an outraged Agamemnon affirms that Zeus, "seething in anger at this deception," will punish the Trojans for violating their oaths (4.157–168). Yet it was Zeus himself who, through his daughter Athena, deceived "blameless" Pandarus into violating his oath (4.89, 4.93–104, 4.127–129). Then, when the fighting has resumed, Agamemnon encourages the most determined Achaians to battle the Trojans by declaring: "Argives, do not let go now of this furious

[50] See Lloyd-Jones 1971, 5. Even Dodds (1973, 32) and Adkins (1960, 66–67) concede this point in some measure.

might. For Father Zeus will not be one who helps liars, but these, who were the first to violate their oaths, vultures will eat their tender flesh, and we will bring their beloved wives and infant children in our ships after we take their city" (4.234–239). Agamemnon, like all the characters in the poem, simply takes it for granted that Father Zeus is just, that he rewards the good and punishes the wicked, and that he specifically punishes those who violate their oaths sworn to him.[51] But Homer reveals here to his audience that Zeus is perfectly willing to deceive men into violating their sworn oaths, that he therefore cannot be trusted to enforce justice, and that he seems, rather, fundamentally indifferent to the longings of men for justice and peace.[52] Homer highlights the shocking contrast between what humans believe about Zeus and his true nature by calling Zeus here, for only the second of thirteen times in the poem, "the Father of Men and Gods," just before Zeus sends Athena to induce the Trojans to violate their oaths and thereby resume what he himself calls "evil war" (4.68, 4.15, 4.82; see also 3.111–112). Homer thereby emphasizes to his audience that it is unreasonable for human beings to believe that "Father" Zeus upholds oaths, enforces justice, or indeed cares at all about human beings.

One might defend the justice of Zeus here by invoking the solemn pledge he made to Thetis, a pledge he claimed "cannot be taken back again," to use the Trojans to punish the Achaians for their injustice to Achilles, so that they will honor him (1.525–527). For even if, in the eyes of all the Achaians and Trojans, it seems just to end the war by returning Helen to her rightful husband and by punishing the deceptive adulterer, the injustice done to Achilles by the Achaians would remain unpunished and the solemn pledge Zeus made to Thetis and Achilles would remain unfulfilled. Perhaps, then, the situation Zeus faces is a tragic moral choice between benefiting the Trojans and the Achaians at the expense of Achilles and Thetis, on the one

[51] Consider as well the statement of Idomeneus to Agamemnon at 4.268–271: "To them [the Trojans] will be death and sorrows hereafter, since they were the first to violate their oaths." The Trojan elder Antenor also evinces the belief that the gods punish those who violate oaths when he urges the Trojans to return Helen to the Achaians, explaining: "Now, having lied about our sworn pledges, we do battle. Therefore I expect nothing at all profitable for us to be accomplished, unless we do this" (7.351–353). See also 7.76, 7.411.

[52] I consequently must disagree with Griffin's contention that, according to Homer, "There is no contradiction" between the belief that the gods "love" human beings and the gods' evident indifference to human beings (1980, 198).

hand, or benefiting Achilles and Thetis at the expense of the Achaians and Trojans, on the other. And once he resolves to benefit Achilles and Thetis, one might argue, that good end justifies the admittedly shocking means of deceiving the Trojans into violating their oaths.

Yet in the account that Homer gives of Zeus's decision to restart the war, Zeus does not even mention Achilles or his promise to Thetis to punish the Achaians for their injustice to him. Zeus does not express concern for Achilles, or for justice, or, ultimately, for any human being whatsoever. In this account, Homer challenges most sharply the conventional pious belief that the gods, led by Zeus, care and provide for human beings. To understand this challenge, let us consider this scene carefully.

As the scene opens, Zeus has assembled the gods in order to decide, as he says, "whether we shall stir up again evil war and dreadful fighting or whether we shall cast friendship between both sides" (4.15–16). By framing the question in this way, Zeus seems to favor deciding in favor of encouraging the Trojans to accept Menelaus's victory and end the war. Although this decision would seem beneficial to both the Achaians and the Trojans, it would mean that the Achaians' mistreatment of Achilles would go unpunished and Zeus's promise to Achilles and Thetis would be violated. Therefore, it is not surprising that Hera, who was said in Book I to "love" and "care" for Achilles (as well as for Agamemnon), objects (1.195–196, 1.208–209). Yet, Homer reveals here that Hera does not object on behalf of Achilles or even on behalf of the Achaians but solely on her own behalf: "How can you wish to make fruitless and unfulfilled the labor, the sweat that I have sweated in toil, and my horses worn out, gathering my people and evils for Priam and his children?" (4.26–28). Hera complains that, by letting the Trojans and Achaians end the war, Zeus will undo all of her efforts to do harm to Priam and his children. She objects, then, not because she loves Achilles but because she hates the family of Priam. But why does she hate them so? The goddess offers no justification whatsoever here for her desire to inflict evils on Priam and his children. Nor does she justify the evils that the Trojans who are not part of Priam's family will suffer or the evils the Achaians as a whole will suffer as a result of the resumption of the war. She simply insists to Zeus that her long-standing desire to hurt Priam and his family be satisfied.

Zeus responds by reasonably demanding to know "what now are such evils that Priam and his children did to you, because of which you are always furious to sack entirely the well-built city of Ilion?" (4.31–33). Now, it is possible that Hera would have a response to this question. Later, Homer explains that "sacred Ilion and Priam and his people incurred the hatred" of Hera and Athena "because of the delusion of Alexandros" who on a certain occasion favored Aphrodite over them (24.25–30). Yet, even if we stipulate that Paris wronged Hera, we must still wonder how it could be reasonable or just for Priam and all of the Trojans to suffer, along with the Achaians, because of the injustice of one Trojan.

Zeus, however, does not wait for Hera to answer but proceeds to denounce her hatred of the Trojans as monstrous: "If you were to go within the gates and long walls and devour Priam and the children of Priam and the other Trojans raw, only then would your rage be healed" (4.34–36). Here, Zeus seems to judge the rage of Hera as simply unjust and malevolent. For what could possibly justify the desire to devour an entire people? He seems to conclude that Hera's rage is simply malicious and even twisted. One would expect, then, that the Father of Gods and Men would resolve to shield the Trojans and also the Achaians from the monstrous hatred of his wife, spare them "evil war" and "dreadful fighting," and establish peace and friendship among them (4.82–84).

But then, in a stunning reversal, Zeus simply yields to Hera and agrees to the destruction of the Trojans! Why does he give in to what he himself has deemed to be her unreasonable, unjustified, and savage rage? Zeus explains:

> Do, however, as you wish. Let this quarrel hereafter not come to be a matter of great strife between us both. But I will tell you another thing, and cast it into your mind. Whenever I myself should be eager to sack completely a city, as I wish, wherein there are men who are loved by you, do not in any way oppose my rage, but let me do it. For I myself willingly granted you this, with my spirit unwilling. For of the cities of earthly men who dwell beneath the sun and the starry heaven, sacred Ilion has been honored most in my heart, both Priam and the people of Priam of the strong ash spear. For never did my altar lack of a fair feast, libation, and savor. For this is what we are due. (4.37–49)

What is so shocking about Zeus's words here is the fundamental indifference they betray toward human beings and especially toward human suffering. As he makes clear, he does not give in to the rage of Hera because he deems it at all just to do so. Zeus remarks here that he is, to some extent, "unwilling" to allow Troy to be destroyed both because he loves the Trojans more than any other human beings and because they have acted justly toward him by always giving him his due. In this way, he reiterates and elaborates on the injustice and savagery of Hera's rage and therefore on the injustice and savagery of his own cooperation with that rage. Nor does he give in because it is necessary for him to do so. Even though Zeus is not all-powerful, he is repeatedly said – by Hera here, for example – to be more powerful than Hera is (4.55–56). And even though she causes mischief later in the poem, Zeus is able to exert his power over her with considerable ease. Zeus gives in to the savage rage of his wife and her malicious desire to destroy Troy simply because he does not want to bother to quarrel with her now and because he does not want to bother to quarrel with her in the future when he feels a similarly savage rage and wishes to destroy some city that she loves. Zeus, the Father of Gods and Men, is willing to sacrifice even just human beings whom he loves and honors more than any other humans simply to avoid the inconvenience of squabbling too much with his wife. He is willing to let the Trojans, who have always been just to him, perish because, it would seem, he does not truly care about justice. He casually sacrifices the lives of mortals he "loves" because, it turns out, he does not genuinely love mortals at all.[53]

One might defend Zeus by arguing that, however hardhearted he might seem here, the true reason he yields to Hera and resumes the war must be to comply with the solemn promise he made to Thetis that he would use the Trojans to punish the Achaians for their injustice to Achilles. In this way, one might argue, Zeus acts on behalf of justice. But even if we stipulate that it would be just for Zeus to sacrifice the well-being of all the Trojans and the Achaians for the sake of Achilles, we must still recognize that Zeus does not mention Achilles or Thetis at all. Furthermore, and perhaps more importantly, Zeus indicates here that he does not genuinely care for justice. For he brazenly affirms that he is willing to let Hera destroy the Trojans, whom he stresses have been just to him and whom he honors beyond all other human beings, simply to avoid bickering with her. But if Zeus is willing to sacrifice the just Trojans for his own convenience, would he not be willing to sacrifice the just Achilles as well for his own convenience?[54]

[53] I consequently cannot agree with Griffin's claim that the gods in Homer truly "love" human beings (ibid.; see also 85–88).

[54] I therefore cannot agree with the claim of Lutz that "Homer shows us a Zeus who limits his actions and his commands to doing what is just" (2006, 129).

Similarly, Hera responds to Zeus by betraying her own astounding indifference even to human beings she claims to love:

> Verily three cities are most loved by me: Argos, Sparta, and wide-wayed Mycenae. These sack completely whenever they become hateful to your heart. I will not stand up for these against you, nor begrudge you. For even if I were to envy you and did not allow you to sack them completely, I would, being envious, accomplish nothing, since you are much greater than I. But you ought not to render my labor unfulfilled. For I myself am also a goddess, my race is even what yours is, and I am the oldest daughter of Cronus of the crooked counsels, both by birth and because I am called your consort and you rule among all the immortals. But verily in these things let us yield to one another, I to you and you to me. The other immortal gods will follow. But you, quickly give orders to Athena, so that dreadful combat may come of the Trojans and Achaians and try to make it so that the Trojans will begin, first, to slay, in violation of their oaths, the highly praised Achaians. (4.51–67)

Homer then pointedly remarks: "So she spoke and he did not disobey her, the Father of Gods and Men" (4.68).

We see here that, even though Hera ostensibly cares for the Achaians, she is willing, not only to prevent them from returning home in peace and hence to sacrifice their lives in battle, but also to let them be annihilated, simply to glut her hatred of the Trojans. Homer offers here the staggering revelation to his pious audience that the gods do not care for human beings. They are willing to inflict untold suffering and sacrifice countless lives on a whim, to satisfy their rages and to avoid squabbling with one another. Once the truce is wrecked and the fighting resumes, the gods urge on both sides to a frenzy of slaughter, with calamitous consequences for each:

> Ares roused them [the Trojans] while the owl-eyed Athena roused the others [the Achaians], and Terror and Fear and Discord, the insatiably eager sister and companion of man-slaughtering Ares, she who ... at that time cast down strife in the middle, equally between for both sides, and she came among the onslaught, enlarging the groaning of men... There arose together the wailing and the boasting of men who were killing and being killed, and the ground flowed with blood. (4.439–451)

Homer's clear lesson, then, to his audience in Book IV is that we should not expect the gods to uphold oaths, to enforce justice, or indeed to protect any human beings at all, even just ones whom they especially honor and love.

One might object that the revelation, in this scene, that Zeus and the gods do not genuinely care for human beings is contradicted by the rest of the poem, in which, as we have seen, Homer portrays the gods on a number of occasions as compassionate and caring beings. Yet, if we consider the rest of the poem more carefully, we must recognize that the gods' feelings toward human beings are not as constant as they may seem at first but are, rather, inconsistent, changeable, and therefore, it would seem, shallow and whimsical. For example, Zeus is said to feel pity and compassion a number of times in the course of the poem, especially for Hector, and he sheds great tears of blood when his own son Sarpedon is slain. But, as Homer indicates, even though Zeus feels affection for Hector and Sarpedon, he allows them both to die simply to avoid squabbling with Hera, Athena, and possibly other gods (4.40–53, 16.431–461, 22.167–185, 24.64–70). Zeus's sacrifice of his "beloved" Trojans here to avoid further bickering with Hera foreshadows his sacrifice of Sarpedon, "most beloved [or dearest] of men" and "beloved" Hector for similar reasons (16.433, 16.447, 16.450, 16.460, 22.168; see also, for example, 6.318).[55]

Similarly, while, as we have seen, the gods do at times heed the prayers of human beings, Homer also highlights five key moments in the poem when the gods refuse to do so. When Agamemnon prays to Zeus for victory over the Trojans in Book II and dedicates sacrifices to him, Homer reveals: "So he spoke, but the son of Cronus did not accomplish any of it; he accepted the sacrifices but increased the unenvied toil" (2.419–420). When the Achaians and Trojans pray in Book III to all the everlasting gods that they enforce the oaths sworn by all to uphold the truce, Homer observes: "So they spoke, but the son of Cronus would not accomplish any of these things for them" (3.302). The Trojan priestess of Athena, Theano, leading the wailing Trojan women, prays that "Lady Athena, Protector of our city," will hold back the attacking Achaians and promises that the Trojans will make abundant sacrifices to her "if only you should pity the town and the wives of the Trojans and their infant children" (6.304–310). Homer remarks: "So she spoke, praying, but Pallas Athena refused her" (6.311). When Hector prays to Zeus and the other gods that he and the Trojans may "drive away" the Achaians, and offers a tremendous sacrifice to them, we learn, "but the blessed gods would not take any part of it, nor did they wish to. For sacred Ilion, both Priam and the people of Priam of the strong ash spear, greatly incurred their hatred" (8.526–528, 8.550–552). Finally, in Book XVI, when

[55] Even Adkins overstates the gods' concern for "their part-human offspring" (1960, 64).

Achilles prays both that Patroclus win glory and that he return from battle safely, Homer tells us: "So he spoke praying, and Thoughtful Zeus heeded him. The Father granted him one [prayer], but refused him the other" (16.249–250). In these instances, Father Zeus and the other gods deliberately deny seemingly just and beneficial prayers for safety and peace without any clear justification. By highlighting these particular instances, Homer warns his audience against relying on divine providence.

Furthermore, it is not clear that Zeus is beneficent toward humans even when he grants their prayers. For example, Zeus grants the prayer of Achilles that he punish the Achaians for their injustice to him. But this punishment leads not only to the deaths of many Achaians but also to the death of Achilles' beloved companion Patroclus at the hands of Hector, and therefore, because Achilles seeks vengeance against Hector and because his death will follow Hector's, to the death of Achilles himself. Homer himself deems the prayer "beyond measure" (15.598–599), perhaps precisely because it leads to a punishment that is more harmful to all concerned than was the original injustice. He thereby invites us to wonder, was it truly provident for Zeus to heed the prayer of Achilles?

HOMER'S TEACHING ON THE NATURE OF THE GODS

Homer does not portray the gods as fundamentally malevolent or misanthropic beings. He rather reveals them to be unpredictable, whimsical, and capricious beings.[56] For example, even though Zeus promises Thetis and Achilles to punish the Achaians by letting the Trojans kill many of them, he permits Athena to stop Ares from killing many Achaians (1.503–530, 2.1–4, 5.755–763). In the midst of the battle he himself has inflicted on them, Zeus mourns for Agamemnon and helps the Achaians (8.245–246). He then pities Hector and helps him and the Trojans (15.12–13, 15.220–235). Moments after thundering Zeus "gave victory to the Trojans and terrified the Achaians," he "mourned" for the weeping Ajax and helps him and the Achaians fight the

[56] I ultimately agree, then, to a large extent, with the characterization of Homer's gods by Vico (1999, 357), Dodds (1977, 32), and Adkins (1960, 62–64), but I think that they do not pay sufficient attention to Homer's human characters' beliefs about the gods and therefore to the larger and deeper significance of Homer's characterization of the gods.

Trojans (15.593–596, 15.648–650). Zeus saves his son Sarpedon from death at the hands of Zeus's grandson Tlepolemus but not from death at the hands of Patroclus (5.630–662, 16.431–507). Zeus refuses to let Patroclus return safely from battle but then feels sorry for Achilles and the Achaian elders as they grieve for the dead Patroclus (16.249–252, 19.338–341). Zeus expresses pity for human beings as a whole: "For there is nothing more full of woe than man, of all the things that breathe and crawl upon the earth" (17.446–447). But it is Zeus who decides to kill many Achaians, who wrecks the attempt by the Achaians and Trojans to end their war, who plunges both the Achaians and Trojans into "dreadful combat," and who "was devising evils" for both Achaians and Trojans (2.1–4, 4.64–72, 7.476–479). In the midst of the battle, "the son of Cronus raised up an evil confusion, and he sent down from on high dew drops dripping with blood out of the upper air, because he was to hurl forth into Hades many mighty men" (11.52–55). Zeus, the "Father," sits "rejoicing in his glory, looking upon the city of the Trojans and ships of the Achaians and the lightning flashes of bronze, and men killing and men killed" (11.80–83; see also 8.49–52). It is Zeus who keeps the battle even between both sides so that they will keep slaughtering each other (11.336–337). As the Achaians and Trojans engage in an exhausting, bloody struggle for the corpse of Patroclus throughout an entire day, Homer remarks, "Such was the evil labor Zeus stretched out for men and horses over Patroclus that day" (17.400–401). And, just as the final, extraordinarily bloody battle of the poem begins, it is Zeus who declares, "I will delight my mind, watching" (20.23).

The other gods are similarly capricious. Even though both Apollo and Poseidon suffered "evils" at the hands of Troy in the past, only Poseidon hates the Trojans, whereas Apollo favors them (21.435–469; see 24.22–30). Poseidon pities the Achaians and comes to their aid against the Trojans (13.10–38). But later he declares his compassion for the Trojan ally Aeneas and saves him from death at the hands of Achilles (20.287–340). Apollo answers the prayers of his priest Chryses, but Athena refuses the prayers of her priestess Theano (1.9–52, 6.297–311). Athena deceives the Trojan Pandarus into shooting an arrow at Menelaus, in violation of the sworn truce between the Achaians and the Trojans (4.86–104). She then protects Menelaus from that very arrow and later helps Diomedes slay Pandarus (4.127–140, 5.290–296). At one point, she rebukes Diomedes for not fighting the gods, even though, as he points out, she herself ordered him not to fight them (5.799–834, 5.124–132). Athena, who hates the Trojans and works against them throughout the poem, "loved" one

Trojan, Phereclus, "especially" but declines to save him from death (5.59–68). Moreover, Athena joins with the pro-Trojan Apollo to stop the war just for a day and to arrange a duel between Hector and one of the Achaians, without any apparent purpose (7.17–43). Hephaestus saves one of the two sons of his priest, but not the other (5.9–24). Artemis declines to save a Trojan she favored in the past with instruction (5.48–58; see also 6.427–428). Hera insists that the gods must help Achilles against Hector because Achilles' mother is a goddess and Hector is purely human (24.55–63). But she sides with Achilles against Aeneas, even though Aeneas's divine mother, Aphrodite, a daughter of Zeus, has a higher stature than Thetis (20.103–131). And of course Hera loves the purely human Agamemnon at least as much as she loves Achilles (1.193–196).

That the gods are capricious, unreliable, and fundamentally indifferent beings proves, then, to be a central teaching set forth by Homer in the *Iliad*. As the poem unfolds, this teaching makes itself increasingly felt. Homer presents most hauntingly the possible implications of his teaching about the gods and the absence of divine providence in a speech by the Trojan ally Glaucus. For Glaucus offers a vision of a world that is fundamentally indifferent to human life: "As is the generation of leaves, so is that of men. The wind scatters the leaves onto the ground, but the forest flourishes and naturally grows, as the season of spring returns. Such is the generation of men: one naturally grows, but the other comes to an end" (6.146–149). Glaucus here suggests that there is no special, privileged status to humans in this world. And he goes on to explain the reason for this vision through his account of his ancestor Bellerephon. For the gods favored him but then, unaccountably, they came to hate him (6.156–204). He was happy, but then his happiness was destroyed, thanks to the immortals. The vision Glaucus presents is bleak, but it may be lightened by the friendship he displays in the poem for Sarpedon, a friendship that may be nourished by his awareness – albeit a partial and inconsistent awareness[57] – that one must look to humans, not gods, for happiness in this life.[58] For Sarpedon is, according to Glaucus, "the best man" (16.521) and Glaucus himself is, in the eyes of Sarpedon, his "beloved companion" (16.491).

57 When Patroclus kills Sarpedon, Glaucus rebukes Zeus for failing to protect his son but then Glaucus prays to another son of Zeus, Apollo, to heal his wound so that he can fight to defend Sarpedon's corpse (16.514–531).

58 In Saxonhouse's words, "It is left to man to provide the order and value the gods deny" (1988, 42).

THE EMERGENCE OF HOMER IN THE ILIAD

Homer presents the implications of his teaching concerning the gods more clearly and less bleakly through his presentation of himself. Homer begins by presenting himself as a human singer who asks the goddess, the divine Muse, for illumination concerning the anger of Achilles and the plan of Zeus. The singer, then, like the other human characters in the poem, begins by assuming that the gods are wise and just and that they care for human beings. The singer turns to the goddess for assistance in Book I just as Chryses and Achilles turn to Apollo and Zeus for assistance in Book I. As the poem proceeds, however, Homer reveals, as we have seen, that the gods do not truly care for human beings, that they are not truly wise or truly just. Accordingly, the singer shifts his focus from the gods to the human characters. In Book I, he asks the goddess, the divine Muse, to share her wisdom with him, and he also addresses her, and the Muses as a whole, whom he describes as all-knowing, twice in Book II (1.1–7, 2.761–762, 2.484–487). However, he only addresses the Muses three more times in the remaining twenty-two books (11.218–220, 14.508–510, 16.112) and Apollo twice (15.365–366, 20.151–152). On the other hand, in Book IV, Homer begins to address human beings – Menelaus, Melanippus, Patroclus, and Achilles – and ultimately addresses them eighteen times in the last twenty-one books of the poem (see footnote 12). Moreover, while Homer stresses early in Book I the divine wisdom of the prophet Calchas, "the best by far of those who interpret from birds, who knew the things that are, that will be, and that were before," in Book XVIII, he highlights the human wisdom of Polydamas, "who *alone* saw before and behind him" (1.68–72, 18.250, emphasis added). In these ways, Homer gently but unmistakably encourages his audience to focus their attention more and more on the humans in the poem rather than on the gods and to look to human beings, including themselves, rather than to the gods, for guidance.

Homer also gradually encourages his audience to look to himself, the human singer of the *Iliad*, rather than to the gods, for guidance.[59] Whereas Homer presents himself in Book I merely as a singer who looks to the gods for instruction, he increasingly makes his independent presence felt in the course

[59] Consider de Jong 1987, 45–53, 228–229; Clay 2010, 22, 26, 62.

of the poem. He asks questions without invoking the Muses, questions that he presumably must address (5.703–704, 8.273, 17.261–262). He also increasingly makes judgments, emphatic and sometimes surprising ones, in his own name. As we have seen, he calls Agamemnon a "fool" for trusting in Zeus. He also criticizes Hector for rebuking Paris "with base words," calls the Trojans "fools" for ignoring the "noble counsel" of Polydamas, calls Patroclus a "fool" for wishing to fight the Trojans and fighting so boldly, calls Tros a "fool" for hoping that the enraged Achilles will spare his life, criticizes Achilles for his "indecent" treatment of Hector's corpse and his "evil" beheading of twelve Trojan youths, and criticizes Priam for rebuking his sons "with base words."[60] In these ways, Homer offers us brief but clear indications of his own understanding of the speeches and deeds of his characters.

Furthermore, through his relentlessly vivid and detailed accounts of death, we also become aware of Homer's extraordinarily austere acceptance of human mortality.[61] For he repeatedly describes the moment of death with calm and precision[62]: "He stabbed him with a spear next to the navel and all of his guts poured out onto the ground and darkness covered his eyes" (4.525–526). "He drew his sharp sword and struck him in the middle of the belly and took the spirit out of him" (4.530–531). "He stabbed him with his sword at the liver. The liver slipped out and from it the black blood drenched the fold of his tunic. Darkness covered his eyes as he was deprived of his spirit" (20.469–472). "He then struck Echeclos, son of Agenor, with his hilted sword in the middle of his head and his entire sword was greatly warmed by the blood. Purple death and mighty fate closed his eyes" (20.474–477). This unflinching resignation in the face of death stands out especially in contrast to such warriors as Hector and Achilles, each of whom is wont, as Homer notes, to speak to a warrior he has slain "even though he was dead" (16.858, 22.364; see also 21.121–125, 21.184–199). Such clear-eyed resignation also stands out in contrast with the god Apollo, who pities Hector "even though he was dead" (24.18–20).

[60] 2.37–38, 3.38, 12.108–115, 12.127–130, 18.310–314, 16.46–47, 16.684–687, 20.463–466, 22.395, 23.24, 23.176, 24.237–238.

[61] As Griffin puts it, "Homer describes hundreds of killings in battle, many of them in pitiless detail, without sliding either into sadism or into sentimentality" (1995, 36; see also 1980, 143).

[62] As Lateiner notes, "Most of the pathophysiological causes of death are precisely recorded and medically sound" (2004, 13).

Through his accounts of death, and especially of the consequences of death for the bereaved, we also become increasingly aware of Homer's tremendous compassion for the victims of this war.[63] For example, after describing how Ajax slays a Trojan youth, Homer observes: "Nor did he pay back his beloved parents for having reared him, but a short-lifetime came to him who was broken by the spear of great-spirited Ajax" (4.477–479). Similarly, in the midst of recounting the martial exploits of Diomedes, Homer pauses to describe his killing of two Trojans, sons of an aged father: "There he slew them and took away the beloved spirit from both, and to their father he left lamentation and miserable sorrow, since he was not to welcome them home alive from the battle" (5.155–158). When Hector enters Troy from the battlefield, "the wives and daughters of the Trojans ran about him to ask after their children and brothers and neighbors and husbands" (6.237–240). Hector tells them to pray to the gods. In his own name, Homer adds, regarding the women: "But sorrows were in store for many" (6.241).[64]

Most strikingly, memorably, and famously, Homer uses similes, beautiful and elaborate similes, that make one increasingly aware of the powers of observation, the rich experience, and the fertile imagination of the mind that composes them. While he uses only three, brief similes in Book I – "He [Apollo] came like the night" (1.47); "His [Achilles'] eyes were like a blazing fire" (1.104); "Swiftly she [Thetis] rose up like a mist out of the grey sea" (1.359) – thereafter he increasingly uses similes – sixteen in Book II, six in Book III, thirteen in Book IV, seventeen in Book V, two hundred and ninety-seven in the entire poem[65]:

[63] As Buxton points out, Homer "goes to enormous lengths to individualise the fates of even the most minor of heroes" (2004, 151). See also Lateiner 2004, 29.

[64] As Scodel observes, "The Homeric epics show an astonishing range of sympathy" (2004, 52).

[65] Here, by my count, is the number of similes given by Homer directly (not through a character) in each book: I (3), II (16), III (6), IV (13), V (17), VI (4), VII (6), IX (2), X (7), XI (30), XII (15), XIII (27), XIV (11), XV (20), XVI (24), XVII (24), XVIII (8), XIX (11), XX (9), XXI (14), XXII (14), XXIII (11), XXIV (5). For an extremely useful catalogue of all the similes in the two poems, see Scott 1974, 190–205; consider also Edwards 1991, 24; Stanley 1993, 264. On the challenge of counting the similes, see footnote 14 in the Introduction. Edwards notes that similes are distinctive to Homer's own narration (or speech) and are consequently "much less common in direct speech... Akhilleus has more than anyone else" of Homer's characters, "and his long similes are all strikingly original in content and highly effective" (1991, 39). According to Moulton, "one seventh of the similes in the *Iliad* occur in speeches" (1977, 118).

Like the nations of swarming bees, always coming out anew from a hollow rock, and in clusters they fly upon spring flowers, and they fly in swarms together this way and that way, so the many nations [of the Achaians] from ships and huts beside the shore of the deep sea were marching forward to the assembly, in order, by companies. (2.87–93)

As when a destructive fire burns an immense forest at the top of a mountain, and far away the glow shines forth, so as they [the Achaians] went, from the divine bronze a radiance, dazzling all, went through the upper air to the heaven. (2.455–458)

As when rivers, flowing with winter force, flowing down from the mountains, throw together at the meeting place of streams the weight of their water, out of the great springs in the hollow gorge, and far away in the mountains a shepherd hears their thunder, so, from the men [the Achaians and Trojans] who mixed together, arose shouting and labor. (4.452–456)

As when a sharp shaft lays hold of a woman, and she suffers piercing pain, which the goddesses of childbirth send forth, the daughters of Hera, who hold the bitter pain, so the sharp pain descended on the furious spirit of the son of Atreus. (11.269–272)

As when the mind of a man leaps, who has gone through much territory and thinks in his thoughtful mind, "Would that I were there, or in that place," and he ponders many things, so quickly in her eagerness did Lady Hera fly. (15.80–83)

They [the Trojans] poured forth, in companies, and in front was Apollo, holding the aegis, highly honored, and with great ease he threw down the wall of the Achaians, as when some child in the sand by the sea makes a plaything in his innocent foolishness and then would wreck it with his hands and feet, still playing. So you, shining Phoebus, wrecked the toil and hardship of the Argives and roused panic among them. (15.360–366)

As in a dream one is not able to pursue the one who flees, nor is he able to flee out from under, nor the other pursue, so he [Achilles] was not able to overtake him [Hector] with his feet, nor was the other able to escape. (22.199–201)

As a father mourns while he burns the bones of his child, newly married, whose dying brought grief to his miserable parents, so Achilles mourned while he burned the bones of his companion and dragged himself by the fire, groaning thickly. (23.222–225)

Through these remarkable similes, these treasures of humane insight and wisdom, the human poet emerges unmistakably out from the shadow of the divine Muse.

Homer is, to be sure, a demure critic of the gods. He does not loudly declare his independence from the gods or loudly claim credit for his poem from the start, lest he awaken the resentment of gods, or of those who believe in gods (see Plato *Protagoras* 316d3–9) and perhaps suffer a fate similar to that of the Thracian Thamyris, who was supposedly silenced by the Muses for claiming to be superior to the goddesses in his singing (2.591–600). But clearly the *Iliad* is a new kind of song. In Book I, the Achaians sing in praise of Apollo and the Muses sing to the gods and hence, it would seem, in praise of the gods (1.472–474, 1.601–604). But Homer's song is not a hymn to the gods. It is not primarily a pious song but rather a song of humane enlightenment. Homer does not justify the gods' ways to men but rather explains the ways of the gods, and the nature of the gods, to men. By demystifying the gods and revealing their fundamentally whimsical nature and hence the doubtful character of their wisdom, justice, and love, Homer teaches his human audience to look to human rather than divine providence.[66]

THE LIMITS OF IMMORTALITY AND THE BLESSINGS OF MORTALITY

Still, we must ask, what is the basis of Homer's teaching about the gods? What is it that leads him to conclude that the gods are, in truth, whimsical beings? To understand the reasoning behind Homer's account of the gods, we must return to the simple observation that, in our experience of listening to or reading the poem, the human beings of the *Iliad* naturally engage our interest more than the divine beings do. Why is this so? The simplest reason that the human characters in the *Iliad* naturally engage our interest more than the gods is that the humans in the poem suffer terrible things but the gods do not, and cannot. As Achilles says to Priam at the end of the poem: "Such is the way the gods spun for wretched mortals, that we live our lives in grief, but they themselves have no sorrows" (24.525–526). The humans in the *Iliad* are emphatically mortal beings, beings who are always aware that death may cut them down at any moment and that death may snatch their loved ones away from them at any moment. And the sheer fact that the humans are so vulnerable to death means that literally everything is at stake for them in their choices and in their actions.

[66] Nietzsche goes so far as to claim that "Homer is so at home among his gods and takes such delight in them as a poet that he surely must have been deeply irreligious" (1984, 88). According to Burkert, "On account of such burlesque treatment of the gods, the *Iliad* has been described as the most irreligious of all poems" (1985, 122; see 397; Mazon 1942, 294). Griffin suggests that "the gods had to pay a certain price" for Homer's depiction of their indifference to humans (1980, 202).

Achilles, for example, must choose between either bowing to the overbearing and unjust Achaian king Agamemnon or withdrawing from the Achaian army and letting countless numbers of his comrades and friends die. Hector's decision to attack the Achaians aggressively, far from the great walls of Troy, means that he must run the risk of letting his warriors be encircled and killed, his city be destroyed, and his beloved wife become enslaved. More generally, every warrior who fights knows that he is putting his very existence at risk. It is the very vulnerability of these human beings that gives them a certain dignity. It is, paradoxically, their very imperfection that gives them a certain capacity for nobility and for greatness, for great courage, great love, and great understanding.

The gods of the *Iliad*, on the other hand, are emphatically *im*mortal beings (see 5.334–342).[67] Their immortality is, of course, a sign of their perfection. And yet, Homer suggests, it is precisely because the gods are such perfect, immortal beings that they are not and cannot be noble or profound beings, beings with our human capacity for courage, for love, and even for wisdom.

Homer's portrayal of the gods takes its bearings from what human beings believe about the gods. As we have seen, humans believe that the gods are, first and foremost, immortal beings and also superlatively noble, loving, and wise beings. But Homer suggests that, if we reflect on what immortal beings must be like, we must conclude that immortal beings cannot, in fundamental respects, be noble, loving, or wise.

In the first place, and most simply, the fact that the gods are immortal beings, the fact that they are invulnerable to death and to the sorrows connected with death, means that hardly anything is at stake for them in their choices or actions. While the quarrel between Achilles and Agamemnon in Book I is tragic, insofar as it leads to tears and terrible suffering for all concerned, the quarrel between Hera and Zeus in that same book is inevitably comic, for it ends with unquenchable laughter and good cheer (1.348–416, 1.595–611).[68] Why in the world should the deathless

[67] In this context, consider Hegel's comment: "But the Greek gods must not be regarded as more human than the Christian God. Christ is much more of a Man: he lives, dies, and suffers death on the cross" (1956, 249).

[68] Clarke remarks on the "jarring disjuncture between the divine and human planes" in this book of the poem (2004, 76). As Redfield points out, "the gods of the *Iliad* are . . . the chief source of comedy in the poem" (1975, 76).

gods make much fuss about a dispute among themselves when they know that they have been bickering for millennia and will do so for the rest of time? And why in the world should the immortal gods quarrel over *mortal* beings, whose lives are but a brief moment in the eternal lives of the gods? As the god Hephaestus remarks to Zeus and Hera, "This will be a disastrous matter and not endurable if you two are to quarrel thus for the sake of mortals... There will be no pleasure in our noble feast at all" (1.573–576). Hera later vows to Athena: "no longer will I allow the two of us to make war before Zeus for the sake of mortals. Let one of them perish, and let another live, who ever shall chance" (8.427–430). And as Apollo points out to Poseidon: "Earth-shaker, you speak to me as though I were not prudent, if I am to make war on you for the sake of wretched mortals" (21.462–464).

Similarly, it is Achilles' wonderful and terrible destiny to choose between living a short but glorious life if he continues to fight at Troy and living a long but inglorious life if he returns home to his father (9.410–416). Throughout the poem, Achilles is aware of the enormous consequences of his choice for his companions, his family, and himself, and he consequently reflects on this grave decision with considerable care. But his is a choice that only a mortal, human being can face. No god – no immortal being – can ever face the choice between a short but glorious life of war with comrades who need your courage and a long and sweet life of peace with a family who needs your love. By definition, no immortal god can ever exhibit the courage or nobility of a mortal being who deliberately exposes himself to the evil of death. Homer suggests that the gods' very immortality – an immortality that is essential to their nature – deprives their lives of the drama, the dignity, and the possible nobility that our human lives possess by virtue of our mortality.[69]

Furthermore, and perhaps more shockingly, Homer suggests that the immortal gods cannot love as deeply as we human beings can. To be sure,

[69] As Clay puts it, "The sublime frivolity of the gods in Homer is the shocking and paradoxical result of the profound and logical reflection on their immortality... Deathless, they cannot risk their lives for anything more precious than life, be it honor, the love of a friend, or the love of home. Their inability to sacrifice themselves for something higher constitutes a limitation of the gods ... The superhuman, then, turns out to be less than the human in an essential respect" (1983, 140–141). Griffin, on the other hand, admits that "the gods live at ease and are strangers to death" but still insists that the gods "suffer" and therefore are, in some sense, "tragic" (1980, 191, 195–196).

the gods of the *Iliad* do exhibit tender feelings for individual human beings. As we have seen, Zeus takes pity on Hector and Sarpedon. But, as we have also seen, he allows them to die simply to avoid squabbling with his wife Hera and the other gods. Similarly, Aphrodite loves her "beloved son" Aeneas and rescues him from certain death at the hands of Diomedes. She tells her mother Dione that Aeneas "is most beloved by me, far beyond all things" (5.377–378). Yet, when Diomedes stabs her hand, she instantly abandons her gravely wounded son to fend for himself on the battlefield and asks her brother Ares to take her to Olympus so that her hand may be treated immediately (5.343–380).

Thetis, the divine mother of Achilles, is, of all the gods, the one who seems to love a human being most deeply. With the exception of Zeus, who weeps once when his son Sarpedon dies, Thetis is the only god who weeps for a human being, and she does so more than once (16.458–461, 1.413, 18.34–94). In contrast to Aphrodite's superficial affection for her son Aeneas, Thetis's love for her son seems powerful, and genuinely comparable, for example, to that of Hecubae's love for her son Hector. Thetis weeps for her son when she learns that Agamemnon has dishonored him, and she weeps again for him when she learns that Achilles plans to kill Hector in vengeance for the death of Patroclus, since she somehow knows that her son's death must quickly follow Hector's (1.413, 18.65–67, 18.94–96; see also 24.83–86). Yet, once Achilles declares that he will go out to fight, the goddess simply accepts his decision, without any effort whatsoever to dissuade him (18.128–129). In contrast, when the mortal Hecubae sees her son determined to fight Achilles on the battlefield, she begs him, pathetically and movingly, to save himself:

> His mother, on the other side, wailed – shedding tears – laid the fold of her bosom bare, and with one hand held out a breast. And shedding tears, she spoke winged words to him: "Hector, my child, revere these and take pity on me, if ever I held you to my breast, to make you forget your sorrows. Remember them, my beloved child, and fight off the man, our enemy, from within the walls." (22.79–92)

Hecubae pleads with him so passionately because, she reminds him, as his entire well-being once depended on her, now her whole happiness, including her very life, depend on him. As she says after Hector dies, "Why now should I live, suffering dreadful things, while you have died? By day and night you were my boast in the town, a benefit to the Trojan men and women throughout the city, who welcomed you as a god" (22.431–435). But Thetis never expresses such a desperate attachment to her son because, being immortal, she never feels so dependent on her son for her own well-being. She compares her son, twice, to a tree that she has nourished, and toward which she feels genuine affection but not profound love (18.54–64, 18.429–443). Homer suggests that the very fact that the gods are immortal means that they are fundamentally self-sufficient, that their happiness does not depend on other beings, and consequently that they can never truly love other beings as we human beings can.

Indeed, Thetis evidently finds it difficult to understand how anyone can love another so deeply. Achilles, for example, loves his friend Patroclus as much as life itself and more deeply than the gods ever love anyone (18.80–82). Achilles' friend Antilochus understands Achilles' love for Patroclus perfectly; when Antilochus tells Achilles that Patroclus has been killed, Homer reports that Antilochus "held the hands of Achilles as he grieved in his proud heart, for he feared that Achilles might cut his [own] throat with the iron" (18.33–34). Antilochus fears that Achilles will respond to Patroclus's death by committing suicide – and rightly so. For Achilles responds to that death by returning to battle against the Trojans even though, or perhaps because, he knows that such a return means certain death for him. So the human Antilochus understands the power of Achilles' love for Patroclus perfectly.

In contrast, the goddess Thetis struggles unsuccessfully to understand her son's love. Right after she learns both that Patroclus is dead and that Achilles knows that Patroclus is dead, she asks Achilles, "Why, then, child do you lament?" She then tells him, somewhat obtusely, that, even though Patroclus has been killed, at least Zeus has answered all of Achilles' prayers for the punishment of Agamemnon and the Achaians (18.72–77). Achilles answers: "But what pleasure is this to me, since my beloved companion has perished, Patroclus, whom I honored beyond all my companions, as greatly as my own self?" (18.80–82). He then tries to explain to his uncomprehending divine mother that he would rather die than continue to live without the companionship of his friend. Later, when Achilles continues to mourn for a number of days for his beloved friend Patroclus, the bewildered goddess asks, again somewhat obtusely, "My child, how long will you mourn and grieve, devouring your heart, remembering neither your food nor your bed? It is a good thing even to mingle with a woman in love" (24.128–131; cf. 24.601–620).[70]

In Book VI, Andromache tells her husband Hector that her entire happiness depends on him alone. After reminding him that Achilles has killed her father and her seven brothers in battle, she concludes: "Hector, thus you are father to me, and honored mother and brother, and you it is who are also my flourishing husband. Come now, take pity upon me, and stay here on the rampart, that you may not make your child an orphan, your wife a widow" (6.429–432). Consequently, when Andromache later learns that Achilles has slain Hector, the news virtually kills her. In Homer's words: "The black night covered her eyes. She fell backward, and gasped her soul away" (22.466–467). But the gods never grieve in this way because they never love in this way. Consequently, their passions always lack the depth of the greatest human passions exhibited in the poem.[71] It is Homer's teaching that the capacity to love is intimately bound up with the capacity to die.

Finally, Homer suggests that, in an important sense, divine beings are less wise than human beings. For since the gods cannot ever truly suffer, since they cannot feel for themselves the terror of death or the misery of losing to death a loved one, on whom one's happiness depends, the gods cannot genuinely understand that terror or that misery when others feel it. The gods do, of course, suffer in their way. Aphrodite is wounded; Ares is wounded; and, according to Dione, Aphrodite's mother, Hera and Hades were once wounded (5.334–354, 5.850–863, 5.392–402). Hephaestus recounts that Zeus once punished him so violently that "there was little spirit within me" (1.593). But none of these hardships is at all serious, for all are softened, and indeed trivialized, by the immortality of the gods. As Homer remarks of the "blessed gods," "For they do not eat food nor do they drink gleaming wine, and therefore they have no blood and are called immortal" (5.340–342). The gods never fear suffering death, they never fear that their loved ones may suffer as a result of their own deaths, as Hector and Achilles do, and they never fear that someone on whom their happiness depends will suffer death, as Andromache, Priam, and Hecubae do (6.450–465, 24.486–512, 6.429–439, 22.33–89). Accordingly, the sufferings of the gods are an occasion for "unquenchable laughter" and smiles

[70] I consequently think that Griffin goes too far in stating that Thetis "mourns as a mortal" (1980, 190).

[71] See Griffin 1980, 93.

rather than tears and sorrow (1.595–600, 5.426–430, 21.388–390, 21.406–409, 21.423–434, 21.505–510). The "sufferings" of the gods always have a comical, histrionic, and hence shallow character, and consequently they cannot truly understand the sufferings of others.

For example, as we have seen, in Book I, when Thetis asks Zeus to punish the Achaians for their outrageous conduct toward Achilles by causing them to suffer many deaths in battle, Zeus responds by expressing concern, *not* for the terrible sorrows the Achaians will suffer – sorrows that Homer devotes the rest of the poem to describing – *nor* for the injustice Achilles is suffering, but rather for the nagging and the reproach that *he* must suffer at the hands of his wife (1.503–527). Zeus simply does not fathom the sorrows of human beings because of his own immunity from such sorrows and hence because of his own divine nature. In this way, Zeus's immortality and his divine perfection paradoxically render his understanding of human things shallow and imperfect. And Homer invites us to wonder whether this imperfect understanding is not a necessary consequence of being a god.

The first example in the poem of a human being whose understanding surpasses that of the gods is, as we have seen, that of Odysseus, who understands far better than Hera and Athena how to induce the Achaians to stay at Troy and continue to fight (2.169–335). But the most moving and memorable examples of a human understanding that surpasses divine understanding may be found at the end of the *Iliad* in the characters of Priam and Achilles.[72] In Book XXIV, the gods command Achilles to return the corpse of Hector to his father Priam, and tell Priam to go alone to the Achaian camp, with a large ransom, and to ask Achilles for the corpse by simply invoking Achilles' family (24.144–158, 24.465–467). The gods are evidently confident that appeals to Achilles' pious reverence for the gods, to his desire for wealth, and to his general love of his family will suffice to induce him to return the corpse of the man who killed his beloved companion. Priam, however, unlike the gods, knows from experience the full power of both human hatred and human love. Even before Achilles kills his son Hector, Priam expresses a bitter and deadly hatred of Achilles for harming other beloved sons of his: "Would that he were as beloved by the gods as he is by me. Soon would the dogs and vultures eat him as he lay, and a dreadful grief

[72] For a fuller discussion of Priam and Achilles in Book XXIV, see Chapter 3.

would leave my heart. For he made me bereaved of sons, many and noble" (22.41–44). Priam understands, then, that Achilles' hatred of Hector for killing Patroclus may well lead him to defy the gods. But he also understands – even in the immediate aftermath of Achilles' killing of Hector and desecration of his corpse – that Achilles' experience of loving and being loved by his father may well lead him to have sympathy for Priam: "I must be a suppliant to this man, a reckless doer of violent deeds, in the hope that he may have reverence for one of my age and take pity on my old age. His father is also of such an age, Peleus, who begot and reared him to become an affliction for the Trojans" (24.418–422). Accordingly, in order to overcome Achilles' hatred and melt his heart, Priam departs from the gods' advice by dramatically appealing to Achilles' sympathetic imagination and to his own experience of love: he kisses the hands of Achilles, implores Achilles to think of his own loving father when contemplating Priam, and thereby urges Achilles to imagine a love so great that it would lead a mighty king not only to risk his life but to sacrifice all of his dignity to recover the corpse of his beloved son (24.476–508). Now, Priam's strategy here is a complete success. Achilles responds to Priam with compassion and understanding and he freely returns the body of Hector to him. But it is important to see that Priam's strategy is based on an essentially human insight that the gods do not and cannot possess. For the gods do not recognize the importance of appealing to Achilles' experience of human love because the gods have never felt such love and therefore cannot appreciate its importance. No god can truly know the heart of Achilles because no god can feel the human passions that burn in that human heart. Only a fellow human being who has felt the hatred and anger that Achilles feels can know how to move Achilles to overcome them.

In Book XXIV, Achilles too exhibits an understanding that, in an important sense, surpasses that of the gods. For Achilles goes well beyond merely returning the corpse of Hector to Priam. Achilles expresses compassion and then, acting on that compassion, he freely grants Priam and the Trojans a twelve-day truce so that they may bury their beloved Hector in peace (24.656–670). And Achilles grants this truce completely of his own free will, without any commandment from the gods.[73] Now, this is an act of human rather than divine compassion. For Achilles' act reflects his

[73] It is therefore not quite accurate to state that the *Iliad* "ends with the gods conducting Priam to Achilles and ordering Achilles to yield him the body of Hector" (Griffin 1980, 144).

understanding of Priam's grief. But the gods cannot know what it means to suffer as Priam has suffered. Only one who has loved as deeply as Priam has and who has suffered a loss as heartbreaking as Priam's loss can genuinely feel for Priam and can genuinely understand him.

Homer suggests, then, that in a certain sense human wisdom eclipses divine wisdom. He suggests that, thanks to our mortality, we human beings may come to have a certain nobility, a certain depth of soul, and a certain wisdom, which divine and immortal beings do not and cannot possess. Therefore, Homer suggests, it is reasonable and just for us to direct our attention to the human tragedy rather than the divine comedy of the *Iliad* and to focus our admiration on the excellence of its human heroes and heroines rather than on the doings of its immortal gods and goddesses. As a result of Homer's influence, two of the distinctive features of Greek civilization were to be its extraordinary celebration of the beauty of the human animal, body and soul – as can be seen in Greek athletics, Greek sculpture, and Greek nudity – and also its singularly questioning posture toward the divine – as can be seen in Greek philosophy. In other words, it is Homer who made possible the liberation from religious awe and the proud, unabashed glorification of human excellence – of the intellectual, moral, and physical excellence of mortal, human beings – that were to become the hallmarks of classical civilization.[74]

[74] Consider Kirk 1974, 179: "The Greeks are a special case. In the mythology of most other peoples, [human] heroes . . . are either inconspicuous or altogether absent."

CHAPTER 2

Achilles and Hector

THE CASE AGAINST ACHILLES: A SELF-INTERESTED WARRIOR

Through his account of the gods in the *Iliad*, Homer seeks to demystify those beings and to expose them as whimsical and improvident. He seeks thereby to liberate his audience from their religious awe and pious belief in divine providence and to inspire in them an admiration for human efforts, for human providence, and, more broadly, for human excellence. But which human being in the poem best embodies human excellence? Whom does Homer hold up to us as a model of human greatness?

The obvious answer would seem to be Achilles, the focus of the poem from the very first line and one who Homer suggests is the greatest human being in the poem. As both the Muse and Homer tell us, "Of men, Ajax the son of Telamon was by far the best of men, while Achilles remained full of wrath, since *he* was by far the greatest" (2.768–769, emphasis added; see also 17.279–280). Later, in his account of Achilles' climactic pursuit of Hector, Homer remarks: "The one in front who fled was noble, but the one pursuing him swiftly was far greater" (22.158–159).

Achilles' greatness would seem to lie most obviously in his martial prowess. Homer illustrates Achilles' greatness as a warrior in a number of ways. After Achilles withdraws from the battle, the Achaians are driven away from Troy by the Trojans for the first time in the nine-year war and are forced to build a wall to protect their ships (7.339–343). When Achilles rejoins the battle, he quickly drives the Trojans back behind the walls of Troy (21.526–538). Indeed, in Book XVIII, the mere appearance of the unarmed

Achilles on the battlefield strikes terror in the hearts of the mighty Trojans. And he need only shout three times to drive the entire Trojan army away from the Achaian camp (18.215–231). Finally, in Book XX, Zeus says that, unless the gods intervene, Achilles will destroy the Trojan army single-handedly and conquer Troy all by himself (20.26–30). Achilles, then, is without a doubt the toughest and most effective of all the warriors in the *Iliad*. No one comes close to rivaling his exploits in battle. Consequently, it is tempting to believe that Homer singles out Achilles for attention and praise because Achilles is the greatest warrior of them all.[1]

There are, however, a number of compelling reasons for resisting this temptation. For even though Homer presents Achilles' amazing exploits in battle, Homer also goes out of his way to provoke our compassion for Achilles' victims, including most emphatically the Trojans.[2] In Books XX and XXI, we see the enraged Achilles slaughter the helpless Trojan soldiers and butcher two of Priam's young sons, one of them as he begs for mercy (20.407–418, 21.134–135). Then, in Book XXII, we see Priam, Hecubae, and Andromache overcome with grief when they learn that Achilles has killed their beloved Hector and is defiling his corpse (22.405–472). Finally, in Book XXIII, at Patroclus's funeral, we see Achilles slit the throats of twelve Trojan youths (23.173–183; see 21.26–33, 18. 336–337). More generally, on virtually every page of the *Iliad*, Homer presents with sorrow and with pity the horrors and the ugliness of war. In his very first accounts of battlefield deaths in the poem, Homer describes how Ajax slew "a flourishing unmarried youth, Simoeis," who consequently "would not pay back to his beloved parents the care which they gave him when they reared him" and also how a Thracian warrior in turn smashed the Achaian Dories with a stone, "and he fell down backward in the dust, reaching out both his hands to his beloved companions, gasping out his spirit" (4.474, 4.477–478, 4.522–524). In these and other ways, Homer humanizes the casualties of war by vividly describing the pain their deaths cause to the living and the painful experience of death

[1] Consider, for example, Nagy's identification of "the heroic worth of Achilles" with "martial . . . superiority" and "might" (1979, 48–49). Consider also Winn 2008, 41–42.

[2] As Segal puts it, "A poet who could create a Hector, an Andromache, a Priam does not simply share his heroes' exultation in bloodthirsty deeds" (1971, 11). And as Lateiner points out, "This epic is not nationalistic" (2004, 20). See also Scodel 2004, 51–52; Clay 2010, 48; Crotty 1994, 98–99; Zanker 1994, 1.

itself.[3] Later, at the climactic moment of the story of the *Iliad*, in Book XXII, when Achilles is chasing Hector across the Trojan plain and is about to kill him and thereby prepare for the final destruction of Troy, Homer interrupts his narrative to describe two springs of water. He then remarks: "Beside these in this place, and close to them, are the beautiful washing-hollows of stone, where the wives of the Trojans and their beautiful daughters washed the clothes to shining, in the old days, when there was peace, before the coming of the sons of the Achaians" (22.153–156). Even in the midst of the high drama of heroic combat, Homer insists on reminding the reader of the terrible price of war, of the sweet pleasures of peace destroyed by the violence of war.[4] The man who composed the *Iliad* could not have regarded the capacity to kill efficiently as the highest human virtue. Consequently, Homer cannot have regarded Achilles as the best of the Achaians simply because he was the strongest and the most warlike.

Furthermore, Achilles is far from being a loyal and dutiful warrior. In the very first lines of the poem, Homer points out that the "destructive" anger of Achilles led to the death of "countless" numbers of his fellow soldiers (1.1–7).[5] In Book I, we see Achilles rebel against Agamemnon, his king (1.277–281). We see Achilles abandon his fellow warriors, in the middle of a war, to the tender mercies of the mighty Trojans (1.240–244). And we see him pray that Zeus bring disaster, not only on Agamemnon, but on *all* of the

[3] See Griffin 1980, 103–143; Schein 1984, 72–75; Buxton 2004, 151; Clay 2010, 51–52. According to Clay, following Mueller, "Of the poem's 360 named characters, 232 are warriors killed or wounded" (Clay 2010, 51–52; see also Mueller 1984, 82). According to Armstrong, there are 238 named casualties and 26 unnamed, 61 of which are Achaian and 208 Trojan (1969, 30; see also Lateiner 2004, 12).

[4] Griffin 1980, 21–22; Schein 1984, 75–76. Similarly, the shield of Achilles, which he will use as he slaughters the Trojans in Books XX–XXII, contains elaborate images of a city at peace (18.490–508, 18.541–605; see Schein 1984, 140–142; Benardete 2005, 54; Griffin 2004, 165). In the words of Sheppard, "At the highest moment of his glory and his sorrow, strong, young and beautiful, and so near death, the hero goes to fight his battle with a shield on which Hephaistos has emblazoned both the sweetness and uncertainty of life" (1969, 10). The similes – which, as Mueller notes, "occur predominantly in battle scenes" (1984, 109) – draw the audience's attention to their world and hence, primarily, "to the everyday world of peaceful human life" (Schein 1984, 140; see Edwards 1991, 39; Lateiner 2004, 20–21; Buxton 2004, 152–153; Redfield 1975, 186, 188). I therefore disagree with Finley's assertion that, in the *Iliad*, "The poet and his audience lingered lovingly over every act of slaughter" (1978, 118).

[5] See Bowra 1977, 17–18; Clay 1983, 37–38.

Achaians (1.407–412; see 1.231). Even if we deem Achilles' anger in some measure justified, his prayer seems, as Homer himself suggests, "beyond measure" in its harshness (15.598–599).[6]

Finally, Achilles is sharply criticized in the course of the poem, not only by Trojans – albeit a surprisingly few of them – but also, and, indeed, above all, by his fellow Achaians.[7] In the first place, Agamemnon denounces Achilles as "most hateful ... For strife is always beloved by you as well as wars and battles" (1.174–177). Agamemnon uses here the very words that Zeus later uses to denounce his "most hateful" son Ares, the most warlike of the gods (5.890–891). He suggests that Achilles loves war and lives for war, that he does not fight out of necessity, for the sake of peace or justice, but because he positively, and insatiably, delights in doing harm to others. Menelaus, Agamemnon's brother, later makes a similar criticism of the "hubristic" Trojans wherein he explains more fully why the insatiable desire for war might seem twisted and unnatural: "they are not able to be satiated with the fighting of war. There is satiety in all things, in sleep and love-making and sweet song and blameless dance. Anyone longs to satisfy his love for these more than for war. But the Trojans are insatiable for battle" (13.633–639). Evidently thinking more of the austere Hector than of the sensualists Paris and Priam (who has, after all, sired sixty-two children – 6.242–250), Menelaus suggests that the Trojans are doubly monstrous, since they love a hateful thing, war, rather than such lovely things as lovemaking, and they love war

[6] Consider Clarke's account of Achilles' "bizarrely exaggerated response to an insult" and "extraordinary vindictiveness" (2004, 74, 82). See also Schein's description of Achilles' "inflexible, irrational anger at Agamemnon's insult to his honor" and his account of Achilles as "inhumanly isolated" (1984, 116, 180). Benardete goes so far as to suggest that, as long as Achilles "believes in his own uniqueness, he is as monstrous as the Cyclops" (2005, 101; see also 105, 114).

[7] Remarkably few Trojans denounce Achilles in the course of the poem, perhaps because he is mostly absent from the fighting but also perhaps because he has the reputation of treating the Trojans with relative mercy (see 21.100–102; consider also 21.34–82, 6.421–428, and, for example, 11.101–112). In the aftermath of Hector's death, his grief-stricken mother, Hecubae, does express hatred for Achilles, "a man who feasts on carrion and is untrustworthy," and warns her husband, King Priam, "he will neither pity you nor treat you with reverence" (24.207–208). But even though Priam too denounces Achilles, both before and after the death of Hector, he also expresses the hope that Achilles will treat him with compassion and reverence when he begs for the corpse of his son (22.38–45, 22.415–422).

more intensely than anyone loves what is truly lovable.[8] In a similar vein, Agamemnon suggests that Achilles craves strife and longs to war with one and all (see also 9.63–64). Agamemnon also contends that, in addition to being monstrously and maliciously eager for battle, Achilles is tyrannically ambitious: "but this man wishes to be above all others, to hold sway over all, to rule over all, and to give orders to all" (1.287–289). Agamemnon, who has been commanding Achilles for nine years at Troy, vilifies him as a violent and tyrannical enemy of human society.

Now, in the light of Agamemnon's bitter dispute with Achilles, it may seem reasonable simply to dismiss Agamemnon's criticisms as expressions of blind hatred. After all, Agamemnon himself goes on to renounce most emphatically, more than once, his quarrel with, and therewith, it seems, his criticism of, Achilles (9.115–120, 19.78–144; but consider 1.492). However, Achilles is criticized most sharply not just by Agamemnon but also by those whom Achilles claims are by him the "most beloved of Achaians" and "the most beloved men" – Odysseus, Phoinix, and Ajax; by his companion Nestor; and, most remarkably, by his most beloved and honored companion, Patroclus (9.198, 9.204, 18.79–82). Patroclus goes so far as to call Achilles "a terrible man" who is given to injustice, since "he might deem guilty even one who is without guilt" (11.652–653). The criticism of Achilles by these men is far more powerful than that of Agamemnon precisely because it comes from his best friends and is therefore far more credible.

The criticism of Achilles by his friends takes place in the aftermath of the Trojans' success in driving the Achaians away from Troy and pinning them against the sea. In Book IX, the Achaians find themselves in a desperate situation. The Trojans have killed them in large numbers, are besieging their camp, and threaten to burn their ships and slaughter them all. Night has fallen before the Trojans can reach the ships, but the next day seems certain to bring defeat and destruction to the Achaians. Agamemnon, overwhelmed with despair, breaks down and cries, just as he had cried piteously in the midst of the Trojan onslaught (8.245–246). The weeping Agamemnon first urges the Achaians to abandon all hope of winning the war and to leave Troy

[8] This statement would seem at least to call into question Griffin's claim that "the archetypal Trojan is Paris," a man who is "glamorous and frivolous" (1980, 5, 9). Benardete suggests that, in apparent contrast with the Achaians, "the Trojans, all of them, are high-spirited in war" (2005, 21; see 18–22).

while they still can (9.13–28). But then, after hearing the rebuke of Diomedes and the advice of Nestor, he resolves to send Odysseus, Phoinix, and Ajax to persuade Achilles to return to battle by offering abundant gifts, the return of Achilles' mistress Briseis, and the promise of extraordinary future gifts and honors, including a princess – one of his daughters – as a future bride and seven cities for him to rule (9.141–156).

Now, Odysseus offers Achilles all of these gifts and honors but also begs him to pity the Achaians in their darkest hour and save them from destruction: "But if the son of Atreus has incurred too much hatred in your heart, both himself and his gifts, take pity on all the rest of the Achaians, who are worn out throughout the army, and who will honor you as a god" (9.300–303). Achilles, however, refuses to help either Agamemnon or the Achaians: "I do not suppose that the son of Atreus, Agamemnon, will persuade me, nor the rest of the Danaans, since there was no gratitude for fighting, unceasingly, always, against enemy men" (9.315–317). He rejects Agamemnon's remorse as insufficient: "Not if he would give me gifts as many as the sand or dust is, not even thus would he persuade my spirit, until he pays for the entire outrage that pains my spirit" (9.385–387). Since Achilles does not specify what Agamemnon must do to satisfy him, one naturally suspects that Achilles will never be satisfied and hence that he will never act to save the Achaians from destruction. Nestor later gives voice to this suspicion: "Will he wait until the swift ships by the sea are consumed by a blazing fire, against the will of the Argives, and we ourselves are killed one after the other?" (11.665–667). Achilles himself appears to confirm this suspicion by declaring, twice, to Odysseus, Phoinix, and Ajax, that he will leave Troy and return to his home on the following day, the day the Trojans will destroy the Achaian army (9.356–361, 9.426–429).[9]

Achilles' astonished friends respond by accusing him of being heartless, unjust, and hypocritical. In the first place, they argue that he is inhumanly hardhearted toward the terrible sufferings of the Achaians. Phoinix, who has known and cared for Achilles since he was a child, who helped raise him,

[9] In Bowra's words, "In this scene Achilles definitely moves a step in the wrong direction . . . and now he alone is to blame for the dire position of the Achaeans" (1977, 19). See also Lloyd-Jones: "when he refused atonement, Achilles puts himself in the wrong" (1971, 26). Consider as well Griffin 1995, 26–27. For a defense of Achilles here, see Lateiner 2004, 25–26.

and who loves him as a son, bursts into tears when he hears Achilles' response and declares: "But Achilles, subdue your great spirit; you ought not to have a pitiless heart. Even the gods themselves may be turned, and their virtue, honor, and might are greater than ours are" (9.496–497). Phoinix acknowledges that Agamemnon, at least, and perhaps the other Achaians as well have wronged Achilles and that his anger toward them has been just. But now that Agamemnon has admitted his wrong, Achilles should soften his justice with compassion:

> For if the son of Atreus were not bringing gifts and naming still more hereafter, but were still swelling with rancor, I myself, at least, would not bid you to cast aside your wrath and defend the Argives, even though they need you. But now he gives you many things immediately, and has promised other things hereafter, and he has sent the best men to supplicate you, choosing them out of the Achaian host, those who by you yourself are the most beloved of the Argives. Do not bring disgrace on their speech or their footsteps, though before this one could not be indignant at your being enraged. (9.515–523)

By persisting in his anger, and letting the Achaians be destroyed for their injustice against him, even after they have repented, Achilles shows himself to be less compassionate to his fellow mortals than even the immortal gods (see also 8.245–246, 350–353).[10]

Indeed, Apollo himself later makes this criticism, when Achilles not only kills Hector in revenge for the slaying of Patroclus but also disfigures his corpse, continually drags it around the tomb of Patroclus, and so prevents Hector's family and people from honoring him, and venting their own grief, with a funeral: "But gods, you wish to aid destructive Achilles, whose mind is not righteous, nor can the thought in his breast be bent, but like a lion he knows savage things, who, once he has yielded to his great strength and manly spirit, goes to the flocks of mortals so that he may feast on them. Thus Achilles has destroyed pity" (24.39–44). Achilles is hard, harder than the gods, inhumanly hard.

Patroclus himself issues the strongest denunciation of Achilles' heartlessness in the poem. At a moment when the Trojans have wounded Odysseus, Agamemnon, and Diomedes; are about to set the Achaian ships

[10] Phoinix's speech here is the longest in the *Iliad*. Nestor's speech to Patroclus in Book XI is the second longest, and Achilles' response to Odysseus in Book IX is the third longest. See Redfield 1975, 3, 226. See also Griffin 2004, 166.

on fire; and Achilles appears to make light of their suffering, a weeping Patroclus chastises him: "Pitiless one, the horseman Peleus was not your father nor Thetis your mother. The gleaming sea bore you and the towering rocks, since your mind is turned away from us" (16.33–35). Patroclus here goes further than Phoinix and Apollo in his criticism, for he suggests that so unfeeling is Achilles' response to the miseries of the Achaians that he is worse than subhuman, even less capable of sympathy than the animals, but comparable only to such inanimate beings as rocks and water.

Achilles' friends also accuse him of being unjust to them. Phoinix suggests that whereas Achilles condemns Agamemnon and the Achaians for their ingratitude toward him, notwithstanding all the painful sacrifices he has made for them, Achilles himself is ungrateful to Phoinix for all the cares he has bestowed on him from childhood: "Thus I have suffered many things for you and endured much toil, considering that the gods would not bring to birth any offspring of my own. But you, godlike Achilles, I made my own child, so that someday you would keep hard destruction away from me" (9.492–495). Now, Achilles does appear sensitive to this charge – in addition to his previous offer to save Phoinix from the Trojan onslaught, Achilles now offers him half of his kingship over the Myrmidon troops and half of his honor, though he had not thought of doing so before (9.426–429, 9.616). But Ajax, perhaps Achilles' most persuasive critic, maintains that Achilles is also ungrateful to his other friends and forgets the benefits conferred on him by men whom he claims to love: "But Achilles has made savage the great spirit in his breast. He is hard and does not have regard for the friendship of his companions, wherein we honored him far beyond others by the ships. He is pitiless" (9.628–632). Achilles remembers only the benefits he has conferred, not those he has received.[11] Ajax does not deny that Achilles is noble or that he has a "great spirit in his breast." But Achilles exaggerates his own nobility and generosity to his friends, dwells on their faults, forgets his debts to them, and heartlessly and unjustly wishes them to suffer. Ajax does not deny that the Achaians, including his best friends, have wronged Achilles. But, he suggests, they have paid a terrible price for their wrongs and are now offering to pay him for them in gifts and honors. As Ajax points out, men accept offerings from those who have murdered their brothers or their children

[11] In this respect, Achilles resembles in some measure Aristotle's description of the great-souled human being in the *Nicomachean Ethics* (1124b12–17).

(9.632–638). They accept payment and remorse from strangers who have committed far graver crimes than robbing one of a captured mistress. But Achilles refuses to accept the return of his mistress, Briseis, and much else besides, from men whom he claims to love. And he refuses to save them from destruction. His anger, then, is unjust, for it is out of all proportion to the wrong that was done and ignores the contrition of the wrongdoers.

Ajax points here to a deeper criticism of Achilles' anger. Achilles claims to be angry because Agamemnon ungratefully and unjustly took from him his beloved mistress Briseis, with the acquiescence of the Achaians: "Since anyone who is a good man and is sensible loves his own wife and cares for her, as I myself loved her from my spirit, even though I acquired her with my spear" (9.341–343). But now the Achaians offer to give his "beloved" Briseis back to him, untouched by any man, and still Achilles refuses to take her back. Why? Was not Chryses willing to accept his beloved daughter back when Agamemnon repented? Would Menelaus not be willing to accept his beloved wife back from the Trojans? Why, then, is Achilles unwilling to accept Briseis back? Does he genuinely love her? It would seem not. Indeed, immediately after his friends leave, Achilles proceeds to sleep with another captured mistress (9.663–665; consider as well 19.56–62; in contrast, see 2.17–46, 10.1–176).

Ajax suggests that Achilles does not truly care for Briseis, any more than he cares for his friends. The Achaians did dishonor him, but now they offer him boundless honor and he refuses to accept it. His beloved Briseis was taken from him, but now the Achaians offer her back to him, and he refuses to accept her. The reasons for his anger are removed, and still he persists in anger. As Odysseus reports to Agamemnon: Achilles "does not wish to quench his rage but still more than ever is filled with fury" (9.678–679). As Patroclus points out, Achilles willfully watches over and cherishes his rage (16.30). Achilles' anger is not provoked any longer by a genuine injustice. Achilles wishes to be angry, he embraces anger even when there would no longer seem to be a justification for it, and therefore he must do so because of the satisfaction and pleasure it gives to him.

Later in the poem, after Hector slays Patroclus, Achilles seems similarly unjust in his anger. Achilles is furious with Hector, "the man who has especially touched my spirit," for having killed his beloved companion (20.425–426). Yet Achilles' anger here would seem at least somewhat unreasonable, inasmuch as Hector simply killed the warrior who was, at least at that point, the most effective warrior the Achaians had. How can Achilles reasonably condemn Hector – as a "dog," for example – for killing an enemy warrior when Achilles himself has been doing so for nine years (22.345–354)? Still, given his apparent love for Patroclus, this anger is understandable (18.114–115). But then, Achilles goes so far as to condemn *all* the Trojans for killing Achaians during the time that he withdrew from battle: "But even thus may you perish in evil doom until you all pay for the murder of Patroclus and the destruction of the Achaians, whom you killed beside the swift ships, away from me" (21.133–135; see also 22.271–272). Yet Achilles himself prayed to Zeus that the Trojans kill the Achaians beside their ships (1.407–412)! He thus condemns the Trojans for doing precisely what he prayed that they would do (18.74–77)! Here, too, it seems that Achilles simply wishes to be angry and to seize on pretexts to fuel his anger. He wishes, as Patroclus said earlier, to hold guilty those who are without guilt so that he may vent his anger on them (11.653). Just as Achilles' anger at the Achaians in the name of his love for Briseis masks Achilles' own grim satisfaction in feeling angry with them, so does his anger at the Trojans in the name of his love for the Achaians mask his own grim satisfaction at being angry with them. Anger, which would seem to be a moral passion, a passion naturally awakened by injustice, in Achilles' case seems to be a selfish passion.

The core of the criticism of Achilles, presented especially by his friends in the poem, is that he is a singularly hardhearted, selfish man. He abandons his fellow Achaian soldiers in the middle of a war so that they might suffer at the hands of the mighty Trojans. When the Achaians, faced with utter destruction, offer him generous tokens of their remorse and beg him for forgiveness and those men who have benefited him in the past and whom he claims to love most of all beg him to save them, he refuses their pleas for help. In response to Ajax's final, desperate plea, in the name of friendship, that he save the Achaians from the Trojan onslaught, Achilles selfishly declares that he will not even think of fighting the Trojans unless they attack *his* huts and *his* ships (9.649–655). If Achilles is not willing to help men he claims to love most of all, in their moment of greatest need, how can we take at all seriously his claim to love them? And if he does not care for these men, for whom does he care, apart from himself? As Nestor remarks to Patroclus, "Achilles, noble as he is, does not care or feel pity for the Danaans" (11.664–665).

It is true that Achilles does evince some concern for the Achaians even after he has withdrawn from battle. He does not leave them at Troy and return home, even though he threatens three times to do so (1.169–171, 9.356–361, 9.426–429). Nestor suggests to Patroclus that, even though Achilles rages against the Achaians, he still cares for them since he will regret their demise: "I suppose he will weep much afterward, once his people are destroyed" (11.762–763). Furthermore, Achilles does send Patroclus twice to the Achaians, first to find out if their principal healer Machaon is wounded, and then, together with Achilles' soldiers, to save them from destruction at the hands of Hector (11.595–614, 16.64–82; see 11.510–518). Still, the fact remains that Achilles himself declines to fight for the Achaians, even in their darkest hour, but only returns to the war to avenge the death of his beloved companion Patroclus.[12]

Achilles might seem to care for his son Neoptolemus and his father Peleus, as well as for Patroclus (19.315–327, 24.511–512).[13] Yet Achilles has stayed away from his father and his son for nine years, even though he believes that his father in particular needs his presence (19.321–337). Even though he repeatedly claims that he will return to his homeland, he never says that he wishes to return in order to be with his father and his son (1.169–171, 9.356–363, 9.393–400, 9.426–429, 19.328–339). And of course he never decides to return home. His feelings for his son and even for his father, then, might seem to be abstract and tepid, especially in contrast with Hector's apparent devotion to his father and his son (6.440–446, 6.466–481).

When Patroclus dies, Achilles explains that the deaths of his father and son would not have affected him more deeply than the death of his beloved companion:

> For I could not suffer anything worse, not if I learned my father had died – who now somewhere in Phthia sheds a soft tear for bereavement of such a son, but in a foreign land, for the sake of the horrible Helen, I make war on the Trojans – or my beloved son [had died], who is reared in Skyros, if somewhere still god-like Neoptolemus lives. (19.321–327)

Patroclus, then, "most beloved of my companions," "whom I honored beyond all my companions, as dear as my own self," would seem to be the

[12] On this point, see Vico 1999, 358; Benardete 2005, 97.

[13] Achilles does express, on one occasion, sorrow for his divine mother, Thetis, though it is in the context of also expressing sorrow for himself, that he must soon die (18.82–93).

clearest example of one whom Achilles genuinely loves and hence the clearest, perhaps the only clear, evidence that he is not simply self-interested (19.315, 18.80–82). Indeed, Achilles goes so far as to utter an astounding – and chilling – prayer in the presence of Patroclus: "Indeed, Father Zeus and Athena and Apollo, if only no one of the Trojans would escape death, as many as there are, nor any of the Argives, but we two would emerge from the destruction so that we alone would undo the sacred headband of Troy" (16.97–100). Achilles here expresses at least the momentary wish that all the Trojans and all the Achaians – including his beloved friends Phoinix, Ajax, and Odysseus – were dead, except for Patroclus and himself, so that the two of them alone could win the glory of capturing Troy. His friendship with Patroclus, then, would seem to constitute the only clear proof that Achilles is not primarily concerned with himself.

Yet, even the example of his friendship with Patroclus does not manifestly refute the accusation that Achilles is primarily self-interested. For Achilles does not join Patroclus in facing Hector and the Trojans but sends him into battle "so that you may win great honor and glory from all of the Danaans for me, so that they may bring back to me the exceedingly beautiful girl and give me splendid gifts as well" (16.84–86; see also 18.101–106). Achilles does advise Patroclus not to fight too boldly in an attempt to conquer Troy on his own. But the primary reason he gives to Patroclus for this advice is a selfish one: "If the loud-thundering husband of Hera should grant to you the winning of glory do not make war on the war-loving Trojans without me. You will make me more dishonored" (16. 87–90). Achilles, it appears, fears lest Patroclus fight too successfully against the Trojans and thereby eclipse Achilles' own glory. Even here, then, in this most moving case of friendship, the apparent self-interestedness of Achilles raises its head.

Achilles comes to sight in the *Iliad* as an unheroic hero, a shockingly disloyal and self-interested warrior. As Nestor succinctly states, in words that Patroclus later echoes: "But Achilles alone will benefit from his virtue" (11.762–763, 16.30–32). Yet, such disloyalty and self-interestedness contradict the dutifulness and devotion we naturally expect from a virtuous human being. So we must ask, why would Homer encourage us to focus our attention and our admiration on one who is capable of turning so sharply against his companions? Why would Homer hold up to us this self-interested man as a model of human excellence?

THE CASE FOR HECTOR: A LOYAL DEFENDER OF HIS PEOPLE

These questions are underscored by the fact that there is, in the *Iliad*, a seemingly shining example of a brave, but also loyal and dutiful warrior, namely, the great defender of Troy, Hector.[14] Hector, although evidently younger, is almost as formidable a warrior as Achilles.[15] When he issues a challenge to the Achaians to select a warrior to duel him, "all were hushed to silence. They were ashamed to refuse it but feared to accept it" (7.92–93). When, after a long silence, Menelaus moves to accept the challenge, his brother Agamemnon denounces his "folly" and reminds him, "even Achilles, in battle where men win glory, shudders at facing this man, who is much better than you are" (7.110, 7.113–114). But even though Hector is evidently inferior to Achilles in martial prowess, he appears to surpass Achilles by far in his noble devotion to others. For, in contrast to Achilles, Hector comes to sight in the poem as one who fights courageously and doggedly in defense of both his family and his city.[16] He never rebels against his king, he never withdraws from battle, and he never seeks to punish his

[14] Scott points out that "Hector has the distinction of being the only person who is named in every one of the twenty-four books of the *Iliad*" (1921, 218). Achilles is mentioned in all but Book III. Redfield reasons that "Hector, a figure less intensely drawn, is in fact more widely present in the *Iliad* than Achilles" and goes so far to contend that Hector "is the true tragic hero of the poem" and that "Hector's ethic" is "the ethic of the *Iliad*" (1975, 229, 109, x; see also the subtitle of the book, iii).

[15] Andromache calls Hector young (νέος) at 24.725. She also describes him as "flourishing" or "in the prime of vigor" (θαλερός) at 6.430. Hector uses this same word to describe himself at 8.190. When Hector dies, "his soul went, flying out of his limbs, into Hades, bewailing his lot, leaving behind his manliness and his youth (ἥβην)" (22.362–363). While Achilles and his companions speak as though he – Achilles – has been with the Achaian army since it first went to Troy nine years ago, it is never said that Hector has been fighting for so long (1.149–160, 2.294–329, 9.252–258, 9.314–338, 9.438–443, 11.764–789, 18.324–337; see also 18.58–59). The fact that Hector's son is an infant but Achilles' son is old enough to take part in the final conquest of Troy shortly after the events recounted in the *Iliad* take place also suggests that Hector is younger than Achilles (6.399–403; *Odyssey* 11.491–537; see also 4.3–10). I therefore am inclined to disagree with Redfield's claim that "It may be that Hector is the eldest of Priam's sons" (1975, 112).

[16] See Nagy 1979, 145–147, for a discussion of the possible meaning of Hector's name as "protector."

fellow Trojans. As Hector explains to his wife, "I have learned to be noble always and to do battle among the first of the Trojans" (6.444–445).

Furthermore, even though he is loyal to Troy, Hector is not a blind partisan of the Trojan cause. As we have seen, in his very first words in the *Iliad*, Hector condemns his brother Paris as being "evil" for having kidnapped Helen, provoked the Achaians to attack Troy, and thereby caused "great sorrow to your father and city and people" (3.39–51). Hector is acutely aware of the injustice of the Trojan cause. He goes so far as to express the wish that the Trojans had executed Paris for having caused the war (3.56–57; see also 6.281–285). Accordingly, in his first noteworthy action in the poem, before fighting in any battle, Hector publicly embraces Paris's proposal to decide the outcome of the war with a duel, explains the proposal to the Achaians, and arranges a truce with them (3.76–120). Nevertheless, when the truce breaks down and the war resumes, Hector fights on, apparently in order to fulfill his duty to protect his city, his family, and his soldiers.

In contrast, then, to Achilles, who is accused by Agamemnon of being a savage lover of war, Hector comes to sight as a would be peacemaker who only continues fighting in order to save his people from destruction. Homer tells us that the Trojans nicknamed Hector's infant son Scamandrios "Astyanax" – Lord of the Town – "for Hector alone protected Ilion" (6.402–403). So vital is Hector to the security of Troy that, later, when his father Priam tries to persuade him to avoid facing Achilles alone in combat by withdrawing into the walls of Troy, he urges him to do so "in order that you might save the Trojans and the women of Troy" (22.56–57; see also 24.242–246). At his funeral, his wife Andromache foretells that Troy will now be sacked, "for you, her guardian, have perished, who protected her and kept safe her devoted wives and infant children" (24.729–730).

Hector's powerful sense of duty is illustrated most dramatically by his conversations in Book VI with his mother Hecubae, his sister-in-law Helen, and his wife Andromache. In each of these exchanges, the women apparently tempt the battle-weary warrior to relax his strict sense of martial duty, and in each case he remains steadfast in his devotion to fighting alongside his soldiers. In the midst of a terrible battle with the Achaians, his brother Helenus, an augur, tells him to go quickly to Troy and bid their mother and the Trojan women to pray to Athena for support (6.73–102). Fresh from battle, "spattered with gore and blood," Hector conveys the message to his mother, but when she offers him a glass of wine, he refuses, "lest it unnerve my furious spirit and

I forget my strength" (6.264–268). When he goes to summon Paris back to the battlefield by reminding him that "it is because of you that clamor and war blaze around the town," the singularly beautiful Helen confides to Hector that she wishes she had married a better man than Paris and then, Siren-like, invites Hector to sit beside her "since labor surrounds your mind most of all, because of me" (6.354–356). Again, Hector resists temptation: "Do not sit me down, Helen, although you love me. You will not persuade me, for already my spirit rushes me so that I might defend the Trojans, who have a great longing for me when I am away" (6.360–362). Before returning to the battlefield, however, Hector visits his "beloved wife and infant son" (6.366). When Andromache tearfully begs him to avoid death on the Trojan plain and to stay within the great walls of the city, Hector, after attempting to reassure her, tells her to return to her wifely household duties and declares: "But the men will concern themselves with the war, all of them, and I most of all, of those who dwell within Ilion" (6.492–493). Taken together, these three scenes, which pit the soft and immediate pleasures of wine, beauty, and love against the austere, self-denying virtues of the dedicated soldier, bear powerful witness to Hector's seemingly selfless dedication to the defense of Troy.[17]

Hector also comes to sight as a warrior who fights not only out of a sense of duty to his city but also out of love for his family. Indeed, Hector's tender feelings for his wife and child might seem to offer an especially sharp contrast with the hardheartedness of Achilles toward his beloved friends. In Book VI, we see him declare to his wife that he would rather die than see her suffer harm at the hands of the Achaians (6.447–465). We see him pity and comfort his distraught, "beloved" wife and laugh, play with, and kiss his "beloved son" (6.482–493, 6.466–475). We see him offer up a tremendous prayer, loving and fatherly, for his boy: "Zeus and the other gods, grant that this child of mine come to be, as I am, pre-eminent among the Trojans, good in his might, and that he rule strongly over Ilion. And someday may someone say: 'far better is he than his father' as he comes back from war" (6.476–480). So great is the heart of this mighty warrior that he prays that his son eclipse his own glory, in contrast with Achilles, who apparently fears lest his beloved Patroclus outshine his own glory.

The clearest evidence of Hector's superior virtue would seem to be the widespread acclaim he receives from the Trojans. In contrast with Achilles, who is sharply criticized in the poem even and especially by those he claims to

[17] See Griffin 1980, 6–7; Clay 2010, 35.

love, Hector enjoys nearly universal praise from his fellow Trojans. From his first appearance in the poem, where we see him in charge of the Trojan assembly and leader of the Trojan army, to the very conclusion of the poem, where we see the entire city of Troy honor him with a splendid and mournful funeral, Hector is repeatedly shown to be celebrated by the Trojans (2.786–808, 2.816–818, 24.692–804).[18] His wife professes her love for him, as she pleads with him to fight less boldly: "Hector, thus you are father to me and honored mother and brother, and you it is who are also my flourishing husband. Come now, take pity upon me, and stay here on the rampart" (6.429–431). Even the handmaidens of his household "wailed for Hector in his home, even though he was still alive, for they said to themselves that he would no longer come back from the war, escaping the furious spirit and the hands of the Achaians" (6.500–502). Later, when Achilles returns to the war, Hector's father and mother beg their "beloved son" to withdraw into the city walls (22.35, 22.38, 22.84, 22.90). When Achilles slays Hector, fastens his corpse to a chariot, and drags it before the walls of Troy, his mother and wife are overcome with grief: "his beloved father cried out piteously, and around him his people, throughout the town, were taken with wailing and crying" (22.405–409, 22.462–474). His father calls him "the best ... child" and goes so far as to say to his other, surviving sons, "Would that all of you had been slain instead of Hector ... who was a god among men" (24.242, 24.253–258). At his funeral, his mother calls him "dearest by far in my spirit of all my children" (24.747). Helen calls him "dearest by far in my spirit of all my brothers-in-law" (24.762). The whole city mourns for him at his death. So great is the love of the Trojans for their defender.

Hector, then, would seem to be the most obviously admirable hero of the *Iliad*. By the standard of sheer might, Achilles is his superior; but by the standard of right, that is, by the standard of duty and loyalty to one's people and one's family, and also by the standard of compassion and tenderness, Hector appears far superior.[19] In our society, perhaps in any society, it is to

[18] The fact that Hector dismisses the assembly without consulting his father suggests that, on this occasion at least, he is in charge of the assembly. See 2.807–808.

[19] Clay contends that "we may admire Achilles, but Hector wins our hearts" (2010, 48). Redfield maintains that, in contrast with Achilles, Hector "has placed his life at the service of others" (1975, 28). Consider Schein's identification of Hector with "duty" and his claim that "Hector is represented as quintessentially social and human, while Achilles is inhumanly isolated and daemonic in his greatness" (1984, 178, 180). See also Schadewaldt 1997a, 133. For the claim that Hector is gentle, consider Griffin 1980, 68.

loyal and dutiful citizens like Hector that all honors go.[20] Why, then, would Homer encourage us to admire the selfish and disloyal Achilles rather than the dutiful and loyal Hector?[21]

THE CASE AGAINST HECTOR, PART I: THE PROBLEM OF LOYALTY

On the surface of the poem, Hector appears, especially in contrast with Achilles, as duty incarnate: a noble, loving, selfless warrior who fights to defend his people and his loved ones. Yet, as we study the poem more carefully, we are led to reconsider this initial impression. For even though Hector is widely praised in the *Iliad*, he is also sharply criticized by three prominent characters in the course of the poem: Homer himself, Andromache, and the Trojan warrior Poulydamas, whose criticisms of Hector Homer explicitly endorses (18.249–253, 18.310–313). These criticisms challenge us to rethink and revise our initial, surface impression of the dutiful Hector and therewith of the stark contrast between the selfless and loyal Hector and the self-interested and disloyal Achilles.

The first criticism of Hector in the poem is a terse one that Homer offers in his narrative introduction to Hector's very first speech. When the Trojans march out to fight the advancing Achaians and Hector sees Paris draw back from doing battle with Menelaus, whom he cuckolded, Hector indignantly denounces the injustice and cowardice of his adulterous brother, "evil Paris" (3.39). Now, given the fact that Paris is indeed guilty of adultery and, here, of cowardice, this denunciation would seem to be altogether just. Indeed, Paris himself agrees with the denunciation his brother makes of him, as one that is "duly" and "not unduly" made (3.59). Yet, Homer calls Hector's words here "base" (αἰσχροῖς): "But Hector saw him and reproached him with base words" (3.38). He thereby suggests that Hector's rebuke is selfish and cowardly as, for example, in the judgment of Agamemnon and Odysseus, it would be "base"

[20] According to Redfield, Hector "embodies the ideal norm of Homeric society" (1975, 119).

[21] Dante, for example, places Hector among the virtuous non-Christians in the First Circle of Hell, along with Homer, but Achilles among the lustful in the Second Circle (*Inferno* 4.88, 4.122, 5.65).

and hence selfish and cowardly for the Achaians to abandon their long, hard-fought war against a smaller army (2.119–128, 2.295–298). Indeed, Homer also calls Hector's denunciation of Paris on two other occasions "base" (6.325, 13.768).[22] Why does the poet sharply criticize Hector for his reasonable denunciation of his seemingly indefensible brother?[23]

To understand Homer's criticism of Hector here, let us consider the context of Hector's denunciation of Paris. Hector issues his denunciation of his brother in the ninth year of the Trojan War. In that denunciation, Hector tells Paris that he has caused "great sorrow to your father and your people" by stealing Helen from Menelaus and thereby provoking the Achaian attack on Troy (3.38-51; see also 6.327–331). He also severely rebukes the Trojans for not having punished Paris by executing him (3.56–57). Yet the question naturally arises, why is it that the Trojans have not put an end to the sorrowful war, not merely by punishing Paris, but also by handing Helen back to the Achaians? Hector implies that the Trojans have not done so for the same reason that they have not punished Paris for causing the war: because they are "frightened" (δειδήμονες – 3.56). But why has Hector, the noble defender of Troy, not rallied his people to overcome their cowardice and save their city from great sorrow? As we have seen at the end of Book II, Hector is the son of the Trojan king, the leader of the Trojans in battle, and also a prominent leader in the Trojan assembly, with the authority to dismiss it. He is both general and champion, fighting among those in the forefront of the army while issuing orders to the rest of the soldiers (11.61–66). When Poulydamas offers advice to "Hector and the other chiefs of the Trojans and their allies," Hector alone decides, on behalf of all, whether or not to follow that advice (12.60–62, 12.80–83). Indeed, throughout the poem, Hector wields unrivalled authority over the Trojans, an authority even greater than

[22] One might argue that the adjective "base" (αἰσχροῖς) here refers to what the speaker is ascribing to the one spoken to, Paris, rather than to the speaker himself, Hector. Yet, on the other occasions in which Homer uses this locution, it seems evident that he means to criticize the speakers, Hector and Priam (6.325, 13.768, 24.238). Perhaps the clearest example is 13.768, where Paris points out the injustice of Hector's rebuke and Hector implicitly admits as much (13.769–788).

[23] Flaumenhaft describes Paris as "every mother's worst nightmare," whereas Hector is "the good brother" (2004, 12, 16; see also 29). For Redfield, Hector is "the worthy son" but Paris "is Priam's most worthless son" (1975, 113). See also Griffin 1980, 8–9, 80; Schein 1984, 22, 24.

that of Agamemnon over the Achaians. While Agamemnon's decisions are repeatedly challenged – not only by Achilles but also by Thersites, Diomedes, Nestor, and Odysseus[24] – Hector's decisions as a leader are only challenged twice, both times by Poulydamas, and on both occasions, he easily makes his decision stand.[25] In response to the first of Poulydamas's challenges, Hector accuses him of cowardice and threatens to have him executed (12.247–250). In response to the second, he confidently declares: "For no one of the Trojans will obey you. I will not let them" (18.296). Why, then, does Hector merely denounce Paris for having caused the war and the Trojans for failing to punish him? Why does he not act on his own words? Why does he not exert his tremendous power and authority to persuade or even command the Trojans to return Helen, end the war, and thereby spare Troy "great sorrow" and destruction? Homer evidently criticizes Hector for basely blaming Paris and the Trojans for the continuation of the miserable war when he has the power to put an end to it himself.

Now, we might defend Hector by pointing out that his authority would appear to be overshadowed by that of King Priam. Indeed, when Hector says that the Trojans do not punish Paris because they are frightened, he must mean that they are frightened of Priam, who is evidently powerful and who evidently uses his power to protect his son Paris (see 7.345–380). Only Priam would seem to have the authority to end the war. However, as we see in Book III, once Paris proposes a truce with the Achaians and a duel with Menelaus to determine the outcome of the war, Hector accepts the proposal and arranges the truce and duel without first consulting Priam. Subsequently, the Trojan soldiers overwhelmingly support the truce and duel and Priam himself agrees to the truce and the duel, albeit with some reservation (3.259–260, 3.304–311). Hector decides as well, on his own, over the opposition of Poulydamas, without apparently ever consulting Priam, to lead a Trojan attack on the Achaian camp and then to keep the Trojan army on the Trojan plain after Achilles has returned to the war (12.210–251, 18.249–350). Finally, before resolving to face Achilles in a final battle, Hector considers

[24] 2.211–242, 9.30–78, 9.92–113, 9.695–709, 14.82–102. See also 1.275–276.

[25] 12.210–251, 18.243–313. The non-Trojan, Lycian leaders Sarpedon and Glaucus do severely rebuke Hector on two occasions for not fighting as hard as he should, but they do not challenge specific decisions he has made (5.470–498, 17.140–187). Consider Flaumenhaft 2004, 4–6.

attempting to end the war by promising, on his own authority, to hand over to the Achaians Helen, all her possessions, and all the wealth that Troy possesses (22.111–122). It is evident, then, that Hector wields considerable independent authority and considerable influence over Priam.[26] The Lycian leader Glaucus goes so far as to tell Hector that the allies of Troy came to her aid, not for the sake of Priam or Paris or the Trojans as a whole, but "for your sake" (16.538–540).

Moreover, as we also learn in Book III and again in Book VII, the leading elders and counselors of the Trojans favor giving Helen back to the Achaians and thereby ending the war (3.146–160, 7.345–353). Idaius, the herald of Priam, whom Homer calls "prudent," suggests that the Trojans as a whole want to return Helen to Menelaus (7.274–278, 7.385–393). Paris must resort to bribery to persuade individual Trojans to oppose returning Helen (11.122–125). Only Priam, it seems, and, of course, Paris, steadfastly refuse to return Helen (see 3.162–165, 7.354–380).[27] It would therefore seem quite possible that, were Hector to urge his father and king to return Helen, he would enjoy strong support from both the Trojan army and the Trojan elders. Yet Hector does not act. He does not support Antenor in his efforts to end the war (7.344–379). He does not even blame Priam for the continuation of the war but confines himself to blaming only Paris and the other Trojans. We must also remember that, even though Hector does gladly support the truce and duel to end the war, it is Paris, not Hector, who proposes the duel and the truce in the first place (3.67–75).[28] For all the time that Hector has been fighting and leading the Trojans, he has evidently never proposed such a way of ending the war. Yet, it would seem to be his duty to act to end the war, since the war has, as he says, caused great sorrow to his people and family and threatens Troy with destruction. Why, then, has Hector, the dutiful warrior, the savior of Troy, not acted to save his city and why does he not act now to save it, by challenging the reckless policy of his king?

This question is all the more powerful if we recall the example of Achilles in Book I. For we must remember that, notwithstanding all the suffering that

[26] See Schein 1984, 171–172. Consider also Flaumenhaft 2004, 7–8.

[27] See Flaumenhaft 2004, 5–6, 14.

[28] I therefore think that Flaumenhaft goes too far in speaking of Paris's "essential passivity" here (2004, 13–14).

Achilles later causes the Achaians, and notwithstanding his apparent self-interestedness, in Book I Achilles single-handedly saves the Achaians from utter disaster. And he does so precisely by challenging the reckless policy of his king. Agamemnon's refusal, in the teeth of opposition from all the Achaians, to return the captured daughter of the priest of Apollo to her father threatens the Achaians with complete destruction at the hands of the wrathful Apollo (1.47–54, 1.380–385). Achilles alone summons the Achaians to an assembly and induces Agamemnon to appease the god by returning the girl to her father (1.53–147). Only Achilles has the courage to challenge Agamemnon's reckless behavior. Even the prophet Calchas, who one would think would trust in divine protection, shrinks from challenging Agamemnon's refusal to return the girl unless Achilles first promises to protect him: "For a king is mightier than a lesser man when he is angry. For even if he should swallow his rage for that day itself, thereafter he holds rancor in his breast until he has brought it to fulfillment" (1.80–83). Achilles alone refuses to obey his king when his king acts foolishly and unjustly. As he later tells Agamemnon: "Then indeed may I be called a coward and of no account, if I were to submit to your every deed, whatever you should say" (1.293). Achilles courageously and dutifully saves the Achaian army from destruction by challenging the folly of his king.[29] Why, then, does the seemingly courageous and dutiful Hector not save Troy by challenging the folly of King Priam?

One significant difference between the two cases is that Priam is not only Hector's king but also his father. On the one hand, it would seem easier for Hector to challenge Priam, since his father evidently loves him and would presumably do him no harm. On the other hand, Hector is evidently reluctant to challenge his father the king because he feels loyalty to his father and also because he identifies his own reputation, indeed his own glory, with that of his father. Hector appears strongly devoted to his father, apparently more devoted than Achilles is to his father. Achilles loves his father and feels compassion for him, but, as we have seen, he also tells the leading Achaians that the death of his father would not be a more grievous blow to him than is

[29] See Whitman 1958, 183–184 and even Redfield 1975, 12–13. Lateiner (2004, 24) argues that Agamemnon's acts at the beginning of the *Iliad* "constitute the paradigm case of *hubris*" in the poem since three-fifths of all appearances of the word in the poem refer to them (1.203, 1.214, 9.368).

the death of his friend Patroclus (19.321–327). Hector, on the other hand, tells his wife that he leads the Trojans in battle to win "great glory for my father and for myself" (6.444–446). Notwithstanding his tender feelings for his wife and child, Hector, by his own words, fights more for his father than for them.

Indeed, as the poem as a whole indicates, Hector feels considerable loyalty to both his father and also his brothers. The Trojan ally Sarpedon complains that Hector has boasted in the past that he, along with his brothers and brothers-in-law, could fight off the Achaians all by himself, without the aid of any other Trojans or Trojan allies (5.471–474). Moreover, while Hector twice rejects the advice of Poulydamas, who is not related to him, he unquestioningly follows the advice of his brother Helenus twice – who says, "obey me, I am your brother" – and of (Athena masquerading as) his brother Deiphobus (6.73–102, 7.44–54, 22.226–247). And even though he sharply criticizes his brother Paris, it clearly pains him to criticize his own flesh and blood. As he says to Paris: "My heart grieves in my spirit, because I hear shameful things about you from the Trojans, who have so much labor because of you" (6.523–525). It would seem that Hector has not seriously attempted to send Helen back to the Achaians, for example, by siding with Antenor against Paris in the Trojan assembly, at least in part out of loyalty to his brother (7.345–379).

In his loyalty to the family, Hector follows the example of his father Priam, who gives the principal leadership of the Trojans to his son Hector; who never sides with Poulydamas, for example, against his son; and who rules, without explanation, in favor of his son Paris in the assembly, over the wise counsel of Antenor (7.345–378).[30] The primacy of family loyalty among King Priam and his sons clearly distinguishes the Trojan ruling class from the Achaian ruling class. To be sure, King Agamemnon has marshaled the massive Achaian expedition against Troy in order to recover the wife of his brother. However, when making important decisions, the king seeks out the advice of Nestor, Idomeneus, Ajax, Odysseus, and Diomedes over that of Menelaus (see, for example, 9.9–173, 10.17–20, 10.53–56, 14.41–134). When Menelaus wishes to duel Hector, Agamemnon denounces the "folly" of his

[30] Schein points out that in the *Iliad*, "familial solidarity and loyalty ... are characteristically Trojan" (1984, 169). Flaumenhaft notes "Priam's unfailing attachment to family" and argues that "his own proud paternity eventually destroys him and his city and all his sons" (2004, 6, 30; see also 13, 24).

brother in seeking to fight a superior man and orders him to sit down among his companions (7.109–119). And when Nestor sharply denounces Menelaus for being lazy and irresponsible, Agamemnon largely agrees (10.114–130). On the other hand, when Priam rebukes his sons, it is only in the name of his other sons, including Hector, who have already died (24.248–261).

Moreover, as becomes evident over the course of the poem, Agamemnon is far less powerful than Priam and his family. Priam and his family dominate Troy politically as his royal family compound – where all his children and their spouses live, apart from the other Trojans – dominates the city physically (6.242–250). Priam automatically commands respect, honor, and obedience. When the Trojan men shed warm tears at the sight of their many fallen on the battlefield, "great Priam did not let them cry out; and in silence they piled the corpses on the pyre, grieving in their heart" (7.425–428). No Trojan or Trojan ally ever even rebukes Priam. Homer does report that Aeneas "was always wrathful toward divine Priam, because he did not honor him at all among his people, even though he was noble" (13.459–461). Achilles speculates that Aeneas hopes to kill him (Achilles) and subsequently "rule among the Trojans, breakers of horses, and over the honor of Priam" (20.179–181). But Achilles insists that his hopes will be dashed, since, even if Aeneas were to kill Achilles, Priam would still remain strong and would always favor his children over Aeneas (20.181–183). At any rate, we never see Aeneas, or anyone else in the Trojan camp, directly challenge Priam, whereas Nestor, Odysseus, Diomedes, and Thersites, not to mention Achilles, severely chastise Agamemnon to his face.[31] Agamemnon proves to be a limited monarch, one who is limited in his power and feels the need to rule together with other rulers. Priam, on the other hand, rules absolutely, together with his son Hector.

Insofar as Hector is especially loyal to his father Priam, it might seem especially difficult for him to challenge his king. Nevertheless, it would seem that both justice and concern for the safety of Troy would require Hector to press for the return of Helen. As Hector admits, Paris is the guilty party who took advantage of his host and stole away his wife, and the subsequent Achaian invasion has caused great woe to the Trojans and their allies and threatens Troy with destruction. Hector's own beloved wife has lost seven brothers and her father in this war, for example (6.414–424). For the good of

[31] See especially 4.349–355, 9.9–64, 9.96–113, 14.64–102, 2.225–242.

his city and for the good of his family, Hector should press his father to end the war by returning Helen. Yet, he does not. Indeed, once the Trojan Pandarus, manipulated by Athena, breaks the truce and almost kills Menelaus, Hector does not even use his tremendous authority to punish Pandarus and maintain the truce that Priam has agreed to. Instead, he does nothing and the Trojans attack the Achaians, at the very least with his acquiescence.[32] Why, then, does Hector not save his city from destruction by opposing the pro-war policy of his father and brother? Does he simply subordinate his concern for the good of his city and family to an ultimately unquestioning loyalty to his father and king? If that were the case, then his condemnation of Paris for causing woe to the Trojans and of the other Trojans for their cowardice in not punishing Paris would itself be cowardly. For while he loudly blames Paris and the Trojans for the war, Hector shrinks from blaming and challenging the one Trojan who persists in continuing the war and protecting Paris: his father and king, Priam.

Hector, in contrast with Achilles, embodies the virtue of loyalty to one's people and one's loved ones. From the first line of the poem, we learn of Achilles' shocking disloyalty; of Achilles' wrath against his own people, the Achaians, who encompass those who are his loved ones; and how he caused tremendous suffering and death among them. We see him quarrel with his king, withdraw from fighting alongside his fellow soldiers, pray to Zeus to punish his people, and reject the entreaties of his friends that he relent. In contrast, Hector is steadfastly loyal to his people and his family. Yet, does his loyalty to his people come into conflict with his duty to benefit his people?

Hector fights for the Trojans, even though he recognizes that the Trojans should not be fighting, that they are in the wrong, that they should not be defending Paris, who is guilty of adultery and deception and abusing the

[32] Shortly after Pandarus wounds Menelaus, the Trojans attack the Achaians (see 4.104–147, 4.220–222). Hector is mentioned only once, briefly (4.505), from just before the duel in Book III (3.314–319) until the middle of Book V, when Sarpedon rebukes him for holding back from the fighting (5.471–493). It is possible that Hector has been reluctant to resume fighting once the truce was broken by the Trojans (consider also 6.526–529). But even if that is the case, he does nothing to restore the truce and, even later, in Book VII, when his brother Helenus urges him to fight a duel with the Achaians, Hector makes it clear that since, as he surmises, the previous truce to end the war was opposed by Zeus, he will only propose a truce and duel to determine who is the greatest individual warrior on the field (7.66–91).

hospitality of Menelaus, but should instead join with the Achaians in punishing Paris and return Helen to her husband. As Hector remarks to Paris, after recounting the chagrin of the Trojans over fighting for his sake, in a cause that is unjust and therefore unworthy of divine support: "But let us go [to battle]. Hereafter we will make amends with the heavenly, everlasting gods, if Zeus ever grant it, setting up to them in our great halls a wine-bowl of freedom after we have driven out of Troy the well-greaved Achaians" (6.526–529). Now, one might argue that Hector here shows the virtue of steadfast devotion, of unconditional loyalty. He defends his country and family even when they are in the wrong. But the question arises, is he truly benefiting his father, his brother, and his people by loyally supporting them and fighting for them here? In the first place, by supporting the war, he is prolonging what he himself acknowledges to be their great sorrow, a sorrow that already includes the deaths of his wife's father and seven brothers, a sorrow that may well culminate with the destruction of Troy (3.39–57, 6.414–424, 6.447–465). Furthermore, by supporting the war, he supports his father, his brother, and his people in what he himself regards as their injustice and cowardice. If Hector were truly to benefit his people and family by saving them from death and destruction and by restoring their noble and just character, would he not have to be willing to quarrel with them? Would he not have to be willing to oppose the self-destructive and unjust pro-war policy of his father and brother and their Trojan supporters, just as Achilles was willing to oppose the self-destructive and unjust refusal of Agamemnon and his supporters to return Chryseis to her father? Indeed, might Hector not have to be willing to oppose the Trojans, even to the point of praying to Zeus that they be punished for their injustice? Hector complains that the Trojans are too cowardly to act justly and save Troy by punishing Paris for his injustice. But, were Hector to act justly and save Troy, would he not have to emulate Achilles in his courageous willingness to oppose his people and his loved ones for their folly and injustice? At first glance, Achilles' anger at his people seems disloyal and therefore unjust. But, insofar as Achilles is angry at the Achaians for their injustice, that is, for supporting the unjust behavior of their king toward the family of Chryses and toward his own subjects, his anger reveals a devotion to justice and a desire that the Achaians live up to the demands of justice.

Hector seems to love the Trojans unconditionally, insofar as he is always loyal to them. Accordingly, although he complains about their cowardice and their injustice, he is never angry with them as a whole. But his loyalty to the Trojans betrays a certain, fundamental indifference to them. For, in his view, even though he believes that they are fighting in an unjust cause and are too cowardly to correct their injustice, he evidently does not expect anything more of them. But how can one truly care for those one thinks so little of that one does not expect them to be anything more than cowardly and unjust? How can one love those who have no lovely qualities?

In this light, paradoxically, the disloyal Achilles reveals himself to be one who, in his way, loves his own people more than the loyal Hector loves his. In the first place, by opposing the foolish and unjust decision of Agamemnon to keep Chryseis from her father, which the Achaians have evidently accepted out of cowardice, Achilles benefits them, not only by saving them from the righteous punishment of Apollo but also by inducing Agamemnon and the Achaians to do what is right and thereby restore their own moral character. But furthermore, when Agamemnon again acts foolishly and unjustly by punishing Achilles – who Nestor points out "is the great bulwark for all the Achaians against evil war" (1.283–284) – and the Achaians again act in a cowardly manner by acquiescing in the outrageous behavior of their king, Achilles again attempts to induce Agamemnon and the Achaians to do what is right, and to honor him as the best of the Achaians, both by punishing them himself by withdrawing from the war and by praying to Zeus to punish them. To be sure, Achilles' concern for the Achaians is not selfless or disinterested. He wants their honor. But he also wants to be worthy of their honor, that is, of their recognition of his virtue. Therefore, he also wants the Achaians to be worthy of giving honor. He wants them to be capable of recognizing his virtue and to be capable of gratitude for his virtuous deeds, and therefore he wants them to be just (9.314–317). Achilles is not content with praise from inferiors, from "those of no account," from men he despises (1.231). He wants genuine honor, a genuine recognition of his excellence from men who are capable of genuinely recognizing excellence. Achilles expects the best of himself and of the Achaians. Therefore, he gets angry with the Achaians when they fall short. He gets angry with the Achaians he loves most of all, but also with Agamemnon and all the rest, even Thersites (2.220). And later he gets angry with himself, bitterly angry, for having sent Patroclus to battle alone (18.98–106; see 18.32–34, 18.231–238). His anger at the Achaians, a harsh and destructive anger, is a sign of his love, his desire that others be good, good for him but also good for themselves.

Hector, on the other hand, never gets angry with the Trojans as a whole or with himself. He never attacks the Trojans as a whole as bitterly as Achilles attacks Agamemnon and the Achaians.[33] He never weeps tears of anger, as Achilles does (1.348–361). But he also never weeps tears of sorrow at the death of a Trojan or even at the prospect of the death of, for example, his father and his wife.[34] Paradoxically, then, the disloyal Achilles would seem to love the Achaians more than the loyal Hector loves the Trojans. The case of Hector suggests that love cannot be unconditional, that it always entails the hope that the beloved will be excellent and noble and worthy of one's love (see 9.613–614). But therefore, love is dependent on the beloved having, and keeping, such qualities.[35] Accordingly, Achilles' anger at the Achaians is a sign of his love, whereas Hector's loyalty to the Trojans, no matter how unjust and cowardly he regards them as being, is ultimately a sign of his indifference to them.

Achilles' anger at the Achaians may well be unjust (see 15.598–599). He may have unreasonably high expectations for them, just as he may have unreasonably high expectations for himself. But Achilles expects the most both from himself and his fellow Achaians. This is a sign that he loves them and that he loves himself.

THE CASE AGAINST HECTOR, PART II: A SELF-INTERESTED LOVER OF GLORY

The most surprising critic of Hector in the poem is his loving wife Andromache. She criticizes him, not for his unquestioning loyalty to the Trojan cause or for his failure to end the war, but for his insistence on fighting the war in a rash and self-destructive way. Andromache weeps with emotion when she sees him, gives a moving account of her love and need for Hector, and later almost dies when she hears of his death (6.404–430,

[33] As we will see, Hector does get angry with the Trojan Poulydamas. But he does so, not as Achilles does with Agamemnon and the Achaians, because they act foolishly and ignobly, but rather because Poulydamas is all too wise in the counsel he gives. See 22.99–103.

[34] According to Lessing, Homer taught "that only the civilised Greek can at the same time weep and be brave, whilst the uncivilised Trojan in order to be so must first stifle all human feeling" (1970, 8). See also Griffin 1995, 44.

[35] Consider Aristotle *Nicomachean Ethics* 1165b13–37.

22.466–474). Yet, precisely because she loves him and needs him so, she criticizes him with singular force, first for pitilessly and recklessly risking his life, and then for pitilessly and recklessly losing it, leaving her and especially their infant son without him, a widow and an orphan, to endure their wretched lot alone (6.406–410, 6.431–439, 22.477–507, 24.725–745).[36]

When Hector returns from the battlefield in Book VI to instruct his mother that the Trojan women should make an offering to Athena, he takes the opportunity to seek out his wife. This is an extraordinarily moving scene, the only scene in the poem between the couple, a singular portrait of a loving family – of a father kissing and playing with his infant son, of a wife and husband in tender conversation – in the midst of the fury of war. Yet, the scene consists primarily of Andromache's critique of her husband and Hector's attempt to defend himself.

Andromache begins by accusing Hector of foolishness with respect to himself and heartlessness with respect to his wife and child: "Daemonic one, your furious spirit will destroy you, nor do you take pity on your child, an infant, nor on me, an ill-fated one, who will soon be your widow. For soon the Achaians will kill you, all rushing upon you" (6.406–410). Andromache, who – unlike the more domestic Helen and Hecubae (3.125–128, 3.383–385, 6.242–252, 6.313–324, 6.369–380) – has been observing the fighting from the great rampart of Troy, criticizes not only Hector's individual conduct in battle but also his overall military strategy (6.372–373, 6.386–389). By fighting on the Trojan plain, away from the mighty walls of Troy, he ensures that he will soon be killed by the Achaians. In this way, he is needlessly throwing away his life and acting pitilessly toward her. For, since she has just lost her parents and her seven brothers during the recent Achaian attack on Thebe (the residence also of Chryseis), her husband's death will destroy all possibility of happiness for her: "there will no longer be any other warmth" for her "but only grief" (6.411–430; see 1.366–369). Andromache does not suggest here that Hector is selfish or cowardly but rather that he is carried away by a frenzied, spirited passion for fighting the Achaians. By allowing his "furious spirit [μένος]" to drive his actions and overpower both his reason and his pity, Hector is foolishly sacrificing his own life and thoughtlessly ruining the

36 I therefore cannot entirely agree with the suggestion of Felson and Slatkin that "with the exception of Hecuba in Book 24, there are no angry, *active* women in the *Iliad*" (2004, 98 – emphasis added).

happiness of his wife and also of his child, who will, if he lives, suffer the wretched life of an orphan (see 22.482–507, 24.732–738).

But furthermore, Andromache argues, Hector is foolishly and pitilessly harming Troy as well. For there is, she claims, a part of the wall that is especially vulnerable to attack, which the Achaians have attacked three times, and which is evidently insufficiently defended (6.431–437). Insofar as his fury leads him to attack the Achaians with reckless aggression, while leaving Troy dangerously vulnerable to attack, his fury is leading him to neglect his duty to protect Troy. Andromache urges Hector instead to move the Trojan army to a more defensive posture, to defend the Trojan walls where they are most vulnerable, and to direct the Trojan efforts from within Troy, standing on the rampart. In this way, by adopting a fundamentally defensive strategy, Hector can effectively fulfill his duty to defend his city, avoid certain death, and thereby avoid making his son an orphan and his wife a widow.

Now, one might be tempted to dismiss Andromache's criticism as the understandable outburst of a distraught and frightened young wife and mother.[37] Hector himself suggests that Andromache, being a woman, understands nothing of war and that, like his mother or Helen, she should leave the fighting and also the strategy to him and confine herself to domestic, womanly concerns, "the loom and the distaff" (6.490–493). Yet, the poem as a whole indicates that the general, defensive strategy Andromache argues for here is indeed the soundest strategy for Troy.[38] In the first place, it is the

[37] Schadewaldt insists that Andromache here is simply "the loving wife" who "speaks from an archetypal calling as a wife, nurturer and preserver of life," who suffers from a "loving lack of understanding" of military matters, and who unreasonably "presumes to dictate to him [Hector] a strategy for defence" (1997a, 133–134). According to Redfield, "Andromache is the faithful wife who completes and motivates the hero" and characterizes her advice here as "mere woman's words" (1975, 122, 152). Griffin goes so far as to suggest that Andromache does not truly wish Hector to follow her advice: "we see from Helen's contempt for Paris and Andromache's love for Hector that what a woman really wants in a man is the strength to resist her and go out among the flying spears" (1980, 6–7; see also 65, 92). Schein argues – apparently overlooking the example of Helen, who left her husband, daughter, brothers, and other relatives to follow Paris (3.172–175, 3.233–242) – that Andromache argues for a more cautious strategy in Book VI simply because "Andromache, like *all* women in the poem, has a primary loyalty to her immediate family" (1984, 173–174 – emphasis added).

[38] Crotty notes that "Andromache . . . presents Hector with a sensible plan to preserve his life and keep Troy safe" (1994, 29). He later speaks of her "sound military strategy" and "the sageness of her advice" (50). See also Clarke 2004, 84.

very strategy that Troy has pursued during all the preceding years of the war against the numerically superior Achaian army (2.119–130, 8.53–57).[39] As Hera, in the guise of Stentor, says to the Achaians: "So long as divine Achilles was joining in the war, the Trojans never would go beyond the Dardanian gates, for they dreaded the mighty spear of that man. But now they battle far from their city, by the hollow ships" (5.787–791; see also 13.94–110, 16.64–73). Hector later complains to his soldiers that the Trojan elders have supported this defensive strategy throughout the war: the Achaian ships "came here against the will of the gods and inflicted much woe upon us, through the evil of the elders, who did not heed me and restrained the army from fighting beside the grounded ships, even though I wished to do so" (15.720–723). But while Troy has suffered economically during the nine years it has pursued this strategy, as Hector also points out, it has also succeeded in thwarting the Achaians so effectively that, as we see in Book II, the war-weary Achaians long to go home (18.287–292, 2.142–156; see also 15.719–723). Indeed, when Hector first boldly decides to let the Trojan army set up camp and besiege the Achaian army, far from the walls of Troy, he himself takes care, in an apparent nod to his cautious wife, to leave a strong guard of youths and elders on the ramparts of the city "lest an ambush enter the city while the soldiers are away" (8.517–522).

Furthermore, the strategy Andromache advocates is the very strategy that Hector's other critic, the "prudent Poulydamas," argues for, especially once Achilles returns to the war (18.249; see also 12.210–229, 13.723–747). For he urges the Trojans to withdraw from the plain into their city, take their stations along the walls and on their towers, and thereby defend the city (18.254–283). Otherwise, he warns, Achilles will slaughter them and "dogs and vultures will devour many of the Trojans" (18.271–272). And Homer himself calls the Trojans "fools" for rejecting this strategy (18.310–313). When Poulydamas's warnings are horribly vindicated, and Achilles slaughters vast numbers of Trojans on the Trojan plain, Hector himself acknowledges that his own rejection of a defensive strategy was foolish: "through my own recklessness I destroyed my people" (22. 99–104).[40] As the rest of the

[39] Consider Clay 2010, 105.

[40] Redfield nevertheless insists, "Polydamas is right and Hector is wrong, but we are on Hector's side" (1975, 146).

poem demonstrates, then, the cautious strategy Andromache urges her husband to adopt is a sound one.

One might offer a qualified defense of Hector by arguing that, even though it is clearly a mistake for the Trojans to continue to fight aggressively once Achilles returns to battle, as Poulydamas argues, it is reasonable for Hector to fight aggressively and attempt to destroy or drive out the Achaians, once and for all, while Achilles remains away from the battle. After all, the Trojans are so successful in their attacks that a despairing, weeping Agamemnon twice calls on the Achaians to flee Troy altogether and return to their homeland and only reverses himself thanks to the spirited Diomedes and Odysseus (9.13–51, 14.64–134; see also 8:212–246). Moreover, just before Patroclus leads the Myrmidons back into battle, Hector and the Trojans do come agonizingly close to setting the Achaian ships on fire and destroying them: "This was in the mind of those fighting: the Achaians said to themselves that they would not escape from the evil, but the spirit in the breast of each of the Trojans was hoping to set fire to the ships and kill the Achaian heroes" (15.699–702). Therefore, one might argue, Hector is right to reject the defensive strategy Andromache proposes at the time – when Achilles is not fighting – that she proposes it and to seize the golden opportunity afforded by his absence to eliminate the Achaian threat to Troy once and for all.[41]

A defender of Andromache might point out, however, that by attacking the Achaians aggressively, Hector inevitably runs the risk of provoking what eventually happens: Achilles' return to the war. It is important to note that, even before Achilles returns to the war, Poulydamas too argues against attacking the Achaians aggressively, smashing down the walls of their camp, and attempting to destroy them beside their ships. Prompted by what seems to be an omen from Zeus, he argues that, by putting the Achaians into a position in which they must fight or be annihilated, the Trojans will embolden the Achaians to fight to the death, will consequently suffer huge losses themselves, and may well provoke Achilles to return to battle (12.211–227, 13.740–747). Inasmuch as the Trojans have succeeded in holding off the Achaians for nine years, and inasmuch as war weariness and homesickness have been evidently growing in the Achaian camp, how can it be reasonable for Hector and the Trojans to abandon their hitherto

[41] Consider Redfield 1975, 152–153.

successful, patient, defensive, Fabian strategy and risk everything on a new, aggressive fight to the finish?

We would naturally expect Hector to respond to Andromache here by justifying his aggressive strategy against the Achaians on the grounds that he will thereby fulfill his duty to save Troy from the Achaian threat. After all, he has just proclaimed to Helen his eagerness to return to the battlefield to defend the Trojans (6.361–362). We would therefore expect Hector to defend himself from the charge of folly and heartlessness by invoking his desire and his duty to defend his city and his people. Yet, astonishingly, Hector never even attempts to persuade his wife that, by boldly attacking the Achaians, he will successfully defend Troy.

In the first place, Hector argues that his noble upbringing and character require him to fight aggressively against the Achaians:

> All these things concern me, woman. But I would quite dreadfully feel shame before the Trojans, and the Trojan women with trailing robes, if, like an evil one, I should shrink aside from the war, nor does my spirit bid me, since I have learned to be noble always and to fight among the first of the Trojans, winning great glory for my father and for myself. (6.440–446)

Hector here simply identifies nobility with boldness. He draws no distinction between a valor that is guided by discretion – and that might entail retreat – and rashness. In a similar vein, later on, when speaking of Diomedes, he remarks: "Tomorrow, he will know his own virtue, if he can withstand my advancing spear" (8.535–536). A noble and virtuous man, Hector evidently believes, may never withdraw. Accordingly, he rejects retreating into the safety of Troy's walls because it is always ignoble to retreat and it is always noble to attack.

At first glance, Hector might seem to suggest that, by fighting so boldly, he is virtually sacrificing his life and acting selflessly for the benefit of his people. Yet, if we examine his words carefully, we see that Hector does not claim here at all that he will benefit Troy by fighting boldly. He does not even claim that he intends to benefit his city by fighting in this way. The only specific reasons Hector gives here for fighting boldly are that he will thereby avoid incurring a shameful reputation for himself, and will win glory for himself, and for his father.[42] But insofar as he admittedly acts here solely out a

[42] I consequently must disagree with Schadewaldt's identification of Hector's self-interested concern for honor here, which Hector mentions, with duty, which he does not mention or refer to here (1997a, 134–135).

concern for his reputation and that of his father, in what sense is his behavior here truly noble? Is it not, rather, self-interested? Indeed, insofar as he is recklessly endangering his people by fighting boldly – either by leaving them vulnerable to attack or, more simply, by exposing himself, their chief defender, to death – is he not ruthlessly sacrificing the good of Troy to that of himself and his father?

Hector implicitly addresses this objection in the remainder of his speech to his wife. In a stunning admission, Hector, the "guardian" of his city, the protector of Troy (24.729), confides to Andromache that Troy will inevitably lose the war:

> For I myself know this well in my mind and in my spirit. The day will come when sacred Ilion, both Priam and the people of Priam of the good ash spear, will perish. But it is not so much the pain hereafter of the Trojans that concerns me, nor of Hecubae, nor of Lord Priam, nor of my brothers who, many and noble, shall fall in the dust at the hands of men who are enemies, so much as your pain, when someone of the Achaians, bronze-tunicked, should lead you off as you shed tears, robbing you of your day of freedom. And when you are in Argos you must weave at the loom of another woman, and carry water from the spring Messeis or Hypereia, and do many things unwillingly, but a strong necessity will lie upon you. And someone, someday, will say, seeing you shed tears: "This is the wife of Hector, he who was the best fighter of the Trojans, breakers of horses, when they fought around Ilion." So someone someday will speak. And for you it will be a new source of pain, to be bereaved of such a man who could ward off the day of your slavery. But may the heaped up earth cover me, being dead, before I hear your cry and your being dragged away. (6.447–465)

Hector here defends himself from the charge that he is recklessly endangering his people and family by pleading impotence. He is powerless, he reveals, to save Troy. No strategy will save Troy from destruction at the hands of the Achaians. His brothers and, presumably, his parents and son, will inevitably be killed, and his wife will inevitably suffer all the horrors a female captive and slave is bound to suffer. Therefore, Hector is not rashly throwing away his life; circumstances have already doomed him to death. He is not acting pitilessly toward Andromache and Astyanax; forces, pitiless forces, beyond his control are sealing their fate. He is not acting irresponsibly or shirking his duty to defend his city and family here, for it is simply beyond his power to fulfill his duty in the situation he finds himself in. Hector does not specifically speak of fate or the gods here, but he suggests that the situation Troy faces is simply hopeless, and nothing he can do will affect the outcome of the war in any way whatsoever.

But why, then, does Hector continue to fight at all? Why not withdraw from the battlefield and spend the precious little time he has with his wife and child, as, for example, Paris, in his way, cherishes his moments with Helen (3.433–448)?[43] Why does Hector worry so about unnerving his spirit and forgetting his strength in battle, as he has just told his mother, if he is powerless to defeat the Achaians (6.264–265)? Why does his spirit rush him to the battlefield, as he has just told Helen, if he has no hope of successfully defending the Trojans (6.359–362)?

Hector gives two reasons here for continuing to fight. First, he says that he fights to win glory for himself and his father. Even though Troy is bound to fall and he and his father are bound to die, Hector can win glory for them both – a glory that will outlast the fall of Troy, a "glory [that] will never perish" as he remarks when he returns to the battlefield (7.91) – as long as he fights boldly, in the front ranks, and never retreats. One might wonder why a bold fighter who knowingly fights for a doomed cause, simply in order to win glory for himself and his father, would *deserve* to win glory. Should not glory go to the dutiful who fight for the sake of others, as Hector at first glance appears to do, rather than to the self-interested? Hector evidently believes that boldness is always rewarded with glory, even boldness in a hopelessly lost cause, while those who retreat, even if doing so is prudent and beneficial to others, are always perceived to be weak and evil by people as a whole. Hence, he condemns Paris for retreating in battle since the Achaians will laugh at him and disdain him as one who is weak-minded and cowardly, and the Trojans themselves will judge him to be a disgrace (3.39–55, 6.521–525). Later, he criticizes the "wickedness" of the Trojan elders (and perhaps, obliquely, his father) for having restrained his boldness (15.719–725). Similarly, he dismisses Andromache's argument here that he should withdraw within the walls of Troy, for the good of his family and his city, since he would feel ashamed if the Trojan men and also "the Trojan women with trailing garments" think him "evil" for retreating (6.440–442). It is not clear that Hector himself believes that it is, in truth, always "disgraceful" and "evil" to withdraw before the enemy. Insofar as Hector believes, as his later remarks

[43] Griffin, in my judgment, overstates "the contrast between the false marriage of Paris and Helen and the true marriage of Hector and Andromache" (1980, 6). Consider also Clay 2010, 35, 41.

to Andromache indicate that he does, that women are, and should be, primarily concerned with household matters rather than war, he would presumably believe that the Trojan women in particular would not be knowledgeable judges of what is or is not bad behavior in war (6.490–493). But Hector evidently cares more about how others judge his behavior than about the intrinsic merit or virtue of his behavior. He evidently cares more about winning honor than about *deserving* to win honor. Accordingly, rather than argue that his boldness truly benefits the city or is truly worthy of admiration, he simply argues that caution and retreat will bring him disgrace, whereas boldness will enable him to win glory for himself and his father. The first reason he gives, then, for continuing to fight in the lost cause of Troy is a self-interested one: to win praise for himself and his father, especially from the men and women of Troy. Even if he is powerless to save Troy, it is still within his power to win glory or suffer disgrace.

The second reason he gives for fighting boldly is his belief that it will be less painful for him to die now than to die later, after Troy has fallen. As he explains at the end of his speech to Andromache, he would rather be dead than endure witnessing the agony of his beloved wife as she is dragged off to slavery. Now, it is true that Hector here expresses grief over the pain that his wife is bound to suffer, a pain that grieves him more than the pain that anyone else will suffer. But it is also true that, by expressing the wish that he die before seeing her suffer, he expresses a wish to spare *himself* the pain of seeing his wife enslaved, rather than a wish that *she* be spared the pain of enslavement. Indeed, as he explains with harsh clarity to his wife here, his seemingly reckless fighting on the Trojan plain is actually based on a calculation of his – but not her – self-interest. For Hector agrees with Andromache that, by fighting so boldly, he is ensuring his death. But he explains that he wants to die soon so as to avoid the pain of seeing his wife suffer, as she surely will.

In the course of defending himself against the charge of Andromache that he is fighting in a reckless and pitiless way, Hector acts rather pitilessly to her. By telling her that Troy is doomed, he dashes any hope she may have for the future, for her husband, her child, or herself. By describing in excruciatingly vivid detail her future plight as a slave, he makes her feel her future pain in the present and consequently deepens her present suffering. Instead of consoling her with false but sweet hopes, instead of lightening her remaining days of freedom in whatever way he can, Hector brutally destroys all her hope. And he does so in order to justify to her, and also to himself, his strategy for acquiring the glory he craves.[44]

Perhaps sensing that he has spoken too harshly, both about the certainty of defeat and about fighting for his glory and that of his father rather than for her and their son, Hector does try to reassure his wife. He offers a prayer for their son that seemingly forgets the dire forecast he has just made and paints instead a hopeful picture of her future:

> Zeus and the other gods, grant that this child of mine come to be, as I am, pre-eminent among the Trojans, good in his might, and that he rule strongly over Ilion. And someday may someone say: "far better is he than his father" as he comes back from war. And may he carry bloody spoils, having killed enemy men, and may his mother be gratified in her mind. (6.476–481)

By expressing love for his son and by conjuring up a picture of the future in which their son is a free man vanquishing his enemies, Hector attempts, it seems, to assure Andromache of his devotion and to offer her hope that Troy will not, after all, be conquered. When she continues to weep, Hector takes pity on her and says: "Daemonic one, do not feel too much grief for me in your spirit. For no man will hurl me into Hades beyond what is destined, and as for fate no man, evil or noble, has escaped it once it has taken its first form" (6.486–489). Here, again, Hector tries at least to qualify, if not take back, his emphatic prediction that Troy will be conquered. But this attempt to comfort his wife seems clumsy and self-contradictory. If he believes, as he claimed before, that the fate of Troy is sealed, he is simply fighting on for the sake of his own glory and that of his father, rather than for the defense of his city and family. But if he believes, as he now suggests, that the fate of Troy is not sealed, is he not, as Andromache argues, actively endangering Troy by fighting so boldly, and thereby sacrificing the good of Troy, and of his wife and child, for the sake of his own glory and that of his father?

We see, then, that the seemingly selfless Hector is, in truth, profoundly self-interested. Rather than fighting to defend his city and family, he is fighting to win glory for himself and for his father and to hasten his own death so as to avoid the pain of seeing his city and family destroyed and enslaved. Yet, his speech here indicates that Hector's overriding motive is not the desire to avoid the pain of seeing his people suffer but his desire to win

[44] I must consequently disagree with Schein's claim that "Andromache . . . is dearer to Hector than anyone in the world" (1984, 174).

glory. For so powerful is his concern for his own glory that even in the midst of imagining the suffering of Andromache as a slave in the future, he cannot help but imagine that her master will identify her as "the wife of Hector, he who was the best fighter of the Trojans" (6.460–461). Even in the midst of grieving in anticipation of his wife's future agony, Hector evidently anticipates the future glory that will be his and to which she will bear witness.

It is true that Hector claims to be fighting for the glory of both his father and himself. In this way, he apparently denies that he is simply or purely self-interested. But the fact that, at the end of his speech to Andromache, Hector imagines his own future fame, without reference to that of his father, suggests that the focus of his ambition is, in truth, his own glory. The rest of the poem confirms this suggestion. Soon after leaving Andromache, when Hector explains to the Achaians that he will permit them to bury the warrior he intends to vanquish in a duel, he declares: "And some day someone of the human beings to come will say, as he sails in a many-oared ship on the wine-dark sea: 'This is the mound of a man who died long ago, who was the best, but whom splendid Hector once slew.' So some day someone will say. And *my* glory will never perish" (7.87–91, emphasis added). On the following day, Hector issues a heartfelt prayer: "If only I were immortal and ageless for all my days and were honored as Athena and Apollo are honored, as surely as the coming day bears evil for the Argives" (8.538–541). Finally, when deliberating whether or not to fight Achilles on the Trojan plain or withdraw into the safety of the Trojan walls, Hector simply ignores the heart-rending pleas of his father and bases his decision exclusively on his desire to win glory for himself and to avoid disgrace (22.33–130). We see, then, that, insofar as he puts his own well-being above the well-being of his loved ones, the seemingly dutiful Hector is no less self-interested than Achilles.

One might defend Hector by arguing that his self-interestedness is less consequential than that of Achilles since the Trojan cause is hopeless. Achilles' withdrawal causes many Achaian deaths. But, as Hector claims to Andromache, Troy will lose the war and hence suffer many deaths whether or not he fights boldly. Therefore, even though he fights boldly in order to win glory, he is not sacrificing the good of Troy for the sake of his glory. But what are the grounds for Hector's claim that Troy will inevitably lose the war? The audience, having heard Hera and Zeus apparently resolve to destroy Troy eventually, may be inclined to think that Hector somehow knows from the gods that Troy is living under a death sentence (4.20–64). Hector, however, never claims that he knows from the gods that Troy is doomed to lose.

Furthermore, it is not altogether clear that the gods are unalterably bent on destroying Troy. Apollo, Artemis, and Ares support Troy in this war, and Zeus himself considers saving Hector, and therewith Troy, just before his death (22.167–185). Homer himself presents the war as one in which human actions play an important, if not always a decisive, role. As we have seen, the war would apparently have come to an end with the flight of the Achaians from Troy had Odysseus not successfully induced them to stay (2.142–210). The war almost comes to a peaceful end as a result of the truce proposed by Paris and the duel between Paris and Menelaus (3.373). Even after the gods wreck the truce, the war might still have ended peacefully had Priam sided with Antenor and agreed to give back Helen (7.345–420). Troy might have avoided destruction if Hector had not rejected Poulydamas's "noble . . . plan" to withdraw from the Trojan plains into Troy once Achilles had returned (18.313). For while Homer says that Athena intervenes to thwart Poulydamas's efforts to persuade the Trojans to follow a defensive strategy, Homer never says that the gods induce Hector to follow a bold strategy or, for that matter, that the gods induce Hector to face Achilles (18.310–313, 22.90–135). Homer suggests, then, that Hector has a free choice whether or not to fight boldly.

Indeed, Hector himself never repeats the claim that he makes to Andromache that Troy is bound to be conquered, but instead he repeatedly speaks as though Troy might win the war. Immediately after speaking to his wife, Hector tells Paris that they will make an offering to the gods "after we have driven out of Troy the well-greaved Achaians" (6.526–529). Moments later, on the battlefield, Hector tells the Achaians that Zeus "considering evil things decrees them for both sides, until that day when you seize well-towered Troy or you yourselves are broken beside your seafaring ships" (7.70–72). Subsequently, Hector tells the Trojans to destroy the Achaian ships, to defend their city and families by driving off the Achaians, and hence to save Troy from destruction (12.440–441, 15.494–499, 15.557–558; see 13.39–43, 16.860–861, but also 13.772–773). Finally, Hector himself, just before his death, claims responsibility for having destroyed the Trojan army and therewith, it would seem, Troy itself (22.99–107). Therefore, it seems that Hector's claim to Andromache that Troy is doomed no matter how boldly or cautiously he fights is both an unwarranted claim and one that he himself makes only this once.

Why, then, does Hector declare so emphatically to his wife that Troy is bound to lose the war? It would seem that he does so to avoid having to admit, to his wife and also perhaps to himself, that he is willing to sacrifice the good of Troy for his own good, in his quest for glory. Hector evidently longs to fight boldly because he thinks that boldness is the path to glory. Andromache, however, is the only character in the poem who specifically accuses Hector of selfishness. Whereas Poulydamas will later stress that Hector is acting recklessly by fighting so boldly, Andromache emphasizes that Hector is pitilessly and therefore selfishly endangering his city and family by fighting so boldly. Andromache thereby challenges not only the prudence but above all the dutifulness and nobility of her husband. Now, rather than admit, to her and to himself, that he may well be endangering the well-being of his city and family for the sake of his glory, rather than attempt to justify placing his own good above the good of Troy, Hector simply insists that Troy is bound to lose, no matter how he fights. In this way, his defeatism gives him license to pursue his self-interest. For, since Troy is doomed anyway, he does no harm to it by pursuing his own glory. But Hector merely asserts here that Troy is doomed. He does not attempt to justify his defeatism, and he therefore does not attempt to justify his self-interestedness, either to his wife or himself. He simply evades the moral challenge of his wife and returns to war. Hector's response to Andromache indicates both that he cares more about his own good than the good of his city and family and that he lacks the courage to acknowledge to others, but also to himself, that he is so self-interested.

Hector's response to Andromache stands in contrast with Achilles' response to his friends when they criticize him for refusing to help the Achaians. Like Andromache, Achilles' friends accuse him of acting pitilessly and selfishly toward his loved ones and his people. However, unlike Hector, Achilles acknowledges the truth of this charge but then attempts to justify, in some measure, placing his own good above the good of the Achaians:

> I do not think that the son of Atreus, Agamemnon, will persuade me, nor that the rest of the Danaans will do so, since there was no gratitude for fighting unceasingly, always, against enemy men. There is an equal portion for the one who stays back and if someone fights hard. The evil and the noble one are held in single honor. He still goes down to death, the man who has done no deeds, and the one who has done many. Nothing more is laid up for me, once I suffered pains in my spirit, always risking my life (or soul) by making war. (9.315–322)

Why, Achilles, asks, should he sacrifice his very self, his very soul, for the sake of an ungrateful, unjust people? Why should he seek honor from an unjust people who either cannot or will not bestow honor on those noble human beings who deserve it? And what is the value of honor in any case, in the light of the death that we human beings must all suffer? Why should he not rather seek his own fulfillment, not only instead of the good of the Achaians, but also apart from and independently of honor from the Achaians?[45] Achilles' honest acknowledgment that he is self-interested[46] and his forthright defense of his self-interestedness lead him to consider, at least, what his genuine interest may consist of and whether, for example, it lies in receiving honor from human beings he looks down on. As we will see, Achilles fluctuates greatly and painfully in his reflections concerning his self-interest. But he does raise and wrestle with the question of whether one should devote oneself to others rather than to oneself and whether human happiness lies in winning glory or not.

Hector's refusal to acknowledge that he is self-interested prevents him from even asking what his true self-interest might consist of. Instead, he simply and, it seems, thoughtlessly identifies his true self-interest with glory, imperishable and universal glory, even if it comes from those who are unjust and ignorant, and even if he must die in order to win such glory. His primary concern is always what the Trojan men, the Trojan women, and human beings as a whole, will say about him, whether they will think him disgraceful or noble. For Hector, the greatest joy imaginable is, quite simply, praise from other human beings. Honor is not primarily for Hector, as it is, for example, for Sarpedon, a means to live on after he dies. Sarpedon explains to his friend Glaucus:

> Dear one, if indeed we two, escaping this war, would be able to live forever, ageless and immortal, I myself would not fight among the first nor would I send you into battle where men win glory. But now, since countless spirits of death stand about us, which it is not possible for a mortal to escape or avoid, let us go, so that we may offer to another a cause for boasting, or do so to ourselves. (12.322–325)

[45] This speech calls into question Clarke's suggestion that until the death of Patroclus, Achilles is simply driven by a "socially determined need for honour" (2004, 82). For Achilles' questioning of honor, consider Griffin 1980, 99–100; Schein 1984, 71, 105; Zanker 1994, 87–88; Burns 1996, 293.

[46] Redfield goes so far as to attribute to Achilles an "absolute incapacity for illusion" (1975, 28).

Sarpedon suggests that, if he were an immortal being, he would find happiness in some other, peaceful and inconspicuous, activity. But since he is mortal, he will seek his happiness in fighting boldly and winning a glory that will enable him to live on, if only in the memory of others, after he dies. Now, Hector too expresses a wish for imperishable glory (7.87–91). But he makes it clear that he would crave such glory even and especially if he were immortal. For twice Hector expresses the wish that he were immortal *and* that he enjoyed honor as a god forever: "If only I were immortal and ageless for all my days and were honored as Athena and Apollo are honored" (8.538–541, 13.825–827).[47] Universal and eternal praise, then, is what he identifies as his self-interest. His goal is honor for himself; he is not concerned with whether he is worthy of honor or whether those giving honor are worthy of giving it.

Like Hector, Achilles wishes to be honored by his fellows. But Achilles, in the first place, understands honor as being valuable only insofar as it is recognition of genuine excellence or as a form of gratitude (9.314–317). Therefore, Achilles does not concern himself primarily with receiving honor from the Achaians but with being worthy of that honor, with being the noblest and best of the Achaians. And when the Achaians do not honor him, Achilles does not simply calculate how he might recover their honor. Instead, he accuses them of ingratitude and injustice and wonders whether their honor, or the honor of any human being, is worth having at all. In this way, however self-interested Achilles proves to be, his self-concern is combined with, and elevated by, a determination to ponder how he might truly fulfill and satisfy himself.[48]

Hector takes it for granted that the path to the greatest honor is fighting boldly and bravely. To win the greatest honor, one must be the best human being, and to be the best human being, one must be the best warrior. When he pictures his wife in slavery, he imagines that someone in the future will say: "This is the wife of Hector, he who was the best fighter of the Trojans, breakers of horses, when they fought around Ilion" (6.460–461). When he

[47] I therefore think that Clarke goes too far in suggesting that "The Homeric warrior" as such seeks "honour in the eyes of other men" in the belief that "fame . . . is a kind of surrogate immortality" (2004, 77–78). That is true of Sarpedon but not Hector. See Benardete 2005, 64–65.

[48] In the words of Griffin, "The deepest reflections on that central theme [namely, what it is to be human] are reserved for the greatest hero, Achilles, in Book 9 and Book 24" (1995, 45).

imagines the grave of a warrior he has slain, he imagines that someone in the future will say, "illustrious Hector slew him," and therefore, Hector concludes, "my glory will never perish" (7.89–91). When he prays to Zeus and all the other gods that in the future someone will say of his son that he was a "far better" man than his father, Hector simply assumes that the best human being must be the best fighter (6.479–481). This is why Hector is always a warrior, even when he is away from the battlefield with his loved ones. He does not take off his armor "spattered with gore and blood," even when he is with his mother Hecubae, the beautiful Helen, or his beloved wife Andromache, and he does not initially take off his frightening helmet even when he is playing with his baby son (6.264–268, 6.466–470). Just as he never questions his identification of his self-interest with the possession of glory, so he never questions his identification of the greatest human being with the greatest warrior.

In contrast, although Achilles is the greatest warrior, he seeks to be, and is, much more than a warrior. He seeks to be "the best of the Achaians," and, for him, that means defending the Achaians from the might of Hector but also defending them from the folly of Agamemnon (1.243–244, 1.165–166, 1.53–129, 1.366–386). Indeed, Achilles' first actions in the poem – saving the Achaian army by summoning the Achaians to an assembly and inducing the Achaian king to return Chryseis to her father – are not acts of battlefield courage but acts of statesmanship and political courage. Similarly, the last actions of Achilles in the poem – returning the corpse of Hector to his father, the king of Troy, and granting the Trojans a twelve-day truce to celebrate the funeral of Hector – are not acts of war but acts of compassion. As his example shows, to be the best of the Achaians entails at times fighting the Trojans but also at times quarreling with the Achaians and showing mercy to the Trojans. In his eyes, the greatest virtue, therefore, encompasses prudence or wisdom, justice, compassion, and political courage, as well as battlefield courage (consider 1.342–344).[49] It is, accordingly, not surprising that, when his beloved companions go to his camp, they find Achilles, together with his beloved companion Patroclus, "delighting his mind with his lyre" (9.186), since "he was delighting his spirit, and he was singing of the

[49] Consider also Idomeneus's account of the importance of thoughtfulness in virtue (13.275–288). Consider as well Achilles' allusions to the manifold character of virtue (22.268–269, 23.276–278).

glories of men" (9.189). For, in contrast to Hector, who vilifies Paris for playing the lyre (3.53–54),[50] and indeed in contrast to every other warrior in the poem, Achilles not only takes pleasure in the beauty of song but also feels a need to think about which deeds win men glory, what makes those deeds worthy of glory, and whether such deeds truly fulfill those who accomplish them (see 9.314–327, 9.401–409).[51] Achilles is the only character in the poem who evidently loves music and poetry and who evidently feels the need for instruction from the man who composes them.[52] In these ways, Achilles demonstrates his singular kinship with the singer Homer himself.[53]

THE CASE AGAINST HECTOR, PART III: A RECKLESS DEFENDER OF HIS PEOPLE

Poulydamas, the most vehement critic of Hector in the poem, criticizes Hector, not primarily for his lack of compassion or concern for others, but rather for his recklessness. On four occasions, he opposes, with varying degrees of success, the rash strategy that Hector is pursuing. First, he successfully urges the "bold Hector" and the Trojans to stop "senselessly" trying to drive their horses over the ditch in front of the wall protecting the Achaian ships, lest the Achaians launch a devastating counterattack, and to attack instead on foot (12.60–80). Then, he unsuccessfully tries to persuade the "bold Hector" to withdraw the army from fighting the Achaians by their ships, lest the Achaians, driven by desperation to fight fiercely, slaughter "many" Trojans and drive them back (12.216–250). Third, Poulydamas urges the "bold Hector" to gather together the Trojan forces that have been scattered by their attack on the Achaian ships and to deliberate with them

[50] Benardete suggests that Achilles "is a mixture . . . of Paris and Hector" (2005, 49).

[51] According to Plutarch, Alexander the Great, who loved the *Iliad*, believed it to be a portable treasure of "military virtue," and slept with it under his pillow, especially admired Achilles for singing of the glorious deeds of good men (*Alexander* 15.4–5; see also 8.1–2, 26.1–2).

[52] Griffin notes regarding Achilles, "His speech is unique for its full flood of images and similes" (1980, 75; see also Edwards 1991, 39). On Achilles' greatness as a speaker, see also Griffin 1995, 17; 2004, 60, 62; Schein 1984, 90.

[53] Crotty suggests as well that "The sense of pity that Achilles attains at the close of the *Iliad* has imbued the poem from its very beginning . . . Achilles expresses a sympathy like that of the poet" (1994, 98–99).

whether or not to continue their attack or withdraw back to Troy, lest they provoke Achilles to return to the war: "For I myself am afraid lest the Achaians exact payment for their debt of yesterday, since by their ships remains a man insatiable for war, who, I suppose, will no longer hold himself from the war" (13.725, 13.735–747). On this occasion, Poulydamas does persuade Hector to assemble the Trojans but fails to persuade him to withdraw to Troy (13.748–757, 13.789–805). Finally, once Achilles does return to the war, Poulydamas attempts, unsuccessfully, to convince the Trojans to reject Hector's bold strategy and withdraw into Troy:

> But now I dreadfully fear the swift-footed son of Peleus. The spirit of that man is so extremely violent that he will not wish to remain in the plain, where both the Trojans and the Achaians divide between them the furious spirit of Ares, but he will be fighting for our city and our women. But let us go to the town! Be persuaded! For thus it will be . . . But if he should overtake us here tomorrow, and attack us with his arms, a man will know him well. For gladly will the one who escapes him come back to sacred Ilion. But dogs and vultures will eat many of the Trojans. (18.261–272)

On each occasion, as Homer stresses, Poulydamas opposes the "bold Hector" for attacking the Achaians passionately and fearlessly, without thinking ahead, without considering the potentially catastrophic consequences of his actions for his army and his people, and above all, without giving due weight to the limits of his power. Poulydamas stresses twice that he fears Achilles and that it is reasonable to fear him, since he is quite simply mightier than the Trojans, including Hector. And since it is reasonable to fear those who are more powerful than you, it is reasonable to retreat to safety to avoid being destroyed by them. Poulydamas does not argue for abandoning the war against the Achaians. He himself fights vigorously and spiritedly, especially when Hector is incapacitated (14.418–474). Poulydamas emphasizes his own martial passions to Hector and the Trojans: "I would wish that this would immediately come to pass, that the Achaians be destroyed here, nameless and, far from Argos" and that, before Achilles returned, "I was rejoicing at sleeping next to their swift ships and was hoping to seize their curved ships" (12.69–70, 18.259–260). But, he indicates, it is not reasonable simply to follow one's wishes and hopes. One must recognize that, as mortal beings, we always have reason to fear mortal threats. In this particular war, the Trojans must fear the numerically superior Achaians and above all the superior power of their champion Achilles (2.119–133, 8.53–57). Poulydamas argues, then, that by retreating within the mighty walls of Troy, the Trojans will protect their city effectively: even Achilles' "spirit will not let him attack within nor will he ever sack it. Sooner the swift dogs will eat him" (18.282–283). Poulydamas urges Hector, not to abandon his defense of the city, but rather to defend it more effectively.

Now, Homer offers singular praise, in his own name, for the prudence of the Trojan Poulydamas. He calls the Trojan warrior Asios a "fool," and his men "fools," for insisting, in defiance of Poulydamas, on attacking the wall and ships of the Achaians with their horses (12.108–115, 12.124–130, 13.383–393). He explains that the counterattacking Achaians would have driven the Trojans to flee "miserably" from the battle "if Poulydamas had not spoken to the bold Hector" and advised him to regroup and reorganize his forces (13.723–725). Finally, Homer highlights the superior wisdom of Poulydamas over Hector when introducing the climactic assembly of the Trojans. In that assembly, they must decide whether to remain on the Trojan plain or withdraw into Troy now that Achilles has returned and, simply by shouting three times, has driven the Trojans away from the Achaian camp (18.215–231). Homer begins by emphasizing the fear that seizes all the Trojans, including, evidently, Hector himself: "The assembly was one in which they stood up, nor did anyone endure to sit. For trembling possessed them all, because Achilles showed himself, after he had stayed so long away from painful battle" (18.246–248). By highlighting the overwhelming terror felt by all the Trojans before Achilles, Homer highlights the compelling force of Poulydamas's argument that the Trojans must either retreat within their city in orderly fashion, under cover of night, or suffer devastating losses in a bloody rout at the hands of Achilles on the following day. Homer then proceeds to explain: "The prudent Poulydamas, the son of Panthoos, was the first to speak to them. For he alone looked before and behind him. He was Hector's companion. They were born on the same night. But this one greatly vanquished the other in speeches, the other this one with the spear. With a good mind, he addressed them and spoke" (18.249–253). As Homer goes on to show, Poulydamas does not, in truth, vanquish Hector with his speech. Hector rejects Poulydamas's advice and the Trojans all side with Hector. But Homer stresses that Poulydamas should have won, that he foresaw that neither the Trojans nor Hector himself would withstand the onslaught of Achilles and that Troy would suffer an irreparable loss. Indeed, Hector's refusal to heed Poulydamas is at least as catastrophic for the Trojans as Agamemnon's refusal to heed the priest Chryses and his subsequent quarrel with Achilles are for the Achaians. As Hector later puts it, by rejecting the plan of Poulydamas, he "destroyed his people" (22.107). Accordingly, Homer calls the Trojans "fools" for rejecting Poulydamas's "noble" plan in favor of Hector's "evil" counsels and claims that Athena took their minds away (18.310–313).[54]

But if Poulydamas's counsel here is so sound, why does Hector reject it? Homer does not claim that Athena took Hector's mind away. Moreover, according to Poulydamas, Hector has always opposed him: "Hector, somehow you always attack me in the assembly, I who speak noble things, since it is not at all seemly for one of the common people to speak mistakenly, either in council or in war, but you always enlarge your might" (12.211–214). Poulydamas suggests here that, even though he consistently proposes to the Trojan assembly a noble course of action, Hector opposes such action because he exaggerates his own power. Hector, he implies, overestimates his ability to vanquish his enemies, does not recognize his own weakness and vulnerability, and hence does not recognize or embrace the nobility of caution and prudence (see 13.726–734).

Now, the claim that Hector opposes the "noble" course of action Poulydamas proposes may seem surprising in the light of Hector's claim to Andromache that he has learned always to be "noble" and hence to fight boldly (6.440–446). But Poulydamas suggests that Hector's boldness is not based on a genuinely noble willingness to face danger but rather on an excessive hopefulness about his own strength and hence on a certain blindness to the dangers he faces. This suggestion, though, also seems surprising. For Hector seems to face danger continuously throughout the poem. It would seem that Hector opposes Poulydamas precisely because, in his view, Poulydamas always favors the ignoble course of action, the course of safety, of saving his own skin by retreating within the safety of the Trojan walls, rather than facing danger. Accordingly, on those evidently rare occasions when Hector accepts Poulydamas's counsel – against driving their horses into the ditch before the Achaian wall or in favor of gathering together the scattered Trojan forces – he does so because it strikes him as a counsel of safety, one that offers a way of avoiding woe and suffering (απήμων – 12.80, 13.748). But, in general, Hector appears to reject the course of safety in favor

[54] Even Redfield acknowledges that Hector's mistake here is "catastrophic" (1975, 155; see 145, 154, but also 146). Consider as well Schein 1984, 185.

of the course of boldness and daring. Accordingly, Hector accuses Poulydamas of sheer cowardice, of a base and selfish desire to flee danger in order to save his own life: "Why are you afraid of war and hostility? For even if all the rest of us are killed by the ships of the Argives, there is no reason to fear that you will die. For your heart cannot endure hostility, nor is it warlike" (12.244–247). Hector suggests that, by arguing for fearful retreat, Poulydamas betrays his fear of danger, whereas, by calling for bold attacks, Hector himself evinces his noble willingness to take risks. Indeed, as we have seen, Hector tells his wife that he knows that the Trojans are bound to lose the war and therefore, it seems, he has no hope for victory (6.447–448). In this light, it would seem that, contrary to Poulydamas's claim, Hector is not excessively hopeful or confident, but defeatist. He simply fights on, boldly and nobly, in what he recognizes to be a hopeless cause.

Yet, as we have seen, Hector's statement to his wife that the Trojan cause is hopeless is one he never repeats. In the rest of the poem, he is much more hopeful. Indeed, Hector tends to reject Poulydamas's advice not only because it seems cowardly to him but also, and above all, because it betrays a lack of faith in Zeus and in his support for the Trojan cause: "If you say this in earnest, then the gods themselves have destroyed your mind, you who bid me to forget the counsels of loud-thundering Zeus, who himself nodded to me and assented ... Let us obey the counsel of great Zeus, who rules all mortals and immortals" (12.233–242). Hector is evidently convinced that the mightiest of gods supports him and therefore he cannot fail (8.172–183, 13.149–154). Indeed, so great is his confidence in Zeus that even after he and his men have fled from the unarmed Achilles, Hector insists that they can still beat him and scornfully rejects Poulydamas's advice that they withdraw into the safety of Troy's walls: "But now, when the child of Cronus of the crooked counsels gave me the glory to win by their ships and to pin the Achaians against the sea, no longer show these thoughts among the people, you fool" (18.293–295). It is, Hector believes, wise to trust that Zeus will protect him and it is foolish of Poulydamas to fear that he will not. The boldness of Hector, then, is not based on a noble willingness to face danger but rather on a confidence – an excessive confidence, Poulydamas suggests – that, thanks to Zeus, he can overcome any danger.

Now, as we have seen, in Homer's account, Zeus does indeed repeatedly help Hector throughout much of the fighting (8.215–216, 11.163–165, 11.299–309, 15.220–280, 15.457–483, 15.592–725, 16.786–850). Zeus even sends his messenger Iris to Hector to assure him of his support (11.195–213). But why is Hector so confident that Zeus will *continue* to support him even, for example, against Achilles himself? As Hector indicates, the basis of his confidence in Zeus is his belief that Zeus is just and that the Trojan cause is just and hence deserving of his support: "I pray, with hope, to Zeus and the other gods, to drive away from here these dogs swept into destruction, whom the spirits of death have brought here on their black ships" (8.526–528). Since justice demands that the vile creatures who have attacked Troy be destroyed, Zeus and all the gods are supporting, and will continue to support, Troy. After reporting to the Trojans that he has seen Zeus thwart the Achaians, Hector declares:

> Easily known is the strength that comes from Zeus to men, either in those on whom he confers surpassing glory, or in those whom he diminishes and does not wish to defend, as now he diminishes the furious might of the Argives and helps us. But fight together by the ships. He who among you is struck or hit and follows his death and fate, let him die. It is not unseemly for one who defends the land of his fathers to die. But your wife and children afterward and home and estate will be untouched, if the Achaians should go with their ships to the beloved land of their fathers. (15.490–498; see also 15.719–725)

Hector, then, is convinced that the gods are supporting the Trojans inasmuch as he is convinced that the Trojan cause simply consists of defending the women and children of Troy from the Achaian invader and hence is simply just.

It is true that, when Hector tells Andromache that Troy is doomed, he himself seems to betray a lack of faith in divine providence. But, again, as we have observed, that instance of defeatism on the part of Hector is singular in the poem and perhaps exhibits a desire to excuse his own seemingly reckless pursuit of glory to his wife. Moreover, his very pursuit of glory may reveal his trust in divine providence. For Hector expresses the hope that "my glory will never perish" (7.91). But how can any mortal, human being be confident that he will receive an imperishable glory unless he is confident that imperishable beings – the immortal gods – will confer this reward upon him?[55]

But is the Trojan cause truly worthy of divine support, in Hector's view? As we have seen, Hector does apparently express severe doubts about the

[55] Unlike Helen or Achilles, Hector never speaks of glory as something conferred by singers or artists of any kind. See 3.125–128, 6.354–358, 9.185–191.

justice of the Trojan cause, in his first words in the poem, when he denounces the "evil Paris," his "woman crazy" brother, and also the cowardice of the Trojans for not punishing "evil Paris" for having stolen Helen (3.39–57; see also 6.279–285). Yet, as we have also seen, Hector never acts on his own initiative to end the war, he never supports the efforts of Antenor to end the war, and he never repeats his criticisms of the Trojans for failing to end the war in the rest of the poem. Hector evidently silences his doubts quite effectively. Just as he tends to focus more on how he can acquire honor rather than on whether he deserves it, he tends to focus more on his hopes for divine support rather than on whether he and the Trojans truly deserve such support.

In contrast, Achilles is much more sensitive to the question of the possible injustice of his own cause than Hector is. Unlike Hector, Achilles vehemently challenges the justice of the Achaian cause: "Why ought the Argives wage war against the Trojans? Why did the son of Atreus bring an army here, having assembled it? Was it not for the sake of fair-haired Helen? But are the sons of Atreus the only ones of mortal humans who love their wives?" (9.337–341). In the presence of Agamemnon and Menelaus, he laments that his old father in Phthia sheds tears in his absence, "But in a foreign land, for the sake of the horrible Helen, I make war on the Trojans" (19.324–325).[56] To be sure, Achilles does fight for nine years against the Trojans without any apparent hesitation. And when he does return to fight against them, after the death of Patroclus, he suddenly speaks as though the Achaian cause is simply just and the Trojan cause is simply unjust: "But even thus may you perish in evil doom until you all pay for the murder of Patroclus and the destruction of the Achaians, whom you killed beside the swift ships, away from me" (21.133–135). But we do learn that Achilles has evidently shown considerable mercy to "many" of the Trojans and their allies – for example, to Lycaon, a son of Priam, and the mother of Andromache – in the course of the war (21.100–105, 21.34–48, 6.414–428, 11.101–112). And he does eventually show tremendous compassion to Priam and all the Trojans by

[56] See, in contrast, the justifications of the war by Nestor and, of course, Menelaus, on the grounds that Helen was kidnapped by Paris (2.354–356, 2.588–590, 3.351–354). But Helen, in her first words in the poem, acknowledges that she freely followed Paris (3.172–180, 6.343–348). Menelaus himself seems burdened by an awareness that the Achaians and also the Trojans have been fighting and dying for his perhaps purely private problems with his wife (3.97–102, 10.25–28, 17.91–93, 17.137–139, 17.555–564, 23.601–611).

freely granting them, entirely on his own initiative, a twelve-day truce so that they may bury their beloved Hector in peace (24.512–551, 24.648–672). In these ways, Achilles betrays a much more serious awareness of the questionable justice of the Achaian cause than Hector ever does regarding the questionable justice of the Trojan cause.

Hector, then, is confident that he and the Trojans enjoy the support of the gods and that, with that support, they can reasonably reject the caution recommended by Poulydamas and boldly attack the Achaians, assured of victory. Poulydamas suggests, however, that Hector rejects his advice and exaggerates his own power out of an excessive trust in the gods and a hope for their assistance. Poulydamas evidently does not share that trust or hope, either because he is not confident that the Trojan cause deserves the support of the gods or because he is not sure that the gods can ever be relied upon. Accordingly, he emphasizes to Hector and the Trojans the need to be rational, to be mindful of threats, to fear them, and to act on such rational fear: "Drawing back, summon all the best ones here, and then we may consider well our entire plan, whether we should fall upon their many oared ships, if a god should wish to give us strength, or whether we should go away from the ships unharmed" (13.740–744). Poulydamas here associates the bold course of action with confidence in divine assistance. But he then proceeds to argue for following the path of caution: "For I myself am afraid lest the Achaians demand payment for their debt of yesterday, since by their ships remains a man insatiable for war, who, I suppose, will no longer hold himself from the war" (13.745–747). In this way, he indicates quite clearly that he thinks it unwise to count on the assistance of the gods.

Poulydamas does invoke the gods on two occasions. But, unlike Hector, he does so in the course of counseling caution, not boldness. On the first occasion, when the Trojans are attacking the wall protecting the Achaian camp, they see an eagle flying with a snake in its talons and then dropping it once the snake bites back (12.200–209). Poulydamas claims that this is an omen warning that, even though the Achaians, like the snake, seem defeated, they still have the power to inflict great harm upon the Trojans. Therefore, he concludes, the Trojans should withdraw back to Troy (12.216–229). Now, on other occasions, Poulydamas argues that the Trojans should withdraw without reference to the gods (13.735–747, 18.254–283). His belief that it is best for the Trojans to withdraw is not based, then, on the purportedly divine omen. But here Poulydamas evidently attempts to appeal to Hector's piety to tame his boldness. The attempt fails because Hector doubts that Poulydamas's pious argument is sincere and because he simply insists that Zeus favors the Trojans in particular (12.233–243). Indeed, so vehemently does Hector reject Poulydamas's advice here that he accuses him of cowardice and threatens to kill him if he holds back from fighting or persuades someone else to do so (12. 244–250).

The second time Poulydamas invokes the gods, he does so again to check the boldness of Hector:

> Hector, it is impossible to persuade you with reasonable words. Because a god gave you surpassingly warlike deeds, you wish in counsel also to surpass others in knowing. But you cannot somehow take all things together for yourself. For the gods give to one warlike deeds, to another dancing, to another the lyre and singing, and to another wide-seeing Zeus puts a noble mind in his chest, which many human beings benefit from and he saves many, and most of all he himself understands. (13.726–734)

By claiming that Hector believes that he is wise simply because he is strong, Poulydamas again suggests here, as he had before, that Hector opposes reason because he exaggerates his own power. But, as we have seen, the cause of Hector's overconfidence is his belief that the gods are on his side. However, rather than challenge that belief directly, Poulydamas asserts that the gods never give more than one excellence to a human being, but rather parcel them out separately to different individuals. Therefore, precisely because Hector is an outstanding warrior, he cannot, Poulydamas suggests, have an outstanding mind. Furthermore, Poulydamas also suggests, an outstanding mind is the greatest gift Zeus can confer on a human being, since through it one can save many.

Now, Poulydamas does not indicate how he knows that the gods parcel out talents in this way. It is also not at all clear why a single human being cannot have more than one excellence. Achilles, for example, is a superb warrior and, unique among the warriors of the poem, sings and plays the lyre (9.185–191; see 3.54–55). Moreover, as we see at the beginning of the poem, when he single-handedly saves the Achaian army from the folly of Agamemnon by inducing him to return Chryseis to her father, Achilles can also excel in offering advice to his fellow Achaians. Poulydamas himself, who excels in offering counsel, is also a leading Trojan warrior. Poulydamas's account here, then, seems more rhetorical than reasonable. He appeals to Hector's piety in order to temper his bold spirit and make it more open to reason. Yet, while Poulydamas succeeds in persuading Hector in this way to regroup his forces, he fails in his efforts to persuade him to save the Trojan army by withdrawing his forces into the safety of Troy's walls. Hector's confidence that the gods support Troy and will grant him the imperishable glory he craves proves impervious to reason.

Hector does eventually acknowledge the wisdom of Poulydamas's counsel of retreat. When the fully armed Achilles returns to battle, Hector and the Trojans run away from him, just as Poulydamas had predicted and just as they had run away in fear from the mere shouts of the unarmed Achilles (20.44–46, 20.364–454, 20.490–503, 21.526–543; see also 18.217–283). Those who are not slaughtered by Achilles rush inside the walls of Troy, but Hector alone stands before the gates of the city, "vehemently eager to do battle with Achilles" (22.36). His father begs him "piteously" to enter the city and thereby avoid certain death at the hands of the "far superior" Achilles (22.37–40):

> But go inside the wall, my child, so that you may save the Trojan men and the Trojan women. Do not extend glory to the son of Peleus and deprive yourself of your beloved life. Take pity on me, an unfortunate one, still mindful, ill-fated, whom the Father, son of Cronus, will destroy, on the threshold of old age, with a hard destiny, after I have looked upon many evils and seen my sons destroyed and my daughters dragged away and their marriage chambers destroyed and their innocent children thrown to the ground with dreadful hostility and the wives of my sons dragged off by the destructive hands of the Achaians. And my dogs will drag me, last, in front of my doorway, eating my raw flesh, since someone will have beaten me and struck me with sharp bronze and will have taken my spirit out of my limbs. And the dogs whom I raised in my great halls, to be at my table and watch my doors, will drink my blood, frenzied in their spirit, and will then lie down in front of my door. (22.56–71)

As Priam stresses here in this heartrending speech, as long as Hector is alive to marshal and lead the Trojans in defense of their city, the city may hope to survive. Priam argues, then, that Hector should save himself for the sake of his family and his city. Yet, Hector entirely ignores the arguments and pleas of his father, as well as those of his mother.[57] Indeed, he does not even

[57] Crotty notes that this is the only time in the poem that Priam addresses Hector; yet, "while Priam addresses Hector in the most poignant terms, the son does not answer a single word to his father's plea" (1994, 24–25).

mention his weeping parents or his wife or his infant son here.[58] Whereas Achilles is later moved by compassion for Priam and the Trojans to grant them a twelve-day truce to bury Hector in peace, Hector, at this critical moment, is wholly unmoved by compassion for his own father or for his own people (24.512–517, 24.650–672).[59]

Why, then, does Hector decide to face Achilles rather than withdraw into Troy? Before giving us the speech in which Hector elucidates this decision, Homer explains that Hector is overcome with anger: "As a mountain snake waits for a man by his hole, having devoured evil poisons, and a dreadful rage descends upon him, and he stares horribly, coiling himself around the hole, so Hector, possessing an unquenchable fury, did not withdraw, but leaned his shining shield against the tower that jutted forth. Distressed, he spoke to his great-hearted spirit" (22.93–98). But against whom is Hector's furious rage directed? One would think it would be directed at Achilles, who has just slaughtered so many of his countrymen, including two of his brothers (20.407–418, 21.34–135). Yet, in his subsequent speech, Hector expresses no anger whatsoever at Achilles. Against whom, then, does Hector direct his anger?

> Ah me! If I go inside the gateway and the walls, then Poulydamas will be the first to lay a reproach upon me, he who bid me to lead the Trojans to the city, on that destructive night, when divine Achilles rose up. But I would not be persuaded by him. That would have been far more profitable. Now, since I have destroyed my people through my recklessness, I feel shame before the Trojan men and the Trojan women with trailing robes, lest someone else, more evil than I, say at some point: "Hector had confidence in his own strength and destroyed his people." Thus they will say. For me, at that time, it would be more profitable, either to go against Achilles and kill him or to be killed by him, with great glory, in front of the city. (22.99–110)

Hector expresses anger here at Poulydamas! And he is angry not because Poulydamas somehow wronged him but precisely because he was all too wise in the advice he offered and consequently his rebuke would be all too justified. Hector admits here that it truly was foolish to have kept the Trojan army on the plain once Achilles had returned and that by doing so he

[58] I must consequently disagree with Schein's claim that "*the* two aspects of Hector" are "his gentleness to his family and his heroic fierceness toward his enemies" (1984, 191 – emphasis added).

[59] See Crotty 1994, 98–99.

inflicted tremendous harm on the city as a whole. One might think that Hector would therefore return to Troy, praise Poulydamas, ask for his advice, and do his utmost to defend the city. For even though the Trojans have suffered terribly, they still have such leading warriors as Poulydamas, Aeneas, Glaucus, Paris, and Hector himself, and they can still follow the defensive strategy that Poulydamas has argued for and that the Trojans have followed with considerable success over the preceding nine years.[60]

Hector, however, refuses to take this course of action because Poulydamas will be the first to reproach him, and because Hector feels shame before the Trojan men and women, since someone will accuse him of having destroyed his people. Now, insofar as the accuser means that Hector has caused the deaths of large numbers of his soldiers, this accusation would be justified, as Hector acknowledges. Hector admits here, then, that he lacks the courage to accept the blame that he deserves. In this way, he would seem to set forth a damning indictment of himself. He, the defender of Troy, destroyed it and he did so foolishly, and needlessly, simply because he would not heed Poulydamas's argument for caution but instead insisted on indulging his confident hope that, with the help of the gods, he would overpower Achilles. Consequently, he has caused untold harm to all who counted on him as their protector, his family as well as his people.

But then, Hector complains about the accusation, since it will, he says, come from someone who is his inferior. Yet, this complaint would seem to be altogether incoherent. In the first place, if the accusation is just, what difference does it make if it comes from someone who might be, as Poulydamas admittedly is, a less talented warrior than Hector? Furthermore, by the standard of the good of Troy, who is inferior to Hector, the man who, by his own claim, destroyed his own people? Hector shows here that he cannot bring himself to accept his folly, to accept his responsibility for doing Troy such harm, and to accept that Poulydamas is wiser than he is. Hector lacks the courage not only to accept blame but also to recognize that he deserves to be blamed. He lacks the courage truly to recognize his folly and to admit that he was mistaken in his trust in the gods and in his confidence that they would support him. He lacks the strength to face the possibility either that he does not deserve the support of the gods or that the gods are

[60] As we learn in the *Odyssey* (4.271–289, 11.523–537), the Achaians finally conquer Troy some time after the deaths of Hector and Achilles, not by an attack, but by a ruse.

not just and provident beings. He lacks the strength to admit his weakness as a vulnerable, mortal human being but still insists, in Poulydamas's words, on exaggerating his might (12.211–214). Accordingly, Hector blames Poulydamas on the grounds that he will, Hector speculates, speak against him and, he implies, turn the Trojans against him.

Hector then proceeds to explain, with a shockingly coldhearted calculation, that it is more profitable for him to face Achilles, since either he will win glory by killing him or he will win glory by being killed by the greatest Achaian warrior. Hector acts with breathtaking selfishness here. So eager is he to avoid disgrace and to win glory that he decides to sacrifice the good of his city and his family in pursuit of his own glory.[61] He almost openly admits here that his overriding concern is himself and his glory, and not at all his family and his city. Yet Hector does not quite admit this. For by insisting, twice, that he has destroyed his people, and hence that the fate of Troy is sealed, he implicitly claims that it is too late to save his family and his people anyway. Now, as we have seen, this claim seems false, insofar as the Trojans still have many mighty warriors, insofar as their walls can effectively keep the Achaians at bay, and insofar as the Achaians never conquer Troy through an attack but only eventually through the ruse of the Trojan Horse. By making this claim, Hector exaggerates the harm he has already done his people. But he also suggests that, since the fate of Troy is already sealed, he would do no further harm to the Trojans now by seeking to die a glorious death. In this way, Hector admits here that he is pursuing his self-interested desire for glory, but he refuses to admit, even to himself, that he is pursuing his own good at the expense of the good of Troy. As in his conversation with his wife, so too here he embraces an unwarranted defeatism to excuse his selfishness. Just as he lacks the strength of soul fully to admit his folly to himself, so he lacks the strength of soul to admit his self-interestedness to himself.

It is true that after appearing to resolve to fight Achilles in order to win glory for himself, Hector suddenly considers the possibility of trying to negotiate a settlement of the war with Achilles:

> But if I should set down my bossed shield and heavy helmet and lean my spear against the wall, and myself go to face blameless Achilles, and I should promise him Helen and all her possessions with her, as many as Alexandros brought in his hollow

[61] I consequently disagree with Flaumenhaft's suggestion that Hector – rather than Poulydamas, for example – is "the most civic-minded" Trojan warrior (2004, 19).

> ship to Troy, which was the beginning of the conflict, to give to the sons of Atreus to take away, and to give as a share to the Achaians as much as is hidden in this city? I would take an oath thereafter for the council of elders, not to hide anything, but to divide everything up, as many possessions as the lovely city keeps within. (22.111–121)

Perhaps mindful that he is almost certain to lose to Achilles in battle and perhaps out of concern for his city and family as well, Hector here contemplates not only returning Helen and all that she has to the Achaians, but also giving them all the wealth that Troy possesses. In other words, he considers giving up all the wealth of Troy, along with Helen, in order to save the lives of the Trojans and his own life. Now, granting that Hector is unwilling to withdraw into the safety of the Trojan walls, attempting to negotiate this virtual surrender to Achilles might seem to be better for Troy than the alternative of fighting Achilles. For even though it is extremely unlikely that the grief-stricken and vengeful Achilles would spare Hector, it would at least do no harm to the Trojans for Hector to try. Yet, Hector decides against taking this drastic measure, not on the grounds that it will fail to help the Trojans but simply on the grounds that it will bring disgrace upon himself:

> But why does my beloved spirit converse about these things? I fear lest I go up to him and he take no pity on me nor revere me at all but kill me, being naked, just as though I were a woman, since I would take off my armor. There is no way anymore from an oak nor from a rock to chat with him as a maiden and a youth, a maiden and a youth who chat with one another. It is better to join in battle as quickly as possible. We will know to which one the Olympian will give a cause for boasting. (22.122–130)

Hector expresses no concern here whatsoever for the fate of Troy, for the fate of his father and mother, his wife and children, the Trojan men, and the Trojan women with trailing robes. Instead, he expresses the fear that he will gain no glory by being cut down unarmed, as though he were a woman. Accordingly, Hector decides to act in accordance with his calculation that, even if he is killed by Achilles in combat, he will still win glory from the Trojan men and women who always praise boldness over caution and who are evidently, he supposes, foolish enough to honor a man who fights and dies boldly, even if he has destroyed his people.

Hector here seems not only harshly self-interested, but thoughtlessly self-interested. In the first place, and most importantly, what value is the honor of the Trojans if they are so foolish as to honor him for fighting Achilles, even though he has destroyed his people? Furthermore, insofar as he truly has destroyed the Trojans and therefore doomed them to oblivion, from whom does he expect glory once Troy is gone? It is possible that he looks to other human beings, to the Achaians, for example, and to the gods, to grant him an imperishable glory. But how can he reasonably hope to win glory from them if, as he claims, he has recklessly destroyed his own people? Finally, how can he reasonably expect to muster the courage to face the armed Achilles in combat now, when he fled with his fellow Trojans from the unarmed Achilles on the previous day? Not only is Achilles far superior a warrior, but he is accompanied by the entire Achaian army, whereas Hector is all alone outside the walls of Troy (22.205–207). How, under these circumstances, can he reasonably hope to win a glorious victory or even die a glorious death? Hector appears to be as reckless in his pursuit of his own self-interest as he is in his pursuit of his people's self-interest.

Once Achilles closes in on him, Hector's resolve to face him in glorious combat collapses. Trembling seizes him and he flees, "being terrified" (22.136–137). Achilles chases after the fleeing Hector and both men "ran for the life [or soul] of Hector" (22.161). Now Hector regrets his decision to fight Achilles, forgets his shame before the Trojan men and women, and desperately tries to find refuge within the walls of Troy (22.194–198). Now the bold warrior embraces, too late, the caution Andromache and Poulydamas had urged on him. Now the awareness of his weakness and the fear of death apparently overwhelm the passion for glory in the soul of Hector.

Yet, at the moment of his death, Hector's hopes for glory reassert themselves. The appearance of Athena in the guise of his brother Deiphobos momentarily emboldens Hector to face Achilles in final combat. But even when Hector recognizes the deception of the goddess and the "evil death" that is near to him, he does not flee but rather boldly rushes against Achilles in the hope that he might garner at least some shred of glory from his death: "But I would not die, indeed, without effort and without glory, but only after doing something great, that those to come will hear of" (22.297–305). In this way, he evidently hopes to erase the memory of his flight from Achilles, and in some measure he succeeds. For, after his death, his mother, at least, insists that Achilles "slew him when he was not evil, but standing before the Trojan men and the deep-bosomed Trojan women, with no thought in his mind for panic or flight" (24.214–216).

Another manifestation of Hector's hope for glory at the moment of his death may be his wish that Achilles return his corpse to the Trojans, a wish that he expresses even when he still believes that Deiphobos has come to help him, and then again when he is dying (22.254–259, 22.337–343). One might think that Hector here is simply eager to respect the customary rituals of burial of both the Trojans and the Achaians. Accordingly, he promises Achilles that should he, Hector, triumph, he will return the corpse of Achilles to the Achaians. Yet, within the *Iliad*, Hector places an exceptional importance on having his corpse buried with honors. When he proposes to duel the bravest Achaian in Book VII, there too he seeks beforehand to extract a promise that his corpse will be returned to Troy so that the Trojans may honor him with a funeral (7.76–86). No other warrior on either side ever makes such a request in a comparable situation. Neither Paris nor Menelaus, for example, makes any such request prior to their duel, nor does Sarpedon when he is facing Patroclus or when he is dying, nor Patroclus when he is facing Hector or when he is dying, nor even Aeneas when he is facing Achilles (3.264–354, 16.419–507, 16.816–854, 20.158–260). Furthermore, the fact that Hector seeks to behead and disfigure the corpse of Patroclus rather than return it to the Achaians suggests that he does not have a general, principled attachment to burying the dead with honors but rather a particular desire to be buried with honors himself (16.836, 17.125–127, 18.172–180). Indeed, on one occasion, Hector goes so far as to threaten to deny burial to any Trojan who shrinks from attacking the Achaians ships (15.346–351; see also 22.41–43).[62] One might also think that Hector wishes to have his corpse returned so that his parents and his people can console themselves with a funeral. But he himself indicates that his primary concern, at least, is that he himself be buried with honors. As he says, in almost his final words, he wishes to have his corpse "so that the Trojans and the wives of the Trojans may give me, in death, a fire" (22.342–343).

One naturally sympathizes with Hector at his death because of the terrible grief his death inspires among his family and people. Yet, Hector evinces no concern for either his family or his people at his death, but only for himself and his glory. Even though Hector comes to sight as a Trojan who loves his people unconditionally, he gradually reveals that he does not truly love them. In his view, the Trojans as a whole are cowards, as he complains

[62] See Segal 1971, 19–20.

in Book III; their leaders are wicked, as he laments in Book XV; and they are foolish enough to confer glory on a man who destroys his people, as he suggests in Book XXII (3.56–57, 15.719–723, 22.99–110). But Hector does not truly expect anything more of them. His attachment to the Trojans is, ultimately, simply instrumental. He wants their praise. But why does he want the praise of people for whom has no respect?

The one Trojan whom one would expect Hector to respect is Poulydamas. After all, Poulydamas is clearly no coward, for he challenges the strategy and tactics of Hector, even after Hector has threatened to execute him (12.248–250). Furthermore, Hector eventually admits that Poulydamas gave him sound advice – advice that would have saved Troy – and hence, it would seem, that Poulydamas is wiser than he is (22.99–105). One might therefore think that Hector would come to admire Poulydamas as one who is wise and would seek his honor, since it would come from someone worthy of giving it. But Poulydamas is precisely the one Trojan Hector seems angry with, not because he is cowardly or wicked or foolish, but precisely because he is wise. Hector angrily imagines that Poulydamas will rebuke him, albeit justly, and that he will inspire the Trojans to rebuke him and disgrace him as well (22.91–108). And, as he shows, Hector would rather die with honor from foolish Trojans, who he believes will grant glory to a man who fights boldly even if he has destroyed his people, than live on, with the truthful criticism of the wise Poulydamas but also with the possibility of earning his honor by saving Troy from further harm.

Like Hector, Achilles longs for honor but, above all, he longs to be virtuous and hence worthy of honor. Accordingly, in sharp contrast with Hector, Achilles admits to faults, sharply blames himself for them, and even seeks to punish himself. When he learns that Hector has slain Patroclus, Achilles resolves to kill Hector even though he learns from his mother that his own death must follow that of the Trojan warrior. As he explains:

> I would die soon, since I was not to protect my companion as he was killed. He perished far away from the land of his fathers, and he did not have me to be his protector from harm. Now, since I am not going to the beloved land of my fathers, since I was not a light for Patroclus, nor for my other companions, so many of whom were broken by divine Hector, but I sit beside my ships, a useless burden on the land, I who am such as no other of the bronze-tunicked Achaians is in war, though there are others better in assembly. (18.98–106; see 18.82)

Here, Achilles emphatically blames himself for the death of his beloved companion and of his other companions and suggests that he may well deserve to die for failing to protect them.[63] He also acknowledges, in passing, that he is inferior to some of his companions in addressing an assembly. Whereas Hector cannot bear to face the justified criticisms of others, Achilles makes such criticisms of himself.

Furthermore, in contrast with Hector, Achilles loves men who criticize him most sharply. We have observed earlier that the most powerful criticisms of Achilles in the poem come from those whom Achilles claims are by him the "most beloved of Achaians" and "the most beloved men" – Odysseus, Phoinix, and Ajax – by his companion Nestor, and by his most beloved and honored companion, Patroclus (9.198, 9.204, 18.79–82). But it is also important to note that, even in the midst of his rage, he expresses love for the men who make those criticisms to his face, he acknowledges much merit to their criticisms, and he yields in some measure to their criticisms.[64] When Odysseus, Phoinix, and Ajax come to beseech Achilles to return to the fighting, he gradually shifts his position in the course of their speeches. Even though Achilles twice vows in response to Odysseus that he will leave Troy the very next day, he responds to the criticisms of Phoinix by saying that he will decide the next day whether or not to go, and then he responds to the criticism of Ajax by expressing his agreement with it – "all that you said seems to have been spoken in accordance with my spirit" – saying that he will not return to the fighting until Hector attacks his ships, and thereby acknowledging that he will not leave Troy on the next day (9.355–361, 9.426–429, 9.617–619, 9.644–655). Even in response to Odysseus, Achilles retreats significantly from his earlier harsh position against the Achaians. For while he had earlier prayed to Zeus to punish the Achaians by using Hector to kill many of them, now he advises Odysseus and the other Achaians to leave Troy, to sail home, and hence to save themselves from further harm at the hands of Hector (1.407–412, 9.417–426). On the very next day, when he believes that the healer Machaon – a key member of the Achaian army, as Idomeneus points out, "for a man who is a healer is worth many others" (11.514) – has been wounded, Achilles sends Patroclus to the Achaians to investigate their predicament. When Patroclus returns and

[63] See Benardete 2005, 112; Lateiner 2004, 26, 28.

[64] See Schein 1984, 113–115; Burns 1996, 293.

sharply criticizes Achilles for refusing to help, Achilles sends Patroclus and all his troops into battle to save the Achaians. Finally, when Patroclus is killed, Achilles blames himself for not having returned earlier to battle – and hence for not having heeded his friends – and effectively punishes himself. In contrast to Hector, then, who attacks Poulydamas for his truthful criticism, Achilles takes the criticisms of his friends to heart and loves them, not in spite of, but in some measure because of, their criticism.[65] Achilles does not want praise from those he does not admire. Accordingly, he hates the Achaian Thersites, even though Thersites does evidently praise him (2.220, 2.239–242). Conversely, Hector is eager for praise from the Trojans he despises but evinces no concern to win the praise of his critics, Andromache and Poulydamas. In the course of the entire poem, Hector mentions Andromache only once, in passing, after she criticizes him (8.185–190). And he lashes out at Poulydamas for having criticized him truthfully. Hector cherishes praise, from others and himself, and turns against or ignores those who suggest that he is not worthy of being praised. But since Achilles wants true honor, since he wants above all to be truly worthy of honor, to be truly virtuous, he loves those who are worthy of giving him honor and whose criticisms help him become worthy of honor.

[65] Schein observes that "The *Iliad* is as much about the *philotēs* [friendship] of Achilles as it is about his *mēnis* [wrath]" (1984, 98; see also 126–127).

CHAPTER 3

Achilles and the Limits of Virtue

THE PROBLEM OF VIRTUE AND HAPPINESS

Achilles is the best of the Achaians and the most virtuous human being in the *Iliad*. Even his critics bear witness to his virtue. Nestor complains to Patroclus, "But Achilles alone will benefit from his virtue" (11.762–763). Similarly, Patroclus declares to Achilles: "May this rage, then, not seize me, which you watch over, a dreadful virtue" (16.30–31).[1] Yet, if Achilles is the most virtuous human being of the poem, if, that is, he is the one who displays most clearly the courage, and also the justice, prudence, and compassion that virtue evidently consists of in the poem, he is also one who suffers terribly in the poem, more terribly than any Achaian and perhaps even more than any Trojan. Andromache and Hecubae do of course grieve terribly over the death of their beloved Hector, and Priam suffers the death not only of Hector, of other sons, and of his many soldiers, but also of his favorite son Polydorus (20.407–410). And, throughout the poem, warriors suffer death and the deaths of companions, and their loved ones suffer the anguish of waiting for news of their bereavement (6.237–241). But Achilles suffers, first, humiliating and enraging treatment at the hands of Agamemnon and his fellow Achaians; then the loss of his beloved companion Patroclus, whom he honored "equal to

[1] The word "virtue" (ἀρετή) is mentioned seventeen times in the poem, twice by Achilles, twice about Achilles, and once to Achilles (22.268, 23.276, 11.762–763, 16.30–31 [αἰναρέτη], 9.498; 8.535, 11.90, 13.237, 13.275, 13.277, 14.118, 15.642, 20.242, 20.411, 23.374, 23.571, 23.578).

his own self";[2] and, finally, and perhaps most painfully, the agony of blaming himself for the death of his friend: "I destroyed him" (τὸν ἀπώλεσα – 18.82; see 18.98–106, 18.324–327).[3] Accordingly, Homer portrays Achilles as weeping more than any other character in the poem, first over the injustice he suffers at the hands of Agamemnon and the Achaians, and then, repeatedly, over the death of Patroclus.[4] What does Homer mean to teach about the virtuous life Achilles leads through this presentation of his suffering? What is the relation between virtue and happiness? Does virtue lead to happiness? Does it protect one from unhappiness or at least mitigate one's suffering? Or does virtue cause unhappiness? Does Achilles suffer in spite of his virtue or because of it?

The most immediate cause of Achilles' suffering is the death of Patroclus, and the most immediate cause of that death would seem to be the wrath of Achilles against Agamemnon and the Achaians, the very wrath that Homer focuses our attention on from the very start of the poem: "Sing, goddess, of the wrath of Peleus's son, Achilles, which was destructive, which put countless woes upon the Achaians, hurled forth many mighty souls of heroes into Hades, and prepared them as food for dogs and all birds" (1.1–5). Homer stresses there that the wrath was "destructive" of the Achaians as a whole, but it proves destructive of Patroclus – the most prominent Achaian hero to die in the poem – in particular, and therewith of Achilles. In order to understand

[2] Crotty suggests, "With the death of Patroclus it becomes clear that the *Iliad* is not, ultimately, a story about the warrior code, or the search for 'unperishable renown,' but rather about griefs and the emotions – especially *eleos* – roused by human suffering" (1994, 59). As Schadewaldt puts it, "the poet increasingly makes us feel the torment Achilles is suffering" (1997b, 159).

[3] "τὸν ἀπώλεσα" could also be translated as "I lost him," but its primary meaning would be "I destroyed him." This reading is supported by Achilles' words of self-reproach at 18.98–106: "I would die soon, since I was not to protect my companion as he was killed. He perished far away from the land of his fathers, and he did not have me to be his protector from harm. Now, since I am not going to the beloved land of my fathers, since I was not a light for Patroclus, nor for my other companions, so many of whom were broken by divine Hector, but I sit beside my ships, a useless burden on the land, I who am such as no other of the bronze-tunicked Achaians is in war, though there are others better in assembly." See also 18.324–327. Consider as well Antilochus's concern that Achilles might kill himself, and hence punish himself, upon hearing of Patroclus's death (18.32–34). Zanker cites Achilles' guilt here to argue against the claim – made most prominently by Dodds (1973, 17–18) – that Homeric characters feel shame but not guilt (1994, 18).

[4] See 1.348–361, 18.22–35, 19.4–6, 19.338, 23.12–18, 23.108–110, 23.152–155, 23.222–225, 24.3–13, 24.507–512.

the relation between Achilles' virtue and his suffering, then, let us consider more carefully the genesis of his anger and what light it sheds on the nature of his virtue.

The apparent beginning of the chain of events that gives rise to Achilles' anger is Agamemnon's outrageously selfish refusal to return Chryseis, the captive daughter of a priest of Apollo, to her father, Chryses. Like all the Achaians except for Agamemnon, Achilles favors returning Chryseis to her father (1.22–23). But unlike all the other Achaians, who are apparently willing to let the army perish as a result of the plague sent by Apollo rather than defy their king, Achilles is unwilling to acquiesce in Agamemnon's decision once it is clear that Apollo threatens the Achaians with destruction. Achilles summons the Achaians to an assembly, urges them to ask a prophet why Apollo is so angry, and promises to protect the prophet Calchas when he expresses fear of antagonizing a powerful Achaian king: "no one, so long as I am living on the earth and see daylight, will lay his heavy hands on you beside the hollow ships, no one of all the Danaans, not even if you speak of Agamemnon, who now boasts to be by far the best of the Achaians" (1.88–91). Once Calchas explains that Apollo demands that Agamemnon return Chryseis, Agamemnon bitterly denounces the prophet and grumbles that he would like to keep the daughter of the priest since he prefers her to his own wife Clytaemnestra (1.106–115). Nevertheless, Agamemnon yields rather quickly to Calchas and Achilles: "But even so, I am willing to give her back, if it is better to do so. I myself want my people to be safe, not to perish" (1.116–117). He does, however, ask for another prize – presumably a captive girl from one of the leading Achaian warriors – to replace Chryseis. At this point, Achilles sharply criticizes Agamemnon for the first time – "greediest of all" – and points out that all the prizes have been distributed and that it would be indecent to take one back from someone to whom it has already been given (1.122–126). But he also promises, on behalf of the Achaians, to pay Agamemnon three or four times the value of his prize whenever they should conquer Troy (1.127–129. This promise might seem sarcastic, since the Achaians have been fighting to take Troy for nine years and therefore it is not clear when they might succeed in conquering the city. On the other hand, Achilles does offer Agamemnon a way of yielding to the Achaians while saving face since he has been promised a much larger future prize. Agamemnon responds by chiding Achilles for trying to deceive him and by insisting that either the Achaians should find and give him a prize – perhaps a newly captured mistress from some neighboring town which they might sack, as they captured Chryseis from the town of Thebe – or "I myself may take your prize or that of Ajax or that of Odysseus, going myself in person, and he whom I come to will be enraged" (1.137–139). After this somewhat general threat against his three principal warriors, Agamemnon proceeds to drop the matter and to instruct one of these same three warriors, or Idomeneus, to undertake the solemn and important mission of returning Chryseis to her father.

Now, Agamemnon's behavior here is outrageously selfish and foolish. For a purely selfish reason – to keep a captive mistress – he has placed at risk the very existence of an Achaian army that has battled for him and his brother at Troy for nine long years. Even now, after yielding to the entirely reasonable and just demands of Calchas and Achilles, he still demands to be given another mistress and threatens to take one from his leading warriors. Nevertheless, if saving the army were Achilles' overriding goal, it would seem that he should rejoice at his success. Agamemnon has agreed to return Chryseis to her father and seems intent on doing so as quickly as possible. Moreover, given that Agamemnon has just behaved so outrageously – endangering the very existence of the entire Achaian army for the sake of keeping a captive mistress – his desire to receive another captive mistress at some future date, a desire that might be accommodated either by another raiding expedition or by one of the leading warriors giving up one of his captive mistresses (Achilles himself evidently has more than one – see 9.663–665), would seem to be a relatively minor outrage.

Yet, this is the moment at which the wrath of Achilles explodes. In response to Agamemnon's vague threat to take away a captive mistress from either Achilles or Ajax or Odysseus, Achilles angrily denounces Agamemnon and suddenly announces that he is returning home. At first glance, Achilles' response seems altogether bewildering. After nine years of fighting, he abruptly decides to stop fighting, to desert his comrades in the middle of a war, and to abandon his life as a virtuous warrior, in response to what would seem to be a relatively petty injustice. Why does he respond in such an extreme and disproportionate manner to Agamemnon here?[5] Let us consider Achilles' explanation more carefully:

[5] Consider, for example, Clarke 2004, 74, 82.

> Alas, you who are covered in shamelessness, with your mind always on profit, how would anyone of the Achaians who has foresight obey your words either to go on a journey or to fight strongly with men in battle? For I myself did not come here on account of Trojan spearmen, since they are not guilty of anything against me. Never have they yet driven off my cattle, nor my horses, never in Phthia, with fertile soil, which feeds men, did they spoil my harvest, since there is much between us, the shadowy mountains and the roaring sea. But for you, great shameless one, we followed, so that you would be gratified, to win honor for Menelaus and for you from the Trojans, you dog-eyed one. But you show no regard at all for these things nor do you have any care for them. And now you yourself threaten to take away my prize, which the sons of the Achaians gave to me, for which I have toiled much. Never is the prize that I have equal to yours, whenever the Achaians sack a well-founded city of the Trojans. But my hands attend to the greater part of the violent war. Indeed, if ever there is a division of spoils, your prize is far greater, but I myself go back to my ships possessing a small yet dear thing, when I tire of waging war. But now I am going to Phthia, since it is much better to go home with my curved ships, nor do I think I will remain here, dishonored, to pile up riches and wealth for you. (1.149–171)

Achilles explains here that he is responding, not only to Agamemnon's threat to take his prize away, but also to his entire rule over the past nine years. Agamemnon's threat is simply the last straw. The fundamental problem with Agamemnon's rule is that it is unjust, so unjust that it is unreasonable for any of the Achaians to obey him. In the first place, Achilles suggests, he and all the Achaians, have been fighting the Trojans for nine years, not out of self-interest, but in a noble spirit of generosity, to gratify Agamemnon and to win honor for him and his brother after Paris (ostensibly) stole away with his sister-in-law Helen.[6] But, as Achilles stresses twice, Agamemnon has no feelings of shame in the face of such generosity, no reverence for such nobility, and no gratitude for such sacrifice.[7] Instead, as Achilles stresses, Agamemnon simply thinks of his own profit, his own prizes, and his own wealth. Accordingly,

[6] Notwithstanding the claim of Nestor and the belief of Menelaus that Helen has been kidnapped and is being held by the Trojans against her will, Helen herself, in her first words in the poem, openly admits that she freely abandoned Menelaus (and her daughter) and followed Paris (2.354–356, 2.588–590, 3.172–175). It is evidently for this reason that Achilles later laments that his father must weep, bereaved of his son: "But in a foreign land, for the sake of horrible Helen, I wage war on the Trojans" (19.324–325).

[7] Achilles may mean to contrast Agamemnon here with his brother Menelaus, who repeatedly expresses gratitude for the sacrifices the Achaians have made for him. See 3.97–102, 10.25–28, 17.91–93, 23.601–611. Consider also 17.137–139, 17.555–564, 7.94–121.

even though Achilles sacrifices much more for the war effort than Agamemnon – indeed, even though Agamemnon hardly fights at all (1.225–227) – Agamemnon always obtains more wealth, more prizes, and more honor. As Achilles remarked earlier, Agamemnon insists on claiming, falsely, that he is the best of the Achaians (1.90–91). By depriving Achilles of the honor he deserves, and by taking more honor for himself than he deserves, Agamemnon acts unjustly. Therefore, since it is "better" for him to leave, Achilles will no longer fight for Agamemnon but will return home.

Achilles suggests here that Agamemnon's behavior toward the Achaians during the plague sent by Apollo is emblematic of his entire rule. Just as he was willing to sacrifice the well-being of the entire army simply to gratify his own selfish desire to have the daughter of the priest of Apollo as his mistress, so has he been willing to take advantage of the sacrifices of his army in order to amass wealth and honor for himself. Yet, whereas Achilles was willing to defy Agamemnon to save the Achaian army from the disastrous consequences of Agamemnon's rule, Achilles now seems to be simply abandoning the Achaians to the misrule of Agamemnon and also to the violence of the Trojans. Insofar as the Achaians are simply innocent victims of Agamemnon, is Achilles himself not acting unjustly toward them here?

Even though Achilles focuses his criticism here on Agamemnon, it is important to see that he also implicitly criticizes the Achaians for acquiescing in the foolish and unjust rule of Agamemnon. As he suggests, they are not simply innocent victims of Agamemnon but have repeatedly permitted their king to take more honor and wealth than he deserves and to deprive others of what they deserve. They have sat by as he has dishonored Achilles as well as themselves. They have endured in silence as he has boasted of being the best of the Achaians (1.90–91). Indeed, as we have seen, the Achaians simply acquiesced in Agamemnon's refusal to return Chryseis to her father, even though his refusal provoked a terrible punishment from Apollo. And now Ajax and Odysseus, for example, sit quietly as Agamemnon arbitrarily threatens to take away their captive mistresses as well as that of Achilles simply in order to gratify himself. Nestor does speak up to urge Agamemnon to let Achilles keep his mistress, and he later claims that all of the Achaians sided with Achilles against their king (1.275–284, 9.102–113). But Nestor and all the Achaians nevertheless acquiesce in silence when Agamemnon insists on taking Briseis from Achilles, just as they did when he insisted on keeping Chryseis from her father. Achilles tells Agamemnon: "Then indeed may I be called a coward and of no account, if I were to submit to your every deed, whatever you should say" (1.293). But since the other Achaians apparently have submitted to even the most outrageous deeds of their king, Achilles must regard them as cowards and of no account. Indeed, Achilles tells Agamemnon, "you rule over those who are of no account" (1.231). Achilles, then, suggests that the Achaians themselves are unjust. Even though Agamemnon is unjust, they simply acquiesce in his rule, perhaps because, like Calchas, they fear his wrath (1.75–83). And even though Achilles has made sacrifices not only for Agamemnon but also for them, even though he has just single-handedly saved them from the terrible plague sent by Apollo, the Achaians continue to obey Agamemnon and hence to side with Agamemnon against Achilles. Achilles, then, is evidently leaving Troy because, in his view, neither Agamemnon nor the Achaians are worthy of his virtuous efforts.[8] For nine years, Achilles has generously toiled and sacrificed for them in war and has nobly endured their injustice and ingratitude. But now, apparently because Achilles finally recognizes the full extent of their injustice and ingratitude, Achilles is returning to Phthia.[9]

This moment marks a crisis, not only in Achilles' devotion to the Achaians, but also in his devotion to virtue. For a certain problematic tension within his understanding of virtue makes itself felt here. On the one hand, Achilles believes the virtuous life to be fundamentally noble and self-denying, since, at its core, it entails making sacrifices for others. Accordingly, he stresses that he has been fighting for Agamemnon in a spirit of generosity rather than out of personal need or self-interest (1.152–160). And he also stresses that, unlike Agamemnon, he is not always thinking of his own profit or his own needs, but rather of the well-being of others (1.149, 1.122). The virtuous life, seen in this light, is essentially painful, since it entails nobly sacrificing one's own good for the good of others. As Achilles stresses, he has "toiled much" for the Achaians and he exhausts himself fighting for others (1.162, 1.168). Yet, on the other hand, Achilles believes that the virtuous man

[8] For Achilles' anger toward the Achaians as a whole, see also 1.407–412, 1.421–422, 1.509–510, 9.314–317.

[9] I consequently cannot agree with Zanker's claim that "Achilles' grievance is with Agamemnon alone" (1994, 75).

deserves to live more than a life of suffering, more than a life of pain and sacrifice and exhaustion. He deserves a "prize," a "dear" token of esteem and admiration (1.163–168). The best of the Achaians deserves to be recognized as such, and honored as such by those who know him and whom he benefits. Achilles, then, believes that the virtuous life is noble and self-denying but also that it ought to be beneficial to the man who leads it. The virtuous life ought to be graced specifically with honor.

Now, this tension within Achilles' understanding of virtue gives rise to two problems. In the first place, given that the virtuous man devotes himself to the good of others rather than to his own good, even sacrificing his own good for others, he would seem to be incapable of securing his own good for himself. Since, for example, he does not focus on acquiring honor but rather on making himself worthy of receiving honor, it would seem that he cannot ensure that he will indeed receive the honor he deserves. Therefore, it would seem that, precisely insofar as the virtuous man is noble, he cannot guarantee that the life he leads will be beneficial to him as well. If, then, the virtuous life is to entail more than pain and suffering, the virtuous man must look beyond virtue and outside of himself in order to ensure that he will receive the fulfillment he deserves.

But furthermore, if the virtuous man benefits from his sacrifices, even in the refined sense of receiving a due recognition of his excellence from those who are themselves excellent, in what sense are his sacrifices genuine sacrifices? In what sense is virtue self-denying if it offers a noble satisfaction to those who possess it? How can the virtuous life combine, as it apparently must, both self-sacrifice and self-fulfillment?

Achilles' failure to receive the honor he deserves from Agamemnon and the Achaians evidently leads him to wonder whether there is anything truly beneficial about the virtuous life, whether that life is not simply a miserable and pointless life of unappreciated sacrifice, and hence whether it is good for him to continue to lead that painful life at all. By declaring that he will return to Phthia because it is "better" – not for Agamemnon or the Achaians, presumably, but for himself – to do so, Achilles appears to indicate that he is now abandoning his devotion to the good of others and dedicating himself primarily to pursuing his own good, a good that is wholly independent of the Achaians – of their honor – and also of what is good for the Achaians (1.169–171). Accordingly, it would seem, then, that by leaving Troy, Achilles intends to leave not only the Achaians behind, but also his whole virtuous way of life behind and to pursue some other way of life, one that focuses on his own good, in Phthia.[10]

But is Achilles willing to leave Troy? Is he truly so indifferent to the Achaians he has fought for, and with, for so long? Is he truly free of the desire for their honor? Is he truly willing to abandon his dedication to virtue? Had Achilles left the Achaians and returned home, he might well have caused them great suffering, though it is not clear how much harm Hector would have done to the Achaians without the aid of Zeus. But Achilles would presumably have avoided suffering himself inasmuch as Patroclus would have accompanied him home. But is Achilles simply willing to leave the Achaians to their own devices?

After Achilles declares that he will leave, Agamemnon responds by daring Achilles to flee. He declares that he has no need for Achilles: "There are others beside me who will honor me, especially Thoughtful Zeus" (1.174–175). Agamemnon then proceeds to denounce Achilles as most hateful to him and to declare that he will take Achilles' captive mistress Briseis from him "so that you may know well how much better I am than you and another man may shrink from making himself my equal and likening himself to me" (1.185–187). Agamemnon here promises to humiliate Achilles by forcing him yield his prize. Now, if Achilles had genuinely decided to abandon his virtuous life, if he had truly become indifferent to the Achaians and to the honor they have given him in the past for his virtue, he would presumably have let Agamemnon take his prize and then would have gone home to Phthia. And he does evidently entertain this possibility when he considers whether "he should put a stop to his rage" (1.191). For to feel anger rather than indifference toward the Achaians, to blame them for dishonoring him, would be tantamount to acknowledging that he still seeks their honor, that he still believes that their honor is worth having and that they are worthy of giving him honor, and that he still hopes to get it from them. Therefore, insofar as Achilles no longer seeks or hopes to win honor from the Achaians, he would yield to Agamemnon here and then leave Troy.

But Achilles decides instead to take the desperate measure of trying to kill Agamemnon on the spot, along with all the Achaians who might take his side (1.188–195, 1.204–205). In the first place, this decision indicates that Achilles is not indifferent to the honor of the Achaians but rather seeks to retain the

[10] See Bolotin 1989, 47.

symbol of that honor – his prize – even if that means trying to kill those who bestowed that honor on him. But Achilles' decision to fight the Achaians here underscores the desperate situation he finds himself in. For the past nine years he has sacrificed for the Achaians with the hope that they would freely recognize and honor his sacrifice. Now the Achaians are attempting to deprive him of the insufficient honor he enjoys and he wants to keep it. But what can Achilles do to retain the honor of the Achaians? He cannot coerce them to honor him since, by seeking their honor, he is seeking their freely given recognition of his excellence. He does not want the false pretense of honor that the Achaians, in their cowardice, give to Agamemnon because they fear him. But how can he force them to honor him freely?

Furthermore, it would seem suicidal for Achilles to kill Agamemnon and to fight the Achaians in the middle of an assembly, since he is one against many. Perhaps he is so enraged that he does not care if he dies as a result of punishing such an outrageously selfish king and such a cowardly people. But if Achilles is not simply suicidal here, he must hope, in his heart of hearts, that since he is fighting against those who have outrageously wronged him, the gods, who are just, will intervene on his behalf, as they intervened on behalf of the righteous Chryses against Agamemnon. For even though Agamemnon claims that Zeus honors him (1.174–175), Achilles has just seen the son of Zeus, Apollo, send a plague to punish the wicked king.

At this point, a daughter of Zeus, the goddess Athena, does indeed intervene, at the behest of Hera, the wife of Zeus. When Achilles sees her, he evidently hopes that she has come to support him: "Why have you come again, child of aegis-bearing Zeus? So that you may know the hubris of Agamemnon, the son of Atreus?" (1.201–203).[11] Achilles, then, must act here against the Achaians with the hope and even the confidence that the gods, at least, will honor his virtue, and that they will help him punish Agamemnon and the Achaians for their injustice and will even somehow induce them to honor him as he deserves. In this way, he must look to the gods to ensure that his noble, self-denying life is one that is also beneficial to him.

But then Athena offers the stunning revelation that she has come to intervene on behalf of Agamemnon! First, she informs him that Hera, who sent her, "loves" and "cares for" both Achilles and Agamemnon "in the same way [ομῶς]" (1.209). This itself is shocking, insofar as Agamemnon has

[11] See Lateiner 2004, 24.

behaved unjustly first to Chryses, the priest of Apollo; then to the Achaians, by endangering them so that he might retain his mistress; and finally to Achilles, who has just saved the Achaians from Agamemnon's folly. But then Athena, speaking on behalf of Hera, orders Achilles to yield to Agamemnon, even though she acknowledges that Agamemnon is guilty of hubris (1.213–214). She orders Achilles to confine himself to criticizing Agamemnon with harsh words and promises him that, in return, he will receive many splendid gifts in the future. In this way, Athena and Hera save the unjust Agamemnon and the Achaians from Achilles' righteous wrath and uphold the authority of Agamemnon over him. Even though they do not praise Agamemnon, by supporting him against Achilles, Hera, the wife of Zeus, and Athena, the daughter of Zeus, would seem to vindicate the claim of Agamemnon that Zeus honors him. This intervention by Athena, then, must be devastating for Achilles. For he learns here that, just as Agamemnon and the Achaians do not honor his virtue, the gods themselves also do not honor his virtue. This divine intervention, then, must deepen the doubts Achilles already has about the life of virtue. For if neither human beings nor gods recognize his virtue, then why should he be virtuous? Why should he make all the painful sacrifices that virtue evidently requires?

Yet, Achilles does not respond to the intervention of Athena by resolving to leave Troy and abandon his life dedicated to virtue. Indeed, Achilles now drops all mention of going home to Phthia. Instead, he responds to the apparent revelation that the gods do not honor virtue by affirming all the more emphatically his hope that the gods will, in the end, honor his virtue and thereby vindicate his belief in the goodness, as well as the nobility, of the life of virtue.

Achilles tells Athena that he will obey her, in the belief that "If a man obeys the gods, they heed him greatly as well" (1.218). Now, the example before his eyes of Agamemnon would seem to call this belief into question. After all, even though Agamemnon has just been defying the god Apollo, Athena and Hera are now intervening on Agamemnon's behalf. Nevertheless, Achilles implicitly affirms here that piety is a part of virtue and evidently trusts that, if he persists in his devotion to virtue, sooner or later, in their sometimes inscrutable manner, the gods will reward him.

Once Athena departs, Achilles fulfills his promise to obey the goddess by confining himself to criticizing Agamemnon. He denounces the king as cowardly – "with the heart of a deer, never armed for war with your people" – and unjust – "a king who devours his people" (1.225–226, 1.231). Achilles then swears a great oath to Agamemnon that

> At some time longing for Achilles will come to the sons of the Achaians, all of them. Then, even though you are grieving, you will not be able to do anything, when many fall dead at the hands of man-slaying Hector. You will then tear at your spirit within, angry, that you did not honor the best of the Achaians. (1.239–244)

Achilles here expresses the confident belief that the Achaians, led by Agamemnon, will come to repent of their injustice to Achilles and will finally come to honor him as the best of the Achaians. In this way, he voices his hope that justice will be done and his dedication to virtue will be crowned with the honor of his companions. But what is the basis of this hope? It might seem that Achilles' hope here is simply based on reason: since he is by far the greatest warrior of the Achaians – "the bulwark of the Achaians," as Nestor will go on to say (1.284) – the Achaians will naturally suffer terrible losses in his absence and will naturally come to regret that they dishonored him. Yet, it is possible that, rather than bestow their honor on Achilles, the suffering Achaians may simply leave Troy, as they almost do in Book II (155–156) and as Agamemnon himself urges them to do in Books IX (26–28) and XIV (74–81). On the other hand, as we have seen, Agamemnon has affirmed that he does not need Achilles since he enjoys the support of Zeus. Even Nestor, who criticizes Agamemnon and stresses the need of the Achaians for Achilles, affirms that Zeus supports Agamemnon (1.277–279). And, as Achilles has just seen, the gods have indeed intervened in support of Agamemnon. Why, then, should they not intervene to protect Agamemnon and the Achaians from Hector in Achilles' absence? Why should the gods not protect Agamemnon from Hector just as they have protected Agamemnon from Achilles? Achilles' hope that the Achaians will suffer in his absence, will repent of their injustice, and will come to honor him as he deserves, must be based entirely, then, on his hope that the gods, in the end, will honor his virtue by punishing the hubris of Agamemnon and inducing the Achaians to recognize and honor Achilles as the best of the Achaians.

We see, then, that, in the first instance, Achilles responds to the apparent revelation of Athena that the gods do not honor virtue by reaffirming his belief that the gods will, in the end, honor virtue. So powerful is his devotion to virtue that he refuses to abandon it, even when both his companions and the gods fail to honor him for his virtue. But, on the other hand, so powerful is his desire to see virtue rewarded that he clings to the hope, notwithstanding the evidence of divine indifference to virtue, that it will be rewarded by just gods who ensure that the self-denying life of virtue is beneficial to those who lead it.

Yet, while he hopes to see his dedication to virtue vindicated by the gods, Achilles also clearly suffers from the agonizing doubt that he will continue to be dishonored and that his life of noble but painful sacrifice will be exposed as foolish and pointless. For once the emissaries of Agamemnon take his prize away, Achilles weeps, just as Chryses wept when Agamemnon refused to return his daughter (1.348–350, 42). Achilles' tears reflect his grief before the triumphant injustice of Agamemnon, but, as in the case of Chryses, they also reflect his unwillingness to accept that triumph. Accordingly, just as Chryses looks to Apollo to right this wrong, Achilles looks to Zeus. He first calls to his divine mother to complain of the injustice of Zeus: "Mother, since you bore me to live for only a short time, the Olympian, high-thundering Zeus ought to confer honor on me, at least. But now he has not honored me even a little. For the son of Atreus, wide ruling Agamemnon, dishonored me" (1.352–356). Achilles clearly blames Zeus here for supporting Agamemnon by at least allowing Hera and Athena to aid him and by allowing him to wrong Achilles with impunity. Nevertheless, Achilles continues to cherish the hope that, since justice demands it and since the greatest of gods must be just, Zeus will ultimately punish Agamemnon and the Achaians and reward Achilles with the honor he deserves. Achilles' hope here evidently draws some strength from the example of Chryses, who successfully beseeched Apollo to punish Agamemnon and the Achaians and thereby induce them to return his daughter Chryseis to him. For Achilles urges his mother to beseech Zeus to punish Agamemnon and the Achaians and thereby induce them to give him the honor he deserves:

> Remind him of these things, sit beside him, and take his knees, if in some way he might be willing to help the Trojans, to pin the Achaians against their sterns and the sea, being killed, so that they may all have profit of their king, and that the son of Atreus, wide ruling Agamemnon, may also recognize his folly, that he did not honor the best of the Achaians. (1.407–412)

Achilles is not simply spiteful or hate-filled here. He does not wish Zeus to kill all the Achaians or even to kill Agamemnon. He rather wishes that Zeus punish the injustice of the Achaians so that they, led by Agamemnon, will come to recognize their injustice and folly and will finally honor him as the most virtuous of the Achaians. Achilles here wishes Zeus to follow the model of his son Apollo: as Apollo sent a plague to kill many Achaians and thereby induced them, led by Agamemnon, to restore Chryseis to her father, Zeus should send Hector and the Trojans to kill many Achaians and thereby induce them, and above all Agamemnon, to repent and right their wrong.

We see, then, that Achilles pins all of his hopes on Zeus to punish the injustice of the Achaians, to induce them to honor him as he deserves, and thereby to vindicate his devotion to virtue. He does not take any action of his own to punish the Achaians. He does not, for example, follow the paths later followed by Alcibiades and Coriolanus of joining with the enemies of his people to punish them and thereby induce them to honor him, both because the gods have prohibited him from doing so and because it is impossible to coerce human beings to honor one freely.[12] More simply, he does not attempt to take any direct action of his own to induce the Achaians to honor him for his devotion to virtue because virtue necessarily requires him to be self-denying rather than self-interested. Virtue means, in his eyes, sacrificing for others, not seeking rewards from others. But it also means being rewarded from others according to one's deserts.

It is Achilles' devotion to virtue and his contradictory understanding of virtue that require him to turn to the gods. Achilles wants both to sacrifice for others and to be benefited for his sacrifices. He therefore turns to the gods to square this circle, to ensure that self-denying virtue is rewarded. The case of Achilles suggests that the life devoted to virtue is radically dependent on divine support.[13] Even Achilles, even the mightiest of men, must wait, idly and impotently, for the gods to vindicate his devotion to virtue. For only the gods can possibly ensure that the self-sacrificing life of virtue is beneficial to the man who leads it. The virtuous man can be noble on his own, but he cannot secure the good, his own good, on his own, without sacrificing his nobility. Therefore, he looks to the gods. But can even the gods truly vindicate the life of virtue as one that is both noble and good, both self-denying and rewarding? Can the gods offer the virtuous Achilles the happiness and fulfillment he seeks?

[12] On comparisons of Achilles and Coriolanus, consider Bowra (1977, 22–23), Redfield (1975, 104, 106), and Benardete (2005, 71–76).

[13] See Bolotin 1989, 47–48; 1995, 86–87.

ACHILLES' DOUBTS ABOUT THE VIRTUOUS LIFE

Fourteen days after Achilles withdraws from the fighting, two days after Zeus agrees to Thetis's prayer, on behalf of her son, that the god use the Trojans to punish the Achaians and make them recognize their injustice to Achilles, the Achaians appear to offer Achilles all that he demands. Faced with the destruction of his army, besieged by the Trojans beside his own ships after nine years of besieging Troy, denounced by Nestor who now claims that all of the Achaians sided with Achilles against him, Agamemnon offers Achilles what would seem to be the pinnacle of human glory. He offers Achilles vast amounts of gold, fine horses, seven beautiful mistresses captured from Lesbos, and Briseis herself right away (9.119–135). After Troy is conquered, Agamemnon promises him even more treasure, the twenty most beautiful Trojan women (other than Helen), one of his own daughters in marriage, along with the honor of being his son-in-law, and seven cities in Argos where the people will honor Achilles as a god (9.135–156). In addition to this, Odysseus promises Achilles that the Achaians themselves will honor him as a god (9.300–303). Short of killing Agamemnon and making Achilles their king, it would seem that the Achaians could offer Achilles no greater honor than they do here.[14] Yet, Achilles rejects their offer and therewith appears to reject the very honor that he had prayed for and the denial of which had prompted him to withdraw from the war. He now rejects the honor from gods and men that he had sought as the crowning benefit of the life of virtue, as the benefit that would vindicate the goodness of the life of virtue. What accounts for this change?

The Achilles we encounter in Book IX appears to be a changed man. In Book I (which takes place fourteen days before), we saw Achilles raging at Agamemnon and the Achaians, weeping in the face of their injustice, and praying that Zeus inflict deadly punishment upon them (1.491–492). In Book II (which takes place two days before), Homer describes Achilles as "angry," "grieving," and "enraged" (2.688–694, 2.768–773). But now, Odysseus, Ajax, and Phoinix find Achilles "delighting his mind with his lyre": "with it he delighted his spirit and sang of the glories of men" (9.186–189). Achilles is the only character in the *Iliad* who is presented as singing, not of gods, but of

[14] See Griffin 1995, 26–27. Lateiner suggests that Agamemnon should have apologized in person (2004, 25).

men (see 1.472–474, 1.601–604). He is the only character in the *Iliad* who is therefore presented as singing a song akin to the *Iliad* itself, the song about the wrath of Achilles sung by Homer.[15] Furthermore, this is the first time and indeed the only time in the *Iliad* in which Achilles appears content, even delighted, and at least momentarily free from the anger and grief that have afflicted him because of the failure of the Achaians and of the gods to honor him.[16] Finally, the fact that Homer says that Achilles delighted his *mind* by singing of the "glories of men" suggests that Achilles has found pleasure and satisfaction in reflecting on men like himself, who have performed deeds that are worthy of glory and who may or may not have received the glory they deserved (see 9.524–525).[17] Thinking about such men has, for the moment, freed him from the pain of nobly sacrificing his well-being for the sake of others and of raging against the ingratitude of others (compare 9.186–189 with 9.321–322). Thinking about honor, rather than seeking it or even possessing it, has, for the moment at least, supplied Achilles with some portion of the happiness that has eluded him.

Achilles' reflections on honor have evidently led him to doubt the goodness of honor and consequently lead him to reject the honor the Achaians now offer him, which he had originally demanded of them. Achilles proceeds to explain to his friends, the men he claims to love most of all of the Achaians, why he rejects the honor of the Achaians. Achilles' explanation here would seem to be an unfriendly act, since he rebuffs the desperate pleas from his friends that he save them from destruction. On the other hand,

[15] Segal notes that the poem "ennobles art by presenting the best of the Achaians in a bardic role" (1992, 21).

[16] The other noteworthy moments when Achilles is said to be delighted are the moment he holds in his hands and beholds the armor Hephaestus has made for him (19.15–20) and during his encounter with Priam. After Priam's plea for compassion moves Achilles to weep for his father and for Patroclus, Homer remarks: "But once divine Achilles delighted himself with lamentation, and longing for it went from his mind and his limbs, he rose from his chair . . ." (24.513–515; see also 23.10–11). Then, Homer later recounts that "Priam wondered at Achilles, both his grandeur and his quality . . . and Achilles wondered at Priam, gazing at his goodly appearance and listening to his speech. But once they had delighted themselves by gazing upon one another, the old man, godlike Priam, spoke to him first" (24.629–634). But perhaps all of these moments of delight, even the last one, are overshadowed for Achilles by his sorrow over the death of Patroclus.

[17] I am therefore inclined to disagree with Benardete's claim regarding Achilles that "As soon as he reflects, he is lost" (2005, 94).

Achilles' explanation is a friendly act insofar as he shares his thoughts about honor and virtue with his friends and urges them to act on his insights by leaving Troy and sailing home (9.417–420).

After Odysseus conveys the offer by Agamemnon and the Achaians of extravagant gifts and honors, Achilles explains why he rejects them all – specifically their offer of honor – and proceeds to raise far-reaching questions concerning the very value of both honor and virtue. In the first place, he observes:

> I do not think that the son of Atreus, Agamemnon, will persuade me, nor that the rest of the Danaans will do so, since there was no gratitude for fighting unceasingly, always, against enemy men. There is an equal portion for the one who stays back and if someone fights hard. The evil one and the noble one are held in single honor. (9.315–319)

Achilles clarifies here that he specifically has sought gratitude from the Achaians for the sacrifices he has made from them. What makes honor valuable is that it is no more and no less than a true and just acknowledgment of one's true nobility and one's true excellence. But the honor that the Achaians are now offering him is both more and less than such genuine gratitude. On the one hand, it is excessive. Agamemnon promises Achilles seven Argive cities in which the men "will honor you as a god" and Odysseus adds that the Achaians "will honor you as a god" (9.297, 9.302–303). But, in contrast with Hector, who declares twice, "I would be honored as Athena and Apollo are honored," Achilles never seeks such flattery (8.540, 13.825–827). He has never wanted to be honored beyond what is called for by truth and justice. Achilles wants to be honored, not as a god, nor even as the greatest human being, but specifically as "the best of the Achaians" (1.243–244, 1.410–412). But furthermore, the honor Agamemnon and Odysseus offer Achilles now falls short of genuine honor because, unlike genuine honor, unlike gratitude, it is contingent and self-serving. Rather than thank him for the tremendous services he has rendered, rather than selflessly recognize his generosity and courage, the Achaians transparently offer him honors and gifts in the hope that he will proceed to save them from the terrible destruction they face. For they are only coming to him laden with honors now, fourteen days after they dishonored him, because they are at the end of their tether. Now that they are so terrified of the Trojans, they are willing, in effect, to pay him to return to work for them as the bulwark of the Achaians. They are therefore only promising to honor him as a god if, and only if, he comes back to fight for them. To be sure, Achilles did pray to Zeus that he use the Trojans to punish the Achaians precisely so that they might feel their need for him and honor him as he deserves (1.407–412; see also 1.239–244). But now, presumably after reflecting on the honor of men he has sung about, Achilles has come to see that such "honor" from self-interested men is not genuine honor, that it is merely the self-serving praise of one whose services they seek to profit from, and hence an instrument through which they hope to save themselves rather than a just and grateful acknowledgment of the virtue of another.

At this point, Achilles goes further to question the value of any form of honor and indeed the value of virtue itself: "He still goes down to death, the man who has done no deeds, and the one who has done many. Nothing more is laid up for me, once I suffered pains in my spirit, always risking my life (or soul) by fighting" (9.320–322). Achilles has suggested that the Achaians are unjust because they do not confer on the noble man the honor he deserves. But now Achilles suggests that it is unjust for the noble to suffer, not only dishonor, but also death. The noble deserve, then, something more than honor as a reward for their sacrifices: the noble deserve everlasting life or immortality. Indeed, Achilles suggests that honor, even gratitude, is not truly worth having when one is dead. The goodness of the noble, virtuous life, then, cannot consist in honor – even genuine honor – but only in immortality. But even though the noble deserve immortality, they do not, according to Achilles, receive it. Death comes to all, noble and ignoble alike. Achilles seems to hint here that, just as the Achaians are guilty of injustice because they do not give the noble the honor they deserve, so the gods are guilty of injustice because they do not give the noble the immortality they deserve.[18]

Here, then, we see more clearly the problem of virtue as Achilles has come to see it. Virtue means devoting oneself to others more than to oneself and therefore enduring pain and even death for the sake of others. Yet, the virtuous human being would seem to deserve some benefit, some reward, for such sacrifice. As Achilles puts it, something more should be gained for him as a result of his continuous suffering for others. Nevertheless, Achilles' reflections

[18] See Bolotin 1989, 47–48. I therefore think that Benardete goes too far in suggesting that "Achilles trusts completely" in the gods here (2005, 97–98). Consider also Redfield's claim that "Achilles never loses his confidence in the gods" except for 21.273–283 (1975, 213–214).

on honor have evidently driven him to the conclusion that honor cannot constitute the crowning benefit of the virtuous life, partly because honor tends to come from selfish men, but mainly because honor is of no benefit to those who are dead. Life, then, he now sees, is the crowning good for human beings, the good that is most to be cherished. And death – the gates of Hades – is that evil most to be hated (9.312–313). But precisely insofar as virtue means devoting oneself to others and putting their good above one's own, it necessarily entails being willing to sacrifice one's very life for others. Now, if the gods rewarded the virtuous with immortality, then the goodness of the virtuous life would be vindicated. But since the gods offer no such reward to the virtuous, we humans must seek to prolong the lives we have and must therefore conclude that the virtuous life is not good for human beings.

One might think that Achilles is not going so far as to suggest that it is unreasonable to devote oneself to others as such but is simply arguing here that Agamemnon and the Achaians in particular are so selfish and unjust that it is unreasonable to devote oneself to them in particular. Yet, by comparing his relation with the Achaians to that of a mother bird with her young, Achilles indicates that he is indeed calling into question the reasonableness of ever sacrificing oneself for another: "As a bird brings morsels to her young who cannot yet fly, wherever she may take them, but for her there is evil, so I have lain for many sleepless nights and passed through bloody days in fighting, struggling with men for the sake of their wives" (9.323–327). Through this simile, Achilles dares to ask whether, even in the clearest example of two beings who are bound together body and soul, even in the case of mother and child, it is reasonable for one to sacrifice for another.[19] For how can it be good to sacrifice one's own good for the sake of another, even for those who need you and count on you? In this way, Achilles calls into question most radically what would seem to be the very essence of virtue.[20]

[19] Homer himself compares the determination of Menelaus and Ajax to protect the corpse of Patroclus from the Trojans to the determination of, respectively, a mother cow and a father lion to protect their young (17.1–5, 17.132–139).

[20] As Gagarin remarks, "It would be hard to show more clearly that what Achilles is here rejecting is a moral sense of distinterested concern for others, as he dismisses even the most minimal, instinctive concern of a mother for her children as unprofitable" (1987, 302). Gagarin goes on to suggest that the loss of Patroclus is Achilles' punishment for this moral error and that his compassionate treatment of Priam in Book XXIV "is intended to compensate for his behavior in Book 9 and reinstate Achilles as a moral hero" (302).

Achilles' doubts about the goodness of the life of virtue lead to the conclusion that one should abandon that life in favor of devoting oneself to pursuing one's own good. But what is that good? What is the primary good for human beings, according to Achilles? What is the happiness he seeks? As we have seen, Achilles here appears to reject honor as the primary ingredient in human fulfillment. By suggesting that it is unreasonable to sacrifice one's life, to suffer physical pain and mental anguish, and to endure sleepless nights for the sake of others, he suggests that the most fulfilling life for a human being is a long, carefree, and restful life.[21] But would such a life, however comfortable, truly satisfy the lion-hearted Achilles (7.228)?

Achilles goes on to suggest that he would find fulfillment in marriage to a woman he loves, his mistress Briseis:

> Why ought the Argives wage war against the Trojans? Why did the son of Atreus assemble and bring here an army? Was it not for the sake of fair-haired Helen? But are the sons of Atreus the only ones of mortal humans who love their wives? Since anyone who is a good man and has judgment loves his own wife and cares for her, as I myself loved her from my spirit, even though I acquired her by my spear. (9.337–343; see also 19.282–300)

Yet, inasmuch as Achilles proceeds to reject once and for all Agamemnon's offer to return Briseis to him and to declare that he will leave Troy when the sun rises in a few hours, and inasmuch as he sleeps with another mistress right after his friends leave, it would seem that Achilles does not pin his hopes for happiness on a loving marriage with his captive mistress (9.356–363, 9.663–665).

At this point in his speech to Odysseus, it would seem that Achilles has firmly resolved to return to Phthia. Having delighted his mind and spirit by singing about and reflecting on the honorable deeds of men, Achilles has evidently concluded that the honor of the Achaians is simply not worth having and, more broadly, that the noble but painful life of the virtuous warrior is an unreasonable one. It would seem, then, that he will now return home to Phthia to devote himself to living a long and comfortable life: "There are very many things belonging to me that I left behind when I

[21] Zanker suggests that "Once Achilles asserts that life is irreplaceable and too valuable for any adequate compensation, he is breathing a different air from Sarpedon, for whom honor actively softens the finality of death" (1994, 88; consider also 81–82, 97–98).

came here and from here I will bring more gold and red bronze and well-girdled women and gray iron, which was allotted to me" (9.364–367).

Yet, it quickly becomes apparent, even before his response to Ajax, in which he reveals that he will stay at Troy, even in his response to Odysseus, that Achilles is not firmly resolved to abandon his dedication to virtue (9.649–655). For even though he decidedly rejects Agamemnon's offer of gifts and honors in exchange for his returning to the war, the reasons he gives for this rejection are contradictory and reveal that he continues to feel an attachment to the virtuous life. On the one hand, Achilles continues to reject the gifts and honors offered by Agamemnon because he rejects the noble life of risking and sacrificing one's very self for the sake of others:

> For not worth my soul are all that they say Ilion, that well inhabited city, possessed, in the old days, when there was peace, before the coming of the sons of the Achaians, nor all that the stone threshold of the archer, Phoebus Apollo, encloses, in rocky Pytho. For cattle and fat sheep can be taken by plunder and tripods and the fair heads of horses may be acquired, but for the soul of a man to come back, this cannot be taken by plunder or seized, once it has crossed the barrier of the teeth. (9.400–409)

No possible good, no possible reward – evidently not even the reward of "imperishable glory" and "noble glory" – can make up for the annihilation of one's being (9.410–416). And Achilles here apparently identifies the preservation and fulfillment of his soul, and hence his happiness, primarily with the preservation and comfort of his body and hence with returning home, living a long life, and enjoying material prosperity and marital comfort:

> For if the gods will save me and I come home, Peleus himself will surely seek out a wife for me. There are many Achaian women throughout Hellas and Phthia, daughters of the best men, who protect their cities, and the one I would wish I would make my beloved wife. There my manly spirit drives me greatly to take a wedded wife, a suitable spouse, to delight in the possessions that old Peleus has acquired. (9.393–400)

Such a life is admittedly not noble or grand, for it does not offer the promise of any satisfaction beyond that of a limited, physical satisfaction. It is not even graced with love, for even though Achilles speaks of making a woman his "beloved wife," the marriage he envisions is an arranged marriage, one of the possessions that his father will bequeath him. Even Achilles' reference to his father is rather businesslike: he does not call him "beloved" or even "father," but merely "Peleus" or "old Peleus." The delights of the life he envisions are material rather than spiritual, ordinary and prosaic rather than grand and heroic. Nevertheless, Achilles apparently embraces this vision of happiness here. Furthermore, insofar as he cares about long life and comfort rather than honor and virtue, Achilles appears to abandon his anger at the injustice of Agamemnon and the Achaians. For if it is better for him to eschew honor and to return home to a long life of peace and material comfort, what harm are the Achaians doing to him by depriving him of honor? Accordingly, he appears to recommend to the Achaians as a whole, in a benevolent spirit, that they too abandon the life of virtue and honor, return to their homes, and devote themselves to living long and comfortable lives (9.417–426). And he appears to speak of his own wrath with a certain distance when he concludes his speech to Odysseus by advising that the Achaians need to devise a better scheme to save themselves than "that which they thought of since I was enraged" (9.426).

On the other hand, Achilles also claims in his speech to Odysseus that he is rejecting the gifts and honors Agamemnon offers to him because he continues to be angry at Agamemnon's injustice. Indeed, so angry is Achilles that he emphatically and unequivocally rejects the material prosperity, the physical satisfaction, and hence, it would seem, the very happiness that Agamemnon offers him:

> Hateful to me are his gifts. I honor them as I would a wood shaving. Not if he gave me ten times and twenty times as much as he possesses now, not if more should come to him from elsewhere, as much as is brought into Orchomenus, as much as is brought into Egyptian Thebes, where greatest possessions lie up in houses, where there are a hundred gates, and two hundred men go forth from each with horses and chariots. Not if he gave me gifts as many as the sand or the dust is, not even thus would he yet persuade my spirit until he should pay for the entire outrage that pains my spirit. Nor will I marry the daughter of Agamemnon, the son of Atreus, not even if her beauty challenged that of golden Aphrodite, or her works equaled those of owl-eyed Athena. Not even thus would I marry her. (9.378–391)

Achilles here vows that he would reject whatever happiness Agamemnon might offer him, even if he offered him infinite wealth and a wife divine in her beauty and works. And Achilles rejects such happiness, not in the name of living a long and comfortable life at home, but in the name of justice. For, Achilles here insists, since Agamemnon took his prize and dishonored him, Agamemnon is guilty of terrible injustice, of hubris, deception, shamelessness, and outrage (9.367–387). Therefore, Achilles will refuse all gifts and even sacrifice his very own happiness so that Agamemnon may pay completely for his injustice. Here, then, Achilles appears to reiterate his noble devotion to virtue, his heroic willingness to sacrifice his own good for the sake of justice, and even his determination to remain at Troy, not to fight the Trojans, but to see that justice is visited once and for all upon Agamemnon. We see, then, that, even though Achilles has come to doubt the goodness of the life of virtue – of devoting oneself to others and sacrificing oneself for others – he continues to feel an attachment to that life.

What prevents Achilles from whole-heartedly rejecting the life of virtue is his doubt concerning the goodness of the alternative to the life of virtue. His reflections about honor and virtue have led Achilles to conclude that it is unreasonable ever to sacrifice one's own happiness for the sake of others, as a mother bird sacrifices her own good for her young, as he has sacrificed for the Achaians. Therefore, his reason dictates that he should pursue his own good. But what is that good that would fulfill him? What is that life that would truly satisfy his soul? The good that Achilles sees most clearly is life itself: nothing is worth the sacrifice of his life since "for the soul of a man to come back, this cannot be taken by plunder or seized, once it has crossed the barrier of the teeth" (9.400–409). The good life, then, in contrast with the dangerous and inevitably short noble life, is a continuous, safe, and, indeed, an endless life. Accordingly, the life he believes to be the clearest alternative to the life of noble sacrifice is a long, safe, and comfortable life: "But if I arrive home to the beloved land of my fathers, my noble fame will be lost, but a long lifetime will be mine, nor would the end of death overtake me swiftly" (9.414–416). Yet the goodness of such a life must inevitably fall short, since it cannot truly fulfill the needs and desires of his soul. In the first place, such a life cannot satisfy Achilles' longing for endless life since death will inevitably bring even that peaceful life to an end. Death will not overtake Achilles swiftly in Phthia, but it will eventually overtake him and thereby deprive him of the goodness of life. Furthermore, a life devoted to merely physical existence and satisfaction cannot fully satisfy the deepest desires of his soul. The delight in material possessions cannot offer his mind and his spirit the delight that they crave and need, a delight supplied, for example, by the activity of singing and reflecting on the honorable deeds of men (compare 9.398–400 with 9.186–189). The comfort of a marriage arranged by his father cannot satisfy his longing for love and friendship. The alternative to the short and painful but noble life of sacrifice, then, does not seem clearly or fully good to

Achilles, since it does not offer him the promise of the deathless existence or the full happiness that he longs for.

At this point, one might wonder whether the activity of singing about and reflecting on the virtue and honor of men could not constitute a compelling alternative to both the long but flat-souled life of material comfort and the noble but painful life of sacrifice. Unlike the life of virtue, it would be a fulfilling life, one that delights his mind and spirit. Unlike the life of physical comfort, it would offer higher, deeper, and more specifically human pleasures than those connected with the body. Would not this life, the life evidently led by Homer himself, offer Achilles the happiness, the fulfillment of mind and spirit, he craves? It is possible that, even though he does cherish the pleasures of singing and thinking about human beings, the active Achilles simply does not grasp that the life of the contemplative singer could constitute a distinct and complete way of life. But it is also possible that he doubts that such a philosophic life would satisfy the deepest longings of his heart. For even if it would satisfy his longing for happiness more fully than the long life of material comfort that he describes awaiting him in Phthia, the life of the contemplative singer would still not satisfy his longing for immortality.

What may ultimately draw Achilles to the life of virtue, notwithstanding his doubts about its goodness, is that it offers the promise of a greater good than that of mere life. As we have seen, the life of virtue seems contradictory, since the virtuous human being both sacrifices his own good for the sake of others and deserves to be rewarded for such sacrifice. Yet that apparent contradiction offers a hope for what might seem to be a true happiness. For the goods that the virtuous man most obviously sacrifices are the material goods of long life and physical comfort. But the goods that such a man deserves would therefore seem to be higher than those material goods, goods of the soul rather than of the body. Therefore, by rejecting goods of the body, by rejecting even, for example, the infinite wealth and beauty that Achilles imagines Agamemnon offering him, Achilles might somehow feel that he deserves an even higher reward than those infinite goods, a higher happiness that would satisfy his soul and not merely his body. Now, again, the question arises, what might such happiness consist of? It would seem that such a happiness would have to encompass an activity that delights and fulfills his whole being, his mind and his spirit. But Achilles does not focus on considering what that activity might be. Instead, by identifying the greatest good for a human being with long life, he suggests that the central element of happiness must be immortality, an immortality that Achilles has suggested the noble man deserves by virtue of his nobility. Achilles, then, must continue to feel attached to virtue because he hopes that, if there are gods who are just, they will reward him with the immortality he deserves and longs for. Now, this hope would seem to be contradictory, since it consists of hoping that he will be rewarded by the gods for sacrificing himself for others. But so powerful is Achilles' hope for immortality that he clings to that contradictory hope.

The manifestation of Achilles' ongoing attachment to virtue and his implicit hope that his virtue will be rewarded with immortality is his anger. Even though Achilles argues that a life devoted to material comfort is superior to the life devoted to virtue, he angrily rejects Agamemnon's offer of tremendous material prosperity. Even though Achilles argues that a long life is superior to a life devoted to honor, he rages at Agamemnon for depriving him of honor and implies that he will sacrifice his homecoming in order to see that Agamemnon is punished for his injustice. Even though, by Achilles' own argument, Agamemnon has not harmed Achilles by dishonoring him – since it is better for Achilles to go home to Phthia to live a long and comfortable life – but has only brought harm to himself by depriving himself of the only warrior who could protect him from the Trojans, even though, by Achilles' own argument, Agamemnon has been robbed of his senses by Zeus and would therefore seem to be an object of contempt or even pity rather than anger and hatred, Achilles persists in raging against him. For by raging at Agamemnon, by insisting that Agamemnon has harmed him unjustly, and by rejecting Agamemnon's material offerings in the name of justice, Achilles can feel that, if there is any justice in this world, the just gods will compensate him for his suffering and reward him for his sacrifice. As Odysseus says, Achilles wants to be angry (9.678–679). And he wants to be angry because he wants to feel deserving of the immortality he craves.

Achilles, then, remains attached to the virtuous life, despite his doubts, because it seems to offer him the promise of immortality. Yet, Achilles does not simply long for an immortal existence. He also longs for the companionship of those he loves and admires, of those who are themselves courageous, just, and thoughtful. Achilles remains attached to the virtuous life because it seems to satisfy his longing for friendship as well as his longing for immortality.

Even though Nestor later complains to Patroclus that "Achilles alone will benefit from his virtue," Achilles is not content to be alone in his virtue (11.762–763). He wishes to share his virtuous life with others, with those whom he loves, to benefit them, to be benefited by them, and to benefit others together. He does not simply want to be the best of the Achaians; he wants to be honored by the Achaians as the best, and he wants the Achaians themselves to be virtuous and hence worthy of honoring his own virtue.

Achilles' very anger at the Achaians and even at Agamemnon reflects his love for them. As he is devoted to virtue, he wants them to be devoted to virtue. As he wishes them to honor him for his excellence – his courage, his justice, his nobility – so does he want them to recognize and appreciate his excellence. As he wants to be worthy of their honor, so does he want them to be worthy of giving him honor. Accordingly, he is disappointed and violently angry when Agamemnon behaves so selfishly and unjustly and when the Achaians shamefully acquiesce in his injustice. But he wants to punish them precisely so that they might recover and renew their devotion to justice.

Even as Achilles withdraws from the Achaians and awaits their chastisement, he is far from embracing a solitary existence, as Nestor suggests. Achilles continues to cherish his long-standing friendship with Patroclus – "you who have given joy to my spirit" (11.607). When delighting his mind and spirit by playing his lyre and singing of and reflecting on the honorable deeds of men, Achilles does so in the presence of Patroclus (9.185–191). He is not content to sing and reflect by himself but wishes to sing for his friend and to share his reflections with his friend, as he goes on to share his reflections on virtue and honor with those he claims to be his dearest friends among the Achaians: Odysseus, Phoinix, and Ajax (9.197–198, 9.204). Furthermore, even when he rejects Odysseus's plea that he return to the war to save the Achaians from destruction, Achilles shows his concern for the Achaians by urging them to join him in leaving Troy and urges his lifelong friend Phoinix in particular to return to Phthia with him (9.417–429). And when Phoinix reiterates Odysseus's plea that Achilles relent in his anger, Achilles again urges Phoinix to join him and offers to share his power and honor with him: "Be king equally with me and take half my honor" (9.616). Finally, when, in contrast with Odysseus and Phoinix, Ajax appeals specifically to Achilles' friendship for his companions rather than to his desire for wealth and honor, Achilles reverses his decision to leave Troy and return to Phthia (compare 9.649–655 with 9.356–368, 9.426–429, 9.617–619). When Ajax complains of

Achilles that "He is hard and does not have regard for the friendship of his companions, wherein we honored him far beyond others by the ships," Achilles accepts this rebuke and agrees with it: "Ajax, seed of Zeus, son of Telamon, ruler of peoples, all that you have said seems spoken after my own spirit" (9.630–631, 9.644–645). And even though Achilles insists that he will not fight the Trojans until they attack his own camp and ships, he thereby indicates that he will stay at Troy, moved by his concern for his friends, and hence offers at least some hope that he will intervene to save the Achaians, as he does on the very next day.[22]

Achilles stays at Troy and persists in his attachment to virtue because he believes that only the life of virtue can satisfy both his longing for immortality and his longing for friendship. Even though he wonders how it can be good to sacrifice one's own happiness – one's very soul – for the sake of others, as virtue demands, Achilles remains drawn to the life of virtue in the hope that the gods may grant the virtuous the immortality they deserve and in the belief that virtue offers the soundest basis for friendship. And Achilles' hope for immortality may seem especially questionable, insofar as it is based on the questionable belief that the gods are just and on the seemingly contradictory belief that those who sacrifice themselves benefit themselves, Achilles' belief in virtue as the soundest basis for friendship would seem to be reasonable.[23] For insofar as virtue means devoting oneself to others and displaying one's courage and generosity on behalf of others, it would seem that the virtuous would be especially good to their friends and hence would be especially good friends. And insofar as the virtuous life is painful, entailing as it does sacrifice for others, it would seem that the virtuous would be especially in need of friends, to share their toils and to compensate them for their toils, and hence it would seem that they would especially cherish their friends. Friendship, then, might seem to be the clearest benefit of the virtuous life, and hence might seem to vindicate the goodness of the virtuous life. The friendship of Achilles for such virtuous Achaians as Ajax, Phoinix, Odysseus, and above all Patroclus would seem to constitute the happiness of the virtuous Achilles, the human happiness of Achilles, apart from his hopes for the divine reward of immortality. And yet it is Achilles' love for Patroclus in particular that leads

[22] See Schein 1984, 113–116; Zanker 1994, 88–90; Griffin 1995, 26.

[23] Consider Aristotle *Nicomachean Ethics* 1155a1–33, 1156b6–1157b38.

to his greatest suffering.[24] The case of Achilles invites us to ask, then, does friendship constitute the crowning benefit of the virtuous human being and thereby vindicate the goodness of the virtuous life? Or does the phenomenon of friendship raise further questions concerning the goodness of the virtuous life? To address these questions, let us turn to examine the friendship of Achilles and Patroclus.[25]

THE PROBLEM OF VIRTUE AND FRIENDSHIP

The pivotal moment of the *Iliad* is Achilles' decision to send Patroclus into battle against the Trojans, with the Myrmidons, but without joining them himself. As a result of this decision, Achilles suffers the terrible loss of his beloved companion, whom he cherished as much as his own self, and also suffers the terrible anguish of blaming himself for the death of his friend (18.80–84; see also 18.98–106, 18.324–327). Insofar as Achilles later sends the Trojans fleeing simply by shouting three times and then proceeds to drive them back to Troy by fighting them virtually single-handedly, it would seem that, had Achilles chosen to fight the Trojans along with Patroclus and the Myrmidons, he would easily have saved the Achaians without losing Patroclus (18.202–238, 21.526–529). Why, then, does he make the disastrous, self-destructive, and seemingly needless choice of sending his dearest companion into mortal peril?

At first glance, Achilles' decision to continue to stay out of the fighting here is simply baffling.[26] As we have seen, the fact that Achilles remains at Troy rather than return home to Phthia, even though he has repeatedly threatened to do so, suggests that he plans to return to the war once Agamemnon and the Achaians have been duly punished for dishonoring him.[27] But Agamemnon has now been seriously wounded and, inasmuch as Hector is about to set the Achaian ships on fire, the Achaians are on the verge of being finally and irreversibly destroyed. This, then, would seem to be the

[24] See Crotty, 1994, 59.

[25] On the centrality of friendship as a theme of the *Iliad*, see Schein 1984, 98, 126–127.

[26] See Alvis 1995, 36.

[27] Compare 1.169–171, 9.356–363, 9.426–429 with 9.617–619, 9.649–655; see also 1.239–244, 1.407–412, 9.379–387, 11.607–609.

last possible moment at which Achilles could still return to battle. Furthermore, Achilles' rage against Agamemnon and the Achaians seems by this point to have faded away altogether. In Book XI, when he sees that Machaon, a key member of the Achaian army because he is only one of two Achaians – in addition to Achilles and Patroclus – who know how to heal the wounded, has himself been gravely wounded, Achilles sends Patroclus to the Achaians, apparently out of concern for their well-being (11.610–614, 11.504–518, 11.827–835). Then, when Patroclus returns and reports the dire condition of the Achaians, Achilles says of the injustice of Agamemnon against him: "But we will let this be a thing of the past. It was by no means in my mind to be enraged forever" (16.60–61). And he then sends his best friend, Patroclus, into battle, armed with his own splendid armor and accompanied by his Myrmidon soldiers, and urges him to save the Achaians from destruction: "But even so, Patroclus, ward off destruction from the ships and fall upon them with your strength, lest they set the ships alight with a blazing fire and take away the beloved homecoming" (16.80–82); "Rise up, Zeus-born Patroclus, rider of horses. I see the sweep of blazing fire beside the ships. Let them [the Trojans] not take the ships so that they [the Achaians] may no longer flee. Don the armor more quickly. I will gather the people [the Myrmidons]" (16.126–129). But if Achilles is willing to go to such lengths to save the Achaians, why does he not go all the way and save them himself?

Achilles does tell Patroclus: "I did say that I would not desist from my wrath until the clamor and war came to my ships" (16.61–63). In this way, he suggests that he is reluctant to go back on his word by unsaying his anger and returning to the war now, before the Trojans have attacked his ships.[28] But it is hard to believe that Achilles, who has already reversed his decision to leave Troy for Phthia, would expose his beloved friend to mortal harm simply in order to avoid reversing his decision to stay angry until the Trojans attacked his ships (1.169–171, 9.357–361, 9.617–619, 9.649–653). Achilles himself apparently acknowledges to Patroclus that he is no longer angry (16.60–61). And the simple fact that he sends Patroclus and all of his soldiers to help the Achaians would seem to demonstrate that Achilles has indeed desisted from his wrath. Finally and perhaps most importantly, Achilles acknowledges to

[28] Consider Redfield 1975, 18; Whitman 1958, 197–198; Janko 1992, 309; Benardete 2005, 112. See also Crotty 1994, 56.

Zeus himself that his prayer that he punish the Achaians for their injustice has been fulfilled: "As once, when I prayed to you, you heeded me and you honored me and strongly smote the host of the Achaians, so too even now bring to pass this wish" (16.236–238). Achilles here acknowledges to Zeus that the cause of his own wrath has been removed and hence that the Achaians have suffered enough for their wrongdoing.[29] Accordingly, he does not repeat the suggestion that he made to Patroclus that he will not desist from his wrath against the Achaians until the Trojans attack his ships. Why, then, does Achilles still stay away from battle? Why does he make the calamitous decision to send Patroclus into battle without the aid of "the bulwark for all of the Achaians" (1.283–284)? Why does Achilles refuse to intervene himself, to save the Achaians without unduly exposing his best friend to the risk of death at the hands of man-slaughtering Hector?

To understand why Achilles sends his best friend into battle without joining him, let us consider more carefully Homer's presentation of Patroclus and of his friendship with Achilles. Homer addresses Patroclus nine times in the poem, more than he addresses Achilles or Hector or any of the other more obviously important characters or indeed any other character at all.[30] In this way, Homer goes out of his way to focus our attention on the easily overlooked friend of the best of the Achaians and to highlight the importance of understanding his key role in the story.[31]

During his first appearances in the poem, Patroclus is wholly overshadowed by Achilles. When Achilles angrily denounces Agamemnon and the Achaians, announces that he is withdrawing from battle, and storms out of the assembly, Patroclus wordlessly follows him (1.306–307). When Achilles enjoins him to hand the unwilling Briseis over to the heralds of Agamemnon, Patroclus silently "obeyed his beloved companion" (1.345;

[29] See Bolotin 1995, 86; Lateiner 2004, 26.

[30] Homer addresses Patroclus nine times, all in Book XVI (20, 584–585, 692–693, 744, 754, 787, 788–789, 812–813, 843). He addresses Achilles once (20.1–3) and he never addresses Hector. Homer addresses Menelaus seven times (4.127, 4.146–147, 7.104–107, 13.602–603, 17.679–681, 17.702–704, 23.600); the Trojan warrior Melanippus once (15.582–583); the goddess (presumably an individual Muse) twice (1.1–7, 2.761–762); the divine Muses as a whole, who dwell in Olympus, four times (2.484–487, 11.218–220, 14.508–510, 16.112); and Apollo twice (15.365–366, 20.151–152).

[31] Scodel nonetheless suggests that "Patroclus's part is always minor" (2002, 110). Benardete, on the other hand, claims, "To no other hero does Homer seem so attached" (2005, 80).

see also 9.205, 11.615). When Achilles delights his mind and spirit by singing of the glorious deeds of men, Patroclus sits before him "in silence" (9.190). And throughout the dramatic scene between Achilles and the men whom he claims to love most, as they beseech him to save them from the Trojans and he refuses to do so, Patroclus confines himself to serving them all, silently, in obedience to "his beloved companion" (9.199–205). The friendship, then, between Achilles and Patroclus comes to sight as one that is radically unequal. Achilles is "the best of the Achaians," "a great bulwark for all of the Achaians against evil war" (1.412, 1.282–283). Patroclus is his faithful and silent companion. Until Book XI, we never even hear Patroclus speak and we never hear of him spoken of as a warrior.[32] Even his mistress is not captured by him nor bestowed on him as an honor by the Achaians for his martial prowess but is simply given to him by Achilles (9.663–668). Patroclus loves Achilles, enjoys the benefits of his friendship, and, it seems, accepts living in his shadow and serving him, silently and unquestioningly.[33]

However, in the conversation he has with Nestor in Book XI and its aftermath, Patroclus reveals that he is not simply satisfied to live in the shadow of Achilles. When Achilles believes that Machaon, one of only two healers in the Achaian army, might be wounded, he asks Patroclus to determine whether this is true and hence, it seems, whether the time has come for Achilles to return to battle: "now I think the Achaians will stand around my knees and beseech me, for a need has come that is no longer to be endured" (11.608–609). At this point, Homer remarks that Achilles' decision to send Patroclus to Nestor "was the beginning of his evil," referring apparently either to Patroclus suffering death or to Achilles suffering the loss of his friend (11.604). Homer indicates here that, by sending Patroclus to Nestor, Achilles sets in motion a chain of events that leads to the death of Patroclus.

[32] Patroclus first speaks at 11.605. Later, after Patroclus's death, Achilles does indicate that Patroclus has fought in battles during their many years at Troy. See 18.338–342, 24.3–8.

[33] According to Crotty, "Patroclus' relationship to Achilles is characterized by a mixture of subservience and intimacy that makes it strangely like the relationship between a wife and a husband" (1994, 58). Crotty also suggests that Patroclus is "woman-like" and possesses "feminine qualities" but is not effeminate and that Achilles' "relationship to Patroclus is charged with an erotic intensity but is without the carnal basis that such intensity implies in the everyday world" (55, 58). Griffin (1980, 104) and Winn (2009, 161–162) follow Xenophon's Socrates (*Symposium* 8.31) in arguing that, in Homer, Achilles and Patroclus are not erotic lovers. See also Schein 1984, 127.

Homer therefore suggests that Achilles' later decision to send Patroclus alone to fight the Trojans, rather than fighting them himself, is a consequence of Patroclus's conversation with Nestor.[34] Let us therefore turn to examine that pivotal conversation.

Now, for the first time in the poem, we see Patroclus apart from Achilles. And in his first words to Nestor, he sharply criticizes his beloved friend. When Nestor invites him to sit down, Patroclus unburdens himself of his misgivings about Achilles in the course of explaining why he must rush back to him:

> Worthy of reverence and quick to indignation is he who sent me forth to learn who is this whom you bring, who was struck. But I myself recognize him and I see that it is Machaon, the shepherd of the people. Now I go back as messenger to Achilles, to tell him. You yourself know well, old man, cherished by Zeus, how terrible a man that one is. He might even deem guilty one who is guiltless. (11.648–653)

Patroclus here goes out of his way to complain to Nestor that Achilles is too quick to blame others, that he sometimes blames the innocent, and hence that he can be unjust in his anger. In this way, Patroclus suggests that he believes that Achilles is wrong to continue to blame the Achaians as a whole for the injustice of Agamemnon and hence, he hints, wrong to continue to stay out of the fighting. We see, then, that even though he loves Achilles, and presumably admires him for his virtue, Patroclus does not revere him unquestioningly or simply defer to him but makes independent judgments about his virtuous character and chides his friend for falling short of the virtue of justice and for failing to help the Achaians.[35]

Nestor now attempts to enlist Patroclus in the cause of saving the Achaians from destruction. Throughout the poem, Nestor, of all the Achaians, recognizes most clearly the military importance of Achilles and therefore strives most energetically first to keep him in the army and then to induce him to return to the army. It is Nestor who intervenes in an attempt not only to persuade Achilles to accept the authority of Agamemnon but also and especially to remind Agamemnon of the crucial importance of Achilles – "who is the great bulwark for all the Achaians against evil

[34] See Redfield 1975, 106; Schein 1984, 117. Consider as well Kim 2000, 104–106.

[35] I am consequently inclined to disagree with those who primarily identify Patroclus as a "ritual substitute" (Van Brock 1959; Nagy 1979, 33, 292–293; Sinos 1980) or even as a "thematic double" for Achilles (Kim 2000, 108–109; see also Whitman 1958, 199–200).

war" – and to induce him to avoid provoking Achilles (1.275–284). It is Nestor who urges the Achaians, in the absence of their bulwark, to build a wall to protect their army and ships from the Trojan onslaught (7.327–343). It is Nestor who persuades Agamemnon to send the embassy of Phoinix, Ajax, and Odysseus, along with abundant gifts and honors, to induce Achilles to return to fighting for the Achaians (9.96–113, 9.163–172). Finally, it is Nestor who gives detailed instructions to each of the ambassadors, "especially to Odysseus, to try hard, so that they might persuade the blameless son of Peleus" (9.179–181). Now, after all efforts to persuade Achilles to return have failed, and the Achaians face imminent destruction, Nestor makes one last attempt to save the Achaians by appealing to Achilles' best friend. What distinguishes Nestor's effort here from his previous efforts is that here he does not confine himself to attempting to bring Achilles back into the fighting but also appeals directly to Patroclus to take Achilles' place and rescue the Achaians, should his friend persist in staying out of the war. Indeed, Nestor concludes his speech to Patroclus by calling on him to come out from under the shadow of Achilles and become the savior of the Achaians – "a light for the Danaans" (11.793–802). In this way, Nestor appeals, not only to Patroclus's compassion for the Achaians but also to his ambition.[36]

Nestor's speech to Patroclus imitates, in some ways quite precisely, Odysseus's speech to Achilles. This is not surprising, since Homer tells us that Nestor especially instructed Odysseus how to persuade Achilles (9.170–181). There are five fairly distinct parts in Nestor's speech to Patroclus, and three of them follow more or less closely Odysseus's speech to Achilles (compare 11.655–667 with 9.225–248 and 9.300–303; 11.761–763 with 9.249–251; and especially 11.764–792 with 9.252–260). However, the other two parts, which constitute two-thirds of Nestor's speech, reveal an entirely new strategy for saving the Achaians (11.667–761, 11.793–802).

Nestor begins his speech by describing the desperate plight of the Achaians and bitterly attacking Achilles for his hardheartedness:

> Why does Achilles lament for the sons of the Achaians who have been struck with shafts? He knows nothing of the grief that has risen throughout the army. For the best ones are lying among the ships, having been struck and stabbed. The son of Tydeus, mighty Diomedes, has been struck, Odysseus has been stabbed, as has Agamemnon,

[36] Lateiner, in contrast, suggests that Nestor simply appeals to Patroclus's loyalty to the Achaians (2004, 26).

> who is renowned for his spear. And Eurypylos has been struck in the thigh with an arrow. And just now I brought this other one out of the war, who was struck by an arrow from a bowstring. But Achilles, noble as he is, does not care or feel pity for the Danaans. Will he wait until the swift ships near the sea are warmed by a blazing fire, against the will of the Achaians, and we ourselves are killed one after another? (11.655–667)

Nestor here echoes the criticism made by Phoinix and Ajax of the pitilessness of Achilles (9.496–501, 9.625–631) and appeals to the compassion of Patroclus for the Achaians, as Odysseus had appealed to the compassion of Achilles (9.227–251, 9.300–303). Similarly, just as Odysseus had warned Achilles that he would regret letting the Achaians be destroyed – "To you yourself it will be a source of grief hereafter, there will be no remedy found to heal the evil once it is done" – so, in the third part of his speech, Nestor warns Patroclus that his beloved friend "will weep much afterward, once his people are destroyed" (9.249–250, 11.762–763). Finally, in the fourth part of his speech, which tracks most closely the speech of Odysseus, Nestor appeals to Patroclus's reverence for his father, in almost the same language as Odysseus had appealed to Achilles' reverence for his father (compare 9.252–259 with 11.764–789).[37] Nestor reminds Patroclus that his father Menoitios had specifically urged him to advise Achilles well. For even though Achilles is of nobler lineage and greater might, Patroclus is older and therefore, Menoitios told his son, "he will be persuaded by you to follow his own good" (11.785–788). And Nestor goes on to urge Patroclus to persuade Achilles to do what Odysseus had directly tried to persuade Achilles to do, namely, return to the war: "But still, even now, should you say these things to fiery-minded Achilles, he might be persuaded. Who knows if, with a deity, you might stir his spirit by speaking? The persuasion of a companion is good" (11.789–792). In all these ways, Nestor follows, indirectly, the strategy for saving the Achaians followed by Odysseus (presumably at the behest of Nestor): to persuade Achilles to return to the fighting by appealing to, in the case of Odysseus, the compassion of Achilles, his fear of regretting the consequences of his anger, and his

[37] For example, both sections begin "dear one [ὦ πέπον]" (9.252, 11.765) and both narrated speeches by Peleus and Menoitios begin "my child [τέκνον ἐμόν]" (9.254, 11.785). Moreover, lines 9.253 and 11.766 are identical: "on the day when he sent you out of Phthia to Agamemnon." Similarly, lines 9.259 and 11.790 are identical: "Thus did the old man bid you, but you have forgotten."

reverence for his father and, in the case of Nestor, the compassion of Patroclus, his fear that his friend will regret the consequences of his anger, and his reverence for his father.

However, in the second and fifth parts of his speech, which together constitute the great majority of his speech, Nestor follows an altogether new strategy for saving the Achaians from the Trojans. In the second part, Nestor echoes, not Odysseus's speech to the angry Achilles, but rather his own speech to the frightened Achaians when Hector had challenged them to select their best warrior to fight him in a duel and all were silent. Just as Nestor had then expressed the wish that he were young – "If only I were in the prime of youth and the strength were steady within me" – in order that he might face Hector, so now Nestor, in the exact same words, expresses the wish that he were young so that he might save the Achaians from Hector and the Trojans (compare 7.157 with 11.670). Just as Nestor had then recounted how he alone among his fellow warriors, even though he was the "youngest," killed the mightiest enemy warrior and "Athena gave me glory [εὖχος]" (7.153–154), so now Nestor recounts how once, when he was so young that his father would not let him fight the enemies of his people – "For he thought that I did not yet know the deeds of war" (11.718) – he nevertheless, in defiance of his father, charged into battle, slew over a hundred warriors, saved his people, "and they all glorified [εὐχετόωντο] Zeus among gods and Nestor among men" (11.760). It would seem, then, that just as Nestor had, on that previous occasion, attempted to induce the Achaians to fight Hector by appealing to their sense of shame and their ambition for glory, so Nestor is now attempting to persuade Patroclus himself to fight the Trojans by appealing to his sense of shame and ambition for glory. Furthermore, Nestor stresses here that by acting boldly and taking the initiative, and by acting contrary to the wishes of his protective father that he refrain from fighting, he was able to come out of the shadow of his brothers and was able to demonstrate his own excellence as a warrior. In this way, Nestor implicitly appeals to Patroclus to come out of the shadow of his illustrious friend and even to defy his protective friend so as to demonstrate his own virtue.

In the conclusion of his speech, Nestor explicitly appeals to Patroclus's ambition to display his virtue and win glory for himself. After urging Patroclus to attempt to persuade Achilles to return to battle, Nestor abruptly suggests that Achilles may have withdrawn from fighting out of fear for his own life and then proceeds to call on Patroclus himself to save the Achaians:

"But if he is escaping something divine revealed to his mind and his esteemed mother has told him something from Zeus, let him send you forth, and let the rest of the Myrmidon people follow you, and you may be a light to the Danaans" (11.793–796). Nestor goes on to explain that Patroclus may reasonably hope to drive the Trojans back from the Achaian ships, especially if Achilles gives him his armor, since Patroclus and his troops are fresh and the Trojans are exhausted: "Easily you unwearied ones might push back those who are wearied toward their town and away from the ships and huts" (11.801–802). Nestor here appeals not only to Patroclus's concern for the Achaians but also to his ambition. By leading the Myrmidons against the Trojans, not only may the Achaians be saved, but *he* may be their savior. After nine years of serving as the faithful companion of Achilles, Patroclus may now himself be Achilles: that is, he may himself be the hero who fights off Hector and thereby rescues the Achaians from destruction and hence may prove himself, at least for this moment, to be the best of the Achaians (see 17.689).

Nestor's appeal here to Patroclus is quite bold. Until now, no mention of Patroclus as a warrior has been made in the poem. The first time in the poem Patroclus performs an independent act, one that is not dictated by Achilles, is when he saves the life of the wounded warrior Eurypylus, not by fighting for him in battle, but by cleaning his wound and treating it with drugs (11.827–847).[38] Nestor's appeal to the compassion of Patroclus for the Achaians is not particularly noteworthy, since a number of characters speak of his compassion and Achilles himself expresses no genuine surprise that his friend should weep out of concern for the Achaians.[39] But Nestor's appeal to Patroclus's passion for glory is a stroke of genius. Homer tells us that Nestor's speech to Patroclus "stirred the spirit in his breast" (11.804). Patroclus immediately leaves to return to Achilles. And though his return is delayed by his compassion for the wounded Eurypylus, Patroclus does persuade Achilles to send him into battle. What no one but Nestor sees is the ambition that burns in the heart of Patroclus. The old man senses that, after

[38] Even when Nestor urges him to beat back the Trojans, he suggests that Patroclus may do so effectively primarily because he is wearing the armor of Achilles – and therefore may be mistaken for him by the terrified Trojans – and because he is well rested, and not because of his skill or courage as a warrior (11.793–802).

[39] 11.805–847, 16.1–19, 17.204, 17.670–672, 19.282–300.

years of loving and serving the best of the Achaians, Patroclus himself must yearn to be the hero of the Achaians. And Nestor may sense as well that, if Achilles will not himself save the Achaians out of love for them, he will let his beloved companion be their savior out of love for him.

Nestor appears to recognize here a fundamental problem that besets the friendship of Patroclus and Achilles. Patroclus loves Achilles, the best of the Achaians, presumably in large part because of his outstanding virtue: his dutiful concern for others, his noble willingness to sacrifice for others, his courage, and his prudence. Similarly, insofar as Achilles himself loves virtue, he must honor Patroclus beyond all his other companions and as much as he honors his own self, in large part because he recognizes in him a deep attachment to virtue (see 18.80–82, 24.3–8). The friendship of the two men is based on their mutual attachment to virtue and their mutual admiration for each other's nobility and dutifulness. Yet virtue proves to be an unstable basis for their friendship. For while both men can be virtuous, their devotion to virtue inevitably leads them to compete with each other.[40] Only one can be the best of the Achaians. Only one can be a light for the Danaans. Only one can be the hero and savior of the Achaian army. Until now, Achilles has clearly been that hero and savior. But consequently, Patroclus's passion to excel as a warrior, to display outstanding virtue, and to win tremendous glory, has been thwarted by the outstanding virtue of his beloved friend. Achilles loves Patroclus and therefore presumably wants him to bring to full flower his own virtue and thereby win his own glory. But Achilles' own virtue prevents Patroclus from fulfilling himself in this way. The case of Achilles and Patroclus suggests, then, that virtue cannot form a stable basis of friendship because it cannot be shared.[41] The outstanding virtue of one stunts the virtue of others. Even though virtue consists in benefiting others, it fails to do so insofar as making others fully virtuous would be the greatest benefit of all.

This problem manifests itself most clearly in the relation between Achilles and the other Achaian heroes. At the beginning of the poem, the Achaians seem cowardly, base, and foolish. They silently acquiesce as Agamemnon foolishly and selfishly risks the destruction of the army at the hands of Apollo by refusing to return Chryseis to her father, the priest of Apollo. Then, they

[40] See Burns 1996, 294–298; Lutz 2006, 116–117.

[41] Consider Aristotle *Nicomachean Ethics* 1169a17–34.

silently acquiesce as Agamemnon threatens to dishonor Achilles, Ajax, or Odysseus by depriving them of the prizes awarded to them. Finally, with the partial exception of Nestor, they acquiesce as Agamemnon again risks the destruction of the army by humiliating the greatest Achaian warrior and prompting him to withdraw from the war against Troy. In Book I, Achilles' description of the Achaians as "those of no account" and his suggestion that they are cowardly since they yield to Agamemnon's every deed and word, no matter how outrageous, seem altogether just (1.231, 1.293–294).

As the poem unfolds, however, it becomes clear that the Achaians are far more impressive than they first appear. We see Odysseus display his remarkable intelligence by single-handedly preventing the army from fleeing Troy (2.166–335). We see Ajax defeat Hector, the best warrior among the Trojans, twice in single combat (7.178–312, 14.402–432; see also 17.119–168). Throughout the ferocious battles during Achilles' absence, we see Achaians demonstrate outstanding courage, martial prowess, and inspiriting leadership while struggling against the mighty Trojans, especially Ajax,[42] but also Odysseus (4.329–363, 5.668–678, 11.310–488), Diomedes (4.365–421, 5.1–6.236, 11.316–400), Idomeneus (4.250–271, 13.210–495), Menelaus (13.581–642, 17.1–112, 17.553–581), and Agamemnon himself (4.223–225, 11.91–283). We even see Agamemnon demonstrate some measure of statesmanship and prudence by seeking to arrange a settlement to end the war (3.76–120); by rallying and urging on his warriors in combat (4.223–421); and, perhaps most importantly, by recognizing his own errors and seeking out and heeding the sometimes brutally frank counsel of Nestor, Odysseus, and Diomedes (9.9–173, 10.1–239, 14.27–134).

Now, what makes it possible for these Achaians to come into their own and to display their virtuous qualities after Achilles withdraws is precisely the absence of the best of the Achaians.[43] For Achilles' virtue is so huge that it crowds out the virtue of the rest.[44] When Achilles is with the Achaians at the beginning of the poem, he single-handedly saves the army from destruction

[42] 4.472–489, 11.485–573, 12.265–276, 12.342–441,13.701–722, 15.300–327, 15.405–483, 15.559–746, 16.101–123, 17.115–168, 17.223–325, 17.626–672, 17.705–761.

[43] As Benardete remarks, "The wrath of Achilles causes great loss of life among the Achaeans and Trojans, but it also allows every hero to win as much glory as he can" (2000, 48–49).

[44] Consider Aristotle *Politics* 1284a4–23, 1284b25–33, 1288a17–29.

by inducing Agamemnon to return Chryseis to her father. And once Achilles returns to the war after the death of Patroclus, one no longer hears of the heroism of the other Achaians, for Achilles crushes the Trojans virtually single-handedly. The heroism of the other Achaians is invisible as long as Achilles is on stage, not because Achilles deliberately suppresses their heroism, but simply because his gigantic virtue inevitably dwarfs theirs. As Homer says of Ajax, he "was by far the best of men, while Achilles remained full of wrath, for *he* was by far the greatest" (2.768–769, emphasis added). And as Homer poignantly remarks of Ajax – in the midst of the dramatic battle over the corpse of Patroclus, in the midst of describing how he single-handedly rallied the fleeing Achaians and heroically scattered battalions of advancing Trojans – "he who, in his form and in the feats he performed, surpassed the rest of the Danaans, *after* the blameless son of Peleus" (17.278–280, emphasis added). The heroic Ajax, Odysseus, and Diomedes evidently do not act to check Agamemnon when his reckless behavior toward the priest of Apollo is imperiling the army because, consciously or unconsciously, they count on Achilles to check him. Similarly, they do not act to check Agamemnon when he acts outrageously toward *them* because, for nine years, Achilles has taken the lead in saving the army from all threats, be they from the Trojans or from Agamemnon. Had Achilles stayed with the army throughout, he – not Odysseus – would have prevented the Achaian army from fleeing (had the Achaians dared to make the attempt), he – not Ajax – would have faced and defeated Hector in a duel (had Hector dared to make the attempt) and would have defended the ships of the Achaians and the corpse of Patroclus from the Trojans (had the Trojans dared to attack them), and he – not Diomedes or Agamemnon or any of the other Achaian heroes – would have bested the Trojans fighting in the Trojan plain (had the Trojans dared to venture out onto the plain). The Achaians of course do, in a way, benefit from the virtue of Achilles, but his superlative virtue inevitably infantilizes them, as – to invoke his own simile – a superlatively solicitous mother bird might harm her offspring by sparing them the need to fly (9.323–327). It is only when Achilles is gone, and they face by themselves the threats of Agamemnon's folly and of the Trojans' might that Ajax, Odysseus, Diomedes, and the others are both prompted and permitted to display their own virtue. The example of Achilles suggests that virtue inevitably pits the virtuous against one another and even leads them to harm one another. For, the most virtuous human being deprives his fellows of the opportunity to be virtuous. Virtue, then, proves to be an unstable basis for friendship because the devotion to virtue inevitably brings friends into conflict with one another.

The most vivid example of the problem posed by Achilles' superlative virtue is the athletic games Achilles holds after the funeral of Patroclus. At the games, the Achaians display their excellence in eight competitions: chariot race, boxing, wrestling, foot race, combat in armor, shot put, archery, and javelin. A variety of heroes win prizes. But the precondition for such displays of excellence and such honors is the forbearance of Achilles. Had he participated in the games, he would have won many, if not all, of the competitions, perhaps by a wide margin (23.272–286, 23.776; consider also, for example, 24.453–456). Achilles' gracious forbearance is itself, to be sure, a virtuous act, but it is more clearly an act of friendship. His forbearance requires him to suppress his own excellence, in order to allow the excellence of others – of his friends – to flourish. But then the pursuit of such excellence cannot form the basis of his friendships. For either he must sacrifice his fulfillment and happiness for theirs or sacrifice theirs for his.

The problem of the conflict between virtue and friendship, and Achilles' sudden recognition of this problem, explain his seemingly incomprehensible decision to send Patroclus to save the Achaians rather than go himself. When he comes to Achilles, Patroclus breaks down and weeps for the first time in the poem. Even though he was moved to compassion for the Achaians, perhaps by the speech of Nestor, and more certainly by the sight of the wounded Eurypylus, only now does he weep, evidently because he sees that the Trojans are about to set the Achaian ships on fire and inflict "disgraceful destruction" upon them (16.32; see 11.803–847). Patroclus's tears move Achilles to pity him (16.5), even as he gently chides Patroclus for showing such sorrow over the just punishment of the Achaians:

> Why, then, are you weeping, Patroclus, like a foolish girl, who runs after her mother and begs to be picked up, and clings to her dress and holds her back as she hurries, and looks up at her, shedding tears, so that she will pick her up. You are like her, Patroclus, shedding a soft tear. Do you have something to tell the Myrmidons or me? Have you alone heard some message from Phthia? They say indeed that Menoitios, son of Actor, still lives, and Peleus, son of Aiacus, lives with the Myrmidons. We would grieve greatly over the death of both of them. Or do you sorrow for the Argives, since they perish by their hollow ships because of their transgression? Speak out, do not conceal it in your mind, so that we shall both know. (16.6–19)

Now, Achilles evidently anticipates that Patroclus – who is frequently said to have a mild and gentle character (17.204, 17.671, 19.287–300)[45] – will, out of compassion for the Achaians, try to persuade Achilles to return to the war and save them from destruction. And Patroclus does evince this intention when, just before returning to Achilles, he tells Eurypylus: "I myself will rush to Achilles so that I may rouse him to wage war" (15.401–402). But in the speech that Patroclus goes on to give – a speech that makes Achilles "greatly distressed" (16.48) – he does not simply or even primarily attempt to persuade Achilles to return to the war.

Homer underscores the importance of this speech, and hence the importance of examining it carefully, for it is the only time in the poem he introduces a speech by addressing the speaker: "Then, groaning heavily, you spoke to him, Patroclus the horseman" (16.20). Patroclus first juxtaposes the greatness of Achilles and the dire condition of the Achaians:

> Achilles, son of Peleus, greatest by far of the Achaians, do not be indignant. Such grief has overcome the Achaians. For all those who were best before lie among the ships struck and stabbed. The son of Tydeus, mighty Diomedes, was struck, Odysseus and spear-famed Agamemnon were stabbed, and Eurypylus was struck in the thigh with an arrow. Around them the healers are working with many drugs to cure their wounds. (16.21–29)

Patroclus then sharply criticizes Achilles for his refusal to help the Achaians:

> But you, Achilles, are impossible! May this rage, then, not seize me, which you watch over, a dreadful virtue. What other one, born hereafter, will profit from you if you do not protect the Argives from a disgraceful destruction? Pitiless one, the horseman Peleus was not your father, nor Thetis your mother. The gleaming sea bore you and the towering rocks, since your mind is turned away from us. (16.29–35)

Here, Patroclus argues, in the first place, that Achilles' rage against the Achaians is due less to their injustice and more to his own delight in feeling rage, in feeling wronged, and hence, perhaps, in feeling that the gods will reward him for the injustice he has suffered. Here, Patroclus echoes his earlier suggestion to Nestor that Achilles can be unjust and also the remark of Odysseus to Nestor that Achilles wishes to be angry (11.647–653, 9.678–679). In this way, Patroclus suggests that Achilles' dreadful virtue is not genuine

[45] See Whitman 1958, 200; Moulton 1977, 104; Zanker 1994, 138–140; Alvis 1995, 65.

virtue, that it does not encompass a genuine justice, but rather that it is selfish and self-indulgent, especially now that the Achaians have suffered so and are on the brink of utter ruin. But furthermore, Patroclus contends that Achilles is inhumanly heartless toward all of his companions, including Patroclus himself. By accusing him of injustice and pitilessness toward his companions, Patroclus, it would seem, attempts to rouse Achilles to return to the war and save the Achaians.

Now, at this point, insofar as Patroclus seeks to persuade Achilles to return to the war, we would expect Patroclus to proceed, for example, to reiterate that the Achaians have already paid for their sins against him and that they have offered to return Briseis along with countless gifts and honors, to invoke Peleus and also Menoitius in the course of arguing that they both would want Achilles to return to battle, or simply to invoke his own friendship by arguing that Achilles should heed the counsel of his most beloved companion and hence should return to battle to save the Achaians from destruction. Instead, Patroclus abruptly shifts from rebuking Achilles as heartless for staying out of battle and stressing that the fate of the Achaians depends entirely on his return to battle to suggesting instead that it would be understandable for Achilles to stay out of battle out of fear for his own life:

> But if you are escaping something divine revealed to your mind and your esteemed mother has told you something from Zeus, send me forth, and let the rest of the Myrmidon people follow me, and I may perhaps be a light to the Danaans. Give me your arms to wear on my shoulders, so perhaps the Trojans might think I am you and hold themselves away from the war, and the warlike sons of the Achaians, who are weary, should take breath again. For there is little breathing space in war. Easily we who are unwearied might push back those who are wearied toward their town and away from the ships and huts. (16.36–45)

Patroclus here abandons his efforts to persuade Achilles to return to battle and even offers Achilles a pretext for staying out. And Patroclus does so because he *wants* Achilles to stay out. For Patroclus himself yearns to be "a light to the Danaans." He wants to be their savior. And he can be their savior only if Achilles, "greatest by far of the Achaians," stays out of the battle (16.21). It is true that Patroclus here repeats the words Nestor had spoken (11.794–803). But he does not attribute those words to Nestor but makes them his own. And he makes them his own because they express his own longing to prove his own independent excellence to one and all, including himself. In this way, Patroclus tacitly but clearly urges Achilles to stay out the battle, and does so by appealing to their friendship.[46]

Achilles responds to Patroclus's speech with great distress. While he feels pity for Patroclus when he observes his compassion for the Achaians, Achilles feels deeply troubled now that he discerns the ambition of his friend. For now Achilles recognizes that Patroclus yearns to be virtuous, that he longs to be a hero. And Achilles recognizes that he has heretofore thwarted and frustrated the honorable ambition of his dearest friend. Accordingly, Achilles now resolves to send Patroclus into battle, with his armor and with the Myrmidons, but without going in himself. As he indicates, Achilles no longer holds back here because he is angry with the Achaians or because they are withholding any honors or gifts. He holds back as an act of love for Patroclus, to let him display his virtue and win the glory of a hero.[47] As he confides to Zeus, when he prays for Patroclus: "Send forth glory to him, Wide-Seeing Zeus, and embolden the heart in his breast, so that even Hector will know whether our attendant knows how to fight by himself, or whether his hands rage invincible only whenever I myself go after the toil of Ares" (16.241–245).[48] And Patroclus does indeed show his excellence at war. He saves the Achaians from destruction by driving the Trojans away from their ships and back to Troy. He slays dozens of Trojan warriors – fifty-four, more warriors than anyone has been said to slay in the poem heretofore – and he slays the greatest hero in the poem to be slain up till now: Sarpedon, the leader of the Lycians – the principal allies of Troy – the best of men and the son of Zeus (16.419–507). Patroclus almost conquers Troy single-handedly (16.698–711). When he is finally stopped, he is stopped by Apollo himself rather than any Trojan. Hector is, as Patroclus points out, only the third one responsible for his death, after Apollo and Euphorbus (16.788–850).

[46] I therefore disagree with Zanker's contention that Patroclus is "given no motive other than pity for his comrades, and the absence of the honor-incentive makes his response [to Achilles] truly disinterested" (1994, 139).

[47] Felson and Slatkin remark that the friendship of Achilles and Patroclus "is by no means unique" in the *Iliad* (2004, 101), but the act of friendship by Achilles here is singular in the poem.

[48] I am therefore inclined to disagree with the intriguing suggestion of Zanker that Achilles stays out of the war here because of "his deepened awareness of the nature of death" and "his personalized realization of the reality of death" that "others may take as a fear of death" (1994, 97).

Menelaus goes so far as to call Patroclus "the best of the Achaians" (17.689). Insofar, then, as Achilles seeks to benefit his beloved friend by allowing him to shine as a warrior and fulfill his ambition for excellence, he succeeds completely.

Yet, three grave problems beset Achilles' act of friendship here. First, precisely because Achilles wishes to allow his beloved friend to display his virtue and win glory as the savior of the Achaians, he must avoid humiliating Patroclus by openly and truthfully declaring that he will stay out of the battle so that his inferior companion can shine on the battlefield. Accordingly, even though he later, in private, acknowledges to Zeus that he has answered his prayer by punishing the Achaians sufficiently, to Patroclus Achilles insists that he will stay out because he still feels grief over the injustice of the Achaians and because he previously vowed that he would not fight until the Trojans attacked his own huts and ships. Achilles, then, must condescend to his friend in order to avoid seeming condescending and be less than truthful, and hence less than friendly, in order to benefit his friend here.

But furthermore, by sending Patroclus into battle to prove his virtue and win glory, Achilles risks diminishing his own glory. For Achilles is himself proud and cherishes his own honor. Consequently, he declares emphatically that he is not staying out of the war because he fears for his life as a result of a prophecy and warns Patroclus not to go too far, lest he diminish his own glory (16.49–51, 16.83–90). Again, the problem that arises here is that virtue and honor cannot ultimately be shared. Only one can be the best of the Achaians, the light for the Danaans, the savior of the army. Insofar as one is devoted to virtue and honor, one is fundamentally in competition, or even in a state of war, with all others, even one's dearest friends. Achilles goes so far as to express the wish that all the Trojans and Achaians were dead so that he and Patroclus alone could win the honor of conquering Troy (16.97–100). But of course, even if the two of them were alone, the question of who is more virtuous would remain.

Finally, by sending Patroclus into battle to prove his virtue, Achilles risks losing his friend and does lose him. As Patroclus's friend, Achilles wants to benefit him and believes that he can do so by letting him demonstrate his own virtue and win his own glory. Yet, Patroclus dies, and even if his death is not simply an evil for him, it most assuredly is for Achilles, as Homer shows through his vivid portrayal of Achilles' grief in the final books of the *Iliad*. As Patroclus's friend, Achilles wants his friend to flourish but also wants to keep his friend for himself and hence to keep his friend alive.[49] Accordingly, Achilles tries – in vain – to persuade his friend to check his drive for glory by appealing to his friendship (16.83–96). Therefore, there is a profound and terrible tension between Achilles' generous desire to benefit his friend and his more self-regarding desire to keep his friend for himself.

Through his moving portrayal of the beautiful and yet tragic friendship, based on virtue, between Achilles and Patroclus, Homer invites us to ask whether there might be a more stable basis for friendship in something other than virtue. The fundamental problem with the friendship based on virtue is that virtue cannot be fully shared. Achilles and Patroclus each strive to be the most virtuous and to be honored as the most virtuous, but only one can be the most virtuous, only one can be the best of the Achaians. Either Patroclus must live in the shadow of his friend and have his ambition thwarted and crushed, or Achilles must sacrifice his own virtue and honor, and even his happiness, for his friend. And to benefit Patroclus, Achilles must suppress himself, he must smother his own longing to shine and excel, and he must even hide from Patroclus that he is benefiting him.

The question arises, then, what good might there be that can be fully shared, that both Achilles and Patroclus might share fully and through which they could be fully happy together? The clearest answer in the poem would seem to be the good that Homer himself possesses to the highest degree: the good of wisdom. For the singer Homer can share his wisdom with others – with his friends or, more broadly, with his audience – without diminishing his own wisdom in any way. Now, the happiest we ever see Achilles in the poem – the happiest we ever see any human being in the poem – is the moment when he comes closest to the life of the wise, contemplative singer, when he is singing in the presence of Patroclus, "delighting his mind with his lyre": "with it he delighted his spirit and sang of the glories of men" (9.186–189). By stressing that Achilles delighted his mind, Homer suggests that through singing, Achilles is reflecting on the nature of honor – of the life devoted to virtue and honor – and that Achilles derives an inner joy and satisfaction through such reflection. Furthermore, in this scene, Achilles seeks to share his reflections with his friends, first and foremost with Patroclus but also with Odysseus, Phoinix, and Ajax. Achilles here appears to divine the possibility of a friendship that is based on shared conversation and shared

[49] Consider Aristotle *Nicomachean Ethics* 1158b29–1159a12.

contemplation, a friendship based on wisdom that would delight him fully, in mind and spirit. In other words, Achilles appears to glimpse here a life that is free of the afflictions that beset the noble life of the virtuous warrior and leader – a life that is graced with a kind of friendship that is free of the tragedy of a friendship based on virtue and honor – namely, the life of the wise singer.

However, Achilles' glimpse of the life and the friendship based on wisdom proves to be limited, for two reasons. In the first place, such a friendship proves elusive, since Achilles' friends evidently do not share or even understand his doubts concerning the goodness of the life devoted to virtue and honor. Phoinix, Odysseus, and Ajax continue to regard honor as an unqualified good, even after hearing Achilles' doubts, and Patroclus, as we have seen, burns to be the savior of the Achaians and to be honored as such (consider, for example, 9.603–605, 10.280–282, 11.404–411, 15.561–564). Second, and more importantly, the fact that Achilles never returns to the activity of singing – the fact that, with the important exception of his encounter with Priam (24.477–674), Achilles does not turn to reflection to calm his fury at Hector after the death of Patroclus, as he had evidently turned to reflection to calm his fury at Agamemnon and the Achaians – indicates that Achilles himself does not fully recognize the life of the wise singer as one that can satisfy his deepest longings, as one that can truly delight his mind and spirit both through the satisfaction of understanding and the pleasure of friendship based on shared understanding. Once Patroclus dies, Achilles gives himself entirely to passion, to rage, and while he eventually overcomes that rage in some measure, he never truly transcends it, as Homer evidently does, by "delighting his mind with his lyre" (9.186).

ACHILLES' RETURN TO THE LIFE OF VIRTUE AFTER THE DEATH OF PATROCLUS

The Achilles we see after the death of Patroclus is a man out of balance, shifting suddenly between terrible grief and friendly affection, and between savage fury and thoughtful compassion.[50] Achilles is evidently a man of great passion, and we have seen him rage and weep in Book I and express tender affection for his friends and anger at Agamemnon in Book IX

[50] See Crotty 1994, 10–11. Consider also Clarke 2004, 84.

(1.149–244, 1.348–361, 9.193–204, 9.369–392). But from the moment he first learns of Patroclus's death, Achilles is overcome, repeatedly, by violent weeping[51] and violent anger,[52] even as he also displays unprecedented consideration for his friends and magnanimity toward his enemies. First, he covers himself with ashes and dust tears at his hair, and weeps (18.22–38). Achilles then offers heartrending lamentations for Patroclus (18.79–93, 18.98–127, 18.324–355, 19.315–337). Thereafter, he enters battle – for the first time in the poem – and proceeds to slaughter countless Trojans, including two of Priam's young sons, one of them as he begs for mercy (21.406–418, 21.34–135), and to defile the corpse of Hector before the eyes of his grieving parents, countrymen, and widow (22.395–474). Subsequently, Achilles mourns movingly for Patroclus at his funeral (23.1–257) – "as a father mourns, burning the bones of his son" (23.222) – while, at the same funeral, savagely beheading twelve Trojan youths – "and he devised evil deeds in his mind" (23.175–177). Thereupon, Achilles graciously organizes funeral games for the Achaians, over which he presides with unfailing good humor, friendliness, and tact (23.258–897). After the games, Achilles returns to grieve over Patroclus (24.1–14) and to outrage the corpse of Hector (24.15–22), but he then agrees without protest to the gods' command that he return the corpse to his father (24.138–140). And finally, Achilles expresses a heartfelt and thoughtful compassion for Hector's father Priam and freely grants a twelve-day truce to the Trojans during which they may bury Hector in peace (24.512–672). Over the course of the final seven books of the poem, we witness Achilles at his most sorrowful and his most gracious, his most savage and his most humane. What are we to make of this bewildering array of moods and dramatic shifts in feeling?

To understand Achilles' response to Patroclus's death, we must first consider the significance of that death for Achilles. In the first place and most obviously, Achilles here loses a friend whom he honored and loved beyond all of his companions, as much as his own life and at least as much as his beloved father and son (18.80–82, 19.321–327). Achilles has long cherished his friendship with Patroclus and, as we have seen, he also expresses his love for Phoinix, Ajax, and Odysseus earlier in the poem. But, as his moving

[51] 18.22–35, 19.4–6, 19.338, 23.12–18, 23.108–110, 23.152–155, 23.222–225, 24.3–13, 24.507–512.

[52] See, for example, 18.333–342, 19.15–20, 19.365–22.24, 22.131–404, 23.17–37, 23.170–191, 24.14–22.

declarations of love for Patroclus show, Achilles evidently feels most powerfully the importance of his friendship with Patroclus only now that he has lost him (consider also 24.1–13). Indeed, Achilles addresses the dead Patroclus as many times (six) as he does the living Patroclus in the course of the poem.[53] The loss of his beloved friend, then, would seem to heighten Achilles' sensitivity to the importance of friendship in his life, to the preciousness of his attachments to other "beloved" companions, such as Antilochus and Automedon, for example, and even to the importance of loved ones in the lives of others, such as, eventually, the importance of Priam's "beloved" son to Priam (23.555–556, 23.563, 24.618–620).

But furthermore, Achilles' increased awareness of the importance of friendship is accompanied by an increased awareness of death. For, even though Achilles has been inflicting death on others and exposing himself to the threat of death for more than nine years at Troy, and even though Achilles has reflected about death in the abstract – including his own death – as we see in Book IX (9.320–322, 9.400–416), the death of Patroclus is evidently his first experience of the actual death of a loved one. Indeed, although the Trojan War has lasted more than nine years, it has evidently been, according to Homer's account, a relatively bloodless war, characterized by a standoff between the besieged Trojans and the besieging Achaians. To be sure, led by Achilles, the Achaians have engaged in bloody attacks on neighboring cities (twenty-three in all), such as the attacks on Briseis's home town and on Thebe, the home town of Andromache and the residence of Chryseis, which occur shortly before the opening of the *Iliad* and in which the families of Briseis and Andromache perish (2.686–694, 19.291–296, 1.366–369, 6.413–428; see also 9.328–329, 20.186–194). Yet, the fact that Homer's Catalogue of Achaian and Trojan forces singles out only the Achaian Protesilaus as a death in the war heretofore suggests that virtually no prominent deaths have occurred among either the Achaians or the Trojans until the withdrawal of Achilles from the war and the subsequent outbreak of fighting on the Trojan plain after the collapse of the truce (2.698–702, 4.457–458). The shock of grief described by Homer among both Trojans and Achaians at the dawn after the first full day of battle, during

[53] Achilles addresses the dead Patroclus six times: 18.333–342, 19.315–337, 23.19–23, 23.94–98, 23.179–183, 24.592–595. He addresses the living Patroclus six times as well: 1.337–344, 9.202–204, 11.607–614, 16.6–19, 16.49–100, 16.126–129.

which over four dozen warriors are specified by Homer to have died, indicates that such carnage is a new experience for the warriors on both sides of this conflict (7.421–432; see also 7.327–335). And Achilles has not taken part in this new, open warfare at Troy, until the death of Patroclus. Achilles' other loved ones – his father, his son, and of course his immortal mother – remain alive, as do his dear friends Phoinix, Ajax, Odysseus, Antilochus, and Automedon.[54]

The death of Patroclus is then, one may say, Achilles' first genuine encounter with the reality of death. For the first time in his life, he mourns for a loved one and he buries a loved one. And quite naturally, seeing his beloved Patroclus die – in Achilles' armor, leading Achilles' men – leads Achilles to reflect on his own death. Moreover, this link between the deaths of Patroclus and Achilles is dramatically reinforced by his awareness that, if he avenges Patroclus's death by killing Hector, he will die shortly thereafter (18.95–96). Accordingly, Achilles' mourning over Patroclus's death is intertwined with his mourning over his own death:

> Now I will go, so that I may overtake the destroyer of the beloved head, Hector, and then I will await destruction, whenever Zeus should bring it about, and the other immortal gods. (18.114–116)
>
> For both it has been decreed to redden the same earth here in Troy, since neither will the old man, the driver of horses, Peleus, receive me, returning, in the great halls, nor my mother Thetis, but here the earth will hold me. (18.329–332)
>
> No, by Zeus, who is the loftiest and best of gods, it is not right that water should come near my head, before I have laid Patroclus on a pyre, and heaped a mound over him, and cut my hair, since there will come no second grief like this to my heart, so long as I am still among the living. (23.43–47)

Indeed, at the very end of Patroclus's funeral, Achilles instructs Agamemnon and the other Achaians to postpone the final burial of Patroclus's bones until after Achilles has died and his bones may be buried with those of his beloved companion (23.236–257; see 23.91–92). By celebrating Patroclus's funeral, then, Achilles is, in some measure, celebrating his own as well.[55]

[54] Achilles' wife, the mother of his son Neoptolemus, is never mentioned in Homer.
[55] See Schein 1984, 132.

Now, Achilles' preoccupation with death in the wake of Patroclus's death causes him turmoil, for he responds to the experience of death by violently refusing to accept the finality of death. Achilles not only laments the loss of his beloved friend, but he also embraces his corpse;[56] he speaks to his corpse;[57] and he beseeches his mother to forestall the decay of the corpse, evidently so that he may cling to the illusion that Patroclus is still, somehow, alive.[58] Furthermore, Achilles insists not only on slaying the man who slew Patroclus, Hector, but also on speaking to him – "though he was dead," as Homer notes (22.364) – and on repeatedly punishing the corpse, not primarily to cause pain to Hector's family and city, but rather, it seems, so that he may cling to the illusion that Hector is also still, somehow, alive (22.395–405, 23.24–26, 24.14–17).

Finally, and most importantly, Achilles responds to the death of Patroclus by appearing to return without qualification to the life of virtue and therewith to the hope that the gods may reward that noble, self-denying life with the good – the everlasting good – that it deserves. By blaming himself for having ever withdrawn from the war and hence failing to defend, not only Patroclus, but all of the Achaians, Achilles appears to renounce all of his previous doubts about the life of virtue (18.98–104; see also 18.82, 18.231–238, 18.324–327). Moreover, Achilles resolves to kill Hector and he insists on portraying this act as an act of virtue, in particular, of justice: Achilles tells his mother that he now chooses to die in his quest to kill Hector, "since the spirit does not bid me to go on living and to be among men unless Hector should first be struck down by my spear and his spirit should perish, and *pay the penalty* for the spoiling of Patroclus, the son of Menoitius" (18.90–93, emphasis added). Even though Hector did nothing more than kill the most dangerous warrior of the Achaians as they were attacking his city, and even though Achilles soon learns that Apollo bore much responsibility for the death of Patroclus (19.409–414), Achilles insists, both here and later, that Hector has acted unjustly – that he is a "slaughterer" and a "dog" (18.335, 20.425–426, 20.449, 22.345) – and must therefore suffer a just punishment. Indeed, Achilles goes so far as to blame Hector and the Trojans for killing Achaians during his absence from the war, even though he himself had

[56] 18.317, 23.18.

[57] 18.333–342, 19.315–337, 23.19–23, 23.179–183. See also 24.592–595 and 23.94–98.

[58] 19.21–33.

prayed to Zeus that Hector and the Trojans would do this very thing (1.407–412, 16.236–238): "But, even so, die an evil doom, *until you all pay the penalty* for the slaughter of Patroclus and the destruction of the Achaians, whom you slaughtered beside the swift ships, *in my absence*" (21.133–135, emphasis added); "Now you will *pay the penalty*, all together, for the sorrows of my companions, whom you killed, raging with your spear" (22.271–272, emphasis added). Achilles willfully convinces himself that his return to war, then, is an act of justice, an act of retribution against those who deserve all the righteous indignation that he can muster (see, for example, 19.15–16, 19.366–367, 20.75–78, 20.381–503, 21.17–33, 21.139–227, 21.520–525).[59] Moreover, when his mother reminds him that he will surely die if he returns to the war and kills Hector, Achilles insists that "Soon I would die, then" (18.98). In this way, Achilles suggests that he will be sacrificing his very life for the sake of justly punishing Hector and the Trojans. For such a noble deed, Achilles expects a just reward: "Now I would win for myself a noble glory" (18.121; see also 20.503, 21.543, 22.18). Later, Achilles suggests that this reward may entail the divine reward of immortality. After killing Hector, Achilles twice suggests that Patroclus lives on in Hades, he has a vision or dream that Patroclus speaks to him from Hades, and he concludes the funeral of Patroclus by declaring that he himself will enfold Patroclus in Hades (23.19, 23.179, 23.65–107, 23.244).

Achilles' refusal to accept the finality of death and his return to the life of virtue do not, however, ease his grief but rather inflame it. For even though Achilles recoils before the harsh truth of human mortality, he also, in some measure, recognizes it. On one occasion in particular, Achilles appears to approach a clear-eyed acceptance of human mortality. When Lycaon, the son of Priam, eager "to escape evil death and black destruction," clasps Achilles' knees and begs for mercy, Achilles responds with words, some of which, in themselves, appear calm and reasonable:

> But, friend, die, even you. Why do you mourn so? Patroclus also died, who was better by far than you. Do you not see what kind of man I am, how noble and great? I am of a good father and a goddess, my mother, bore me, but for me, as for you, there is death and an overpowering fate. (21.106–110)

[59] Benardete remarks of Achilles, "His fury against Hector far exceeds the fury of an innocent man. He exacts from Hector the penalty he feels that he himself should pay" (2005, 112).

Achilles' words to Lycaon here echo the words he spoke to his friends in Book IX: "He still goes down to death, the man who has does no deeds, and the one who has done many" (9.320). Read literally, Achilles' words here seem to offer friendly and wise counsel: that Lycaon and all human beings should accept the finality of death with resignation, as a necessity of their nature.[60] Yet Achilles does not himself heed this counsel, for he proceeds both to kill Lycaon in anger and to explain to his lifeless corpse that he has done so in order to exact just retribution from "all" the Trojans "for the slaughter of Patroclus and the destruction of the Achaians" (21.114–135). This episode indicates that Achilles both recognizes the finality of death and recoils at that recognition, apparently because he cherishes in his heart a longing for immortality. Similarly, Achilles grieves over the loss of Patroclus and refuses to accept that loss, and he slays Hector and refuses to accept his death. Achilles evidently experiences within his mind and his heart a gnawing, embittering, and agonizing conflict between his awareness, and his denial, of the finality of death.

One might think that Achilles would turn in his agony to song, to calming – if not delighting – his mind and his spirit by singing of, and reflecting on, the deaths – if not the glories – of men. For, as we have seen in Chapter 1, the singer Homer himself, through his at once sorrowful and thought-provoking, clinical and compassionate depictions of death throughout the poem, points us toward acceptance of the finality of death. For example, Homer's graphic description of Lycaon's death highlights its finality and therewith the unreasonableness of Achilles continuing to speak to the lifeless body: "Achilles drew his sharp sword and struck him at the collar-bone, beside the neck, and the double-edged sword plunged in. He dropped to the ground, face downward, and lay at length, and the black blood flowed out, and soaked the ground" (21.116–119). Homer thus faces death more clear-sightedly than does the hero who inflicts it. Perhaps the most memorable image of the finality of death in the *Iliad* is to be found in a speech of the Trojan ally Glaucus: "As is the generation of leaves, so is that of men. The wind scatters the leaves onto the ground, but the forest flourishes and naturally grows, as the season of spring returns. Such is the generation of

[60] Schein goes so far as to suggest, "For all its brutality, the scene with Lykaon serves to remind us of the hero's humanity and tenderness" (1984, 149). Whitman comments, "There is little rancor in such hatred, only an engrossing vision of death" (1958, 207).

men: one naturally grows, but the other comes to an end" (6.146–149). This simile invites us to ask, are not corpses mere things, mere remnants of beings who were once alive, as dead leaves on the ground are mere remnants of the leaves on trees that were once alive? Yet, even though Achilles had pondered such questions earlier in the poem, even though he had affirmed to his friends that "for the soul of a man to come back, this cannot be taken by plunder or seized, once it has crossed the barrier of the teeth" (9.408–409), after the death of Patroclus, Achilles apparently forswears such questions, along with his questions about the goodness of the life of virtue. By embracing a fierce rage against the Trojans in the aftermath of Patroclus's death, along with a fierce rejection of the finality of death, it might seem that Achilles abandons all of his doubts about the goodness of the life of virtue and embraces that tragic life wholeheartedly at the end of the poem.

Yet, Achilles' tremendous fury gives way, in the first place, to his singularly gracious behavior toward the Achaians in Book XXIII and then to his singularly compassionate behavior toward Priam and the Trojans in Book XXIV. The poem whose theme is the destructive wrath of Achilles ends with Achilles, to a significant degree, overcoming that wrath. Achilles' graciousness at the end of the poem appears to reflect his increased awareness of the importance of friendship and love in the light of his beloved friend's death. But it also reflects his abiding and even deepening awareness of the limits of the honorable life of virtue.

ACHILLES' GRACIOUSNESS TOWARD THE ACHAIANS

Achilles is singularly courteous and generous toward the Achaians in the aftermath of Patroclus's funeral. First, by organizing games – eight competitions in all (chariot race, boxing, wrestling, foot race, combat in armor, shot put, archery, and javelin) – Achilles gives his fellow Achaians the opportunity to demonstrate their virtue and to win honor. Indeed, virtue is mentioned more times in Book XXIII than in any other book of the *Iliad*: once by Achilles when speaking of the virtue of his horses (23.276) and twice by Menelaus when speaking of his own virtue (23.571, 23.578).[61] Furthermore, and more importantly, by declining to participate in the

[61] See Note 1.

games himself, Achilles allows the Achaians to win honors that they would have otherwise failed to win. Achilles, whose horses are divine, who is famous for his fleetness of foot, and who is the best of the Achaians in combat, would certainly have won many of the eight competitions – at least the chariot race, the foot race, and combat in armor – and perhaps all of them (23.272–286, 23.776; consider also, for example, 24.453–456). But in his absence, such a formidable but secondary hero as Diomedes wins the prizes for chariot race and combat in armor (23.506–513, 23.802–825), Odysseus triumphs in the foot race (23.777–779) and ties Ajax for wrestling (23.700–737), and Agamemnon receives the first prize for javelin (23.884–894). Moreover, relatively minor figures are allowed to shine: Epeius carries off the prize for boxing, Polypoites for shot put, and Meriones for archery (23.664–699, 23.830–883). Finally, many other Achaians, renowned and not so renowned, receive honors from Achilles, for he is careful to give prizes even to those who do not win.

Achilles presides over these games with considerable tact and humanity. He diplomatically resolves a quarrel between the lordly Idomeneus and Ajax, son of Oileus, who foolishly abuses Idomeneus and speaks "shamefully," according to Homer (23.455–498). Achilles compassionately awards second prize in the chariot race to Eumelus – the best charioteer, according to Homer – who came in last because of a wholly unprovoked punishment by Athena (23.288–289, 23.382–397, 23.532–538). Then, when Antilochus, who actually came in second, "with justice" objects, Achilles graciously grants him the second prize and Eumelus another, special prize (23.539–565). Achilles deftly prevents the spirited and bloodied Odysseus and Ajax from seriously harming one another in their quest to prove who is the better wrestler by declaring a tie for first place and giving each first prizes (23.700–739). Later, Achilles similarly joins in preventing Ajax and Diomedes from harming one another in their armed combat competition and in giving ostensibly equal awards to each, while at the same time recognizing Diomedes' superiority (23.798–825). Achilles also gives Antilochus, his "beloved companion," a prize simply out of pleasure for his praise (23.555–556, 23.786–797). And Achilles grants two prizes to men who do not even compete! To Nestor, Achilles grants fifth prize for charioteering, on the charitable assumption that, were he younger, he would have won (23.615–653). And to Agamemnon, he grants first prize in javelin – and cancels the competition – with the generous and tactful claim that since

Agamemnon would surely win the contest, there is no need to hold it (23.884–897)!

Achilles exhibits here the greatest benevolence and affection toward his fellow Achaians as a whole – beyond the four friends whom he dines and converses with in Book IX – that he ever displays in the poem. At the beginning of the poem, Achilles saves the Achaians from the wrath of Apollo and the folly of Agamemnon, and he has evidently been fighting on their behalf for more than nine years; but here Achilles seems genuinely affectionate in his benevolence and seems to take pleasure in helping his fellow Achaians to win honor for themselves. Now, Achilles' graciousness here would seem to constitute an unambiguous ascent from his destructive anger throughout much of the poem. But it is important to note that Achilles' graciousness and generosity toward the Achaians here are based on a certain indifference to their honor and to virtue, especially to the virtue of justice. For his decision not to compete indicates that he no longer seeks to win from the Achaians the recognition that he is the best among them. Furthermore, Achilles' willingness to confer rewards on the basis of something other than merit suggests that he no longer believes that honor should simply go to those who deserve it. This is shown most clearly in the case of his awards to Nestor and Agamemnon, even though they do not even compete. We may feel inclined to praise Achilles here for exhibiting such tact, delicacy, and graciousness toward men who are conventionally superior to him due to their age and position, even if they are inferior to him due to their merit. But Achilles' graciousness here is based on and made possible by a certain indifference to justice. For he gives prizes and honors to men who do not, strictly speaking, deserve them.[62] Insofar, then, as Achilles acts graciously toward his fellow Achaians during the funeral games of Patroclus, he does so because he has come to accept, calmly and without any trace of bitterness, the limited goodness of virtue, the inevitable disproportion between honor and virtue, and the inevitability of injustice in human life.[63] And to the extent that he accepts the limited goodness of virtue, it might seem that Achilles has come to accept the limited character of human life and hence to forswear the hope for an unlimited, divine reward after death. Yet, insofar as

[62] See Saxonhouse 1988, 40.

[63] I consequently disagree with Benardete's suggestion that Achilles does not participate in the games out of guilt (2005, 127–128).

Achilles continues to punish the lifeless corpse of Hector even after the funeral of Patroclus and continues to speak to the dead Patroclus, he evidently falls short of reconciling himself to the finality of death (24.1–22, 24.591–595).

It is also true that Achilles' graciousness toward his companions at the funeral games is based on a sharp awareness of the gulf that separates them. Achilles benefits them by keeping his distance from them, by allowing them to compete on a more or less equal footing with their peers, and hence by recognizing how vastly superior he is to them. As he sought to benefit Patroclus by staying out of battle and letting him win honor for himself, so does Achilles benefit his fellow Achaians by letting them win honor for themselves in the games. Moreover, his refusal to participate in the funeral games reflects his indifference to their honor and gratitude. Achilles has come to see that the honor of the Achaians is not worth having, because they are not truly worthy of honoring him. He feels good will toward them, and hence takes the trouble to provide them with opportunities to win honor for themselves. But his is a good will borne of a magnanimous appreciation of his own superiority to them rather than a true feeling of kinship with them. Achilles does not even attempt to share his thoughts with the Achaians here, as he had tried to with Patroclus, Odysseus, Phoinix, and Ajax in Book IX. It is therefore not surprising that, at the end of the games, we see Achilles alone, without any companionship, cherishing in his solitude his memories of his friendship with Patroclus (24.1–13). It is also not surprising that Achilles' final act in the poem is to grant a twelve-day truce to the enemies of the Achaians – the Trojans – without asking permission from or consulting any of the Achaians and without even taking into account their interests (24.650–670; see also 24.683–688). Both his graciousness toward the Achaians in Book XXIII and his compassion toward the Trojans in Book XXIV reflect Achilles' fundamental independence from, and considerable indifference to, his fellow Achaians.

THE HUMANE PROVIDENCE OF ACHILLES

The very end of the *Iliad* seems to present Achilles at his most admirable. The wrath of Achilles, which was condemned so sharply by Homer at the beginning of the poem and which has caused so much suffering for so many, including Achilles himself, now gives way to the compassion of Achilles.[64] The *Iliad* closes, as it opens, with a suffering father pleading with a mighty Achaian ruler for the return of his child. But while the poem begins with the cruel rebuff by Agamemnon of the Trojan ally Chryses, it concludes with the kindly sympathy of Achilles for the Trojan king Priam (1.8–42).[65] Achilles comes to recognize at the very end of the poem what Homer has taught us to recognize throughout the poem: the common humanity shared by the Achaians and the Trojans, the nobility of the Trojans, and the piteousness of their suffering.[66] It seems altogether fitting, then, that the compassionate singer Homer should teach that the best of the Achaians is the most compassionate of the Achaians.[67]

Yet, the reason that the grieving Priam receives the corpse of his son is not, in the first place, the compassion of Achilles but rather the compassion of the gods. At the opening of the final book of the *Iliad*, we learn that Achilles continues to punish the lifeless corpse of Hector, day after day, even after the funeral of Patroclus (24.1–31). We then see the gods, prompted by Apollo, decide to order Achilles to return the corpse of Hector to Priam (24.32–120). Just as Apollo induced the Achaians to return the child of Chryses to her father at the beginning of the poem, so now does Apollo intervene to induce Achilles to return the child of Priam to his father (1.35–52). It is true that, in contrast to Agamemnon, Achilles does not defy the gods but promptly obeys their commandment (24.126–140; see also 24.559–570). But does the *Iliad* conclude, then, by celebrating the reverence of Achilles for the gods rather than his own sympathy for Priam? Does Homer finally highlight the compassion of the gods rather than the compassion of Achilles and finally teach that piety is the greatest virtue of the best of the Achaians? To examine these questions, let us consider the conclusion of the poem more carefully.

Apollo eloquently denounces Achilles for his lack of compassion for Priam and his family, for his lack of reverence toward the gods, and for his unreasonable refusal to accept the death of Patroclus:

[64] See MacLeod 1982, 32–35 and, as a whole, Kim 2000.

[65] Consider also Zanker's illuminating comparison of Achilles' generosity toward Priam with his (relative) generosity toward Eetion, Andromache's father, recounted by her at 6.416–428 (1994, 123–125). See also Segal 1971, 65.

[66] See Griffin 1980, 69.

[67] See Crotty 1994, 98–99.

> Thus Achilles has destroyed pity, nor is there any reverence in him, which harms men greatly, but also profits them. Someone, I suppose, must lose another even more beloved, a brother from the same womb or even a son. But once he weeps and mourns, he relaxes. For the Fates put an enduring spirit in humans. But he, once he has wrested away his beloved heart, attaches divine Hector to his horses and drags him around the tomb of his beloved companion. It is neither nobler nor better for him. (24.44–52)

Yet, Apollo's denunciation of Achilles is itself pitiless, for the god belittles Achilles' love for Patroclus as inferior to that of a father for a son, even though Achilles declares that his love for his companion is at least as great as that for his son (19.321–327; see also 23.43–47). Apollo's exhortation to Achilles to show compassion for the grieving Priam and to cease mourning for Patroclus might also seem capricious, inasmuch as it was Apollo himself who pitilessly abandoned Hector to Achilles and who pitilessly slew Patroclus (22.212–213, 16.804–805, 16.844–850, 18.453–456).

Nevertheless, the most powerful aspect of Apollo's denunciation of Achilles here would seem to be his demand that Achilles feel compassion for Priam. With the possible exception of Andromache, Priam would seem to be the most sympathetic character in the final books of the *Iliad*. In Book XXII, we see the old man "piteously" plead with his "beloved son" Hector to retreat within the walls of Troy, away from the oncoming Achilles, and thereby save himself, his family, and his city (22.33–76). We then see him cry out "piteously" at the sight of Achilles desecrating his son's corpse (22.407–429). Finally, as both Priam and Achilles go on to observe, Priam has fallen from the pinnacle of prosperity to the depths of misery (24.497–506, 24.543–548). While the *Iliad* opens with the moving spectacle of an innocent father begging for the return of his daughter, it concludes with the even more moving spectacle of the great king of a fabled city with fifty sons now covered with filth and bereft of his most heroic sons, as he begs for the corpse of his greatest son of all from the killer of that son.

Unlike Chryses, however, Priam is not simply an innocent victim of malefactors. For it was Priam, the mighty king of Troy, who prolonged the war by, for example, siding with his son Paris against his counselor Antenor and refusing to return Helen to her lawful husband (7.345–380; see also 7.381–393, 3.146–160). It was, moreover, Priam who evidently entrusted his son Hector with absolute command of his army and who never intervened on behalf of the prudent counsels of Poulydamas to fight the Achaians from behind the great walls of Troy (2.816–818, 12.195–250, 18.243–314; consider also 20.178–183). As the virtually absolute ruler of Troy, Priam bears ultimate responsibility for the destruction of Troy's prosperity wrought by the war he chose to prolong, and for the deaths of his sons caused by the folly of his chosen general.[68] Furthermore, in contrast to Achilles, who does blame himself for the death of Patroclus, Priam never blames himself at all for his grievous errors and even goes so far as to revile his surviving sons as "scoundrels ... evil children of mine, disgraces ... liars and dancers," for daring to survive when his "best sons" perished (24.239–264). What is more, insofar as Priam bears responsibility for the prolongation of the war, he bears some responsibility for the death of Achilles' beloved companion Patroclus in that war. The case of Priam, then, is morally complicated – certainly more so than that of Chryses – and therefore it is perhaps understandable that Achilles hesitates to show compassion for him.[69]

It is a testimony to Priam's tremendous shrewdness that, in contrast to the gods, he recognizes how difficult it will be to induce Achilles to overcome his anger at Hector and hand over the corpse of the killer of Patroclus to his father. Zeus is confident that a large ransom and fear of the gods will "melt" Achilles' spirit, "for he is not mindless nor unwatchful nor a transgressor but will with all kindness spare the man who is a suppliant" (24.111–119, 24.144–158). Hermes assures Priam that a ritual invocation of Achilles' family will suffice: "go in yourself [to Achilles' hut] and clasp the knees of Peleus's son and beseech him in the name of his father, of his fair-haired mother, and of his child, and so rouse the spirit within him" (24.465–67). Priam, however, departs from the gods' advice in three crucial respects. First – in stark contrast especially with Odysseus's attempt to sway Achilles in Book IX – Priam says almost nothing to Achilles about the gifts he brings, lest any direct appeal to Achilles' self-interest backfire, as Odysseus's appeal evidently does (compare 9.260–299 with 24.502; see also 9.378–429). Second, Priam not only clasps the knees of Achilles, but he also kisses his hands, the very hands that killed his son. Finally, Priam is silent about Achilles' divine mother and speaks to him *only* of his mortal father.[70] These are Priam's words:

[68] Consider Flaumenhaft 2004, 5–6, 24, 28–30.

[69] I am therefore inclined to think that Zanker goes too far in arguing that, according to Homer, "To pity is a morally right response, and not to pity is wrong" (1994, 24).

[70] For Priam's knowledge that Peleus is Achilles' father, see 22.38–41, 22.56–58. For Priam's son Hector's knowledge that Thetis is Achilles' mother and Peleus is his father, see 16.860–861, 20.366–372, 20.431–437, 22.250–253. For the evidently general knowledge

"Achilles like the gods, remember your father, one who is of years just like mine, and on the destructive door-sill of old age. And they who dwell nearby encompass him and afflict him, nor is there anyone to defend him against harm and disaster. Yet surely, when he hears of you and that you are still living, he rejoices within his spirit and all his days he hopes that he will see his beloved son come home from the Troad. But I myself had no such destiny. For I have sired the best sons in wide Troy, but I say not one of them is left to me . . . Have reverence, then, for the gods, Achilles, and take pity on me, remembering your father. Yet I am still more pitiful. I have endured what no other mortal on earth has endured; I put my lips to the hands of the man who killed my children." So he spoke and stirred in him a longing to grieve for his own father . . . and Achilles wept now for his own father, now again for Patroclus. (24.486–512)

Priam evidently reasons that the only way that he can melt Achilles' heart and overcome his anger and hatred toward Hector and Priam and all the Trojans is by appealing to his sympathetic imagination and to his own experience of love. Priam must induce Achilles to see in Priam the image of his own father, Peleus, and to imagine the sorrow that Peleus will feel when he, Achilles, is dead.[71] Priam must induce Achilles to think of the love his father bears for him and even to think of the love he himself bears for his beloved friend Patroclus and, drawing on that experience of love, to imagine a love so great that it can inspire the king of Troy to risk his life and to sacrifice every shred of his dignity, honor, and pride in order to recover the corpse of his son. The only way, then, that Priam can arouse such humanity and pity in Achilles is by reminding him of the experiences of human love and human sorrow that he shares with Priam and hence by speaking to him of his *human* father and not at all about his divine mother.[72] And this strategy of Priam's is a complete success.[73] For, as Homer specifies, Achilles goes on to weep both for his loving father and his beloved friend and to feel genuine sympathy for the aged king Priam (24.511–516).

Achilles, however, goes beyond expressions of pity for Priam and even beyond acting to return the corpse. In the first place, Achilles offers singularly thoughtful and friendly advice to Priam – advice that matches in its thoughtfulness the advice he gave his companions in Book IX, but here

among the Trojans and their allies that Thetis is a goddess, see 20.206–207 (and also 1.357–358, 18.35–49, 18.138–142).

[71] Priam recognized the need for this very appeal to Achilles' sympathetic imagination immediately after Hector's death. See 22.415–422.

[72] See Crotty 1994, 75–77.

[73] MacLeod suggests that this scene is Priam's *aristeia*, that is, the scene in which he demonstrates his excellence (1982, 127).

without any trace of the anger he showed then.[74] After marveling at the power of Priam's heartfelt love for his son that enabled him to come alone to the ships of his enemies and to face the man who slew "your many noble sons," Achilles remarks: "But come, sit down on the chair, and we will even let our woes lie down in our spirit, even though we are grieving" (24.518–523). Achilles not only identifies their woes as common to them both – their painful sorrow for the suffering of their loved ones – but also indicates here that the advice he is about to give is meant for himself as well as for Priam. In other words, Achilles goes beyond expressing compassion for Priam by sharing thoughts that are of common benefit to them both. Achilles then goes on to explain: "For there is nothing to be accomplished by numbing lamentation. For such is the way the gods spun for wretched mortals, that we live our lives in grief; but they themselves have no sorrows" (24.524–526). Achilles highlights here, not only the common condition that he shares with the Trojan king, but also the gulf that separates them, as mortals, from the gods. Because humans are destined to suffer all the painful longing and the painful grief that mortals must suffer, humans must accept their suffering and their mortality with a measure of calm resignation rather than endless, excruciating lamentation. But because the gods inflict such sorrows on humans, and because the gods themselves have no sorrows, humans must not look to the gods for relief from their sorrows, for the carefree gods, Achilles suggests here, neither care for humans nor understand them.

Achilles goes on to affirm that Zeus does offer some benefits to humans, but he stresses the evils that the god metes out:

> For two urns lie on the door-sill of Zeus that give evil gifts, but the other one, good things. Should Zeus who delights in thunder mingle these and give them to someone, he sometimes encounters something evil, sometimes something noble. But when Zeus gives from the urn of sorrows, he makes one the victim of outrageous deeds, and the evil hunger drives him over the divine earth, and he wanders, honored neither by gods nor by mortals. (24.527–533)

Even Zeus, then, cannot be counted on by humans for assistance. And Achilles goes on to highlight the harsh indifference of the gods through the examples of Peleus – whom the gods blessed with happiness and wealth but also gave a son, Achilles, and "Now I do not take care of him as he grows

[74] As MacLeod notes regarding Achilles' pity here, "It is not only an emotion, but an insight" (1982, 27). Consider as well 34–35; Schein 1984, 159–162; Griffin 1995, 45.

old since, very far from the land of my fathers, I sit in Troy, bringing sorrows to you and your children" (24.540–542) – and Priam himself, whose happiness the gods destroyed by inflicting war (24.543–548). Achilles goes on to conclude by urging Priam explicitly, and himself implicitly, to accept the finality of their loved ones' demise and to reconcile themselves to their sorrows rather than look to the gods for providence (24.549–551).

Yet, a further piece of advice lies buried in this speech of Achilles to Priam about the gods. By blaming himself for failing to take care of the father who needs him and for inflicting sorrow on Priam, Achilles indicates that he himself has needlessly compounded the sorrows of both his father and Priam. The gods, then, are not the sole cause of the two men's sorrows or of any human being's sorrows. Achilles has caused harm to Peleus and Priam and, we might add, Peleus and Priam have caused harm to themselves – Peleus perhaps by sending his son to fight at Troy (9.252–259, 9.438–443) and Priam certainly by prolonging the war and entrusting command of his army entirely to his son Hector. And furthermore, insofar as humans cause themselves some sorrows, they can also desist from harming themselves and can even assist and provide for themselves. Achilles, then, implicitly advises Priam, and perhaps especially himself, not only to accept the sorrows that our mortal condition inflicts upon us and not only to refrain from looking to the carefree gods for assistance, but also to look to human beings – to themselves – for assistance and for providence.[75]

Now, Achilles proceeds to act on this advice by taking care, not of his father, but of Priam. When Priam abruptly demands the immediate return of Hector's body in return for the ransom he has brought, Achilles sternly but sagely warns the old man against provoking his deadly wrath (24.552–570). Achilles then thoughtfully prepares Hector's body for conveyance back to Troy and deliberately does so out of the eyesight of Priam lest the sight of the corpse enrage the old king and thereby move him to provoke the always simmering wrath of Achilles (24.571–586). Achilles goes on to warn Priam – and himself – against neglecting to take care of himself while mourning his beloved dead son: "But now let *us* remember our supper" (24.601, emphasis added). And while explicitly reiterating this warning through the story of the

[75] I therefore think that Scodel goes too far in claiming that "Achilles completely ignores human responsibility" here (2002, 211–212). As Saxonhouse observes, Achilles concludes that "It is left to man to provide the order and value that the gods deny" (1988, 42).

sufferings of Niobe at the hands of the gods, through that story Achilles also implicitly reiterates his advice against trusting in divine providence (24.602–620). Finally, after feeding Priam and just before he puts him to bed under his protection against the other Achaians, Achilles offers Priam a great gift, one that perhaps surpasses the gift of returning the corpse of Hector: addressing him as "dear old man," Achilles asks Priam how many days he would wish for to celebrate the funeral of Hector and vows to hold back the Achaians during that time (24.650–672). This benefaction is entirely free on the part of Achilles: the gods do not command it and even Priam had not dared to ask for it. Achilles would seem to derive no benefit from it whatsoever, no honor, for example, from the Achaians and none from the gods. This, the noblest and most compassionate act in the poem, is entirely independent of the gods, an act of human rather than divine compassion, an act of human rather than divine providence.[76]

Rather than an act of virtue, Achilles' final act in the poem seems to be one of friendship for Priam.[77] Achilles has of course not shared his life with Priam as he has with Patroclus. But they do have in common the experience of heroic love and grief over the loss of a loved one. Achilles evidently feels closer to Priam at this moment than he does to the other Achaians. It is with Priam, not with them, that Achilles shares his reflections concerning the indifference of the gods and the need for humans to accept their mortal sorrows and to provide for themselves. Achilles attempts to articulate his insight, his understanding, and his counsel to Priam and, through, Priam, to himself. Moreover, Achilles and Priam evidently admire one another and derive pleasure from contemplating one another: as Homer recounts, "Priam wondered at Achilles, both his grandeur and his quality . . . and Achilles wondered at Priam, gazing at his goodly appearance and listening to his speech. But once they had delighted themselves by gazing upon one

[76] Saxonhouse points out that Achilles "does not call on the gods to witness" the truce he offers to Priam and the Trojans as Hector had when he proposed a covenant with Achilles (22.254–259). We might add that Achilles does not call on the gods to witness this truce, in contrast to all the Achaians and Trojans, who invoked the gods to enforce the earlier truces between the two armies (3.95–112, 3.249–301, 7.76–86, 7.408–411). Saxonhouse concludes: "The truce is Achilles' assertion of man's ordering of his own world" (1988, 44).

[77] Crotty notes that Achilles' "attainment of self-understanding seeks expression in forming a friendship or *philotēs* with Priam" (1994, 83; see also 86). See as well Schein 1984, 159–162.

another, the old man, godlike Priam, spoke to him first" (24.629–634). Through this brief interaction between the Achaian warrior and the Trojan king, Homer offers a glimpse of the beauty and the delight of a friendship based on the common good of shared understanding.

Achilles' graciousness and sympathy at the end of the poem reflect his awareness of the limits and the problem of virtue and therewith a certain acceptance of death. But it is important to recognize that that awareness is itself limited and fragile.[78] Just as, after his kind and calm demeanor during the games in honor of Patroclus, Achilles returns to punishing the lifeless corpse of Hector, so, even in the midst of his humane and wise advice to Priam, does Achilles show that he does not fully accept that advice. Even as Achilles expresses compassion and understanding for the grief of Priam, he also warns Priam against provoking his deadly rage (24.560–571).[79] Even after he urges Priam to reconcile himself to the finality of the death of his beloved son – since "you will not raise him up" (24.551) – Achilles speaks to his beloved companion – "Do not be angry with me, Patroclus" (24.592) – though his beloved companion is dead. And even though he warns against trusting in the gods for assistance, he still holds out some hope that Zeus – with his urn of "good things" – may bestow something "noble" upon humans (24.527–530). Achilles goes very far in overcoming his anger but never quite frees himself from it. He calls into question the goodness of the life of virtue and honor but feels a powerful attachment to it. He sees but does not fully recognize and accept the finality of death. In Achilles, then, we have a man who glimpses the alternative way of life represented by the wise singer Homer but who does not quite recognize it or embrace it. Nevertheless, more than anyone else in the *Iliad*, Achilles points beyond himself to the fullness of soul, the clarity, the calm, and the humane understanding of Homer himself.

[78] Consider MacLeod's observation that "the *Iliad* is great not least because it can speak authentically for pity or kindness or civilization without showing them victorious in life" (1982, 16).
[79] See Segal 1971, 65.

CHAPTER 4

Odysseus and Achilles

THE CASE FOR ODYSSEUS: THE RATIONAL HERO

If the teaching of the *Iliad* is that the greatness of Achilles lies in his mind rather than in his physical strength, and in his thoughtfulness rather than in his martial prowess, then must we not conclude that the greatest Homeric hero of all is not Achilles but Odysseus? After all, it is Odysseus who is the most evidently brainy, wily, and resourceful Homeric character.[1] The *Odyssey* virtually opens with Zeus praising Odysseus as outstanding among humans for his intelligence (νόον), as well as his piety (1.66–67). Later, Athena herself – by her own account, famous among all gods for counsel and cunning – proclaims Odysseus "best by far of all mortals in deliberation and speeches" (13.296–299). If the Homeric poems teach that wisdom is the cardinal human virtue, do they not teach that Odysseus is the most excellent of human beings?[2] Is this not why Homer follows his poem on the anger of

[1] Consider Nagy's claim that "the reference in *Odyssey* viii 78 to the quarreling Achilles and Odysseus as the 'best of the Achaeans' seems to be based on an epic tradition that contrasted the heroic worth of Odysseus with that of Achilles in terms of a contrast between **mêtis** [which Nagy translates here as 'artifice, stratagem'] and **bíē** [which Nagy translates here as 'might']" (1979, 45). Heitman contends that, "If the true subject of the *Iliad* is force, the true subject of the *Odyssey* is mind" (2005, 104–105).

[2] According to Vico, the *Iliad* celebrates Achilles, "the hero of violence [*eroe della forza*]," but the *Odyssey* celebrates Ulysses, "the hero of wisdom [*eroe della sapienza*]" (1999, 383; 1977, 579). Clay maintains that "Homer does not caricature the figure of Achilles but gives him the honor due his greatness. In the final analysis, however, the

Achilles with his poem on Odysseus – the man of many ways (πολύτροπος),[3] many counsels (πολύμητις),[4] many schemes (πολυμήχανος),[5] and much wisdom (πολύφρων)?[6]

At first glance, the *Odyssey* presents Odysseus as an obviously more rational hero than Achilles. Odysseus is the hero who leads the Achaians to victory over Troy through his brilliant stratagem of the Trojan Horse. When he returns home, the cunning Odysseus vanquishes the overbearing suitors even though he is vastly outnumbered. Most remarkably of all, Odysseus defeats the monstrous, physically overpowering Cyclops, against seemingly hopeless odds, thanks to his outstanding guile, self-control, and foresight. On other occasions as well, Odysseus displays his capacity to reason his way to a successful outcome, by assessing the obstacles he faces, weighing his possible choices, and deliberately choosing the best, most effective remedy (5.464–487, 6.142–185). In contrast to Achilles, who defeats his enemies through sheer force of passion and might, Odysseus demonstrates the power of brains to beat the brawniest of foes.[7] In this way, Odysseus would seem to exemplify most vividly the tangible goodness – the practical power and benefits – of the life of reason.

To be sure, Odysseus's life is not simply happy. As Homer tells us in the opening of the *Odyssey*, Odysseus failed to save his companions and their homecoming, "even though he was eager" to do so (1.6). And he himself fails

humane heroism of Odysseus, based as it is on intelligence and endurance, is set above the quicksilver glory of Achilles" (1983, 96; see also 132, 244).

[3] Odysseus is referred to as πολύτροπος twice in the *Odyssey*, once by Homer and once by Circe: 1.1, 10.330. Consider Clay 1983, 29–32.

[4] Odysseus is referred to as πολύμητις sixty-eight times in the *Odyssey*: 2.173, 4.763, 5.214, 7.207, 7.240, 7.302, 8.152, 8.165, 8.412, 8.463, 8.474, 8.486, 9.1, 11.354, 11.377, 13.311, 13.382, 13.416, 14.191, 14.390, 14.439, 15.380, 16.201, 17.16, 17.192, 17.353, 17.453, 18.14, 18.51, 18.124, 18.312, 18.337, 18.365, 19.41, 19.70, 19.106, 19.164, 19.220, 19.261, 19.335, 19.382, 19.499, 19.534, 19.582, 19.585, 20.36, 20.168, 20.183, 20.226, 21.274, 21.404, 22.1, 22.34, 22.60, 22.105, 22.170, 22.320, 22.371, 22.390, 22.430, 22.490, 23.129, 23.247, 23.263, 24.302, 24.330, 24.356, 24.406.

[5] Odysseus is referred to as πολυμήχανος seventeen times in the *Odyssey*: 1.205, 5.203, 10.401, 10.456, 10.488, 10.504, 11.60, 11.92, 11.405, 11.473, 11.617, 13.375, 14.486, 16.167, 22.164, 24.192, 24.542.

[6] Odysseus is referred to as πολύφρων five times in the *Odyssey*: 1.83, 14.424, 20.239, 20.329, 21.204. Regarding all of the πολυ-compounds applied to Odysseus, see Stanford 1950, 108–110.

[7] Heitman suggests that "In the Odyssey, nearly every battle is won by outsmarting the enemy" (2005, 105).

to reach home for ten long years, "longing for his wife and his homecoming" (1.13). Homer repeatedly reminds us throughout the poem that Odysseus is a man who "endured many things" (πολύτλας).[8] But, in contrast with Achilles, Odysseus's hardships do not appear to be self-inflicted. The opening of the *Iliad* stresses that Achilles' anger causes "countless woes (ἄλγεα) for the Achaians" (*Iliad* 1.1–2), perhaps above all for himself, since it eventually leads to the death of his beloved friend Patroclus who is as dear to him as life itself (18.80–82). Odysseus, on the other hand, comes to sight as one who "*suffered* many woes (ἄλγεα) in the deep sea" (*Odyssey* 1.4) as a result of the actions of others: his companions, the proemium tells us, who "perished through their own folly – the fools! – who ate the cattle of the Sun God, the son of Hyperion" (1.7–8); the love-sick nymph Calypso, who "detained" Odysseus on her isle against his will for eight years (1.14–15); the wrathful god Poseidon, who persecutes him (1.19–21); and the overbearing suitors, who consume his home and torment his family (1.159–162).[9] Odysseus, then, is not responsible for his suffering. His intelligence enables him to avoid avoidable evils. But Odysseus is, through no fault of his own, the victim of the passions and the follies of those who are less wise than he is.

Indeed, Odysseus comes to sight as being morally as well as intellectually superior to Achilles. For while both heroes display the moral passion par excellence of anger, Odysseus's anger seems both more sensible and more just.[10] Achilles' fury leads him, first, to expose his fellow Achaians to the

[8] Odysseus is referred to as πολύτλας thirty-seven times in the *Odyssey*: 5.171, 5.354, 5.486, 6.1, 6.249, 7.1, 7.133, 7.139, 7.177, 7.329, 7.344, 8.199, 8.446, 13.250, 13.353, 14.148, 15.340, 16.90, 16.186, 16.225, 16.258, 16.266, 17.280, 17.560, 18.90, 18.281, 19.102, 21.414, 22.191, 22.261, 23.111, 24.176, 24.232, 24.348, 24.490, 24.504, 24.537.

[9] Clay suggests that, in the opening of the *Odyssey*, "Homer reveals his partisanship for his hero" (1983, 34; see 35–38 and also Bolotin 1989, 41).

[10] As Benardete puts it, the *Odyssey* "seems to share in Odysseus's wrath more than the *Iliad* does in Achilles'" (1997, 1). Consider also Dimmock's claim: "the *Odyssey* is a poem about right and wrong, in a sense that the *Iliad* is not . . . The *Odyssey* . . . unabashedly exhibits the triumph of life over death in terms of the triumph of good over evil: quite simply, it suggests that Odysseus vindicated justice so strikingly that his name will never die" (1989, 25). Similarly, Lloyd-Jones contends, "The survival of Odysseus and his triumph over the suitors are the reward of *arete* [virtue]" (1971, 29). Lateiner remarks, "If you seek moral satisfaction, like T. S. Eliot you will prefer the Odyssey" (2004, 27). Crotty states more cautiously, "The slaughter of the suitors by Odysseus may seem at first glance to be an emphatic vindication of the moral vision of the world" (1994, 151).

onslaught of the Trojans, then to slaughter not only Trojan soldiers on the battlefield but also twelve Trojan youths at the funeral of Patroclus, and finally to punish – repeatedly and pointlessly – the lifeless body of Hector. Achilles' anger leads him to act disloyally, senselessly, and self-destructively, as he acknowledges by repenting of and eventually abandoning his anger in the final books of the *Iliad*.[11] In contrast, Odysseus's anger leads him to act in a seemingly loyal and prudent fashion, since it leads him to kill the suitors who pose a dangerous threat to his family and himself and therefore, it would seem, leads him to benefit his loved ones and himself.

Finally, and most simply, Odysseus seems to understand thoroughly, throughout the *Odyssey*, what Achilles comes to understand only intermittently in the course of the *Iliad* – the blessings of peace, shared with loved ones, at home.[12] What is the story of the *Odyssey* – what is the key to its timeless and universal appeal – if not that of a man longing with all his heart and striving with all his might to reach his beloved home? In the first description of Odysseus in the poem, Athena explains how Odysseus, in hopeless captivity to Calypso, "eager even for the smoke rising up from his land, yearns to die" (1.55–59). Homer describes him on Calypso's isle: "Nor were his eyes ever dry of tears, but the sweet life ebbed away from him as he wept for his return" (5.151–153). In Odysseus's words to his Phaiacian hosts: "Let life leave me once I have seen my possessions and my household servants and my great-high-roofed house" (7.224–225).

Odysseus's longing for his home seems above all to consist of longing for his wife (1.13).[13] To Nausicaa, he declares, "Nothing is mightier than this, nor better, than when a man and woman have a home, like-minded in their thoughts" (6.182–184). Such seems to be the marriage Odysseus enjoys with the "surpassingly wise" (περίφρων)[14] Penelope, who evidently matches him

[11] Consider, for example, 18.98–113, 19.54–75, 23.257–897, 24.507–672.

[12] In Nagy's words: "unlike Achilles, who won **kléos** but lost **nóstos** . . . Odysseus is a double winner. He has won both **kléos** and **nóstos**" (1979, 39). See also Schein 1996, 12–13.

[13] According to Felson and Slatkin, the *Odyssey* "puts marriage at the centre" and, through its account of Odysseus and Penelope, "idealises it" (2004, 104; see also 112).

[14] Penelope is referred to as περίφρων fifty times in the *Odyssey*: 1.329, 4.787, 4.808, 4.830, 5.216, 11.446, 14.373, 15.41, 15.314, 16.329, 16.409, 16.435, 17.100, 17.162, 17.306, 17.492, 17.553, 17.498, 17.528, 17.562, 17.585, 18.159, 18.177, 18.245, 18.250, 18.285, 19.53, 19.59, 19.89, 19.103, 19.123, 19.308, 19.349, 19.375, 19.508, 19.559, 19.588, 20.388, 21.2, 21.311, 21.321, 21.330, 23.10, 23.58, 23.80, 23.104, 23.173, 23.256, 23.285, 24.404. The only other characters referred to as περίφρων in the poem are Queen Arete once (11.345) and

in stratagems,[15] patience, and wisdom and with whom she shares the pleasures of body and soul.[16] As Homer describes their reunion, after twenty years apart: "Once the two delighted themselves in passionate love, they delighted themselves with tales, which they told to one another" (23.300–301).[17] So great is the happiness that Odysseus finds in such a marriage of true minds that he prefers it to the divine, immortal existence offered him by the goddess Calypso (5.203–224, 7.245–260, 23.333–337).[18]

In his embrace of a life of reason and love over a life of anger and war, Odysseus seems not only to surpass the excellence of Achilles but also to approach the wisdom of the singer of these poems, Homer himself. Indeed, Odysseus is himself, like the singer of the *Odyssey*, a singer of the deeds of men: one-sixth of the poem consists of Odysseus's own recounting of his adventures to the Phaiacians in Books IX–XII. Moreover, Odysseus displays the imagination and inventiveness of a singer by repeatedly concocting fictitious tales about himself that he tells to the Cyclops, to Athena, to Eumaeus, to the suitor Antinoos, to his wife, and to his father.[19] Finally, Odysseus is compared to a singer of tales by Alcinoos (11.366–369), by Eumaeus (17.513–521), and by Homer himself (21.404–409). By emphatically linking Odysseus to the activity of singing tales, the *Odyssey* suggests a close kinship between the rational heroism of Odysseus and the humane wisdom of Homer.[20]

Eurycleia four times (19.357, 19.491, 20.134, 21.381). The word appears only once in the *Iliad*, to describe the wife of Diomedes (5.412).

[15] The word δόλος (stratagem, guile) is used to describe, for example, both the Trojan Horse scheme devised by Odysseus through which he conquers Troy and the plot of weaving and unraveling of Laertes' shroud, hatched by Penelope, through which she keeps the overbearing suitors at bay for three years (8.492–495, 2.93–126, 24.126–146). It is also used to describe the treachery of Circe toward Odysseus's companions (10.232).

[16] See Schein 1996, 27.

[17] Felson-Rubin goes so far as to claim that "Homer sets forth the reunion as the climax of the *Odyssey* plot" (1994, 65). Crotty compares the reunion of Odysseus and Penelope with the meeting of Achilles and Priam at the end of the *Iliad* and also to the relationship between the poem and its listeners (1994, 181–184, 199–203).

[18] Schein (1996, 22) and Benardete (1997, 2–3) compare Odysseus's choice of Penelope over Calypso with Achilles' choice of a short but noble and glorious life over a long but ignoble and inglorious life. See also Felson and Slatkin 2004, 106.

[19] 9.280–286, 13.250–286, 14.192–359, 14.468–503, 17.415–444, 18.138–140, 19.165–202, 19.269–307, 24.258–314. See Saïd 2011, 183–188.

[20] See Moulton 1977, 147; Schein 1996, 19; Saïd 2011, 235–237.

THE WRATH OF ODYSSEUS

The ending of the poem, however, calls into question our initial impression of Odysseus as a man of reason who knew the mind of many men and who surpasses all men in intelligence and deliberation (1.3, 1.66–67, 13.296–299). For the poem ends with Odysseus in the grip of violent passion, killing all 108 of the largely unarmed suitors (along with eight male servants) – even those who beg for mercy – ordering the killing of all of his disloyal maidservants and attempting, even in defiance of Athena, to kill "all" of the brothers and fathers of the dead suitors, even as they are fleeing (24.528).[21] At a particularly dangerous moment in his fight with the suitors, when the suitors have managed to obtain a number of weapons and when Odysseus would seem to need each of his three allies – his son, his swineherd, and his oxherd – to help him, Odysseus instead commands his two servants to withdraw from the fight and take the time to tie up the disloyal and insulting goatherd so that he may be tortured later: "thus he may suffer harsh woes for a long time, while he is alive" (22.177). During the battle with the suitors, Odysseus angrily cuts off the head of the prophet Leiodes – "to whom alone their [the suitors'] wicked follies were hateful and he [Leiodes] was indignant at all the suitors" (21.146–147) – as Leiodes rightly protests his innocence (22.320–329). Once the suitors are slaughtered, Odysseus needlessly and, it would seem, imprudently, tortures and kills two children of a faithful servant whose family – not

[21] Crotty deems the "slaughter ... one of the most deeply troubling aspects of the *Odyssey*" and observes that "Odysseus not only outwits Antinous but outdoes him in ruthlessness" and that "Odysseus' vengeance bears a striking and troubling resemblance to Aegisthus' ambush of Agamemnon and his companions while they sat at table" (1994, 154, 153). Saïd, who calls the killing of the suitors a "massacre," notes that the characters of the *Odyssey* "display a cruelty that goes far beyond anything in the *Iliad* when it comes to punishing the suitors' lowly accomplices: the maidservants are hanged and Melanthius' genitals thrown to the dogs (while in the *Iliad*, Hector's body is not touched by dogs)" (2011, 213–214). Even Dimmock, who defends the justice (in the view of Homer) of the slaughter of the suitors – including Leiodes – the torture and killing of Melanthius, and the killing of the maidservants, notes that Odysseus here is "deaf to pity" (1989, 298; see 295–297, 301–302, 306–315). Pucci observes that "the *Odyssey* is almost explicit in denying *kleos* – that is, the specifically epic fame and renown – to Odysseus' return and revenge" (1987, 216).

yet aware of the killing – later provides valuable support to him against the relatives of the suitors.[22] Odysseus seems to be possessed by a blind fury throughout the last books of the poem,[23] especially in the final book, where he "shouted horribly" as he attacked the fathers and brothers of the dead suitors (24.537). Odysseus's rampage is only stopped by the forceful intervention of Zeus himself (24.536–544). Perhaps Odysseus's fury is definitively quelled by this intervention (see 24.545–548). But does not the fact that the gods must intervene so forcefully demonstrate the degree to which Odysseus is possessed by a zealous anger at the end of the poem?

The contrast with the end of the *Iliad* is dramatic.[24] There, in the final two books, the hitherto wrathful Achilles overcomes his wrath for both the Achaians and the Trojans, first by demonstrating a gracious forbearance and friendliness toward Agamemnon and the Achaians (in Book XXIII), and then by demonstrating genuine compassion and understanding for Priam, the father of the enemy he slew (in Book XXIV). But the *Odyssey* ends with the ostensibly self-controlled and thoughtful Odysseus blindly succumbing to his vengeful passion – against the suitors and their fathers – and slaughtering without discrimination or calculation. The theme of anger unites both the *Iliad* and the *Odyssey*. The hero of each poem displays a righteous, ferocious fury against his enemies.[25] But only one hero rises above his fury. And that hero is not Odysseus.[26]

[22] Melanthius and Melantho, both of whom are insulting and abusive toward Odysseus and supportive of the suitors, are the children of Dolios, who is especially devoted to Penelope and who, along with his other sons, later helps Odysseus against the relatives of the suitors. See 17.212–216, 22.131–141, 18.307–336, 19.65–95, 23.417–476, 4.734–741, 24.386–411, 24.489–501.

[23] Ruderman characterizes Odysseus's anger against the suitors and servingwomen as "almost limitless" (1995, 47).

[24] Homer goes out of his way to encourage us to think of the contrast between Achilles in Book XXIV of the *Iliad* and Odysseus in Book XXIV of the *Odyssey* by presenting the character of Achilles in Book XXIV (15–97) of the *Iliad* and perhaps also by describing old Laertes in Book XXIV of the *Odyssey* (226–317, especially 315–317) in a way that echoes his descriptions of old Priam in Book XXIV of the *Iliad* (161–165, 476–517).

[25] Consider Clarke 2004, 87.

[26] Benardete goes so far as to suggest that "the anger of Odysseus . . . is inseparable from who he is" (1997, 44). On the possible derivation of Odysseus's name from the word for anger, see Benardete 1997, 44, 130; Clay 1983, 60; Ruderman 1995, 47; 155.

The ending of the *Odyssey* compels us to examine afresh, and more carefully, the complex character of Odysseus, the man of many ways.[27] In the course of the poem, Odysseus displays a tremendous capacity for reason and self-control and also a tremendous capacity for unbridled rage and vengeance. Is his fury at the end of the poem a temporary lapse from his sovereign reasonableness? Or does the fact that the poem culminates with his rage and vengeance reveal that his rational self-control is ultimately in the service of his passions?

IS ODYSSEUS RESPONSIBLE FOR THE DEATHS OF HIS COMPANIONS AND THE POSTPONEMENT OF HIS HOMECOMING?

One might defend and excuse Odysseus's rage at the end of the poem on the grounds that he has suffered so long and so terribly during the ten years that he has struggled for the return home of his men and himself. Telemachus, Eumaeus, Eurycleia, and Laertes (though not perhaps Penelope) are also quite vehement in their demand for vengeance against the suitors who have tormented them (22.194–199, 22.285–291, 22.401–476, 24.351–352; cf. 19.535–558). It only seems human for those who have innocently endured cruel injustice for so long to lash out, even recklessly and at times cruelly, at their tormentors. Is it not understandable that Odysseus, who, as Homer stresses in the opening of the poem, has "suffered many woes on the deep sea" (1.3) and through no fault of his own – thanks to the "wicked folly" of his companions, the unrequited love of Calypso (1.14–15), the fury of Poseidon (1.19–21), and the outrages of the suitors – has been deprived of his cherished homecoming for ten bitterly long years, should succumb to a righteous, and even a blind, fury?[28] Would it not be natural, given the experience of such long, innocent suffering, and given his longing for his home and his wife, that his moral rage should well up and, at least temporarily, overthrow his reason?

Yet, even though Homer, in the opening of the poem, initially gives the impression that Odysseus's homecoming was delayed because of the folly of

[27] Stanford suggests that the most important aspect of Odysseus's character is "the fundamental ambiguity of his essential qualities" (1963, 79).

[28] Consider Dimmock 1989, 295–315.

his companions, and even though Odysseus himself gives that overall impression in his account of his years of wandering to the Phaiacians and later to his wife, Homer goes on to show quite unmistakably that Odysseus himself bears considerable responsibility for the delay of his homecoming. For example, the poem begins by explaining that Odysseus was not able to secure a homecoming for his companions because "they perished through their own wicked folly – the fools! – who ate the cattle of the Sun God, the son of Hyperion" (1.7–8). Yet, the companions referred to here are only a small fraction – less than one-twelfth – of the companions who were with Odysseus "after he sacked the sacred city of Troy" (1.2).[29] As we learn over the course of Books IX through XII, the vast majority of Odysseus' men perished *through no fault of their own*. They perished at the hands of the Ciconians, the Cyclopes, Scylla, and above all at the hands of the Lastrygonians, who destroyed eleven of Odysseus's twelve ships with all their crew (10.112–132, 9.159–160). In the case of the Ciconians, Odysseus does claim that the men perished through their own folly, but even he makes no such claim in the other, much more costly episodes (9.43–44). Furthermore, Homer's overall account indicates that Odysseus himself bore considerable responsibility for his men's loss of life, most clearly in the episode of the Cyclops, but in other episodes as well. When studying the *Odyssey*, then, we must keep in mind the wiliness of its author as well as of its hero. While Homer's artful narrative begins by encouraging us to admire and sympathize with Odysseus, it subsequently compels us to wonder about and to question ever more deeply the wisdom and moral character of the hero. This complex poem unfolds in stages, and it thereby leads us through multiple stages of appraising and assessing the complex character of Odysseus.[30] By prompting us to identify and strip away the many layers of this man of many ways, Homer prompts us to consider and reconsider our initial impressions of his heroism and indeed

[29] As Benardete puts it with respect to Odysseus's companions, "That Homer began the Odyssey with their wicked folly, from which Odysseus could not save them, now seems trivial in comparison with the losses Odysseus had already sustained" (1997, 83). See also Bolotin 1989, 48.

[30] As Clay notes, "The *Odyssey*, like its hero, is multifaceted, diverse, and varied" (1983, 6). She later describes the poem as a "labyrinth" and "At its center is Odysseus, the man of many wiles" (1983, 54). Consider also Slatkin's observation: "The narrative of the *Odyssey* ... embodies, in its many weavings, its reversals, its twisting of time, a *mētis* of its own" (1996, 237). Consider as well Schein 1996, 17–18.

of human heroism as such. In this way, Homer leads us to undertake, one might say, an intellectual odyssey of our own.

After being told in the opening lines of the poem that Odysseus's companions perished through their own folly and that Calypso has detained him against his will for a number of years, we learn that the final obstacle to Odysseus's return is the fury of Poseidon (1.16–21). But why is Poseidon furious with Odysseus? Some fifty lines later in Book I, Zeus reveals that Odysseus blinded the one-eyed Cyclops Polyphemus, the mightiest of all the Cyclopes and the son of Poseidon (1.68–75). And even though Zeus offers no explanation for Odysseus's action, Homer himself informs us still later, at the beginning of Book II, that the "savage" Cyclops killed and ate a number of Odysseus's companions (2.17–20). We are left with the impression from the early books, then, that Poseidon is unjust in his anger at Odysseus, and this impression is confirmed by the full account Odysseus himself gives of his encounter with the Cyclops in Book IX. Yet, even though we learn there of Odysseus's great achievement in outwitting the Cyclops and in saving his own life and the lives of six of his best companions, we also learn there of Odysseus's own great folly, a folly that leads to the deaths of his other six best companions and the subsequent persecution by Poseidon of him and all of his men (9.193–196). For it was Odysseus who insisted on visiting and exploring the island of the Cyclops in the first place, for no apparent need (9.166–176, 9.193–196). It was Odysseus who insisted, contrary to the urging of his, in this case, more prudent companions, on waiting for the Cyclops in his cave, even though they all knew that the Cyclops was a monstrously huge man and even though they all, including Odysseus, instantly regretted this decision (9.224–236). Finally, after the deaths of six of his men at the hands of the Cyclops and after his brilliant rescue of his remaining men, it was Odysseus who insisted, contrary to the pleading of his companions after he and his men had escaped, on boasting to the Cyclops of his accomplishment and on telling the Cyclops his name (9.473–525). By needlessly telling the Cyclops his name, Odysseus enables the Cyclops to pray to his father Poseidon – apparently successfully – that he destroy all of Odysseus's companions, delay his homecoming for many long years, and ensure that Odysseus encounter troubles in his homeland when he finally returns (9.526–536).

To be sure, it is not clear that Poseidon's opposition to the homecoming of Odysseus and of his men is insuperable. According to Odysseus's account of his adventures to the Phaiacians, for example, Odysseus and his men come within sight of Ithaca after they leave the floating island of Aeolus (10.28–30). And the soul of the prophet Teiresias speaks as though it were possible for Odysseus and his (then surviving) men to arrive safely in Ithaca, notwithstanding the fury of Poseidon (11.100–109). What does seem clear is that Odysseus makes a number of mistakes that imperil and delay both his homecoming and that of his men.[31]

Odysseus makes it difficult to identify these mistakes because his less-than-completely-candid narration of his adventures to the Phaiacians deliberately and artfully obscures his mistakes while highlighting what he at least perceives to be his successes.[32] For example, his narration of his voyage home from Troy begins with his sacking of the city of the Ciconians. Odysseus urges his men to withdraw immediately, but the "great fools" refuse to heed him (9.43–44). When the Ciconians counterattack, Odysseus and his men are forced to flee (9.39–61). Now, Odysseus does not explain why he decided to attack the Ciconians in the first place (they were allies of the Trojans – *Iliad* 2.846) rather than sail directly home, nor why his men should so casually and foolishly disregard the orders of their leader for the past ten years. Odysseus does, however, imply through his narrative that his encounter with the Ciconians was a relatively minor affair, for he devotes only 22 lines to it. In contrast, he spends 463 lines on his encounter with the Cyclops (*Odyssey* 9.104–566). Yet, while Odysseus lost six men in total at the hands of the Cyclops, he lost six men from *each* of his ships at the hands of the Ciconians (9.287–291, 9.310–314, 9.343–344, 9.60–61). How many of Odysseus's men in total did the Ciconians kill? How many ships did he have with him? Odysseus does not say, at first, but almost a hundred lines later, he reveals that he had twelve ships (9.159). Therefore, we may deduce,

[31] In the words of Felson and Slatkin, "Odysseus has arrived home alone, moreover, having lost every single member of his crew: he did not sustain solidarity with them, did not succeed in protecting their homecoming, and was (in short) not a successful leader" (2004, 104).

[32] Schein observes, "Odysseus' penchant for lying and the poem's general atmosphere of disguise and deceit help make the *Odyssey*, unlike the *Iliad*, a poem in which the characters offer narratives against which a reader or listener must be constantly on guard" (1996, 18). As Griffin notes of Odysseus's account of his adventures, "These are sailors' stories; who knows how much truth they contain?" (2004, 159). See also Benardete 1997, 63–64, 82; Slatkin 1996, 231–232.

notwithstanding his evasions, that the Ciconians inflict heavy losses on Odysseus – seventy-two men, twelve times as many as he lost from the Cyclops incident. The whole episode calls into question Odysseus's judgment in attacking the Ciconians in the first place and his ability to inspire trust and confidence in his longtime followers. Yet Odysseus's narrative obscures the magnitude of his losses and leaves one with the impression that he and his men suffered as much in the Cyclops incident as they did in the Ciconian fiasco. For Odysseus uses the identical two lines to describe the grief of his men after each of the two episodes (9.62–63, 9.565–566). Of course, the Cyclops affair deserves great attention, and Odysseus does acknowledge that he made mistakes there (9.228–230; cf. 9.491–501). But Odysseus also (rightly) takes pride in his success in outwitting the huge monster and therefore highlights the incident, here and elsewhere, whereas he cannily obscures his much bloodier encounter with the Ciconians.[33]

Similarly, the greatest disaster Odysseus and his men suffer in the poem is in the land of the Lastrygonians. There, Odysseus suffers the loss of eleven of his twelve ships at the hands of tens of thousands of giant cannibals. The episode raises grave questions about Odysseus's prudence and also about his devotion to his men. Why did he decide to visit this land? Why did he order eleven of his ships to enter the harbor with a narrow entrance but keep his ship outside of the harbor? If he suspected danger, why did he visit the land at all or allow any of his ships to enter the harbor? If he did not suspect danger, why did he keep his ship outside?[34] Yet, again, Odysseus is tight-lipped about this catastrophic episode, devoting only 53 lines to it, compared to the subsequent 432 lines (in Book X alone) devoted to his stay on the isle of Circe (10.80–132, 10.133–574). Moreover, here too, Odysseus is evasive concerning his losses with the Lastrygonians. We may infer, given that he later reveals that there are 46 men remaining on his ship (10.203–209) and given that his ship alone lost 6 men in the land of the Cyclopes, that, on the

[33] See 9.413–414, 9.473–479, 9.500–505, 9.522–525, 10.431–442, 12.209–213, 23.312–313; see also 20.18–21. Odysseus later tells Penelope that he "subdued" the Ciconians, presumably referring to his sacking of their city, but omits telling her of his bloody defeat at their hands, in which they "subdued" his men. Compare 23.310 with 9.58–59.

[34] Benardete goes so far as to suggest that Odysseus here is guilty of "criminal negligence" (1997, 114). Bolotin suggests that Odysseus's behavior here is "perhaps the most striking evidence of his selfish concern for mere survival, and of his being at least neglectful of his men" (1989, 48).

assumption that each of his ships originally had an equal number of men, Odysseus suffered the loss of 572 men (11×52) at the hands of the Lastrygonians, a far heavier loss than is suffered in any single incident recounted in the *Odyssey* or, for that matter, the *Iliad*. Yet Odysseus downplays this catastrophe, while he celebrates his ultimately triumphant stay on the isle of Circe (see also 9.29–33).

Odysseus stresses the responsibility of his companions for their failure to reach home on two occasions in particular: after their departure from the island of Aelous and at the island of Thrinakia. In each case, his companions commit mistakes, on the verge of reaching Ithaca, that thwart their homecoming. Nevertheless, those mistakes underscore Odysseus's striking inability to inspire trust and confidence in his men, an inability already evident in the episode of the Ciconians.

At the isle of Aeolus, after the Cyclops episode but immediately before the Lastrygonian catastrophe, Aeolus gives Odysseus a magical bag of winds with which to direct his twelve ships. Odysseus successfully leads the ships, after nine days, to their homeland of Ithaca. But just when he and his men are within sight of their island, Odysseus, who has insisted on handling the bag of winds by himself, falls asleep, and his men, wrongly suspecting that Odysseus is greedily keeping treasures from Troy in this bag, open it, thereby releasing a storm that blows them back to a horrified and now hostile Aeolus. Odysseus highlights the folly of his men here and his own innocence: "For we were destroyed through their folly . . . the evil counsel of my companions prevailed . . . I pondered in my blameless spirit . . . I answered . . . 'my evil companions brought me to ruin'" (10.27, 46, 50, 68). Yet, while Odysseus's men are unreasonably distrustful of Odysseus here, it would seem that Odysseus himself is also unreasonably distrustful of his men. Why, after all, should he not confide in them regarding the bag of winds and even share control of it with them? Is it not foreseeable that he will need to sleep and will therefore need their assistance? Odysseus may distrust his men because of their foolish refusal to leave the land of the Ciconians before being attacked. But, on the other hand, his men were more prudent than he was during the Cyclops episode, both in urging him to leave the cave before the Cyclops returned and in urging him to keep quiet after their escape. It would also seem to be in their clear interest, as well as his, to return home. Therefore, his distrust of his men seems unreasonable in this case, and it has terrible consequences for them all. Finally, even if it were reasonable for Odysseus to distrust his men as a whole,[35] it is astonishing that, after ten years with these companions, he cannot find a single friend or subordinate whose judgment or loyalty he can trust. In the *Iliad*, wounded commanders, on either side of the war, are regularly replaced by able lieutenants and comrades.[36] When Achilles sends his Myrmidons into battle, he entrusts Patroclus with overall command and five others as his lieutenants (*Iliad* 16.64–82, 168–197). Even young Telemachus has a "trustworthy companion," Peiraius, who sailed with him to Pylos, "who especially obeys" him, and who can be counted on to take Telemachus's guest, the fugitive prophet Theoclymenos, into his own home (*Odyssey* 15.539–541). But Odysseus cannot find it within himself to trust a single companion to handle the bag of winds for a few hours.

It is also true that, even though his men are wrong here to suspect that he is selfishly keeping treasure to himself, they are not altogether wrong in questioning his leadership. In the first place, they might reasonably conclude that Odysseus's foolish curiosity and boldness in the land of the Cyclopes led to the deaths of six of his men and that his reckless boastfulness and unbridled anger almost led to the destruction of his ship. As Eurylochus later says on the isle of Circe, "it was by this man's wicked folly that those men [in the Cyclops's cave] perished" (10.437). Furthermore, it was Odysseus who decided to linger at the palace of Aeolus for an entire month, apparently without consulting his men, because Aeolus "lovingly entertained *me* and asked *me* everything about Ilion and the ships of the Argives and the return of the Achaians" (10.14–15, emphasis added). Is it not reasonable for them to doubt the judgment and character of their commander?

More generally, Odysseus's men might reasonably wonder how strongly he cares about their well-being. As we have noted, in the land of the Lastrygonians, he lets eleven of his ships enter the harbor but he keeps his ship outside, apparently in case trouble arises. Odysseus does express feelings for his men on occasion, especially when he grieves over their suffering (10.375–405). But it is a striking fact that, in the course of his entire narrative, he names only four of them. We never learn from Odysseus the names of any of the men who perish among the Ciconians, the Lastrygonians, Scylla, or the

[35] Dimmock maintains that the companions here are simply untrustworthy (1989, 120–122).

[36] See, for example, 5.655–691, 11.264–335, 11.369–501, 11.565–594, 13.306–575, 14.440–522, 16.394–428.

Cyclops, even though Homer does inform us of the name of one – Antiphus – who was eaten by the Cyclops Polyphemus (2.17–20). Even the examples of the four whom Odysseus names highlight the remarkable coldness that exists between Odysseus and his men. Polites, in Odysseus's words, "whom I cared for most of my companions and who was most considerate," is mentioned only this once by him in the whole course of the poem (10.224–225)! Elpenor dies in a drunken accident on Circe's isle and Odysseus does weep tears of pity at the sight of him in Hades. Yet so apparently negligent is Odysseus of his men – at this point, only forty-five are left – that he is wholly unaware for at least one entire day on board of his ship that one of his men is missing (10.550–560, 11.51–58).[37] Perimedes is mentioned twice, without comment (11.23, 12.195). Finally there is Eurylochus, Odysseus's chief lieutenant and relative by marriage, who is far more prominent than any of his other companions. Odysseus, however, portrays him as a villain, the companion who criticizes Odysseus most sharply on the isle of Circe and who finally leads his men to destruction by rebelling on the isle of Thrinakia.[38] Yet, it is important to note that Eurylochus's criticisms of Odysseus on the isle of Circe are not unreasonable.[39] Odysseus and his men reach this island after losing 72 men to the Ciconians, 6 to the Cyclopes, and 572 to the Lastrygonians. When Odysseus sees that the island of Circe is inhabited, he insists on sending out a party of twenty-three, headed by Eurylochus, to investigate, over the objections of his terrified companions. Eurylochus leads his companions to the house of the welcoming goddess Circe but stays outside because he rightly suspects treachery (10.232). When he sees his companions vanish (for Circe magically turns them into animals), he returns to Odysseus, reports what happened, and urges that they flee (10.244–269). Instead, Odysseus goes off to confront Circe by himself. Now, it is true that Odysseus goes on to vanquish the goddess and to rescue his men, thanks to the divine intervention of Hermes. But it is also true that Odysseus's behavior here would seem to be utterly foolish and irresponsible, given all the disasters his men have suffered and given that he has no way of

[37] It is possible that Odysseus knew that Elpenor was dead when he left Circe's isle for Hades, but in that case he would have been negligent in failing to bury him (11.51–80). Elpenor, at any rate, feels he must threaten Odysseus in order to induce him to bury his corpse (11.71–76).

[38] See Dimmock 1989, 129–130, 171; Saïd 2011, 239. Consider Crotty's more qualified appraisal (1994, 149–150).

[39] See Benardete 1997, 90.

anticipating that Hermes will intervene as he does. Eurylochus's advice to Odysseus to flee the island therefore seems reasonable. Later, when Odysseus reappears to his companions and peremptorily tells them to join him with Circe, without any explanation whatsoever, it would again seem reasonable for Eurylochus to object and to remind his companions of Odysseus's reckless boldness on the isle of the Cyclopes (10.406–437). And yet, Odysseus responds savagely, by attempting to behead Eurylochus, only to be stopped by his other companions (10.438–445)!

The case of Eurylochus points to a striking contrast between Achilles' relations with his companions and Odysseus's relations with his. On the one hand, if one considers Achilles' companions in a broad sense as encompassing the Achaians as a whole, Achilles' relations would seem to be much worse. Early in the *Iliad*, Achilles almost kills Agamemnon and prays to Zeus to punish the Achaians as a whole, even though he also plausibly claims to love the Achaians Antilochus, Ajax, and Odysseus (1.188–195, 1.407–412, 9.192–204, 23.555–557). On the other hand, if one considers Achilles' companions as his countrymen, the Myrmidons, then his relations with his companions are much closer than Odysseus's with his followers from Ithaca. For Achilles clearly loves two of his companions from his homeland, Patroclus and Phoinix and he never violently quarrels with or experiences insubordination from any of the Myrmidons (18.80–82, 9.606–616). Moreover, Achilles' two most beloved companions, Patroclus and Phoinix, are precisely his most independent-minded companions, the ones who criticize him to his face most vehemently (16.29–35, 9.496–523). In contrast, Odysseus evidently enjoys no genuine friendship with any of his companions, and Eurylochus, Odysseus's most independent-minded and reasonable companion, is the one whom Odysseus hates the most.[40]

The final destruction of Odysseus's men on the isle of Thrinakia illustrates most clearly Odysseus's failure as a leader of men, especially the baleful consequences of his distrust of his men. Odysseus learns from Circe, in private, that, to reach Ithaca, he and his men will have to sail past the six-headed monster Scylla, who will snatch at six of his men as they pass. They will then have to pass by the isle of Thrinakia without eating any of the cattle or sheep there that are sacred to the Sun God (12.85–142). Now, Odysseus

[40] See Ruderman 1995, 36, 39; Alvis 1995, 93. T. E. Lawrence goes so far as to describe Odysseus as "that cold-blooded egotist" (Shaw 1932, iii).

proceeds to announce to his men, "Friends, neither one nor two alone ought to know the divine sayings which Circe told me, she who is divine among goddesses. I will tell you, so that, knowing them, we may avoid death and escape destruction" (12.154–157). Yet, while Odysseus claims here that he will confide in them completely, in truth, he lies here to his men, for he goes on to conceal from them Circe's revelations concerning Scylla and Thrinakia. Odysseus justifies this deception in his narrative by explaining that he feared that they would be paralyzed by terror and thereby would doom their homecoming (12.222–225). However reasonable that concern may be, the consequence of this brazen lie, once it is – inevitably – exposed, is to destroy virtually all trust his men may still have had in him. In the first place, the men, without having been warned by their leader, see the monster Scylla snatch up and devour six of their companions as they sail by – "screaming and reaching out their hands to me in dreadful struggle" (12.256–257). Furthermore, the fact that Odysseus insists on arming himself – but not his men – *before* they are attacked by Scylla, must signal to his men that Odysseus knew of, and deliberately concealed from them, the deadly threat from the monster (12.225–233). Accordingly, once the men pass Scylla, they know that Odysseus lied to them, and they might understandably conclude that he sacrificed their well-being for his (though consider 12.108–110).[41] Consequently, when their ship leaves Scylla behind and arrives at Thrinakia, and now Odysseus reveals that both Circe and Teiresias foretold that they would reach home as long as they sailed past the island and did not eat of the cattle or sheep of the island, his disheartened and distrustful men quite naturally rebel (12.270–294). They insist on landing on the island over the somewhat half-hearted protests of Odysseus. Then, when winds have kept them on the island for a month and they are close to starvation, Odysseus separates himself from his men, who predictably proceed to kill the oxen.[42] Finally, once they leave the island, Zeus, at the behest of the Sun God, destroys the ship, kills the men, but allows Odysseus to float to the isle of Ogygia where the goddess Calypso takes care of him (12.295–453).

Homer's account suggests that Odysseus is a flawed leader of his men and that his failures lead to disaster for them and for himself. In the first place, he

[41] For an argument that Odysseus here acts "primarily out of concern for his men," see Bolotin 1989, 50–51.

[42] See ibid., 48.

at times exhibits disastrously poor judgment, most clearly in staying in the Cyclops's cave and revealing his name to the Cyclops, who thereby brings down on him and his men the wrath of Poseidon. But furthermore, Odysseus is unreasonably and transparently distrustful of his men, he exhibits considerable – and again, transparent – coldness and indifference toward them, and he therefore is incapable of inspiring trust or devotion among his men, most disastrously after leaving Aeolus and on the isle of Thrinakia. It would seem, then, that Odysseus bears considerable, and even the primary, responsibility for destroying the homecoming of his men and postponing his own.[43] As the Ithacan Eupeithes, the father of Antinoos puts it, harshly but not entirely unreasonably, after learning that Odysseus has returned home to Ithaca, alone, and slaughtered all the suitors: "Friends, this man devised a great deed for the Achaians. He took many noble ones with his ships, he lost the hollow ships, he lost the people, and he has come and killed those who were by far the best of the Cephallenians" (24.426–429).[44]

As Eupeithes reminds us, Odysseus's failings cause great suffering to the families of his companions who are lost. But Odysseus's failings also cause great suffering to the members of his own family, who suffer not only from his absence but also from their ignorance of his fate. His son suffers ten more years without a father;[45] his father Laertes pines terribly for him;[46] his mother dies out of grief for her absent son; and his wife not only misses him and his protection but cannot know whether, if she remarries, she will be a victim of his vengeance (11.181–203, 23.213–224).[47] The suitors certainly bear considerable responsibility for the sufferings of his family and therefore Odysseus's anger at them is at least somewhat understandable. But insofar as Odysseus is himself largely responsible for the postponement of his homecoming and the

[43] See Alvis 1995, 86–87; Schein 1996, 30.

[44] Haubold suggests, "Eupeithes' version of events is by no means absurd. Rather, it articulates a highly plausible, forcefully traditional alternative to the official version, an alternative which needs to be rejected precisely because it sounds so convincing. It is hardly a coincidence that the speaker who puts forward this anti-Odyssean Odyssey is called 'he who persuades well'" (2000, 108). In Benardete's judgment, Eupeithes speaks here "strongly and irrefutably" (1997, 10).

[45] See Crotty 1994, 115–116.

[46] For this reason, among others, I cannot agree with Benardete's intriguing suggestion that Odysseus usurped his father's rule before he left for Troy (1997, 4; see also 111–112).

[47] On the uncertainty and peril of Penelope's position, see Felson-Rubin 1994, 15–16, 19–20, 56; 1996, 165–166; Felson and Slatkin 2004, 107. Consider also Katz 1991, 80–93.

subsequent suffering of his family, our sympathy for his righteous fury against the suitors must be at least somewhat qualified.[48]

HOW EAGER IS ODYSSEUS TO GO HOME?

One might still defend Odysseus's rage against the suitors at the end of the poem by arguing that it simply reflects his devotion to his family and his long thwarted desire to come home. Yes, Odysseus's mistakes lead to the destruction of his men and a ten-year separation from his family and his country. He thereby causes harm to his men and his loved ones but also, insofar as he himself is eager to return home, to himself. Is it not understandable, then, that this long suffering man, who endured so many things, above all the separation from his beloved family, should explode in rage against their persecutors when he returns home? Is this passionate anger not a reflection of his passionate devotion to his family and his frustration at having failed to come home and protect them for so long?[49]

But are we right to assume that Odysseus is so very eager to return to Ithaca? Is his devotion and loyalty to his family unqualified? Is he averse to visiting strange and distant lands? Or indeed might his very reason – his passion for wisdom – impel him to see the cities of many men and to know their mind, even at the cost of risking his homecoming, and the homecoming of his men?

One might think that Odysseus is himself a primary victim of his failure to secure his homecoming. Yes, he survives to return, ultimately, in triumph over his enemies. But he is forced to endure ten years of misery, pining away for his family and his home, as both Athena and he stress over and over again.[50] Homer opens the poem by presenting Odysseus as a homesick wanderer: "many were the woes he suffered in the deep sea in his spirit . . . he was longing for his homecoming and his wife" (1.4, 13). Athena stresses to her father Zeus

48 Consider Bolotin 1989, 51; Ruderman 1995, 47.

49 Heitman insists that "no one doubts that he [Odysseus] is eager to return home" (2005, 9). Saïd claims that "Odysseus never forgets Ithaca" (2011, 277). Dimmock denies that Odysseus forgets Ithaca even on Circe's isle, where his men emphatically remind him of their desire to go home (1989, 131). In Crotty's words, "The family is the focus of . . . Odysseus' desire in the *Odyssey*" (1994, 211).

50 1.48–59, 5.7–17, 7.151–152, 7.211–225, 7.241–260, 8.154–157, 8.477–478, 9.21–38.

that Odysseus "suffers sorrows, far from his loved ones" on Calypso's isle (1.48–50). And Homer himself describes Odysseus on that same island, "sitting on the shore crying, there where he had even before, shattering his spirit with tears and groaning and woe" (5.83–85).

Yet, here too, Homer's artful narrative impels us to reconsider this initial impression. Indeed, the more carefully we study the *Odyssey*, the more we must wonder whether Odysseus has always been so eager to return home. Unlike Nestor, Diomedes, Idomeneus, Agamemnon, and Menelaus, Odysseus does not try to return home immediately (3.130–192, 3.276–303, 4.351–352, 4.495–521). First, he stops to sack the city of the Ciconians (9.39–40). Then, he pauses to explore the land of the Lotus Eaters and, more extensively, the land of the Cyclopes (9.87–90, 9.166–196). He then freely spends one month with Aeolos before leaving (10.14–15). And most shockingly, he freely and gladly spends one year on the isle of Circe, sharing the bed of the goddess (10.467–471; see 10.333–347, 10.476–482).[51] Odysseus apparently would have stayed longer if his companions had not urged him to think of returning home: "Daemonic man, now is the time for you to remember the land of your fathers!" (10.472). Furthermore, even though we see him weeping on Calypso's isle at the beginning of the poem, Homer immediately explains his weeping with the arresting statement: "since the nymph *no longer* pleased him" (5.153, emphasis added). But for how long during his eight years on her isle *did* Calypso please him? Did she please him as much and as long as that other goddess, Circe, pleased him? Even now, after weeping for so long, he and Calypso, in Homer's words, "delighted themselves in lovemaking" (5.227). Homer also reports that while he was with Calypso, "his care was continuous, as though he were a god" (8.450–453). It would seem, then, that, for some indeterminate amount of time, Odysseus was pleased to stay with Calypso, as he had been pleased to stay with Circe.[52]

[51] In contrast, Homer implies that Laertes was tempted to sleep with the young Eurycleia but never did: "he honored her equally to his careful wife in his great halls, but he never mingled with her in bed, fleeing the rage of his wife" (1.428–433). Consider Benardete 1997, 151–152.

[52] See Ruderman 1995, 37. Even Dimmock acknowledges that Odysseus "liked" Calypso and her surroundings "at first" (1989, 66–67). See also Vernant 1996, 189. Benardete suggests that, "at the heart of" the "labyrinth" of the *Odyssey*, "there is a double mystery, the missing seven years with Calypso and the second journey to a people who do not know the sea. It is these two experiences . . . that define Odysseus and the *Odyssey*" (1997, 38).

More generally, it would seem that, throughout his time with Circe and Aeolus and for some period of time with Calypso as well, Odysseus did not long for his home.

Indeed, Odysseus seems rather distant in his feelings toward his family throughout both the *Iliad* and much of the *Odyssey*. In stark contrast with Achilles, who speaks movingly of his concern for his father, Odysseus never even mentions his father in the *Iliad*, he never speaks of his wife or mother there either, and he refers only twice in passing to his son (2.260, 4.354; cf. 18.329–332, 24.533–542).[53] Odysseus also does not mention his son, mother, or father at all in the *Odyssey* until his account to the Phaiacians of his journey to Hades from the isle of Circe in Book XI (66–68, 84–87, 170–179) and he never mentions his sister at all (see 15.352–370). His encounter with his mother in Hades highlights the asymmetry between his feelings for his family and their feelings for him. It is true that Odysseus says that, upon seeing the soul of his dead mother, Anticleia, whom he has not seen for more than ten years, "I burst into tears when I saw her and pitied her in my spirit" (11.87). But it is also true that Odysseus uses these very words to describe how he feels when he sees the soul of his dead companion Elpenor, who died on the previous day and whose death he evidently ignored (11.55). Furthermore, Odysseus rather easily restrains his feelings for his mother, for he prevents her from approaching until he has first learned from the soul of Teiresias how he may reach Ithaca (11.88–89). We then learn from Anticleia of Penelope that "full of woe, the nights and days always waste her away as she sheds tears," of his father Laertes that "sorrow grows great in his mind as he longs for your return," and of herself that "longing for you, illustrious Odysseus – for your counsels and your gentle thoughts – wrested away from me my sweet spirit" (11.181–183, 11.195–196, 11. 202–203). The juxtaposition in this section of the poem between Anticleia's moving account of how his family painfully yearns for his return with Odysseus's admission (some 300 lines earlier) that he forgot his family for a whole year while partaking of the pleasures of Circe's isle highlights Odysseus's relative coldness toward his family (11.150–203, 10.467–474).

Book XI offers as well an illuminating contrast between Odysseus's aloofness toward his family and Achilles' devotion to his. Whereas Odysseus asks his mother briefly "about my father and my son, whom I left behind" and then

[53] Benardete suggests that "Odysseus most distinguishes himself from Achilles by his relationship to his father" (1997, 150).

proceeds to ask whether someone has taken his property and his wife, Achilles asks Odysseus first whether his son Neoptolemus shone in battle at Troy and then, at length, about his father Peleus, "if he still has honor among the Myrmidons or they dishonor him throughout Hellas and Phthia, because old age holds down his hands and feet" (11.174–179, 11.492–497). Achilles goes on to lament that he left his father behind without being able to defend him against his enemies (11.498–503). And when Odysseus reports to him that Neoptolemus both excelled in fighting at Troy and escaped unscathed, Achilles is, in Odysseus's words, "joyful because I said that his son was conspicuous" (11.538–540). While Odysseus's interest in his family here is narrowly bound up with his concern for his own inheritance and matrimony, Achilles' concern is more generously focused on the well-being and also the honor and of his father and son and is mixed with regret (never voiced by Odysseus) that he has caused his father in particular harm through his absence from home.

Even when Odysseus finally returns to Ithaca, he continues to exhibit considerable self-restraint toward his family. He represses any urge he may have to see them all right away. He insists on hiding his identity from his son, his wife, and his father even when he does see them. There are of course reasons for Odysseus to be on guard when he returns home after twenty years, given the presence of the suitors and the fate of Agamemnon at the hands of his faithless wife and her lover. But given Odysseus's own infidelity toward his wife and apparent indifference toward his family for a significant portion of his absence from home, one must wonder whether Odysseus is able to restrain his feelings for his family because those feelings are simply not very strong. For example, although he knows from his mother that his father Laertes is grieving terribly for him – tormented with longing for his son and by the uncertainty of his son's fate – he makes no effort whatsoever to see him or to send him a message, in contrast with both Telemachus and Eumaeus, who are eager to reassure the anxious Laertes of Telemachus's safety (16.135–153). And when Odysseus finally does see his visibly suffering father – after twenty years – and does shed tears for him, Odysseus still insists on testing even further the depth of his father's feelings for him, at considerable length, and thereby increases his father's suffering in order to satisfy his own curiosity and perhaps his vanity (24.226–317).[54]

[54] See Bolotin 1989, 55. For a defense of Odysseus here, see Dimmock 1989, 329–330.

With regard to Telemachus, Odysseus does weep uncontrollably when he finally reveals himself to the son he left as an infant twenty years before: "he kissed his son, and let a tear go down his cheeks to the ground; before, he had been holding himself back ceaselessly, always" (16.190–191). Yet, Odysseus only reveals himself to Telemachus at the prompting of Athena. Homer's magnificently artful portrayal of Odysseus's response to seeing his son for the first time in twenty years sheds light on Odysseus's character and how we should think about it. At the moment when Telemachus returns from his voyage of several weeks to Pylos and Sparta and approaches the swineherd Eumaeus and the disguised Odysseus at the swineherd's hut, Homer uses the following remarkable simile: "As a father, whose mind is full of love for his child, welcomes him when he comes back from a distant land in the tenth year – his only one, grown big, for whose sake he has endured much sorrow – so then did the divine *swineherd* kiss godlike Telemachus altogether and cling to him" (16.17–21, emphasis added). Homer first leads the reader to think that he is using this simile to describe Odysseus's heartfelt love for his son. But he then reveals that he is describing Eumaeus's great love for Telemachus, not Odysseus's love for him. And Homer thereby leads us to wonder how great Odysseus's undescribed love for his son truly is.

But what of Penelope? Odysseus's control over his feelings here is especially great. Odysseus represses the urge to go to her once he arrives at Ithaca, even though, as Athena points out, "another man, having come from wandering, would gladly go to his great halls to see his children and wife" (13.333–334). When he sees her for the first time in twenty years, as she speaks to the suitors, he is not overcome with erotic passion – as the suitors are – but rather responds in an appreciative but also seemingly calculating spirit: "divine Odysseus, who endured many things, rejoiced because she drew out gifts from them and enchanted their spirit with mild words, but her mind was eager for other things" (18.212–213, 18.281–283). When describing Odysseus, disguised as a vagabond, conversing with his wife for the first time, Homer stresses how skillfully he lies to his weeping wife and how perfectly he masters his feelings before her: "He made the many lies he spoke resemble the truth . . . Odysseus pitied his sorrowing wife in his spirit, but his eyes stayed, as if of horn or iron, steady in his eyelids. He concealed his tears with guile" (19.203, 19.209–212). One might of course argue that Odysseus is simply containing his powerful love for his wife because he fears that she no longer loves him or because he fears that she may inadvertently divulge his identity to the suitors and thereby help them. However, it is important to note that Odysseus's ability to control his feelings for his wife is not new. Menelaus reports that, ten years earlier, near the conclusion of the Trojan War, when Helen was trying to determine whether the Trojan Horse contained Achaian warriors, she walked around the horse three times, calling the names of the best warriors, and "likening her voice to the wives of all the Argives" (4.277–279). Diomedes, Menelaus, and Anticlus were all moved by the precious sound of their wives' voices to respond, but Odysseus, evidently unmoved by the sound of Penelope's voice, restrained them (4.280–289). And of course Odysseus goes on to forget Penelope in particular during the year he is with Circe and, it seems, at first, with Calypso.

Now all of these questions about Odysseus's feelings for Penelope might seem petty and low-minded in the light of the poignant and moving reunion of the two, in which Odysseus reveals not only that he remembers how he constructed their marriage bed, but also reveals how "troubled" he is at the possibility that the bed was moved and therefore how much that bed, the symbol of their marriage, still means to him after all these years (23.181–182).[55] Yet, even at this dramatic reunion of this heroic couple, Homer calls into question the strength of Odysseus's feelings for his wife in two ways. First, as in his account of Odysseus's first encounter with his son, Homer here uses a simile in his account of Odysseus's first embrace of his wife, but again with a surprising twist:

> He wept as he held his wife, so well fitted to his spirit, she whose thoughts were full of care. As when the land appears, welcome to men who are swimming, whose well-made ship Poseidon has smashed on the deep sea, pounded by wind and hard waves, and a few escape the grey sea swimming toward land, and much salt has caked their skin, and gladly they go onto the land, having escaped the evil; so then was *her husband* welcome to *her*, as she looked upon him, and she did not let go at all of his neck with her powerful white arms. (23.232–24, emphasis added)

The focus of the poem on Odysseus and the evident similarity between the simile and Odysseus's swimming ashore, after his ship was destroyed by Zeus and Poseidon, onto Ogygia, the isle of Calypso, and Phaiacia, lead one to expect that Homer is finally permitting us, at this climactic moment, to witness the tremendous love that this heroic husband feels in his heart for his

[55] Consider Silk 2004, 38–39.

heroic wife (12.415–449, 5.282–463). Yet, Homer denies our expectation, letting us peer only into the heart of Penelope. In this way, he heightens our uncertainty concerning the depth of Odysseus's feelings for his wife.

Furthermore – astonishingly – Odysseus's very first words to Penelope, after their tearful reunion, are to announce to her that he must leave home again. He reports that the soul of Teiresias told him that – apparently in order to appease the wrath of Poseidon – Odysseus must find a land where the inhabitants know nothing of the sea and there make large sacrifices to the god of the sea, perhaps in order to spread the worship of Poseidon (23.248–281, 11.101–137). Now, why does Odysseus make this abrupt announcement to Penelope that he must depart soon on an evidently long journey – an announcement Odysseus acknowledges will give her no joy (23.266) – at this particular moment? Odysseus does say to his wife that he himself takes no joy from the prospect of this journey either (23.266–267). And yet the fact that, rather than immediately speak of all that has happened during their years apart, Odysseus informs her that he must soon leave again, suggests that he is instinctively uneasy about the prospect of simply remaining at home and even perhaps that he welcomes the prospect of a further adventure.[56] After all, as we have seen, Odysseus betrayed no impatience to go home when he was on the island of Aeolus and evidently forgot about Ithaca when he was on Circe's isle for a year. Moreover, when Teiresias's soul first announces that he must go on this journey, Odysseus does not respond with sorrow, as he had, for example, when Circe informed him that he had to voyage to Hades – "so she spoke and my beloved heart was broken; I sat down on the bed and wept and my heart no longer wished to live nor to see the light of the sun" (10.496–498) – but rather with equanimity: "Teiresias, this, then, I suppose, is what the gods have spun" (11.139). Indeed, when Odysseus repeats Teiresias's words to Penelope, he alters those words, for he adds that Teiresias bid him "to go to *very many towns of mortals*" and thereby suggests both that he anticipates a longer and more far-ranging journey than Teiresias had prescribed and that he relishes the prospect of such a journey (compare 11.121–123 with 23.267–270, emphasis added; see also 1.3). And when Odysseus speaks in the guise of a vagabond to Eumaeus and invents tales about himself, he makes the intriguing

[56] See Bolotin 1989, 55–56. Benardete goes so far as to claim, regarding Penelope, "That Odysseus will leave again seems decisive for her acceptance of him ... He cannot be an impostor if he has no interest in staying" (1997, 146; see also 35, 113).

confession – on his first day in his homeland, after twenty years of war and wandering – that he is dissatisfied with home life and always delights in the adventure of war and travel. First, he tells the swineherd:

> Work was not beloved by me, nor benefiting my home, which rears splendid children, but always ships driven by oars were beloved by me, and wars and well-polished javelins and arrows, miserable things, which to other men are frightening. But they were beloved by me, which, I suppose, a god put in my mind. For another man delights himself in other deeds. (14.222–228)

He then remarks that once he returned home after fighting ten years at Troy, "for one month only I remained, delighting myself with my children and my wedded wife and my possessions. But then my spirit bid me to sail to Egypt" (14.244–246). One might of course object that Odysseus is here speaking of his fictitious self – a pseudo-Odysseus – rather than of the man who has just returned home to his beloved family after a long separation. Yet, the true Odysseus did also leave home to go to war for ten years; did enjoy his stays in the isles of Aeolus, Circe, and, to begin with, Calypso; and is not distressed at the prospect of leaving home again. Does the true Odysseus not share with his fictitious self a certain restless spirit and delight in war and adventure?[57]

ODYSSEUS'S LOVE OF GLORY

If Odysseus's ruling passion is not the longing for home and family, what might it be? The passion most evident in Odysseus's heart is the passion for glory. After he has left Ogygia, the isle of Calypso, and Poseidon has destroyed his raft, and Odysseus believes that "now my towering destruction is certain," he gives voice to what is apparently the deepest desire of his heart:

> Three times blessed were the Danaans, and four times, who perished then in wide Troy, bringing favor to the sons of Atreus, as I wish I too had died and followed my destiny on the day when most of the Trojans hurled their bronze-fitted spears at me over the dead son of Peleus. I would have received my funeral rites and the Achaians would have brought me glory. But now, with a miserable death, it is ordained that I be taken. (5.305–311)

[57] Consider Dante's *Inferno*, 26.55–142, and Alfred Lord Tennyson's poem *Ulysses* (2007, 49–51). Benardete suggests that the lies of Odysseus "reveal the man himself" (1997, 107; see also 113).

At the critical moment when Odysseus faces certain death, his deepest regret is not that his death will deprive him of his homecoming or deprive his beloved family of his protection. Nor does the prospect of certain death lead him to express any regret whatsoever that he left Ogygia and rejected the offer of an immortal, ageless existence with the goddess Calypso. Odysseus's deepest regret is rather that an ignominious death in a sea storm will deprive him of the glory that death in battle would have given him. Glory, rather than a shared mortal love with his family or a shared immortal pleasure with Calypso, would seem to be the object of his heart's desire.

Similarly, when Odysseus requests that the Phaiacian Demodocus sing, he asks him to sing of his most glorious stratagem, the wooden horse, filled with men, who sacked Troy (8.492–495). When Demodocus recounts this glorious story, Odysseus weeps uncontrollably, more so than when he is reunited with Penelope. Moreover, here, in contrast with his account of that tearful reunion, Homer offers a direct description of Odysseus's own inner feelings by means of an extremely moving simile:

> Odysseus melted and his tear wet his cheeks under his eyelids. As a woman weeps, falling about her beloved husband, who fell before his city and people, warding off the pitiless day for his town and his children; she sees him dying and quivering, winds herself around him, and wails in a high, shrill voice. But they beat her with their spears, from behind, on her back and shoulders, and lead her into bondage, to have labor and misery, and her cheeks waste away with most pitiable anguish. So Odysseus shed a pitiable tear under his brow. There he escaped the notice of all the rest as he shed tears. (8.521–532)

Homer suggests here that Odysseus's most powerful passion is his love of glory. For Odysseus loves glory as deeply as a woman loves her noble husband. Odysseus evidently weeps in response to Demodocus's account of his past glory because his longing to win further glory by performing glorious deeds has been thwarted so long, above all on the isle of Ogygia, and he fears that he may be unable to perform such deeds in the future. He grieves, then, over the corpse of his ambition as Andromache grieved over the corpse of Hector.[58] Indeed, it would seem that Odysseus weeps so bitterly on that isle and rejects the offer of immortality from Calypso precisely

[58] I am inclined, then, to disagree with the suggestion of Pucci and Crotty that Odysseus here "weeps out of pity" for "those who were destroyed by" his victory over Troy and thereby resembles Achilles in his compassion for Priam at the end of the *Iliad* (Pucci 1987, 222; Crotty 1994, 125, 127).

because, after eight years there, his longing for glory craves satisfaction through the performance of glorious deeds, in Ithaca, to be sure, but more broadly in the world outside of the isolated island (compare 8.521–531 with 5.81–84).[59]

Odysseus's love of glory is evident in a number of ways throughout the poem. When he reveals his identity to the Phaiacians, he declares: "I am Odysseus, the son of Laertes, who worry all human beings through my stratagems, and my glory reaches the heaven" (9.19–20).[60] His glory – that he is known by others, far and wide – defines him, in his eyes, as much as his intrinsic craftiness. When he makes the fateful mistake of revealing his name to the Cyclops, he does so, in part, for the sake of spreading his fame: "Cyclops, if someone of mortal humans should ask about the hideous blinding of your eye, tell him that Odysseus, the sacker of cities, the son of Laertes, who has his home in Ithaca, did the blinding" (9.502–505).[61] Even Odysseus's praise of marriage to Nausicaa is couched in terms of fame as well as love: "Nothing is mightier than this, nor better, than when a man and woman have a home, like-minded in their thoughts: a thing that brings many woes to their enemies, joy to those who wish them well, and they themselves especially are renowned" (6.182–186).[62]

Odysseus's concern for his own glory is manifest, in a general way, in his account of his adventures to his Phaiacian hosts. Not only does he highlight his own successes and downplay his failures, as we have seen, but Odysseus also tries to omit from his account any possible competitors for glory. His account of his adventures focuses on goddesses – Circe, the Sirens, Calypso – and such quasi-divine or monstrous characters as Aeolus, the Cyclopes, the Lastrygonians, Scylla, and Charybdis. We hardly learn the names of any of his companions, and we never learn, for example, the names of his human

[59] As Vernant points out, "Sharing divine immortality in the nymph's arms would constitute for Odysseus a renunciation of his career as an epic hero... he would have to allow his memory to be erased in the minds of humans and his posthumous fame to be taken from him; and though still alive, he would have to allow himself to sink into the depths of oblivion" (1996, 188). See also Alvis 1995, 86; Schein 1996, 23.

[60] Consider Segal 1996, 203–205.

[61] See Clay 1983, 121–122.

[62] In Ruderman's words, "It is not so much domestic happiness that will content Odysseus as it is winning fame for having such a household (an accomplishment denied Agamemnon, Menelaos, Hephaistos, and others)" (1995, 42).

adversaries among the Ciconians. It is also noteworthy that, while Odysseus is glad to describe the famous human heroines whose souls he encounters in Hades, he abruptly stops his narrative of his adventures before describing any famous human heroes whom he meets there. It is only thanks to the insistent intervention of the Phaiacian queen Arete, the Phaiacian king Alcinoos, and the oldest Phaiacian hero Egenor that Odysseus goes on to describe his encounter with the glorious human heroes – above all, Achilles, "by far the best of the Achaians," and Ajax, "best in form and stature of all the other Danaans, after the blameless son of Peleus" (11.478, 11.469–470; see 11.326–384). Odysseus's love of glory is so adamant that it will not brook any competition, even from the memory of men who were ostensibly his friends. In contrast with Achilles, who delights in singing of the glory of *other* men, who loves such glory-loving heroes as Ajax, Odysseus, Antilochus, and Patroclus and who, in the *Iliad*, holds himself back both from athletic competition and from war in order to let his friends win glory for themselves, Odysseus never subordinates his love of glory to his love for another (*Iliad* 9.185–204, 23.555–557, 18.80–82, 16.241–245). Perhaps Odysseus's most memorable relations in the *Odyssey* are with female (Nausicaa, Circe, Calypso, Penelope) rather than male characters because he does not regard them as rivals for fame. For example, while he is perfectly gracious and courtly with Nausicaa, the daughter of the Phaiacian king, he allows himself to be needlessly and imprudently drawn into quarreling and competing with the vain and petty young men of the Phaiacian court – including the son of the king (compare 6.149–185, 8.464–468 with 8.131–234). Odysseus does not even permit his own son Telemachus to have the honor of winning the bow contest when he is, Homer stresses, on the verge of doing so (21.128–129).[63] And their last exchange in the poem – in which Odysseus extravagantly boasts of his and his ancestors' deeds ("we have surpassed the whole earth in might and courage") and sharply urges "his beloved son" not "to shame" them – is described by Laertes as "strife" (δῆρις) between father and son (24.505–515).

Odysseus's passion for glory runs deeper in his character than even his love for his family. It inspired him to be the "first" to attack the great boar of Parnassus when he went hunting as a boy with his grandfather (19.447–467).

[63] Consider, in contrast, Hector's prayer to Zeus and the other gods that someone might some day say of his son, "much better is he than his father" (*Iliad* 6.473–481).

It presumably prompted him to go to Troy with the rest of the Achaians to win the great glory that he did.[64] And it apparently moves him to reject the immortal existence offered him by Calypso. Yet, even this passion does not fully explain the multifaceted character of this man of many ways, for two reasons. First of all, Odysseus does not seem to reflect on his love of glory, and especially on the kind of glory that is worth having, as one would expect him to do if he loved glory deeply. In contrast with Achilles, Odysseus's passion for glory does not seem discriminating in any way. He wishes to be honored, not only by those who know him and whose respect he cherishes, but by the Achaians as a whole, by the Phaiacians as a whole, by the Cyclopes, and indeed by "all human beings," regardless of how noble or ignoble, wise or foolish they are (9.19–20). But furthermore, Odysseus's love of glory does not seem to hold a constant sway over him. During his month on Aeolus's isle and his year on Circe's isle, he evidently forgot about his pursuit of glory just as completely as he forgot about his family. At the beginning of his stay on Calypso's isle, when the goddess still pleased him, he presumably forgot about his interest in glory as well. Moreover, his initial hesitation to return home and his initial exploration of the lands of the Lotus Eaters and the Cyclopes, and perhaps of the Ciconians as well, do not seem clearly motivated by a love of glory. All these episodes seem to be animated by a certain curiosity about the strange and distant lands he visits and their strange inhabitants. Might not Odysseus, then, be motivated by a general curiosity – a love of wisdom – in addition to his love of family and his love of glory? Might his desire for home and his love of glory not even be subordinated to a desire for wisdom – a desire to know the cities and minds of many men, a desire that may prompt him also to embrace the later journey prescribed by Teiresias? Might Odysseus, then, for all his anger, his love for his family, and his passion for glory, not ultimately prove to be the rational hero, the thoughtful hero, the proto-philosophic hero, and therefore the greatest hero of Homer's poems?[65]

[64] Benardete remarks that "the only hint Odysseus ever gives that his going to Troy was not entirely voluntary" is in a lie (14.239 – 1997, 113).

[65] Ruderman suggests that "It is precisely Odysseus' curiosity to learn about the gods and the minds of men (1.3) that makes him a hero for Homer" (1999, 147). See also Hall 2008, 147–159; Saïd 2011, 231. Consider as well Strauss 1987, 2–3.

ODYSSEUS AND THE QUESTION OF DIVINE PROVIDENCE

Odysseus's curiosity is focused on one particular question, the question with which the *Odyssey* virtually opens: the question of divine providence. Do the gods care about humans? Do they reward the righteous and punish the wicked? Or do they allow the wicked to run roughshod over the good? Now, at first glance, the poem appears to teach unambiguously that the gods do indeed provide for righteous human beings. Zeus, whom Homer introduces here as "the Father of Men and Gods," opens the first speech in the poem with a complaint: "Alas, how the mortals blame the gods! For they say that evils come from us. But they themselves, through their reckless folly, have woes beyond their fate" (1.28, 1.32–34). Zeus cites the example of the "blameless" Aegisthus who, despite the warnings of Hermes, foolishly committed adultery with Clytaemnestra and murdered her husband Agamemnon, only to be killed in turn by their son Orestes. Since one human being, Aegisthus, freely brought evils upon himself beyond what was fated – beyond, for example, the natural death that is fated for all mortal beings – Father Zeus argues that it is unreasonable for humans to blame the gods for their evils (1.28–43). Athena, however, challenges her father by citing the counterexample of Odysseus, who suffers evils beyond what is fated and hence, she implies, innocently (1.44–62). Zeus immediately decides that all the gods must come to the rescue of Odysseus, and the rest of the poem recounts their divine providence. In the first four books of the poem, Athena helps Odysseus's son learn the fate of his father and gain confidence and experience in the company of the old heroes Nestor and especially Menelaus. In the next four books of the poem, Hermes induces Calypso to release Odysseus from his captivity on her island, and Athena helps Odysseus gain the assistance of the Phaiacians. Finally, in the last twelve books of the poem, Athena helps Odysseus and his son slay the overbearing suitors of his wife Penelope. As the poem ends, we see Father Zeus and his daughter Athena, the two gods with whom the poem began, intervene to protect Odysseus from the vengeful relatives of the slain suitors and establish peace between them. Zeus's last words in the poem are "Since divine Odysseus punished the suitors, let them [the relatives of the dead suitors and Odysseus] make their oaths of faith and let him always be king, and we will make them forget the slaughter of their children and brothers. Let them love one another, as before, and let them have prosperity and peace in abundance" (24.482–486). On the surface, then, the *Odyssey* vindicates entirely the justice of the gods. As Laertes declares when he learns that his son has returned and has killed all the suitors, "Father Zeus, there are indeed still gods in tall Olympus, if truly the suitors paid for their reckless hubris" (24.351–352). The poem seems simply to assure its audience that the gods not only "range at large through the cities, looking upon the hubris and the lawfulness of humans," but also that they punish their hubris and bless their righteousness (17.485–487).[66]

The surface of the *Odyssey*, however, is only so reassuring on the question of divine providence because the narrative structure of the poem is *not chronological*.[67] In other words, even though the poem indicates in its opening lines that the *story* of Odysseus properly begins "once he sacked the sacred city of Troy," the poem does not narrate that story from the beginning (1.2). The poem opens toward the end of the story of Odysseus, ten years after the end of Trojan War, at the very moment when Zeus and Athena decide to provide assistance to Odysseus. In this way, the poem artfully focuses on only a part of the story of Odysseus: his divinely assisted homecoming, which dramatically culminates with his divinely assisted punishment of the suitors and his divinely assisted re-enthronement in Ithaca.[68] This narrative structure begins with Odysseus the weeping captive and, thanks to the gods, ends with Odysseus the triumphant king.

However, the narrative structure of the *Odyssey* points beyond this reassuring surface account of divine providence to the much more unsettling story of the gods' abandonment of Odysseus from his sacking of Troy to their decision to come to his aid. During those ten years, Zeus and Athena did not reward the lawful and punish the hubristic but rather deserted the lawful Odysseus, leaving him, for example, to the tender mercies of the hubristic and lawless Cyclopes and leaving his family to the tender mercies of the hubristic and lawless suitors.[69] The poem points to this story most dramatically through Odysseus's own vivid narration of those ten years of wandering

[66] See Lloyd-Jones 1971, 28–32; Edwards 1987, 130; Dimmock 1989, 25–26, 30–31; Schein 1996, 15; Kearns 2004, 67–69.

[67] See Slatkin 1996, 223–223; Silk 2004, 43; Saïd 2011, 110–116. Saïd notes that there are both "flashbacks" and "flashforwards" (2011, 110, 112).

[68] See Clay 1983, 39–41, 51–53.

[69] See Bolotin 1989, 44.

to the Phaiacians in Books IX–XII, but it also points to crucial stages and aspects of that story in remarks that are scattered throughout the poem. The surface of this artful poem, then, is a theodicy, but the story at the heart of the poem is more akin to the story of a Greek Job: the story of a man who was first abandoned and even punished by the gods for no clear reason, but then finally helped by them. The story of Odysseus proves to be one, not of divine providence, but of divine caprice.[70]

The beginning of the story of Odysseus as the poem identifies that beginning – just after the sacking of Troy – is not easy to uncover, for neither Homer's narrative nor Odysseus's narrative begins at this beginning. However, through artfully scattered accounts – the accounts of Phemius, Nestor, Menelaus, and Hermes – Homer's narrative does indicate that the story of Odysseus begins with the gods' abandonment of him, along with a number of other Achaians.

Homer first briefly tells us of a song sung by Phemius to the suitors, in the house of Odysseus in Ithaca, "of the miserable homecoming of the Achaians from Troy, which Pallas Athena inflicted on them" (1.326–327). Here, we learn that Athena punished all the Achaians, including Odysseus, but we are not told why. And so we are left to wonder, why did Athena, who always favored Odysseus throughout the war,[71] suddenly turn on him?

We then learn from the account Nestor gives to Telemachus that, when the Trojan War came to an end and the Achaians prepared to return home, it was Zeus who devised evils for them because "not all were lawful nor just" (3.132–134). In this way, Nestor suggests that the punishment of the Achaians was an act of divine justice. Yet, the rest of his account does not explain what specifically the Achaians were punished for and why some were punished severely but others not at all. Nestor explains that Athena, evidently in league with her father, also became angry with the Achaians and specifically caused Agamemnon and Menelaus to quarrel with each other. The Achaian army split into two groups, one stayed with Agamemnon at Troy to make sacrifices to Athena to appease her anger, and the other followed Menelaus, who tried

[70] As Clay points out, "to view the Odyssey as a poem of divine justice ignores the darker moral contained in the wanderings of Odysseus, his experiences at the hands of the gods, and the very character and qualities of the hero of the poem" (1983, 235; consider 217–235; Crotty 1994, 132–133).

[71] See 3.218–224, 3.377–379, and also *Iliad* 10.241–245.

to sail directly home. Now, those who sailed with Menelaus evidently all reached home safely – Nestor himself, Diomedes, Achilles' son Neoptolemus, Philoctetes, and Idomeneus – except for Menelaus, who was blown off course because of Apollo and Zeus (3.165–192). Menelaus, however, after wandering for eight years and gathering much wealth, did return safely home (3.276–312). Odysseus originally joined the portion of the army that followed Menelaus, but he then decided to return to Agamemnon. Nestor implies, but does not explicitly state, that on his way to Agamemnon, Odysseus was somehow blown off course and failed to join him (3.83–95, 3.162–164). Agamemnon, Nestor reports, did arrive home quickly, only to be murdered by his unfaithful wife and her lover (3.134–200, 3.254–312).

Nestor's account of Zeus's justice here is extremely unclear. The one prominent Achaian who seems clearly punished here is Agamemnon, who also seems especially pious, inasmuch as he tries to appease the wrath of Athena with sacrifices. Furthermore, even though he is killed, he dies, not at the hands of the gods, but at the hands of Clytaemnestra and Aegisthus – who, according to Zeus at the beginning of the poem, killed Agamemnon of his own free will and contrary to the counsels of the gods (1.28–43). Menelaus is punished, insofar as he is forced to wander and thereby deprived of the opportunity to avenge the murder of his brother. But on the other hand, he gathers great wealth during his eight years in Egypt. The clearest victim of the gods' punishment – other than the steersman of Menelaus slain by Apollo (3.278–281) – is Odysseus, who simply vanishes as he is returning to Agamemnon. But why should Zeus and Athena single out Odysseus for punishment for seeking to rejoin the head of the Achaian army, who was at that time making sacrifices to Athena herself? And why should Athena in particular turn against Odysseus, especially given that, as Nestor himself stresses, she had always singled out Odysseus for favor (3.218–222)?

Menelaus's account of the justice of the gods is also most puzzling. Menelaus reports to Telemachus that he heard from a god – Proteus, "the truthful elder of the sea" – that his homecoming was delayed by the gods because he failed to "make noble sacrifices to Zeus and the other gods" after the sacking of Troy (4.472–473). Yet this divine punishment seems capricious for two reasons. In the first place, we learned from Nestor that after the sacking of Troy, Agamemnon, in contrast to his brother Menelaus, did make sacrifices, to the goddess Athena (3.141–146). Yet, Nestor stresses that Athena was not pleased with the sacrifice and Agamemnon went on to arrive home quickly, only to die at the hands of Aegisthus and Clytaemnestra. And even though Zeus stresses, at the opening of the poem, that the gods warned Aegisthus not to kill Agamemnon, they did decline to protect Agamemnon from harm. Why, then, do the gods punish the more reverent Agamemnon more severely than the less reverent Menelaus? Furthermore, Menelaus's "punishment" turns out to be mild indeed. Not only do Menelaus and Helen – who we only now learn has returned to him after the sacking of Troy (compare 3.254–327 with 4.120–146, 4.219–232) – gather considerable wealth and "skillful drugs" during their wanderings in Egypt and other African lands (4.81–91, 4.226–232), but Proteus tells Menelaus that when he dies, the immortal gods will escort him to the Elysian Fields, "where life for human beings is most easy . . . because you possess Helen and are, in their eyes, a son-in-law of Zeus" (4.561–569). Menelaus, then, will enjoy the divine reward of everlasting comfort, notwithstanding his failure to make sacrifices to the gods, simply because his wife – who had abandoned him for more than ten years – is a daughter of Zeus. And he will enjoy this reward from the gods, even though Zeus was unable to save, for example, his own son Sarpedon from destruction (*Iliad* 16.431–461). Finally, Menelaus's account from Proteus of the two other Achaian heroes, besides himself and Agamemnon, who did not immediately return home after the Trojan War ended, also presents the justice of the gods in a mysterious light. Ajax, the son of Oileus, was, for no stated reason, hated by Athena, then punished by Poseidon, and then saved by Poseidon. Subsequently, when Ajax boasted that he had survived in spite of the will of the gods, Poseidon killed him (*Odyssey* 4.499–511). As for Odysseus, Proteus reports that he was not killed in accordance with the will of the gods, as were Ajax and Agamemnon, but he is detained by the goddess Calypso, without his ships or his companions, against his will (4.555–560). Of the four heroes whose homecoming was prevented by the gods, Odysseus's fate, in this account, is clearly superior to that of Ajax and Agamemnon, who are killed, but would seem to be inferior to that of Menelaus, who has lost his brother but has gained wealth, has regained his wife, and may look forward to eternal comfort. Most importantly, in contrast with Proteus's account of Ajax and Menelaus and with Nestor's account of Agamemnon, no explanation is given here of why the gods have deprived Odysseus of his homecoming. Menelaus hints to Telemachus that Odysseus may have done something to provoke the anger of a god, but he offers no suggestion as to what he might possibly have done to provoke – or deserve – such punishment (4.181–182).[72]

The final account given of Odysseus's fate immediately after the sacking of Troy is by Hermes. He reports to Calypso that Zeus says that Odysseus is the "most wretched man" of those who fought at Troy, that the Achaians "offended Athena in their homecoming, who roused an evil wind and tall waves against them, and all his other noble companions died, but a wind and wave brought him here" to the isle of Calypso (5.105–111). Hermes' account of what Zeus said suggests that Odysseus and his men in particular offended Athena and therefore that the god most responsible for Odysseus's wandering is not Poseidon, as the opening of the poem suggests, but the goddess who always seemed to favor him in particular, Athena. But, again, this account sheds no light on what Odysseus may have done to provoke or deserve this punishment.

Taken together, these accounts indicate that, after the Achaians sacked Troy, thanks to Odysseus's stratagem of the wooden horse, the gods as a whole and Athena in particular turned against Odysseus and prevented his homecoming.[73] Indeed, inasmuch as Odysseus must not have known of the sufferings inflicted on Ajax, Menelaus, and Agamemnon, he must have felt that he was singled out by the gods for punishment. And this punishment must have come as a terrible shock. For the gods as a whole, and Athena in particular, had always singularly favored Odysseus. As Nestor says to Telemachus: "If only owl-eyed Athena should wish thus to love you, as then she cared so surpassingly for glorious Odysseus in the land of the Trojans, where we Achaians suffered woes – for I never saw gods love so openly as Pallas Athena openly stood beside that man" (3.218–222; see also 3.377–379). But now, after the moment of his greatest triumph, when he had led the Achaians to conquer Troy at long last, the gods as a whole and Athena in particular either abandoned him or punished him. As Odysseus later remarks to Athena, once he is back in Ithaca:

> This I know well: that in former times you were kind to me, when we sons of the Achaians were fighting war in Troy. But once we sacked the towering city of Priam

[72] Clay contends that Athena's wrath is provoked by the fact that "Odysseus is too clever; his intelligence calls into question the superiority of the gods themselves" (1983, 209).
[73] See Clay 1983, 43–53. I therefore disagree with Dimmock's claim that "In the Odyssey . . . Athena clearly has no fault to find with Odysseus" (1989, 65).

> and went on to our ships, a god scattered the Achaians, and then I did not see you, daughter of Zeus, nor did I notice you going onto my ship, so that you might ward off some woe from me, but always I had a heart torn in my breast as a I wandered, until the gods released me from evil. (13.314–321)

Odysseus reveals here that he suffered profound anguish after the sacking of Troy, when he was forsaken by Athena and the other gods. So great was this anguish that, even at the court of the Phaiacians, Odysseus cannot bring himself to begin his account of his travels with the sacking of Troy but only with the sacking of the city of the Ciconnians (9.39–40). For the gods' desertion of him at the end of the Trojan War was evidently a true crisis for him. Why did the gods desert him? What wrong had he done? Or were the gods simply indifferent to right and wrong? These are the questions that haunted him then. And these are the questions that inspired him to explore the land of the Cyclopes.

Once Odysseus and his companions arrive at an uninhabited island that is singularly favored both by nature and the gods, and they see nearby, across the water, another well-endowed land that is inhabited, he decides to sail there and explore it. More precisely, as Odysseus explains to his companions, "I will test these men, who they are, whether they are hubristic and savage and not just or are hospitable to strangers and their mind is godlike" (9.174–176). Odysseus's decision to explore this land that is favored by the gods is motivated, not by general curiosity – to know the towns and mind of many humans (1.3) – but specifically to determine whether the inhabitants of this favored land are just and hence whether or not they deserve such favor. In the wake of the gods' abandonment of him after the sacking of Troy, Odysseus evidently attempts now to discover whether the gods are just – whether they truly "range at large through the cities, looking upon the hubris and the lawfulness of humans" and punish hubris when they find it (17.485–487, 24.351–352) – as humans generally believe and as he has evidently believed until now, and hence whether he is somehow at fault for their desertion, or whether they are indifferent to justice. He tests here, then, not only the moral character of the inhabitants of this land but also the moral character of the gods. This man who always seeks to test the justice of those near to him – who later will "test" his servants, the suitors, his wife, and his father to learn "which are upstanding and which lack righteousness" – here tests the justice of the very gods.[74]

[74] 17.350–363; see also 13.333–338, 14.459–461, 15.303–306, 16.303–307, 17.411–414, 24.232–240. See Bolotin 1989, 44–45; Ruderman 1999, 153. Stanford maintains that

By any measure, the gods fail this test. For the monstrously huge Cyclops Polyphemus would seem to be clearly deserving of divine punishment. He "lacks righteousness," is "pitiless," and hubristically defies the gods (9.106, 9.189, 9.272, 9.287). When Odysseus meets him, he declares to the Cyclops: "Have reverence for the gods, most excellent one. We are your suppliants and Zeus is the avenger of suppliants and strangers, the protector of strangers, one who accompanies strangers who are reverent" (9.269–271). Yet Polyphemus responds by expressing brazen contempt for the gods: "For the Cyclopes do not care about aegis-bearing Zeus nor about the blessed gods, for we are far superior! Nor would I, for fear of the enmity of Zeus, spare either you or your companions, unless my spirit bid me" (9.275–278). He then proceeds to kill and eat two of Odysseus's companions for dinner, then two more for breakfast, and again two more for dinner. And even though Odysseus and his men hold out their hands to Zeus – the avenger of suppliants and strangers – in prayer, Zeus does nothing to punish such flagrant injustice and impiety (9.294; see also 9.317). Indeed, the gods go on to side with Polyphemus, for his father Poseidon heeds his prayer for vengeance after Odysseus blinds him (9.526–536). And although Odysseus and his men sacrifice to Zeus, "who rules over all," after their escape, "He did not care for the sacrifices but pondered how all my well-benched ships and trusty companions would be destroyed" (9.551–555).

Odysseus's test of the gods would seem clearly to demonstrate that they are not true enforcers of justice. They have cared for Odysseus in the past and they may care for him in the future, but fundamentally they are indifferent to human beings. As Achilles suggests at the end of the *Iliad*, the cause of such divine indifference may ultimately be the gulf between immortal beings and mortals: "For such is the way the gods spun for wretched mortals, that we live our lives in grief, but they themselves have no sorrows" (*Iliad* 24.525–526). The gods have their own ways and cannot be trusted to understand and care about our ways.[75] Therefore, since humans cannot rely on divine providence, we must rely on human providence, and hence on human reason.

Odysseus seems to accept this conclusion and act on it, brilliantly, in the cave of the Cyclops. Odysseus coldly and clearly analyzes the complicated

Odysseus is motivated here by "acquisitiveness as well as inquisitiveness" (1963, 76). See also Clay 1983, 74, 116.

[75] Dimmock observes, "Odysseus has correctly read the situation: no human can be certain of divine help" (1989, 185).

problem he faces. Since Polyphemus always blocks the cave with a huge stone that only he can move, Odysseus must disable the monster so that he cannot kill the surviving men but must not kill the monster lest he and his men be fatally trapped in the cave. Therefore, he must blind the Cyclops (9.298–305, 9.315–333). Since the Cyclops is overwhelmingly strong, he can only subdue the monster by guile. Therefore, he will get him drunk (9.345–354). Since the Cyclops has fellow Cyclopes who live around him – and since he is not at all smart – Odysseus must give Polyphemus as his name one – Nobody – that will neutralize the call for help that he will inevitably make once he is blinded (9.355–367, 9.401–414). Then, when the blind monster removes the stone, as he inevitably will, so that the sheep that he lives off of can go out and graze, Odysseus must keep his men silent and tie them to the bellies of the sheep so that they can all escape and reach their ship (9.415–470). Odysseus here displays careful deliberation, subtle analysis, keen foresight, resourcefulness, and imagination. Above all, he displays the virtue of self-control. For, realizing that he cannot indulge his anger at the Cyclops's injustice, realizing that the gods will not support that anger in any way, Odysseus understands that he must be guided by his reason alone if he is to provide for his men and himself.[76]

ODYSSEUS'S PERSISTENT BELIEF IN DIVINE PROVIDENCE

Yet, Odysseus ultimately fails to accept the conclusion that we humans must fend for ourselves without relying on divine providence. For, once he has brilliantly saved himself and his men from the clutches of the wicked Polyphemus through his own wits, Odysseus insists to the Cyclops that he was merely an instrument of the gods' justice: "Cyclops, you were not to eat the companions of a defenseless man in the hollow cave, with mighty violence! Indeed, evil deeds were to overtake you, hard one, since you felt no shame to eat guests in your own home. Therefore, Zeus and the other gods punished you!" (9.475–479). Odysseus offers here what might seem to be a surprisingly humble and pious account of his own heroism. After all, Odysseus is a lover of glory and he is happy to claim credit, for instance, for the stratagem of the wooden horse, which enabled the Achaians to sack Troy (8.492–495, 9.19–20).

[76] Clay deems this "the most 'Odyssean' of all the adventures" (1983, 112; consider also 125).

However, he insists on claiming that his own rescue of his men and punishment of the Cyclops was an act of divine justice. And his insistence on making this claim to the Cyclops demonstrates the sincerity of this claim. For Odysseus acts quite boldly and even recklessly here, as though he has little to fear from the Cyclops because he is confident that the gods will protect him. Even after the Cyclops almost destroys his ship and his men beg him to hold his tongue, Odysseus indulges his anger – "I spoke back to him with a spirit that was angered" – by speaking to the Cyclops again and revealing his own identity (9.500–505). In this way, Odysseus acts as though he believes that he can afford to indulge his anger at the injustice of the Cyclops because he believes that he can rely on the gods to support his righteous anger.[77]

We see, then, that Odysseus's attachment to the belief in the justice of the gods is so powerful that, when confronted by the painful truth that gods are fundamentally indifferent to justice, he recoils. Even though Odysseus has just experienced most dramatically the gods' abandonment of him to face evil triumphant all by himself, Odysseus affirms that the gods have never abandoned him. Even though Odysseus vanquished the monstrous Cyclops by his own reason, he insists on attributing his triumph to divine providence. Indeed, even ten years after the gods' abandonment of him in the cave of Polyphemus, after he has seen the gods side with the Cyclops and answer his prayer that all of Odysseus's men be destroyed and that Odysseus's own homecoming be postponed, Odysseus insists, in his narration to the Phaiacians, on leaving open the possibility that the gods may have helped him in that cave. He remarks that the Cyclops brought all his sheep, including the rams, into the cave on the night Odysseus was planning to blind him – the very sheep Odysseus planned to use as a way to escape – "either thinking of something or even a god so urged him" (9.336–339; see 9.237–239). He later claims that, at the moment when he and his men were about to blind the drunken, sleeping Cyclops, "a great deity breathed boldness into us" (9.381; see also 9.317).[78] Odysseus clings to the comforting belief in divine providence, notwithstanding ten years of evidence to the contrary.

[77] See Ruderman 1999, 154–156.

[78] I therefore think that Clay goes too far in claiming that Odysseus's account of his adventures "is singularly free of references to divine activities" and in suggesting that Odysseus fully accepts that "the Cyclops adventure … constitutes a feat accomplished without divine assistance" (1983, 24, 125).

As we have seen, Odysseus is animated by great curiosity about the justice of the gods. After their desertion of him once Troy was sacked, when they drove him off course rather than let him return quickly home, Odysseus comes to doubt that the gods are reliably provident, that they reward the good and punish the wicked. Therefore, when he sees the blessed land of the Cyclopes, he explores it to learn whether the inhabitants are good and therefore deserving of such prosperity. In this way, he conducts a kind of scientific experiment, to gather evidence to determine whether or not the thesis that the gods are just is correct. But once the results of this experiment appear to demonstrate conclusively that the gods are indifferent to justice, Odysseus turns his back on those results and passionately affirms that the gods must be just. Odysseus is extremely smart, and extremely curious, but he ultimately lacks the strength to face the painful truth of the gods' indifference to human beings.

One might think that Odysseus's belief in divine providence would finally collapse under the weight of the Lastrygonian disaster, when eleven of his ships and all their men are destroyed, without provocation, by the monstrous Lastrygonians. Indeed, at first it might seem that Odysseus has come to the conclusion that he cannot count on the gods to protect the righteous and punish the wicked but must rather rely on his own prudence. For he does not express any anger at the Lastrygonians' wickedness or any hope that the gods will punish them, as he had regarding the Cyclops; he only thinks of how he and his surviving companions might escape (compare 10.125–134 with 9.294–295, 9.473–505, 9.522–525, 9.550–555). However, when they arrive at Circe's isle, half of Odysseus's men vanish in their encounter with the goddess, and Odysseus's companion Eurylochus reasonably argues that the remaining men should flee the island, Odysseus rejects this advice and insists on confronting the goddess, even if he must do so alone. Now, it is important to see that Odysseus here has no plan whatsoever to vanquish the goddess who has effortlessly overpowered – and as far as he knows destroyed – twenty-two of his men. In contrast to the Cyclops episode, Odysseus does not deliberate at all here but seems rather to act blindly, out of an irresistible anger – he tells Eurylochus, "a mighty compulsion is on me" and he later says twice that his heart is in turmoil (10.273, 10.309, 10.313) – and, it would seem, out of hope that the (other) gods will come to his aid and punish this unjust goddess or woman (see 10.254–258).[79] It is true that that a god – Hermes – does come to his aid and enable him to overcome Circe and save his men. Circe later surmises that Odysseus overcame her because of his mind – "There is a mind in your breast that cannot be bewitched" (10.329) – but Odysseus here does not rely on his mind at all but rather, entirely, on the gods. And the gods do save him here. But it is also true that we never learn why Hermes helps Odysseus here, whether Zeus sent him – as he later sends Hermes to Calypso's isle to help Odysseus (5.28–148) – or whether Hermes acted on his own – as Circe later suggests (10.330–332). Most importantly, we never learn why the gods did not help Odysseus save his men in the Cyclops's cave or in the land of the Lastrygonians. Odysseus, however, does not ask Hermes this or any other questions but simply obeys him here wordlessly and blindly (cf. 13.316–323).

What is more, in his narrative to the Phaiacians, Odysseus appears to interpret Hermes' intervention in a distinctively pious fashion. For Hermes helps Odysseus here by revealing to him the "nature" of a drug that will render powerless the dangerous magic of the goddess Circe (10.303). In this way, Hermes clearly reveals that there is a certain fixed order in the world – a natural order – that limits the power even of the gods. This revelation is of paramount significance, for it shows that the gods are not all-powerful and that humans may, armed with the knowledge of nature, fend for themselves without supernatural assistance.[80] However, in his narrative to the Phaiacians of Hermes, Odysseus draws the opposite conclusion and affirms that the gods are indeed all-powerful. For, after explaining that it is hard for humans to dig up the drug Hermes shows that he can use to defeat Circe, Odysseus says, "The gods are capable of everything" (10.306). Here, too, when confronted with evidence that would seem to challenge his piety, Odysseus emphatically reaffirms it (see also 10.573–574). Indeed, the more reason Odysseus is given to doubt the justice and the power of the

[79] It is possible that Odysseus here is simply suicidal. It is true that Odysseus does consider committing suicide on two occasions in Book X, after his men open Aeolus's magical bag of winds just as they are on the verge of returning to Ithaca and after Circe informs him that he must journey to Hades to confer with Teiresias (10.46–55, 10.488–498). Yet, the fact that he seeks to act against Circe – who may be a goddess according to Eurylochus's report (10.254) – rather than simply kill himself, suggests that he does somehow cherish a hope that he will somehow prevail with some kind of divine assistance.

[80] This is the first appearance of the word "nature" (φύσις) in extant Greek literature. See Strauss 1987, 2–3.

gods – their abandonment of him and his men in the cave of the Cyclops and to the Lastrygonians, the revelation by Hermes of their limited power – the more Odysseus doubles down on his faith.

ODYSSEUS'S RELIANCE ON DIVINE ASSISTANCE RATHER THAN HUMAN PRUDENCE IN ITHACA

The clearest and most detailed example in the *Odyssey* of Odysseus's blind embrace of piety and reliance on divine assistance rather than his own wits is his behavior once he has returned to Ithaca. Odysseus returns home after a twenty-year absence to an extraordinarily complex situation. As he learns from Teiresias (11.113–117), a large number of "overbearing" men – 118, counting the suitors and their attendants (he later learns from Telemachus – 16.245–253) – from Ithaca and neighboring lands are wooing his wife and consuming the goods of his household. In order to benefit himself, his family, and his realm, he must somehow free his home from the overbearing suitors. Now, from the beginning of the poem, a number of characters speak as though the clearest and perhaps only solution to the problem of the suitors is to kill them. For example, when Athena first comes to Telemachus in Book I, she encourages him to consider how he will kill the suitors (1.293–296; cf. 1.113–117). Telemachus tells the suitors he wishes for their destruction (2.145, 2.314–317). Halitherses, Odysseus's old friend, predicts that Odysseus will kill all of the suitors (2.163–167). At Sparta, Menelaus tells Telemachus that, were Odysseus to return to Ithaca, he would single-handedly destroy the suitors (4.333–350). Teiresias seems to urge Odysseus to kill the suitors when he returns home and, when Odysseus does return home, he urges Athena to advise him how to wreak vengeance on the suitors (11.112–120, 13.386–396).

However, it is not altogether clear that attempting to kill all of the suitors is in truth in the best interest of Odysseus and his family. In the first place, as Telemachus later points out, it is not clear how he, alone, or even with his son, can overcome 118 men (16.233–257). But furthermore, even were Odysseus to slay all the suitors, how should he and his family avoid the vengeance of the suitors' families (see 23.117–122)? How should Odysseus secure his family and his kingdom in the face of such hostility, especially insofar as he must undertake a long journey away from home hereafter, if he is to obey Teiresias (11.119–137)?[81]

There would seem to be an evident parallel between the challenge Odysseus faces from the suitors and the challenge he faced once he was trapped in the Cyclops's cave. After the Cyclops reveals his wickedness and devours two of his men, Odysseus's first impulse is to find a way to kill him. However, he quickly realizes that, were he to kill the Cyclops, he would doom himself and his men to destruction since they lack the strength to remove the stone blocking the entrance of the cave (9.296–305). Accordingly, Odysseus devises a brilliant scheme to blind the Cyclops and escape from the cave when the Cyclops removes the stone himself. Now, killing all the suitors by himself is evidently a much harder task than killing the Cyclops. But furthermore, it would seem that it would be similarly self-destructive for him to kill them all even if he could, for he would then doom himself and his family to destruction at the hands of the vengeful relatives of these 118 men. As Odysseus himself remarks to his son – *after* they have already killed 116 of the 118 men – "Let us consider how it would be best. For even if one kills one mortal in a land, for whom there are not many defenders, one flees and abandons one's kinsmen and the land of one's fathers. But we have killed the pillar of the city, by far the best of the young in Ithaca" (23.117–122; see also 15.222–224). Just as Odysseus needed to disable the Cyclops by blinding him, but not kill him lest he doom himself and his men to destruction by being trapped in the cave without escape, so, it would seem, Odysseus must neutralize the threat of the suitors without attempting to kill them all, lest either he fail in his attempt to kill them or he doom himself and his family to destruction at the hands of their surviving fathers and brothers. Reason, then, would seem to dictate that he find some middle path between surrendering to the overbearing suitors and attempting to kill them all. More specifically, reason would seem to dictate that he attempt to gain the support of at least some portion of the suitors, even a large majority of them, rather than attempt to kill them all.

One might object that it is impossible for Odysseus to gain the support of the suitors because they are simply wicked.[82] Therefore, he has no alternative

[81] Consider Benardete 1997, 8–9.

[82] Clarke maintains that "the punishment of the suitors is more than an example of reciprocal vengeance: it is an enactment of absolute and timeless justice . . . Their folly . . .

but to try to kill them all. But how uniformly and incorrigibly wicked are the suitors in Homer's account? Homer himself stresses the folly of the suitors, and of their relatives, rather than their wickedness (22.31–33, 24.469).[83] Moreover, it is important to keep in mind that, like everyone else, the suitors believe that, since no one has heard any news of Odysseus for ten years, he must be dead. Even though Leocritus claims that the suitors might well kill Odysseus were he to return home, they seem to maintain the view of Telemachus, for example, that Odysseus is surely dead after so many years of absence (2.242–251; 1.166–168, 1.353–355, 1.394–396, 1.413, 2.182–183). Their behavior, then, is at least somewhat different from that of Aegisthus, who wooed Clytaemnestra knowing that Agamemnon was alive, with the intention of killing him on his return (1.32–43, 3.193–198, 3.232–235, 3.261–272, 4.512–537). It is true that the suitors place tremendous pressure on Penelope by coming to her home each day for three years, consuming vast quantities of goods, and demanding that she agree to marry one of them. But it is also true that Penelope has given them some encouragement, perhaps because she herself wonders whether her absent husband is alive or will ever return (2.91–92). Indeed, Homer informs us that one of the leading suitors, Amphinomos, "especially pleased Penelope with his words, for he wielded a good mind" (16.397–398). Odysseus too admires Amphinomos and warns him to separate himself from the suitors and go home, but Athena somehow induces him to remain (18.119–157). Homer also informs us of the suitor Leiodes: "to him alone their follies were hateful and he was indignant with all the suitors" (21.146–147). In these ways, Homer stresses that at least some of the suitors are not simply wicked.[84] The most clearly wicked act the suitors undertake is their plan to kill Telemachus, a plan devised by Antinoos, but one to which they "all" consent (4.669–674; 20.240–242; but see 16.363–406). Yet, insofar as they do not carry out the plan successfully, the suitors do not actually do any irreparable harm to Odysseus's family.[85] And one

is sufficient to justify their wholesale destruction" (Clarke 2004, 88–89). According to Schein, "all" the suitors "are conceived as thoroughgoing villains" (1996, 9; but see 30). In a similar vein, see Lloyd-Jones 1971, 31; Dimmock 1989, 295–307; Lateiner 2004, 22, 25; Saïd 2011, 249–250.

[83] See Silk 2004, 36–37.

[84] See Felson-Rubin's excellent account of how "Homer lessens the suitors' automatic blameworthiness by diverse ploys" (1994, 111; 111–123).

[85] Consider Benardete 1997, 131.

must remember that, insofar as the suitors do inflict harm on Odysseus's family during his absence, Odysseus himself bears considerable responsibility for that harm, insofar as he tarried on his way home from Troy and even, for a time, forgot about returning home.[86]

Could Odysseus have induced many or even all of the suitors to leave his home and accept his return without resorting to mass slaughter? In the first place, Odysseus might have focused from the beginning on acquiring allies apart from the suitors, not only by appealing to his son, Eumaeus, the oxherd Philoitios, and Eurycleia, but also Penelope, Mentor, Halitherses, and Antiphos – Odysseus' faithful companions of old (2.252–254, 17.68–69); Peiraios and other faithful companions and friends of Telemachus (17.71–85, 15.495–546); and Laertes and Dolios and his sons (24.489–525). Then, Odysseus, with the aid especially of such respected elders as Laertes, Mentor, Halitherses, and Antiphos, might have won over the Ithacans as a whole and subsequently a significant number of the suitors themselves – most clearly Medon, Phemius, Leiodes, and Amphinomos, but perhaps others as well. Antinoos himself expresses the fear that Telemachus alone might rally the people against the suitors and consequently drive them out of his house (16.370–392; see also 2.80–81). Would not Odysseus have been able to accomplish this task even more successfully? Even after Odysseus has slaughtered all of the suitors, Medon and Phemius – who were only spared thanks to Telemachus – play a crucial role in his ultimate victory by persuading a sizeable minority of the angry relatives of the dead suitors to relent in their hostility (see 22.330–380, 24.412–471, especially 24.463–466). Would they not have been even more effective with the families of the suitors and even with the suitors themselves before Odysseus killed so many? Perhaps Antinoos is irreconcilable, but might not Eurymachus – who offers peace and reparation after Odysseus kills Antinoos and reveals himself (22.44–59) – and

[86] After describing Odysseus's justification of killing Leiodes on the grounds that he must have often prayed that Odysseus would never return and that Penelope would "marry him instead and bear him children (XXII 310–329)," Bolotin asks, "is it reasonable or just for a husband who has been absent from home for twenty years, and missing without a trace for ten of them – in part, moreover, because of his own dalliance – to kill a harmless man on these grounds?" (1989, 51).

the other suitors, out of contrition or fear, relent once they see that Odysseus has come home and enjoys broad support?[87]

Given the overbearing character of the suitors and their willingness to kill Telemachus and even Odysseus, a violent conflict with them, and therefore with their families, might well have been inevitable. Nevertheless, given the complexity of the challenge of both killing them and somehow pacifying their families, one would at the very least expect Odysseus to analyze the situation, weigh his options, and deliberate about his choices, as he has done so brilliantly in the past (9.298–305, 9.315–470; see also 5.464–487, 6.142–185). It is therefore simply astonishing that Odysseus does not deliberate at all concerning whether to kill the suitors, how to kill them, or how to pacify their relatives. Instead, when he arrives in Ithaca, he simply puts himself in the hands of Athena, who comes to him and claims that he should trust her since she has "always" stood by him in the past and protected him (13.299–301). And even though Odysseus himself points out that he knows well that, for some ten years, he "never" saw Athena or received her assistance, he proceeds to put his faith in her and even to declare that, with her help, he would gladly face three hundred men (13.314–321, 13.386–391). His trust in the evidently unreliable Athena is especially striking in contrast with his distrust of those human beings who would seem to be his natural allies. He confides in Telemachus only at the behest of Athena; he confides in Eumaeus, Philoitius, and his father Laertes only after he tests them; he confides in Penelope only after the suitors are all dead; and he makes no effort whatsoever to contact such potential allies as Mentor, Halitherses, and Antiphes. But his trust in Athena is absolute and complete.

When Athena tells him to trust no human being, disguises him as an old beggar, and orders him to go to Eumaeus, Odysseus unquestioningly obeys (13.307, 13.396–439). When Odysseus reveals his identity to his son – at Athena's behest – and declares his intention to kill all the suitors, Telemachus objects that his famously prudent father's desire for revenge against the 118 suitors and their attendants will simply prove self-destructive (16.233–256). Odysseus replies: "Consider whether Athena and her father Zeus will suffice for the two of us, or whether I must think of some other

[87] Crotty remarks, "It is characteristic of the ironic mode of the *Odyssey* that the sanest plan for resolving the suitors' crime is put forth by Eurymachus, one of the most villainous suitors" (1994, 154).

defender" (16.260–261). Now, it is true that Odysseus proceeds to set forth a plan of his own to Telemachus: Odysseus will go to his house in his disguise as a beggar, Telemachus must not intervene when the suitors abuse his father, Telemachus must hide all the weapons in the great hall where the suitors pass their time, and then he and Telemachus will slaughter all the now partially disarmed suitors (16.270–297). But it is also true that Odysseus himself acknowledges that the only way that he and Telemachus could possibly hope to kill 118 suitors and their attendants all by themselves is with the miraculous intervention of Athena and Zeus (16.267–269, 16.297–298). And since Odysseus pins his hopes on the gods rather than on any possible human allies, he follows Athena in insisting to Telemachus that no one – not even Penelope or Laertes – be trusted (16.299–304). Later, on the eve of his vengeance, as Odysseus contemplates killing the suitors, he only ponders how he will do so with Athena as his partner (19.1–2, 19.50–52). He takes it for granted that Athena will not abandon him – even though she had abandoned him for ten years – and consequently makes no plans of what to do if she should abandon him yet again. Odysseus does worry how he and his son might defeat so many suitors and escape from their vengeful relatives, but when Athena simply insists that he will be invincible with her assistance, he simply believes her (20.36–53). Accordingly, when Odysseus kills Antinoos, and Eurymachus offers, on behalf of the remaining 117 suitors and their attendants, to make peace and to pay reparations for the harm they have done, Odysseus declares: "Eurymachus, if you gave me all that belongs to your father, as much as you have now and what you could add to it from elsewhere, even so I would not stay my hands from slaughter until I had punished the suitors for their entire transgression" (22.61–64). Odysseus is absolute in his vengeance here because he is absolute in his faith that the gods will grant him a miraculous victory over 117 men.

Odysseus's recklessness is especially evident after the suitors have been killed. Even though he points out to Telemachus that they are vulnerable to the vengeful wrath of the relatives of the suitors, his only plan is to pretend that Penelope is celebrating her engagement with one of the suitors so that no one learns that evening of the deaths of the suitors, then to go to Laertes' country home with Telemachus (but without Penelope), and then "consider what gain the Olympian may put in our hand" (23.139–140). When Odysseus leaves for the country the next day with Telemachus, Eumaeus, and Philoitius, he does so in broad daylight, without any effort at all of concealment, and is only hidden from view thanks to Athena (23.366–372). When the relatives discover the deaths of the suitors and resolve to kill Odysseus, it is only thanks to the intervention of Medon and Phemius – two men who were spared at Telemachus's insistence and who were left no instructions at all by Odysseus – that nearly half of the relatives stay home (24.412–471). As the relatives approach Laertes' country house, Odysseus makes no plans for defense but rather spends an inordinate amount of time testing his father's affection (24.213–326). Finally, when the relatives appear, Odysseus attacks them, without any evident thought concerning how he might defeat them, how he might rule Ithaca in the wake of such bloodshed, and how he might safely leave his realm and his family when he departs on the voyage Teiresias has ordered him to undertake (24.489–540). Odysseus evidently dismisses from his mind all the times that the gods abandoned him – most notably in the Cyclops's cave and the land of the Lastrygonians[88] – and trusts that the gods will protect him from harm and allow him to surmount all of these seemingly insurmountable challenges – as they did once, on the isle of Circe.

THE PROVIDENCE OF PENELOPE

One might argue that Odysseus's faith in the gods is entirely vindicated by their intervention against the suitors and their families. After all, thanks to Athena, Odysseus slays 108 suitors (and presumably eight of their attendants as well) and thanks to Zeus and Athena, peace is apparently established in Ithaca between Odysseus and the relatives of the dead suitors – though one cannot help but wonder how firm such a peace could possibly be. However, even in the light of the gods' providence here, the lesson of the Cyclops's cave would seem to remain: the mysterious and whimsical gods cannot be counted on to care for human beings and therefore humans should rely on human rather than divine providence.

Furthermore, human providence does play a significant role in Odysseus's triumph over both the suitors and their relatives. At the last minute, Odysseus on his own, without prompting from Athena, enlists the

[88] Consider Clarke's comment that Odysseus "has experienced to the full the inexplicable fickleness of the gods" (2004, 87).

aid of Eurycleia, Eumaeus, and Philoitius, and they provide valuable assistance in both killing the suitors and concealing their slaughter from the rest of Ithaca overnight (21.188–244, 21.378–395, 22.160–204). As we have seen, Telemachus on his own induces Odysseus to spare Medon and Phemius and they in turn, on their own, persuade a sizeable minority of the relatives of the dead suitors to refrain from joining in attacking Odysseus (22.354–377, 24.439–466).

Finally, Penelope provides crucial assistance to Odysseus by proposing the bow contest. For it is the bow contest that gives Odysseus a vital weapon with which to kill multiple suitors from a safe distance while Telemachus runs to get swords, spears, and armor (22.1–25, 22.70–125). In the absence of the bow contest, it is hard to see how Odysseus could have initially withstood the onrush of up to 118 hostile men, unless Athena had simply destroyed them on her own from the beginning (22.205–309). The soul of the dead suitor Amphimedon plausibly suggests that it was the bow contest, along with the removal of the armor from the great hall and the assistance of the gods, that enabled Odysseus to kill the suitors (24.154–185). Now, Amphimedon surmises that Odysseus must have instructed Penelope to set up the bow contest as part of the plan to destroy the suitors (24.167–169). But Homer's text shows quite clearly that the bow contest is a scheme that is hatched, not by Odysseus or by Athena, but exclusively by the "surpassingly wise [περίφρων]" Penelope (19.570–581). The bow contest is one of two great stratagems Penelope devises in the poem, the other being her weaving and unweaving of Laertes' shroud. Through the latter, she holds off the suitors for three critical years, until the time when her son reaches manhood and the moment her husband arrives home; through the former, she contributes significantly to the destruction of the suitors – a goal that Amphimedon claims, in retrospect, she was always striving to achieve, "considering our death and destruction" (24.127; 24.125–148).[89]

But does Penelope propose the bow contest with the intention of helping Odysseus? Does she know that Odysseus has returned, even though he – at the behest of Athena – does not confide in her? Homer never unambiguously shows Penelope recognizing Odysseus, as he does Argos and Eurycleia, for example, until Book XXIII, after the killing of the suitors. Moreover, when Eurycleia comes to Penelope to tell her that Odysseus is home and has

[89] See Felson and Slatkin 2004, 110–111; Crotty 1994, 196–197.

killed all the suitors, Penelope initially doubts her words (23.1–24). Yet, surprisingly, Penelope abandons her skepticism quickly. Moreover, she apparently wonders primarily, not whether Odysseus himself had returned, but – quite reasonably, given that Eurycleia says nothing about the role of Telemachus, Eumaeus, Philoitius, or Athena – how Odysseus, "being alone," could have killed all the suitors (23.38; 23.32–84). Once she sees Odysseus, even though he is still in the guise of the old beggar, she evinces little doubt of his identity (23.85–95, 23.104–110). Penelope does, of course, test Odysseus – even once he and Athena have removed his disguise – before throwing herself into his arms (23.152–180). But what she apparently tests here is not merely or primarily his knowledge that their marriage bed cannot be moved and hence his identity, but whether he will be distressed that their marriage bed has been uprooted and hence whether – after a twenty-year absence – he still cares for their marriage and for her (23.181–230). She tests here not merely who he is but how he feels.[90] The test is not only a memory test but also, and above all, a love test.

Homer's portrayal of Penelope is singularly subtle, complex, and enigmatic.[91] Penelope is, for example, deeply devoted to her son and husband, but she also expresses a certain sympathy for the adulterous Helen (23.215–224) and feels some affection at least for Amphinomos and perhaps for other suitors as well (16.397–398, 19.535–550).[92] Moreover, Penelope is a victim of the overbearing suitors, but she is also their formidable adversary, deploying stratagems (δόλοι) and beguiling (θέλγει) the suitors as, for example, the goddesses Circe, Calypso, and the Sirens deploy stratagems and beguile their male victims (compare 2.93–126, 24.126–146, 18.281–283 with 10.232, 10.291, 10.318, 10.326, 1.55–57, 12.39–46).[93] The clearest manner in which Homer signals the ambiguity of his portrayal of Penelope is by comparing her alone, of all his characters, simultaneously to two other characters – two goddesses with dramatically different traits: "Surpassingly wise Penelope went out of her chamber, resembling Artemis

[90] As Dimmock observes, "The anger of Odysseus" here "is the measure of his love for her" (1989, 319). Consider as well Heitman 2005, 99–100; Crotty 1994, 197–199.

[91] Consider Felson-Rubin 1996, 164; Katz 1991, 93–113..

[92] See Felson-Rubin 1996, 168–179; Felson 2004, 111–112; Crotty 1994, 189, 193–196; Murnaghan 1987, 141–143.

[93] See Pucci 1987, 193–195. Felson-Rubin notes, "The suitors are no match for Penelope" (1994, 111). See also Dimmock 1989, 61.

or Golden Aphrodite" (17.36–38; see also 19.53–54). Which is Penelope, the cold divine huntress or the soft, seductive goddess of love? Penelope is famously devoted to her husband and might therefore seem especially loving, but she is also a formidable adversary of the suitors and the only character in either the *Odyssey* or the *Iliad* who prays to the goddess Artemis (20.60).[94]

Does Penelope suspect that the old beggar is Odysseus? Does she recognize that Odysseus is planning revenge against the suitors and therefore help him by proposing the bow contest?[95] Homer's narrative offers considerable evidence that Penelope does indeed suspect that Odysseus has returned at long last in the guise of a beggar. First, she learns from Telemachus that Odysseus is reportedly alive and then, from the prophet Theoclymenus, that Odysseus is already in Ithaca, informing himself of the evil deeds of the suitors and devising evils for all of them (17.142–161). Now, if she deemed Theoclymenus's prophecy credible, she might reasonably surmise that Odysseus was in Ithaca in disguise. When Penelope subsequently learns that a stranger has appeared in her house – an old beggar, who claims to be a friend of Odysseus and to have news of him – and that he has been struck, she appears extremely indignant on his behalf and also singularly insistent on meeting him, urging Eumaeus three times to send him to her (17.492–550; see also 18.215–225). Does she suspect that the stranger is Odysseus?

The dramatic interview between Odysseus and his wife is especially suggestive. The most obvious question to ask is, does Penelope recognize her husband after twenty years? We know that his dog Argos recognizes him, and so does Eurycleia (17.290–327, 19.392–394). Moreover, even before seeing his telltale scar, Eurycleia remarks that the stranger closely resembles Odysseus in his form, voice, and feet (19.379–381). Penelope herself remarks

[94] See Felson-Rubin 1996, 181.

[95] Harsh argues that Penelope – "a keen and intelligent woman" whose character is marked by a "cautious conservatism" – recognizes Odysseus, or at least harbors "secret suspicions of the stranger's identity," and that the final scene of Book XIX is consequently "an exciting duel of indirectness, subtle and brilliant in its execution" (1950, 6, 4, 19, 18). Consider also Winkler 1990, 129–161. On the other hand, Murnaghan maintains that Penelope does not suspect that the stranger is Odysseus and attributes her proposal of the bow contest at this very moment to "lucky chance" (1987, 134–139, 139). See also Schein 1996, 29; Saïd 2011, 286–289. On this whole question, consider as well Felson-Rubin 1994, 3–5, 16–18; Crotty 1994, 191–192; Thalmann 1998, 232–233.

to the stranger, "I suppose Odysseus is already such in his feet and his hands" (19.358–359). Is it credible that Argos and Eurycleia would recognize Odysseus but "surpassingly wise" Penelope – who has heard the news of Telemachus and the prophecy of Theoclymenus – would not?

Now, if Penelope were to suspect that her husband is before her, after twenty years – part of which, she knows, was spent with a nymph (17.142–144) – she would naturally want to test the stranger, not only to confirm that he is Odysseus but also to determine whether he still cares for her. Penelope does, as she herself says, "test" the stranger, ostensibly to determine whether, as he claims, he truly met Odysseus twenty years before, by asking him to describe what he was wearing. The stranger then accurately describes in particular Odysseus's mantle, brooch, and tunic, all of which were given to him by Penelope when he left her for Troy. Homer describes Penelope's response as follows: "So he spoke, and still more did he arouse in her a longing for weeping, since she recognized the sure signs that Odysseus showed" (19.249–250). Ostensibly, the stranger's account moves her because it confirms that he did in truth meet her husband – albeit twenty years ago. And yet, if Penelope suspects that the stranger is her husband, would she not be especially moved that he remembers so clearly and specifically what she gave him twenty years ago? Might such a remembrance on his part not seem to signify an abiding love for her? Is Penelope's test here, then, not simply a memory test for a stranger but rather a love test for her long absent husband – akin to her later love test concerning their marriage bed?

The remainder of the interview increasingly suggests that Penelope recognizes her husband. Odysseus, in disguise, proceeds to assure Penelope that her husband is nearby and will be home very soon (19.300–307). Penelope does reply by claiming that Odysseus will never return (19.312–316). But she then remarks to Eurycleia that the stranger resembles Odysseus in his hands and feet (19.358–360). Subsequently, after Eurycleia has recognized Odysseus as she bathed him – apparently in front of Penelope (19.386–394, 19.467–479, 19.503–507) – Penelope shares with this stranger, whom she has just met, her uncertainty as to whether or not she should marry one of the suitors and then her rather straightforward dream that signifies that Odysseus will return home and kill the suitors (19.509–553). When Odysseus insists that Odysseus will indeed come soon and destroy the suitors, Penelope suddenly declares that she will hold a bow contest the very next day. Does she not do so to supply Odysseus with the means for killing the suitors? And by declaring his enthusiastic approval of this plan and thereby suggesting that Odysseus himself will be there on the next day, does Odysseus not confirm her suspicions that her husband is indeed before her (19.583–587)? Homer remarks that, during the ensuing night, Odysseus suspected that his wife "already recognized" him (20.93–94).

Penelope, then, provides crucial assistance to her husband here. Moreover, given her wisdom, and given the fact that she has been in Ithaca while he has been gone and knows the situation there intimately, it would seem that she would be able to provide Odysseus with crucial advice.[96] Which of the suitors, if any, can be won over by persuasion? Who among the Ithacans has been loyal? Odysseus, however, rejects any possible advice his wife might give him, just as surely as he initially rejects the offer of the "surpassingly wise" Eurycleia to tell him who of the female servants has dishonored him and who has been without fault, instead urging her: "Hold your speech in silence and turn to the gods" (19.491–502). Odysseus forgoes the counsel of his wise and faithful wife and instead trusts entirely in the gods, even though he knows all too well how untrustworthy they are.[97] He rejects human providence in favor of divine providence. And while it is true that the gods do provide him with crucial assistance in this case against the suitors, it is also true that Penelope in particular provides him with invaluable aid.

CONCLUSION

In contrast with Odysseus, Achilles openly, forthrightly, and courageously faces his doubts concerning the providence of the gods. Like Odysseus, Achilles comes to question the justice of the gods and like Odysseus he tests the justice of the gods – in particular by praying that Zeus punish the Achaians for their injustice toward him. In Book IX of the *Iliad*, he raises questions about the gods that we never see Odysseus explicitly raise: do the

[96] See Alvis 1995, 91. Consider also Heitman's comment: "In the poem of mind, the *Odyssey*, it is wisdom, whose depth is for Penelope to sound" (2005, 111).

[97] I therefore think that Felson-Rubin goes too far in claiming, with regard to Odysseus and Penelope, that he "apprehends her strength and thrives on her wiliness" and that "The reunion of Odysseus and Athena on Ithaka rehearses the reunion between husband and wife" (1994, vii, 50).

gods reward justice, inasmuch as both the just and the unjust must die? Is it reasonable to be just if there are no divine rewards for justice (9.314–343, 9.400–420)? It is true that Zeus appears to answer Achilles' prayer and thereby appears to assuage his doubts (16.236–238). Yet the chain of events that follows Achilles' prayer leads to the death of Patroclus and that death leads Achilles again to raise questions about the gods and their providence. In particular, Achilles wonders whether there is not an inseparable gulf between the immortal gods, who never sorrow, and sorrowful mortal human beings. Accordingly, at the end of the *Iliad*, Achilles displays a certain humane independence from the gods. He freely expresses compassion for Priam and gives content to that compassion by freely granting a truce to the Trojans (24.507–672). While Odysseus ends the *Odyssey* in the grip of savage anger at the relatives of his dead enemies and in the grip of pious zeal, Achilles ends the *Iliad* by freely expressing compassion to the relatives of his dead enemy and by giving voice to a humane understanding of the limits of divine providence. Achilles proves to be more self-reliant, more humane, and more rational at the end of the *Iliad*, whereas Odysseus proves to be less so at the end of the *Odyssey*.

Why does Achilles go further down the path of reason than Odysseus? Achilles is a man of greater passion than Odysseus. He rages more, he weeps more, but he also loves more deeply. Achilles' passions, especially his love, make him more sensitive to the suffering of others – of Patroclus and Priam, for example – and make him more aware of the lack of compassion of the gods. In the case of Achilles, at least, an openness to the passions and to the sufferings of others and himself leads him to question himself more deeply and to think more deeply. Odysseus never blames himself for the sufferings of his companions or family, as Achilles blames himself for the sufferings of Patroclus and the Achaians and his father. Similarly, Odysseus expresses no compassion or understanding for his enemies, and little for his family and companions, in stark contrast with Achilles. In the case of Odysseus, at least, coldness does not lead to greater rationality.

Achilles also seems stronger than Odysseus in his capacity to endure pain, and this strength proves to be an intellectual virtue, for it enables Achilles to endure more manfully than Odysseus the pain of doubt. In contrast to Odysseus, Achilles questions not only the gods but also the value of honor and the goodness of virtue. Achilles wrestles with painful doubts concerning his own beliefs and his own virtue. In contrast with Achilles, Odysseus evinces a strong taste for pleasure, both in body and spirit. His love affairs with Circe and Calypso seem loveless, but they are a source of pleasure, a pleasure that in the case of Circe leads him to forget everything else for a year. It seems that Odysseus may have had a similar experience with Calypso, at first. It is true that he eventually tires of this life. But would Achilles have abided such a loveless, empty life at all? Odysseus's taste for pleasure leads him to shy away from doubting himself and from doubting, for example, the value of honor. Above all, it leads him to shrink from his all too reasonable but painful doubts about the justice of the gods. Odysseus is curious, but he lacks the austerity necessary for the life of reason. In the end, Homer's description of Odysseus as a man of many ways may well be a criticism. Odysseus is manifold – the man of many ways, many schemes, many counsels, many thoughts – but he lacks the lion heart, the single-minded passion and courage, of Achilles.[98] Odysseus's character oscillates between prudence and recklessness, pleasure-seeking and glory-seeking, self-restraint and fury, skepticism and piety.[99] His character lacks focus perhaps because it lacks inner strength and ultimately his thought lacks penetration.

One might still argue that Odysseus is wiser than Achilles because he is more of a singer and is therefore closer to the wise singer, Homer himself. Odysseus's recounting of his adventures in Books IX–XII is much more elaborate a song than any Achilles or anyone else in the Homeric poems sings. Odysseus is also compared to a singer, unlike Achilles (11.366–369, 17.513–521, 21.404–409). And Odysseus's inventiveness – his repeated fabrication of elaborate and detailed fictitious tales – certainly reminds one of the inexhaustibly fertile imagination of Homer.

However, Achilles delights his *mind* by singing the famous deeds of men (9.180–185). He sings rarely, but he views song as a source of instruction – of wisdom – and of intellectual pleasure. Telemachus delights in the speeches of Menelaus and the suitors delight in song, but Achilles delights his mind through song (4.597–598, 17.605, 18.304). Hermes delights his mind by contemplating the beauty of Calypso's cave and the Phaiacians delight

[98] The epithet "lionhearted" or "lion-spirited" [θυμολέοντα]" appears five times in Homer's poems. It is applied once to Achilles, by Ajax (*Iliad* 7.228); twice to Heracles, by his son Tlelopolemus in the *Iliad* (5.639) and by Odysseus in the *Odyssey* (11.268); and twice to Odysseus by Penelope (*Odyssey* 4.724, 4.814). It is worth noting that Penelope has not seen her husband for twenty years at the time that she calls him lionhearted.

[99] See Alvis 1995, 86–87.

their minds through athletic contests, but Achilles finds intellectual joy specifically in song (5.74, 8.131). In this respect, Achilles appears singularly close to Homer, whose own singing is both delightful and enlightening.[100]

It is not at all clear that Odysseus regards song as a source of instruction or wisdom. Odysseus seems to use song as an instrument – to gain the assistance of the Phaiacians and Eumaeus, for example, or to win glory, as, for example, when he asks the singer Demodocus to sing about his own famous deed, the stratagem of the Trojan Horse (8.487–498). It is also not clear that Odysseus derives great pleasure from song. Two of the three songs Demodocus sings cause Odysseus to weep – including the one he requests – and he is somewhat reluctant to recount and to continue to recount the tales of his adventures to the Phaiacians (8.72–95, 8.485–534, 11.328–384). One of Demodocus's songs – his song about Hephaestus – does, according to Homer, delight Odysseus's mind (8.367). However, it is not clear what lesson Odysseus derives from this tale. There is a certain parallel between Hephaestus and Odysseus. Both are husbands who are distrustful of their wives, both are vengeful, and both deploy stratagems. Now, Demodocus seems to criticize Hephaestus. He seems to present him as both spiteful – if Aphrodite will not love him she will not love anyone – and contradictory – he demands that she love him while acknowledging that she does not (8.270–281, 8.303–366). But given that Odysseus proceeds, in the rest of the *Odyssey*, to take vengeance against all those who wooed his wife, it is not clear that Odysseus understands the apparent lesson of Demodocus's tale.[101]

A comparison of Achilles and Odysseus highlights the importance of courage as an intellectual virtue. Odysseus is extremely smart, but he

[100] Within the *Iliad*, Achilles' speech is singularly poetic (see Griffin 1980, 75; Edwards 1991, 39): for example, he composes more similes than any other character in the *Iliad* (four of fourteen), all of which are quite arresting: 9.323–327, 16.6–10, 21.281–283, 22.262–267; for the others, see 3.59–63 (Paris), 3.195–198 (Priam), 4.243–246 (Agamemnon), 6.146–150 (Glaucus), 12.167–172 (Asios), 13.99–110 (Poseidon), 17.20–23 (Menelaus), 20.251–255 (Aeneas), 21.462–466 (Apollo), 24.39–45 (Apollo). Odysseus does produce many more similes in the *Odyssey*, but only one – the last – occurs outside of his narration of his adventures or of his lies to Nausicaa, Eumaeus, and Penelope: 6.166–169, 9.4, 9.51–53, 9.287–291, 9.291–293, 9.310–314, 9.382–390, 9.391–394, 10.118–123, 10.123–124, 10.210–219, 10.410–418, 11.205–209, 11.605–606, 11.606–608, 12.237–239, 12.251–256, 12.411–417, 12.417–419, 12.431–436, 12.438–441, 14.307–309, 14.476–477, 19.107–114, 19.233–234, 23.190–191.

[101] Consider Ruderman 1995, 42–43; 1999, 155, 158–159.

ultimately lacks the courage to wrestle with painful doubts and to face painful truths. Achilles is certainly not wise in the manner of Homer. While he does delight his mind through song, he ultimately prefers the life of the warrior to that of the singer. And while he does display tremendous compassion and understanding for Priam and all the Trojans, Achilles ultimately returns to the war against them. But in his capacity to rise above his anger and his courageous willingness to question his cherished convictions about the life of virtue and the justice of the gods, it is the lion-hearted Achilles rather than the wily Odysseus who comes closest to the wise singer Homer.

Bibliography

Adkins, Arthur. 1960. *Merit and Responsibility: A Study in Greek Values*. Oxford: Clarendon Press.

Alvis, John. 1995. *Divine Purpose and Heroic Response in Homer and Virgil: The Political Plan of Zeus*. Lanham, MD: Rowman and Littlefield.

Ambler, Wayne. 2009. "On Strauss on Vico: A Report on Leo Strauss's Course on Giambattista Vico." *Interpretation* **36**: 165–187.

Armstrong, C. B. 1969. "The Casualty Lists in the Trojan War." *Greece and Rome* **16**: 30–31.

St. Augustine. 1984. *City of God*. Trans. Henry Bettenson. London: Penguin Classics.

Bacon, Francis. 1974. *The Advancement of Learning and New Atlantis*. London: Oxford University Press.

Barchilon, Jacques and Flinders, Peter. 1981. *Charles Perrault*. Boston: Twayne Publishers.

Benardete, Seth. 1997. *The Bow and the Lyre*. Lanham, MD: Rowman and Littlefield.

Benardete, Seth. 2000. *The Argument of the Action: Essays on Greek Poetry and Philosophy*. Chicago: University of Chicago Press.

Benardete, Seth. 2005. *Achilles and Hector: The Homeric Hero*. South Bend, IN: St. Augustine's Press.

Bentley, Richard. 1713. *Remarks upon a Late Discourse of Free-Thinking: in a Letter to F.H. D. D. by Phileleutherus Lipsiensis*. Printed for John Morphew. London.

Berlin, Isaiah. 2000. *Three Critics of the Enlightenment: Vico, Hamann, Herder*. Ed. Henry Hardy. Princeton: Princeton University Press.

Berlin, Isaiah. 2002. *The Power of Ideas*. Ed. Henry Hardy. Princeton: Princeton University Press.

Bolotin, David. 1989. "The Concerns of Odysseus: An Introduction to Homer's *Odyssey*." *Interpretation* **17**: 41–57.

Bolotin, David. 1995. "The Critique of Homer and the Homeric Heroes in Plato's *Republic*." In *Political Philosophy and the Human Soul: Essays in Memory of Allan Bloom*. Eds. Michael Palmer and Thomas L. Pangle. Lanham, MD: Rowman and Littlefield. Pp. 83–94.

Borges, Jorge Luis. 1971. "El hacedor." In *El hacedor*. Buenos Aires: Emecé Editores. Pp. 9–11.

Borges, Jorge Luis. 1974. "El inmortal." In *El Aleph*. Madrid: Alianza Editorial. Pp. 7–28.

Bowra, C. M. 1977. *Tradition and Design in* The Iliad. Westport: Greenwood Press.

Browning, Robert. 1992. "The Byzantines and Homer." In *Homer's Ancient Readers: The Hermeneutics of Greek Epic's Earliest Exegetes*. Eds. Robert Lamberton and John J. Keaney. Princeton: Princeton University Press. Pp. 134–148.

Burkert, Walter. 1985. *Greek Religion*. Trans. John Raffan. Cambridge, MA: Harvard University Press.

Burns, Timothy. 1996. "Friendship and Divine Justice in Homer's *Iliad*." In *Poets, Princes, and Private Citizens*. Eds. J. Knippenberg and P. Lawler. Lanham, MD: Rowman and Littlefield. Pp. 289–303.

Buxton, Richard. 2004. "Similes and Other Likenesses." In *The Cambridge Companion to Homer*. Ed. Robert Fowler. Cambridge: Cambridge University Press. Pp. 139–155.

Clarke, Michael. 2004. "Manhood and Heroism." In *The Cambridge Companion to Homer*. Ed. Robert Fowler. Cambridge: Cambridge University Press. Pp. 74–90.

Clay, Jenny Strauss. 1983. *The Wrath of Athena: Gods and Men in the Odyssey*. Princeton: Princeton University Press.

Clay, Jenny Strauss. 2010. *Homer's Trojan Theater: Space, Vision, and Memory in the* Iliad. Cambridge: Cambridge University Press.

Collingwood, R. G. 1956. *The Idea of History*. Oxford: Oxford University Press.

Croce, Benedetto. 1964. *The Philosophy of Giambattista Vico*. Trans. R. G. Collingwood. New York: Russell and Russell.

Crotty, Kevin. 1994. *The Poetics of Supplication: Homer's* Iliad *and* Odyssey. Ithaca: Cornell University Press.

d'Aubignac, François-Hédelin. 1925. *Conjectures académiques, ou Dissertation sur l'Iliade*. Paris.

Deneen, Patrick J. 2000. *The Odyssey of Political Theory*. Lanham, MD: Rowman and Littlefield.

Dimmock, George E. 1989. *The Unity of the* Odyssey. Amherst: University of Massachusetts Press.

Dobbs, Darrell. 1987. "Reckless Rationalism and Heroic Reverence in Homer's *Odyssey*." *American Political Science Review* 81: 491–508.

Dodds, E. R. 1973. *The Greeks and the Irrational*. Berkeley: University of California Press.

Edwards, Mark W. 1987. *Homer: Poet of the* Iliad. Baltimore: Johns Hopkins University Press.

Edwards, Mark W. 1991. *The* Iliad*: A Commentary, V: Books 17–20*. Cambridge: Cambridge University Press.

Farrell, Joseph. 2004. "Roman Homer." In *The Cambridge Companion to Homer*. Ed. Robert Fowler. Cambridge: Cambridge University Press. Pp. 254–271.

Felson, Nancy and Slatkin, Laura. 2004. "Gender and Homeric Epic." In *The Cambridge Companion to Homer*. Ed. Robert Fowler. Cambridge: Cambridge University Press. Pp. 91–114.

Felson-Rubin, Nancy. 1994. *Regarding Penelope: From Character to Poetics*. Princeton: Princeton University Press.

Felson-Rubin, Nancy. 1996. "Penelope's Perspective: Character from Plot." In *Reading the* Odyssey. Ed. Seth L. Schein. Princeton: Princeton University Press. Pp. 163–183.

Finley, Moses I. 1978. *The World of Odysseus*. New York: Viking Press.

Fisch, Max Harold and Bergin, Thomas Goddard. 1963. "Introduction." In *The Autobiography of Giambattista Vico*. Trans. Max Harold Fisch and Thomas Goddard Bergin. Ithaca, NY: Great Seal Books.

Flaumenhaft, Mera. 2004. "Priam the Patriarch, His City, and His Sons." *Interpretation* **32**: 3–32.

Fowler, Robert. 2004. "The Homeric Question." In *The Cambridge Companion to Homer*. Ed. Robert Fowler. Cambridge: Cambridge University Press. Pp. 220–232.

Fradkin, Hillel. 1995. "Poet Kings: A Biblical Perspective on Heroes." In *Political Philosophy and the Human Soul: Essays in Memory of Allan Bloom*. Eds. Michael Palmer and Thomas L. Pangle. Lanham, MD: Rowman and Littlefield. Pp. 55–66.

Fustel de Coulanges, Numa Denis. 1900. *La Cité Antique*. Paris: Libraire Hachette.

Gagarin, Michael. 1987. "Morality in Homer." *Classical Philology* **82**: 285–306.

Grafton, Anthony. 1992. "Renaissance Readers of Homer's Ancient Readers." In *Homer's Ancient Readers: The Hermeneutics of Greek Epic's Earliest Exegetes*. Eds. Robert Lamberton and John J. Keaney. Princeton: Princeton University Press. Pp. 149–172.

Grafton, Anthony. 1999. "Introduction." In *The New Science* by Giambattista Vico. Trans. David Marsh. London: Penguin Books. Pp. xi–xxxiii.

Grafton, Anthony, Most, Glenn W., and Zetzel, James E. G. 1985. "Introduction." In *Prologomena to Homer (1795)* by F. A. Wolf. Trans. Anthony Grafton, Glenn W. Most, and James E. G. Zetzel. Princeton: Princeton University Press. Pp. 3–35.

Graziosi, Barbara. 2002. *Inventing Homer: The Early Reception of Epic*. Cambridge: Cambridge University Press.

Griffin, Jasper. 1980. *Homer on Life and Death*. Oxford: Clarendon Press.

Griffin, Jasper. 1995. *Homer: Iliad IX*. Oxford: Clarendon Press.

Griffin, Jasper. 2004. "The speeches." In *The Cambridge Companion to Homer*. Ed. Robert Fowler. Cambridge: Cambridge University Press. Pp. 156–167.

Grote, George. 1861. *History of Greece*, vol. **1**. 2nd ed.. New York: Harper and Brothers.

Hall, Edith. 2008. *The Return of Ulysses: A Cultural History of the Odyssey*. Baltimore: Johns Hopkins University Press.

Harsh, Philip Whaley. 1950. "Penelope and Odysseus in *Odyssey* XIX." *American Journal of Philology* **71**: 1–21.

Haubold, Johannes. 2000. *Homer's People: Epic Poetry and Social Formation*. Cambridge: Cambridge University Press.

Haugen, Kristine Louise. 2011. *Richard Bentley: Poetry and Enlightenment*. Cambridge, MA: Harvard University Press.

Hegel, Georg Wilhelm Friedrich. 1956. *Philosophy of History*. Trans. J. Sibree. New York: Dover Publications.

Heitman, Richard. 2005. *Taking Her Seriously: Penelope and the Plot of Homer's* Odyssey. Ann Arbor: University of Michigan Press.

Hobbes, Thomas. 1894. *The Illiads and Odysses of Homer*. London: Longman, Brown, Green, and Longmans.

Homer. 1976. *Opera: Odysseae*. Vols. III–IV. Ed. Thomas W. Allen. Oxford: Oxford University Press.

Homer. 1988. *Opera: Iliadis*. Vols. I–II. Eds. David B. Munro and Thomas W. Allen. Oxford: Oxford University Press.

Homer. 1992. *The* Iliad. Trans. Richmond Lattimore. Chicago: University of Chicago Press.

Homer. 1999. *The* Odyssey. Trans. Richmond Lattimore. New York: Perennial Classics.

Horkheimer, Max and Adorno, Theodor W. 1972. *Dialectic of Enlightenment*. Trans. John Cumming. New York: Herder and Herder.

Hunter, Richard. 2004. "Homer and Greek literature." In *The Cambridge Companion to Homer*. Ed. Robert Fowler. Cambridge: Cambridge University Press. Pp. 235–253.

Janko, Richard. 1992. *The* Iliad: *A Commentary, IV: Books 13–16*. Cambridge: Cambridge University Press.

Jong, Irene J. F. de. 1987. *Narrators and Focalizers: The Presentation of the Story in the* Iliad. Amsterdam: B. R. Grüning.

Jullien, Dominique. 1995. "Biography of an Immortal." *Comparative Literature* 47: 136–159.

Katz, Marilyn. 1991. *Penelope's Renown: Meaning and Indeterminacy in the* Odyssey. Princeton: Princeton University Press.

Kearns, Emily. 2004. "The Gods in the Homeric epics." In *The Cambridge Companion to Homer*. Ed. Robert Fowler. Cambridge: Cambridge University Press. Pp. 59–73.

Kim, Jinyo. 2000. *The Pity of Achilles: Oral Style and the Unity of the* Iliad. Lanham, MD: Rowman and Littlefield.

Kirk, G. S. 1962. *The Songs of Homer*. Cambridge: Cambridge University Press.

Kirk, G. S. 1974. *The Nature of Greek Myths*. Harmondsworth, UK: Penguin Books.

Lateiner, Donald. 2004. "The *Iliad*: An Unpredictable Classic." In *The Cambridge Companion to Homer*. Ed. Robert Fowler. Cambridge: Cambridge University Press. Pp. 11–30.

Lattimore, Richmond. 1992. "Introduction." In *The* Iliad *of Homer*. Trans. Richmond Lattimore. Chicago: University of Chicago Press. Pp. 11–55.

Lessing, Gotthold Ephraim. 1970. *Laocoon*. Trans. W. A. Steel. London: J. M. Dent and Sons.

Lilla, Mark. 1993. *G. B. Vico: The Making of an Anti-Modern*. Cambridge: Harvard University Press.

Lloyd-Jones, Hugh. 1971. *The Justice of Zeus*. Berkeley: University of California Press.

Locke, John. 1988. *Two Treatises of Government*. Ed. Peter Laslett. Cambridge: Cambridge University Press.

Long, A. A. 1992. "Stoic Readings of Homer." In *Homer's Ancient Readers: The Hermeneutics of Greek Epic's Earliest Exegetes*. Eds. Robert Lamberton and John J. Keaney. Princeton: Princeton University Press. Pp. 41–66.

Lord, Albert Bates. 1960. *The Singer of Tales*. Cambridge, MA: Harvard University Press.

Lord, Albert Bates. 1991. *Epic Singers and Oral Tradition*. Ithaca: Cornell University Press.
Lukàcs, Georg. 1977. *The Theory of the Novel: A Historico-Philosophical Essay on the Forms of Great Epic Literature*. Trans. Anna Bostock. Cambridge, MA: MIT Press.
Lutz, Mark. 2006. "Wrath and Justice in Homer's Achilles." *Interpretation* 33: 111–132.
Macaulay, Thomas Babington. 1903. *Critical and Historical Essays*, vol. 2. Ed. F. C. Montague. New York: G. P. Putnams's Sons.
Machiavelli, Niccolo. 1966. *Il Principe, Discorsi Sopra La Prima Deca di Tito Livio*. Ed. Piero Gallardo. Milano: Edizioni per il Club del Libro.
Machiavelli, Niccolo. 1998. *The Prince*, 2nd ed.. Trans. Harvey C. Mansfield. Chicago and London: University of Chicago Press.
MacLeod, Colin. 1982. *Homer:* Iliad: *Book XXIV*. Cambridge: Cambridge University Press.
Manent, Pierre. 2010. *Les Métamorphoses de la Cité: Essai sur la dynamique de l'Occident*. Paris: Flammarion.
Mazon, Paul. 1942. *Introduction à* l'Iliade. Paris: Les Belles Lettres.
Michelet, Jules. 1971. *Oeuvres complètes*, vol. 2. Ed. Paul Viallaneix. Paris: Flammarion.
Montaigne, Michel de. 1976. *The Complete Essays of Montaigne*. Trans. Donald M. Frame. Stanford: Stanford University Press.
Moulton, Carroll. 1977. *Similes in the Homeric Poems*. Göttingen: Vandenhoeck and Ruprecht.
Mueller, Martin. 1984. *The* Iliad. London: G. Allen & Unwin.
Murnaghan, Sheila. 1987. *Disguise and Recognition in the* Odyssey. Princeton: Princeton University Press.
Murray, Gilbert. 1924. *The Rise of the Greek Epic*. 3rd ed. Oxford: Clarendon Press.
Myres, John L. 1958. *Homer and His Critics*. Ed. Dorothea Gray. London: Routledge and Kegan Paul.
Nagy, Gregory. 1974. *Comparatives Studies in Greek and Indic Meter*. Cambridge, MA: Harvard University Press.
Nagy, Gregory. 1979. *The Best of the Achaeans: Concepts of the Hero in Archaic Greek Poetry*. Baltimore: Johns Hopkins University Press.
Nagy, Gregory. 1996. *Homeric Questions*. Austin: University of Texas Press.
Nagy, Gregory. 2004. *Homer's Text and Language*. Urbana: University of Illinois Press.
Nagy, Gregory. 2009. *Homer the Classic*. Cambridge, MA: Harvard University Press.
Nagy, Gregory. 2010. *Homer the Preclassic*. Berkeley: University of California Press.
Nietzsche, Friedrich. 1954a. "Thus Spoke Zarathustra." In *The Portable Nietzsche*. Trans. Walter Kaufmann. New York: Viking Press. Pp. 103–439.
Nietzsche, Friedrich. 1954b. "Twilight of the Idols." In *The Portable Nietzsche*. Trans. Walter Kaufmann. New York: Viking Press. Pp. 463–563.
Nietzsche, Friedrich. 1967. *The Birth of Tragedy*. Trans. Walter Kaufmann. New York: Vintage Books.
Nietzsche, Friedrich. 1968. *The Will to Power*. Trans. Walter Kaufmann, R. J. Hollingdale. New York: Vintage Books.
Nietzsche, Friedrich. 1969a. *Genealogy of Morals*. Trans. Walter Kaufmann. New York: Vintage Books. Pp. 15–163.

Nietzsche, Friedrich. 1969b. *Ecce Homo*. Trans. Walter Kaufmann. New York: Vintage Books. Pp. 217–335.

Nietzsche, Friedrich. 1974. *The Gay Science*. Trans. Walter Kaufmann. New York: Vintage Books.

Nietzsche, Friedrich. 1984. *Human, All Too Human*. Trans. Marion Fabor, with Stephen Lehmann. Lincoln and London: University of Nebraska Press.

Nietzsche, Friedrich 1989. *Beyond Good and Evil*. Trans. Walter Kaufmann. New York: Vintage Books.

Pangle, Thomas L. 2003. *Political Philosophy and the God of Abraham*. Baltimore and London: Johns Hopkins University Press.

Parry, Adam. 1971. "Introduction." In *The Making of Homeric Verse: The Collected Papers of Milman Parry*. Ed. Adam Parry. Oxford: Oxford University Press. Pp. ix–lxii.

Parry, Milman. 1971. *The Making of Homeric Verse: The Collected Papers of Milman Parry*. Ed. Adam Parry. Oxford: Oxford University Press.

Passannante, Gerard. 2009. "Homer Atomized: Francis Bacon and the Matter of Tradition." *ELH: English Literary History* 76: 1015–1047.

Porter, James I. 2004. "Homer: The History of an Idea." In *The Cambridge Companion to Homer*. Ed. Robert Fowler. Cambridge: Cambridge University Press. Pp. 324–343.

Pucci, Pietro. 1987. *Odysseus Polutropos: Intertextual Readings in the* Odyssey *and the* Iliad. Ithaca: Cornell University Press.

Redfield, James M. 1975. *Nature and Culture in the* Iliad: *The Tragedy of Hector*. Chicago: University of Chicago Press.

Reinhardt, Karl. 1960. *Tradition und Geist: gesammelte Essays zur Dichtung*. Göttingen: Vandonhoeck & Ruprecht.

Reinhardt, Karl. 1997a. "The Judgement of Paris." In *Homer: German Scholarship in Translation*. Trans. G. M. Wright and P. V. Jones. Oxford: Clarendon Press. Pp. 170–191.

Reinhardt, Karl. 1997b. "Homer and the Telemachy, Circe, Calypso, and the Phaeacians." In *Homer: German Scholarship in Translation*. Trans. G. M. Wright and P. V. Jones. Oxford: Clarendon Press. Pp. 217–248.

Richardson, N. J. 1992. "Aristotle's Reading of Homer and Its Background." In *Homer's Ancient Readers: The Hermeneutics of Greek Epic's Earliest Exegetes*. Eds. Robert Lamberton and John J. Keaney. Princeton: Princeton University Press. Pp. 30–40.

Richardson, Scott Douglas. 1990. *The Homeric Narrator*. Nashville: Vanderbilt University Press.

Rorty, Richard. 1989. *Contingency, Irony, and Solidarity*. Cambridge: Cambridge University Press.

Rorty, Richard. 1991. *Objectivity, Relativism, and Truth*. Cambridge: Cambridge University Press.

Rousseau, Jean-Jacques. 1979. *Emile*. Trans. Allan Bloom. New York: Basic Books.

Rousseau, Jean-Jacques. 1986. *Discourses and Essay on the Origin of Languages*. Trans. Victor Gourevitch. New York: Harper & Row.

Ruderman, Richard S. 1995. "Love and Friendship in Homer's Odyssey." In *Political Philosophy and the Human Soul: Essays in Memory of Allan Bloom*. Eds. Michael Palmer and Thomas L. Pangle. Lanham, MD: Rowman and Littlefield. Pp. 35–54.

Ruderman, Richard S. 1999. "Odysseus and the Possibility of Enlightenment." *American Journal of Political Science* **43**: 138–61.

Saïd, Suzanne. 2011. *Homer and the* Odyssey. Oxford: Oxford University Press.

Saxonhouse, Arlene. 1988. "Thymos, Justice, and Moderation of Anger in the Story of Achilles." In *Understanding the Political Spirit*. Ed. Catherine Zuckert. New Haven and London: Yale University Press. Pp. 30–47.

Schadewaldt, Wolfgang. 1997a. "Hector and Andromache." In *Homer: German Scholarship in Translation*. Trans. G. M. Wright and P. V. Jones. Oxford: Clarendon Press. Pp. 124–142.

Schadewaldt, Wolfgang. 1997b. "Achilles' Decision." In *Homer: German Scholarship in Translation*. Trans. G. M. Wright and P. V. Jones. Oxford: Clarendon Press. Pp. 143–169.

Schein, Seth L. 1984. *The Mortal Hero: An Introduction to Homer's* Iliad. Berkeley: University of California Press.

Schein, Seth L. 1996. "Introduction." In *Reading the* Odyssey. Ed. Seth L. Schein. Princeton: Princeton University Press. Pp. 3–31.

Schiller, Friedrich. 1981. *On the Naive and Sentimental in Literature*. Trans. Helen Watanabe-O'Kelly. Manchester, UK: Carcanet New Press.

Scodel, Ruth. 2002. *Listening to Homer: Tradition, Narrative, and Audience*. Ann Arbor: University of Michigan Press.

Scodel, Ruth. 2004. "The Story-Teller and His Audience." In *The Cambridge Companion to Homer*. Ed. Robert Fowler. Cambridge: Cambridge University Press. Pp. 45–55.

Scott, John Adams. 1921. *The Unity of Homer*. Berkeley: University of California Press.

Scott, John. 1963. *Homer and His Influence*. New York: Cooper Square Publishers.

Scott, William C. 1974. *The Oral Nature of the Homeric Simile*. Leiden, the Netherlands: Brill.

Scott, William C. 2009. *The Artistry of the Homeric Simile*. Hanover, NH: University Press of New England.

Segal, Charles. 1971. *The Theme of the Mutilation of the Corpse in the* Iliad. Leiden, the Netherlands: Brill.

Segal, Charles. 1992. "Bard and Audience in Homer." In *Homer's Ancient Readers: The Hermeneutics of Greek Epic's Earliest Exegetes*. Eds. Robert Lamberton and John J. Keaney. Princeton: Princeton University Press. Pp. 3–29.

Segal, Charles. 1996. "Kleos *and Its Ironies in the* Odyssey." In *Reading the* Odyssey. Ed. Seth L. Schein. Princeton: Princeton University Press. Pp. 201–221.

Shaw, T. E. [Lawrence, T. E.] 1932. *The* Odyssey *of Homer*. New York: Oxford University Press.

Sheppard, John Tresidder. 1969. *The Pattern of the* Iliad. London: M. S. G. Haskell House.

Silk, Michael. 2004. "The Odyssey and Its Explorations." In *The Cambridge Companion to Homer*. Ed. Robert Fowler. Cambridge: Cambridge University Press. Pp. 31–44.

Silk, M. S. and Stern, J. P. 1981. *Nietzsche on Tragedy*. New York: Cambridge University Press.

Sinos, Dale. 1980. *Achilles, Patroklos, and the Meaning of "Philos."* Innsbruck: Institut für Sprachwissenschaft der Universität Innsbruck.

Slatkin, Laura M. 1996. "Composition by Theme and the Mētis of the Odyssey." In *Reading the* Odyssey. Ed. Seth L. Schein. Princeton: Princeton University Press. Pp. 223–237.

Stanford, William Bedell. 1950. "Homer's Use of Personal πολυ-Compounds." *Classical Philology* 45: 108–110.

Stanford, William Bedell. 1963. *The Ulysses Theme: A Study in the Adaptability of a Traditional Hero*. Oxford: Basil Blackwell.

Stanley, Keith. 1993. *The Shield of Homer: Narrative Structure in the Iliad*. Princeton: Princeton University Press.

Strauss, Leo. 1964. *The City and Man*. Chicago: University of Chicago Press.

Strauss, Leo. 1971. *Natural Right and History*. Chicago: University of Chicago Press.

Strauss, Leo. 1987. "Introduction." In *The History of Political Philosophy*, 3rd ed. Eds. Leo Strauss and Joseph Cropsey. Chicago: University of Chicago Press. Pp. 1–6.

Swift, Jonathan. 1975. "A Full and True Account of the Battel Fought Last Friday Between the Antient and the Modern Books in St. James's Library." In *A Tale of a Tub and Other Satires*. Ed. Kathleen Williams. London: J. M. Dent and Sons. Pp. 137–165.

Tennyson, Alfred Lord. 2007. *Selected Poems*. London: Penguin Classics.

Thalmann, William G. 1998. *The Swinherd and the Bow: Representations of Class in the* Odyssey. Ithaca: Cornell University Press.

Van Brock, Nadia. 1959. "Substitution rituelle." *Revue hittite et asiatique* 65: 117–146.

Verene, Donald Phillip. 1981. *Vico's Science of the Imagination*. Ithaca: Cornell University Press.

Vernant, Jean-Pierre. 1996. "The Refusal of Odysseus." In *Reading the* Odyssey. Ed. Seth L. Schein. Princeton: Princeton University Press. Pp.185–189.

Vico, Giambattista. 1963. *The Autobiography of Giambattista Vico*. Trans. Max Harold Fisch and Thomas Goddard Bergin. Ithaca: Great Seal Books.

Vico, Giambattista. 1977. *La scienza nuova*. Ed. Paolo Rossi. Milano: Rizzoli Editore.

Vico, Giambattista. 1999. *The New Science*. Trans. David Marsh. London: Penguin Books.

Voeglin, Eric. 1957. *Order and History II: The World of the Polis*. Baton Rouge: Louisiana State University Press.

Wade-Gery, Henry Theodore. 1952. *The Poet of the* Iliad. Cambridge: Cambridge University Press.

Weber, Max. 1958. *From Max Weber: Essays in Sociology*. Trans. H. H. Gerth and C. Wright Mills. New York: Oxford University Press.

Whitman, Cedric H. 1958. *Homer and the Homeric Tradition*. Cambridge, MA: Harvard University Press.

Winkler, John Jay. 1990. *The Constraints of Desire: The Anthropology of Sex and Gender in Ancient Greece*. New York: Routledge.

Winn, James Anderson. 2009. *The Poetry of War*. Cambridge: Cambridge University Press.

Wolf, F. A. 1985. *Prologomena to Homer (1795)*. Trans. Anthony Grafton, Glenn W. Most, and James E. G. Zetzel. Princeton: Princeton University Press.

Zanker, Graham. 1994. *The Heart of Achilles: Characterization and Personal Ethics in the* Iliad. Ann Arbor: University of Michigan Press.

Zuckert, Catherine. 1988. "On the Role of Spiritedness in Politics." In *Understanding the Political Spirit*. Ed. Catherine Zuckert. New Haven and London: Yale University Press. Pp. 1–29.

Index